The Ethics of Representing Organizations

The Ethics of Representing Organizations

Legal Fictions for Clients

LAWRENCE J. FOX  SUSAN R. MARTYN

OXFORD

UNIVERSITY PRESS

UNIVERSITY PRESS

Oxford University Press, Inc., publishes works that further Oxford University's objective of excellence in research, scholarship, and education.

Oxford   New York
Auckland   Cape Town   Dar es Salaam   Hong Kong   Karachi   Kuala Lumpur   Madrid   Melbourne
Mexico City   Nairobi   New Delhi   Shanghai   Taipei   Toronto

With offices in
Argentina   Austria   Brazil   Chile   Czech Republic   France   Greece   Guatemala   Hungary   Italy
Japan   Poland   Portugal   Singapore   South Korea   Switzerland   Thailand   Turkey   Ukraine
Vietnam

Copyright © 2009 by Oxford University Press, Inc.

Published by Oxford University Press, Inc.
198 Madison Avenue, New York, New York 10016

Oxford is a registered trademark of Oxford University Press
Oxford University Press is a registered trademark of Oxford University Press, Inc.

Library of Congress Cataloging-in-Publication Data

Fox, Lawrence J., 1943-
  The ethics of representing organizations : legal fictions
for clients / Lawrence J. Fox, Susan R. Martyn.
    p. cm.
  Includes bibliographical references and index.
  ISBN 978-0-19-537154-3 ((hardback.) : alk. paper)
1. Legal ethics—United States. 2. Attorney and client—United States.
3. Practice of law—United States. 4. Lawyers—United States.
I. Martyn, Susan R., 1947- II. Title.
  KF306.F687 2009
  174'.30973—dc22   2009007275

1 2 3 4 5 6 7 8 9

Printed in the United States of America on acid-free paper

Note to Readers
This publication is designed to provide accurate and authoritative information in regard to the subject matter covered. It is based upon sources believed to be accurate and reliable and is intended to be current as of the time it was written. It is sold with the understanding that the publisher is not engaged in rendering legal, accounting, or other professional services. If legal advice or other expert assistance is required, the services of a competent professional person should be sought. Also, to confirm that the information has not been affected or changed by recent developments, traditional legal research techniques should be used, including checking primary sources where appropriate.

(Based on the Declaration of Principles jointly adopted by a Committee of the American Bar Association and a Committee of Publishers and Associations.)

To Susan, the most talented (and charitable) collaborator and dedicated friend one could ever have. None of this would be possible without her good will and energy. ✻ LJF

To Larry, creative (and gracious) collaborator and unwavering friend. None of this would have happened without your vision and perseverance. ✻ SRM

Contents

Detailed Contents

Preface

THE AUTHORS HAVE BEEN ENGAGED in a twenty-year journey together exploring the law governing lawyers and debating the contours of the rules of professional conduct. The journey began in the windowless conference room at the American Law Institute's headquarters in West Philadelphia, where the authors both served as advisors to the ALI project The Restatement of Law Governing Lawyers. This followed almost equally long dedication to Ethics 2000, the American Bar Association's multiple year review and revision of the Model Rules of Professional Conduct originally adopted in the early '80s.

Then the authors turned to what has become a wonderful collaboration of publications in their mutual field of endeavor. First came a casebook for students, *Traversing the Ethical Minefield*, published by Aspen in 2004, a book now in its second edition (2008). Then came *The Law Governing Lawyers: National Rules, Standards, Statutes, and State Lawyer Codes*, also published by Aspen on an annual basis, with a third author, W. Bradley Wendel. Third was a handbook for lawyers called *Red Flags: Legal Ethics for Lawyers*, published by American Law Institute in 2005 and just supplemented in 2009. Fourth, the team of Martyn and Fox authored *Your Lawyer, A User's Guide*, published by Lexis-Nexis in 2006 and subsequently rewritten and published by Oxford University Press in 2008 under the new title *How to Deal with Your Lawyer: Answers to Commonly Asked Questions*.

And now we have the authors' latest effort *The Ethics of Representing Organizations: Legal Fictions for Clients*, which is an attempt to focus on the particularly knotty ethical dilemmas faced by lawyers who represent legal entities. The authors hope you find this volume as useful and entertaining as we have found it rewarding to produce.

Needless to say, no publication of this scope would be possible without the splendid assistance of many. At the top of the list, the authors must acknowledge the sage and dedicated review of the manuscript by our great friend, Harry Bryans, now Senior Vice-President of Aon Risk Services Northeast. Next on the kudos list is the wise and wonderful Bea Cucinotta,

Larry Fox's long-suffering assistant, who not only, to the extent possible, helped keep the authors organized but also provided rich editorial comments when the authors' prose went astray. Larry Fox specifically acknowledges the assistance of his research assistant at Harvard, Juan Lázaro Peña, as well as the advice he received from his colleagues at Drinker Biddle & Reath, David Kessler, Douglas Raymond, and Kathryn Doyle. Susan Martyn especially wants to recognize her colleagues at the University of Toledo College of Law and her research assistants, Jocelyn N. Cubbon and Jeanette M. Kuhn.

As with most authors, the credit for the good in this volume goes to the foregoing. Any lapses are the sole responsibility of the authors who remind our readers that we welcome comments and criticisms for what we hope will be the second edition of the volume after we recover from this invigorating albeit exhausting experience. We also remind you that the problems in this book are works of fiction. Any similarity to actual persons or occurrences is entirely coincidental and not intended by the authors.

PART ONE

Understanding the Law
Governing Lawyers

"Don't get me wrong. Legality has its place."

Beginning Your Representation

⧫ Legal Fictions for Clients

Clients are clients. Who needs a special ethics book about representing companies?

Not just companies—any organization or entity. A family business, a publicly held corporation, a nonprofit, even the government. And why? Because when you represent a person, life is simpler. You know whom to talk to. You know where to get clarification. You know who decides the client's best interests.

But when you represent an organization, life is not so straightforward. Your client is a legal fiction, an entity, an abstraction, a construct. And it can only operate through individuals, usually many individuals with different roles and different responsibilities and different interests of their own. Entities act through employees, officers, members, directors, trustees, agents, shareholders, on and on. So when you represent an organization, oppose an organization, or otherwise are involved with one as a lawyer, there are special professional responsibility issues you must identify and address.[1] And because organizations are so pervasive in American life—with few lawyers not dealing with them one way or another—a special volume dedicated to these matters should prove helpful. This volume is also prompted by a second reason: organizations often employ their own inside counsel. The special ethics issues facing in-house counsel are certainly worthy of careful analysis and explication.[2]

---

1. MODEL RULE 1.13; RLGL § 96.

2. *E.g.,* JOHN K. VILLA, CORPORATE COUNSEL GUIDELINES, Chapter 3 (West 2007).

𝓜 Framing the Issues

It seems so simple. You earn fees by representing clients. But representing organizations can be daunting. Of course, many of your professional obligations are shaped by the organic law that governs the entity you represent, whether an unincorporated association, a public or private corporation, a government, or a nonprofit. We will refer to this law, but in this volume we will primarily focus on the vast body of law and ethical discretion that shapes your professional obligations to all clients, including organizations. This law, which may be a bit less familiar, includes the lawyer disciplinary codes (each jurisdiction's Rules of Professional Conduct),[3] common law (such as agency and malpractice law), a few statutes (such a fee-shifting provisions), and court rules (such as Rules of Civil Procedure).[4] Your license to practice and your income depend on your understanding of all these bodies of law, as adopted in each jurisdiction. In this volume, we refer collectively to all of this law as "the law governing lawyers."

Lawyer disciplinary codes govern the conduct of all lawyers admitted to law practice. Violation of your jurisdiction's Rules of Professional Conduct subjects you to professional discipline, with sanctions ranging from disbarment, suspension from practice, and fines, to public and private reprimand. Because nearly every jurisdiction has patterned its Rules of Professional Conduct on the ABA Model Rules of Professional Conduct, we cite to the ABA Model Rules in this volume, noting some significant departures where relevant.

Most of the common law that governs lawyer conduct has been collected in the recent Restatement (Third) of the Law Governing Lawyers. When we refer to this common law, we rely on the Restatement. We do so because it is quite recent (2000), does an admirable job of restating and organizing both

---

3. State lawyer codes generally follow the template of the American Bar Association's MODEL RULES OF PROFESSIONAL CONDUCT, available in law libraries and at: http://www.abanet.org/cpr/mrpc/mrpc_toc.html. We include in Appendix A a few representative state rules of professional conduct organizational lawyers should keep in sharp focus. We cite the 2008 ABA Model Rules in this volume as "MODEL RULE __." You can find the most recent iteration of your state lawyer code at: http://www.abanet.org/cpr/links.html.

4. The common law, statutes, and court rules that govern lawyer conduct are collected in the American Law Institute's RESTATEMENT (THIRD) OF THE LAW GOVERNING LAWYERS (2000), available in law libraries and on Westlaw and Lexis. We include portions of the RESTATEMENT relevant to organizational lawyers in Appendix B. We cite the RESTATEMENT in this volume as "RLGL § __."

the lawyer disciplinary codes and the common law, and has been cited and relied on in hundreds of court opinions.

Which leads us to one final observation: DO NOT RELY ON THIS BOOK FOR LEGAL ADVICE. We have used a question and answer format here to invite you into a conversation about your professional responsibilities, not to offer you answers to any specific legal problem. As every lawyer knows, the exact requirements of all of the legal rules we discuss in this volume will differ from jurisdiction to jurisdiction. Further, a slight change in facts can make a huge difference in outcome. With these caveats in mind, we hope to engage you in a fascinating subject, and by citing Model Rules and Restatement sections, we hope to facilitate your further research.

Our first two topics illustrate the hidden traps that can ensnare a lawyer who assumes too facilely that the law governing lawyers is obvious and intuitive. Chapter 1 explores the ways—some unexpected—that lawyers can take on clients, including accidental clients you may not intend or anticipate. Chapter 2 addresses fees and explores the manner in which the law governing lawyers has laid a patina of fiduciary duty on contract law, even in the bargaining stage.

Who Is Your Client?

ℳ Introduction: Identifying Your Clients

LET'S START BY DEFINING YOUR CLIENT. It seems axiomatic that lawyers owe fiduciary duties to clients, and only very limited duties to non-clients. But in the context of representing an organization, identifying who is who can be very dicey indeed.

Your role as an officer of the legal system creates primary obligations to clients, as well as responsibilities to courts and third parties. All of these obligations require you to identify your clients, an inquiry that can produce unanticipated results.

In most situations, you know who your clients are because you have expressly agreed to represent them.[1] Increasingly, however, the law governing lawyers also has recognized clients that lawyers may think of as "accidental" clients, those you do not expect, but nevertheless recognized by law as being owed the same fiduciary duties that lawyers owe intended clients.[2]

Once a legally recognized client-lawyer relationship begins, the law governing lawyers obligates you to fulfill five fiduciary duties, which we call the "Five C's": client control over the goals of the representation, communication, competence, confidentiality, and conflict–of-interest resolution.[3] Lawyers who fail to recognize those who are clients easily can ignore one or more of these obligations. If this occurs, you set yourself up for trouble because the law governing lawyers provides for multiple and overlapping

---

1. RLGL § 14(1)(a).

2. LAWRENCE J. FOX & SUSAN R. MARTYN, RED FLAGS: A LAWYER'S HANDBOOK ON LEGAL ETHICS, Chapter One (ALI-ABA 2005); Susan R. Martyn, *Accidental Clients*, 33 HOFSTRA L. REV. 913 (2005).

3. RLGL § 16.

remedies[4] for the breach of these duties—remedies such as professional discipline,[5] malpractice,[6] breach of fiduciary duty,[7] fee forfeiture,[8] and disqualification.[9]

In this chapter, we will identify several situations where you can take on an incidental, accidental, or even unintended representation that binds you legally. We will, of course, explore organizations and their constituents, as well as court appointments (which you usually have a duty to accept); implied client-lawyer relationships (created by conduct from the viewpoint of the reasonable client); prospective clients (those who discuss the possibility of creating a client-lawyer relationship); third-party payment or direction (including accommodation clients); joint clients; clients who change (such as by merger, reorganization, or bankruptcy); imputed clients; and quasi-clients (such as third-party beneficiaries).

Throughout this chapter, it will be clear that you cannot recognize or solve any legal ethics issue until you first learn to identify your clients, including those you may consider to be "accidental" clients. Once you understand the necessity of properly identifying clients, you will be in a position to avoid client-lawyer relationships you do not wish to create, and to recognize the moment when fiduciary duties attach to client-lawyer relationships you intend to undertake. In other words, the first step to addressing any legal ethics issue is to know your clients, so that you will be able to observe the Five C's for all legally recognized clients and avoid interference by those who are not.

𝕸 Language Matters

I got a call from my client the other day. He told me to prepare the necessary documentation for the company to merge with its 80 percent-owned subsidiary.

---

4. RLGL §§ 5, 6.

5. RLGL § 5.

6. RLGL §§ 48, 50, 52–54.

7. RLGL § 49.

8. RLGL § 37.

9. RLGL § 6, cmt. i.

Isn't that an interesting assignment. But what is more interesting is your description. You said you got a call from your "client." But, of course, your client isn't a person; it's a company.[10] The call you got was from a client representative, or constituent.

Constituent?

Yes. A constituent can be an officer, director, employee, shareholder, or other agent of the organizational client. Lawyers regularly refer to the officers and employees of their entity clients as "my client," both in speaking to third parties as well as to the "clients" themselves. "I'm playing golf with my client" and "Can we get my client's kid a summer job?" and "That client is a pain the way he audits my bills" are all statements that trip easily off the tongue. And in some ways they should. We want these individuals to trust us. We want them to provide us with everything we need to be effective lawyers. We want to foster a long-term relationship. So we refer to them as clients.

The problem is they are not clients. And there are certain situations where we want them to recognize that they are not clients.[11] For example, we do not want them to think they are clients when they tell us something they think we are going to keep confidential from the company.[12] Nor do we want them to think they are clients when they think they are in need of personal legal services, and we do not believe we are acting as their lawyer (as opposed to the organization's lawyer).[13] But all this "client" talk could mislead them. If someone is misled into thinking that we are acting as his or her lawyer, we can be deemed to have been acting as that individual's lawyer.[14] In that case, in the event of a legal malpractice suit, the first thing the plaintiff will assert is that you called him "my client," not once as a slip of the tongue, but over and over again across a number of years. Therefore, the plaintiff will argue that he was entirely justified in believing you were his lawyer, in relying on the advice you unknowingly provided, and that the flawed advice caused "your client" harm, so pay up![15]

---

10. MODEL RULE 1.13(a); RLGL § 96(1).

11. MODEL RULE 1.13(f).

12. MODEL RULE 1.13, cmt. [2]; RLGL § 96, cmt. e.

13. MODEL RULES 1.13(g), 4.3; RLGL §§ 103, 131.

14. RLGL § 14, § 131, cmt. e.

15. *See, e.g., Hopper v. Frank,* 16 F.3d 92 (5th Cir. 1994) (individual partners had no standing as clients to sue for legal malpractice by hiring lawyer to represent limited partnership); *Meyer v. Mulligan,* 889 P.2d 509 (Wyo. 1995) (husband and wife incorporators of corporation had standing to sue lawyer who represented corporation in legal malpractice action).

🏛 Appointed Pro Bono

I don't believe it! I'm in a medical malpractice defense firm. We represent both individual docs and hospitals. Another firm in town represents a different insurer, arguing that they have no duty to pay a judgment against a doc who skipped the jurisdiction and refused to cooperate in the defense of his case. Plaintiff asked the court to appoint a lawyer to represent the absent doc. You can guess who got appointed? Surely I cannot be conscripted to provide civil pro bono.

Although such appointments in civil cases are rare, judges indeed have the inherent authority to appoint lawyers where necessary to ensure a fair and just proceeding and the integrity of the justice system.[16] We're sorry to tell you that yours just might be such a case. The court needs the absent doc's interests to be fairly represented in determining whether the plaintiff is entitled to the insurance coverage.[17]

But don't I have some right to claim that I'm not the right lawyer for the job?

You could. But what would happen if this were a paying client?

Well, I'm not sure I know that much about insurance law.

When was the last time you confessed ignorance to someone who would pay your hourly rate?

What if I feel conflicted?

You could assert an ethical objection, but the burden rests on you to show good cause, which requires a demonstration that you would in fact violate the rules by taking on the case, say, by a conflict of interest.[18]

How about poverty? This case could take way too much of my time.

That reasoning works only if the financial burden is unreasonable.[19] The same is true if the matter is repugnant to the lawyer. Absent a real showing, you must accept the appointment, even though the court has created an actual, albeit involuntary client-lawyer relationship.[20]

---

16. *Bothwell v. Republic Tobacco Co.*, 912 F. Supp. 1221 (D. Neb. 1995).

17. *Burke v. Lewis*, 122 P.3d 533 (Utah 2005).

18. MODEL RULE 6.2.

19. *E.g., Synergy Assocs. v. Sun Biotechnologies, Inc.*, 350 F.3d 681 (7th Cir. 2003) (court could not reappoint lawyer on pro bono basis where lawyer was owed nearly $100,000 in fees and costs and previously was allowed by court to withdraw from the representation).

20. RLGL § 14(2).

⅍ Implied Clients: The Speech

The Chamber of Commerce sponsored a "Start Your Own Business" forum. I was lucky enough to be one of the presenters. My topic: how to choose the right vehicle—partnership, L.L.C., corporation—for your start-up. At the beginning and at the end I gave my usual disclaimer. "This is not legal advice. For that, you need to consult your own tax advisor . . . or me." I thought I was pretty good that day.

Did you get any business?

Two follow-up calls. And one lawsuit.

A lawsuit?

Yep. A guy in the audience claims he followed my advice. He and his buddy formed a partnership. Now the business has gone south, and he's personally liable for the business's debts. Had to declare personal bankruptcy. And it's all my fault.

What a shame. The disclaimers you made should protect you—as long as you acted accordingly. So we hope you offered legal information, but not legal advice, tailored to this fellow's individual situation. If so, the guy has no claim to being an accidental client.[21] Was your disclaimer in writing?

Not on my slides. But the Chamber had a disclaimer on the registration page.

That'll be helpful. As with all protective actions, to the extent they are in writing, you are far more likely to be able to rely upon them. People's memories fade . . . perhaps conveniently.

⅍ Prospective Clients: Casual Advice

One of those long flights to San Diego. Lucky to get an upgrade. My seat companion is lost in his spreadsheets for the first hour. Then he says, "damn board," loud enough for the whole cabin to hear. "You're a CEO?" I ask, figuring I'll flatter him. Turns out he is. What an opportunity. And he starts spinning this tale of woe.

---

21. *E.g.*, RLGL § 14 (1); Md. Op. 2007-18 (2008) (lawyer conducting domestic relations law seminars for the lay public who wants to avoid creating a lawyer-client relationship must offer only general legal information as opposed to advice targeted to a particular attendee's situation); Wis. Op. E-95-5 (lawyer-volunteer at organization that provides information about landlord-tenant law must emphasize that only general information is provided and that advice specific to a certain set of facts is beyond the scope of representation).

He thinks things are under control. Turns out they're not. But he wants to solve the problem himself, and not aggravate the board. Not jeopardize his bonus. Or the stock price. I listen carefully. I know some SEC stuff. Our firm specializes in it. So I advise him that he's okay. And I wish him good luck. When I tell my partner the story at lunch the next day, he is horrified. "You gave him bad advice," he says, "and you better call him right away." My answer: "The advice is worth what he paid for it. And if he's ever going to hire us, that chance will evaporate if I admit error." I don't owe him a call, right?

Your colleague has it right. This fellow did not become a client. But he was a prospective client.[22] While you had no obligation to give him any advice, once you offered it, it had better be right.[23] We call these folks "accidental clients." and the absence of a fee, a conflicts check, or an engagement letter doesn't absolve you of responsibility. It's time to make that call. You can couch it in a positive way. Tell him that you were concerned and that you did some further research.

🏛 Prospective Clients: E-Lawyering

Our firm just came up with a great idea. We'll use our Web site to advertise our services to small businesses, complete with an e-mail feature that invites readers to "ask the lawyer."

We'll call the service "BizHelp."

What a great idea. Everyone's online today. You can be as accessible as anyone. Just three things to worry about.

First, be as careful on your Web site as you would be if you were advertising—because that's what the discipline folks will say you are doing. This means no false, fraudulent, or misleading communications.[24] No promotionals, no promises about results, no boasting about prior victories, no superlatives you cannot substantiate.[25] Just because your target audience consists of businesses does not change the rules.

---

22. MODEL RULE 1.18; RLGL § 15.

23. *Nelson v. Nationwide Mortgage Corp.*, 659 F. Supp. 611 (D.D.C. 1987) (lawyer who volunteered to answer questions and explain document to opposing party in transaction undertook a client-lawyer relationship and a duty of care to opposing party).

24. MODEL RULE 7.1; *Fla. Bar v. Went for It, Inc.*, 515 U.S. 618 (1995); *Shapero v. Ky. Bar Ass'n*, 486 U.S. 466 (1988); *Bates v. State Bar of Ariz.*, 433 U.S. 350 (1977).

25. MODEL RULE 7.1, cmts. [2]–[3].

Second, business clients present a far wider and, in many cases, far more specialized range of problems than individual clients. If you are offering soup-to-nuts legal services to these businesses, you'd better be in a position to provide them (a) because of your own experience, (b) by getting yourself a quick but sufficient tutorial, or (c) by associating yourself with, or referring these clients you've caught in your web to, someone who has the necessary expertise.[26]

Third, we worry about "Ask the Lawyer." We know, we know—you thought, lure'em in with a little free advice, and they'll beat a track to your paying-client door. Almost a public service. But how does it look to your visitors? Like you are acting as their lawyer. Forming a lawyer-client relationship. Providing free legal services. Realize that offering legal advice to someone who asks is enough to bind you to a client-lawyer relationship, even if you don't know who they are, the nature of their matters, whether they present a potential conflict of interest, or how the advice you are providing fits into their needs.[27] All opportunities for you to get sued[28] and, worse yet, disciplined[29]—with no income to show for your efforts. A risky proposition to be sure.

If you are going to offer free advice, you must remember to treat the people who are going to receive that advice exactly as you treat full-fledged, paying clients. You should expect to be held to the exact same standard of care regarding the Five C's: control, communication, competence, confidentiality, and conflict-of-interest resolution, just as if you had entered into a formal full-scale agreement after consultation. So make sure you know what you are saying, because it can be dangerous to give advice on incomplete facts. Equally important, make sure that the client understands the scope of

---

26. MODEL RULE 1.1; RLGL § 48; *Horne v. Peckham*, 158 Cal. Rptr. 714 (Cal. Ct. App. 1979) (lawyer who acknowledged need for tax expertise had a duty to refer client to an expert in the field or to comply with the specialized standard of care).

27. RLGL § 14; Ver. Op. 2000-04 (the more e-mail responses to Web site inquiries address specific facts, the greater the risk a client-lawyer relationship will be formed; Web site disclaimer does not necessarily preclude client-lawyer relationship); Ariz. Op. 97-04 (just as lawyers should not answer specific legal questions in giving a legal seminar to lay people, lawyers should not answer specific legal questions from lay persons through the Internet unless the question presented is of a general nature, and the advice given is not fact specific).

28. *E.g., Togstad v. Vesely, Otto, Miller & Keefe*, 291 N.W.2d 686 (Minn. 1980).

29. MODEL RULE 1.1.

your undertaking,[30] because it can be dangerous to give advice on one part of a matter when you don't know how the client intends to use it in another. And don't forget to be sure that you are not violating the conflict-of-interest rules[31] in taking on this "albeit informal" representation, and that you hold confidential everything you learn during the course of your work.

✄ Prospective Clients: Beauty Contests

Those damn companies. They don't just call a lawyer up and hire her. No. They have to hold beauty contests. Gives the general counsels something to do. And makes'em feel real important. So there's this big class action suit. Sued every-body—the company, its officers, its auditors, its banks, its accountants, and they're all blaming each other. Yesterday my partner went to the company's swimsuit competition. Met with them for three hours. Thinks it went well, but the company's interviewing ten—count'em, ten—law firms. Today I get a call from the company's accountants. They want to hire us ... me. What a great deal. Since we won't hear from the company for a week, the case is mine, right? A bird in the hand and all that.

Not so fast. It all depends on what happened yesterday. Or the day before. Did your colleague have any understanding with the company before he met with them?

How do you mean?

Did the company agree you could represent one of the other defendants if they didn't choose your firm?

I doubt it. That would be a helluva way for a lawyer to start the talent show. "You don't mind if we represent someone else, do you?" Doesn't sound warm and fuzzy, and my colleague was so desperate for this new matter, I'd be shocked if he started off that way. Would it have worked?

Know what you mean. It is a hard question to ask. But if the question were asked, and the prospective client agreed to the condition, the waiver the lawyer received would likely be enforceable, especially in the case of a sophisticated client and assuming the meeting progressed as the client anticipated.[32]

---

30. MODEL RULE 1.2(c); RLGL § 19.

31. MODEL RULES 1.7–1.12; RLGL §§ 121–135.

32. MODEL RULE 1.18, cmt. [5]; RLGL § 15, cmt. c.

But what about me? Assume no agreement.

Then the question is whether the company will object to your firm's representing the accountants.

How could they? They aren't a client. Just another one of those high falutin companies that makes a big deal about selecting counsel.

That may be true. But no matter how high falutin they are, they are still a prospective client who provided a prospective lawyer with all kinds of confidential information. Didn't you mention that your colleague met with them for three hours?

Something like that.

Anyway, no matter how long they met, the company is entitled to protection of the confidential information that was discussed. And to not have it fall into the hands of the accountants.[33]

I promise not to talk to our pageant team.

That promise won't solve the problem. Whatever your partner learned is imputed to you.[34] And I'm afraid that three-hour meeting will not bring you within Model Rule 1.18.

Rule 1.18? What's that?

It's a part of the Model Rules; it came out of the ABA Ethics 2000 project that rewrote the Model Rules. It provides a reminder and a little gift.

The reminder?

Yes. It's a reminder to lawyers of the existing law. That is, prospective clients are entitled to confidentiality, and your obligation—to keep the prospective client's confidences—can disqualify a prospective lawyer from taking on another representation, particularly in the same matter.

And the gift?

The Rule provides that if a prospective client provides confidential information to a lawyer but then does not retain that lawyer, the lawyer's firm may take on the representation of a conflicting client with two conditions: (1) that the lawyer or lawyers who participated in the initial conversation "took reasonable measures to avoid exposure to more disqualifying information than was reasonably necessary," and (2) that the lawyer who learned confidential information is screened from the firm's representation of the second client.[35]

---

33. MODEL RULE 1.18(b); RLGL § 15(1)(a).

34. MODEL RULE 1.10; RLGL § 123.

35. MODEL RULE 1.18(d); RLGL § 15(2).

So, if my colleague just had a short phone call with the company about the basis: the parties, the nature of the matter, I'd be home free?

If your jurisdiction has adopted Rule 1.18, that's generally correct; but I'm afraid with a three-hour song and dance, you only have one chance to waltz.

What's that? Tell me. Tell me.

Your colleague can call the company to determine whether the company will waive the conflict and permit your firm to take on the representation.[36] But don't make that call quite yet.

Why not?

Because you first need the permission of the accounting firm to clear the conflict.[37] Without that permission, you cannot start the process.

All because my friend got called first?

And went to the beauty contest.

〽 Third-Person Influence: Dealing with Constituents

So, you say the organizational client acts through people. True enough. How, then, do I decide who I deal with? The person who called me? The CEO? His secretary? In-house counsel and their paralegals? The company's HR rep?

Great question. And an important one too. When a lawyer is assigned to represent a company, the rules tell us that the lawyer is to take instruction from the person the entity directs you to deal with.[38] Sometimes it's the CEO, Chairman, or head of a government agency. Sometimes it's general counsel. Sometimes it's the plant superintendent or the head of the lab. It is the pre-rogative and responsibility of the client to identify the contact. But it is your responsibility to clarify who that is.[39] So when that settlement offer comes in or you need guidance on how to handle a knotty problem, you know whom to call.

What if I'm told that my contact person is the general manager of sales and I get a call from the Comptroller?

---

36. MODEL RULE 1.18(d)(1); RLGL § 15(2)(b).

37. MODEL RULES 1.18(b), 1.6(a); RLGL §§ 15(1)(a), 60.

38. MODEL RULE 1.13, cmt. [3]; RLGL § 96(1)(b) & cmt. d.

39. MODEL RULE 1.13(a), (g); RLGL § 14, cmt. f, § 96, cmt. d.

Unless it is clear that the latter is authorized to pull rank to give you instructions, it is no different from a representation drafting dad's estate plan in which son calls you up to "clarify instructions." Son may be dad's authorized agent,[40] but son also may wish to interfere.[41] It's your job to clarify the situation. Here, you have to call the general manager to confirm that the general manager approves of the new instructions.

𝑀 Accommodating Clients' Employees at a Deposition

It's a great case. So much at stake. And the key witnesses are the CEO, the CFO, and the board. A chance to represent the great and near great. Show our stuff.

It's a journey fraught with peril.

There you go again. Just when I am on top of the world, you have to be the ink droplet in the cold glass of milk.

Just want you to be careful.

Oh, I will be, you can be sure. With clients like these, how can I miss?

Let me count the ways. You said "clients."

I mean the company and the big cheeses.

Do you represent them all?

Well, I represent the company, of course. There are no individual parties in this matter.

So you only have one client.

Hadn't really thought about it.

Start thinking now.

Well, I heard some big ethics guy talk about "accommodation clients." I think that's what these other folks are.

And what does that mean?

I don't really know. I guess it means I represent these guys at their deps as a favor to my real client.

Does that make them clients?

I don't know.

Well I suggest you find out.

There's no time like the present.

---

40. MODEL RULE 1.14; cmt. [3], RLGL § 24, cmt. c.

41. MODEL RULES 1.8(f), 5.4(c); RLGL § 134.

The rules say nothing about "accommodation clients." Even thought the Restatement mentions it,[42] courts have refused to accept the label.[43] We have clients,[44] prospective clients,[45] former clients,[46] adverse parties,[47] and other represented[48] and unrepresented persons.[49] So calling someone an "accommodation client" does not answer any question whose answer you need to know.

Does it really matter? I'm just taking them to a deposition.

And preparing them for that deposition?

Of course. What do you think I am?

An effective lawyer. A conscientious lawyer. A well-prepared lawyer. As a result, when you sit in that conference room going over the upcoming deposition, you will not just be representing the company, you may be representing the soon-to-be deponent.

Not really.

Okay, let's assume that person is not a client. What does that mean?

It means I don't have a joint representation.

True enough. But what else?

That's why I came to you.

It means that this person is unrepresented. And under our rules, it means that you can't give this person any legal advice. Except for one thing.

What's that?

The advice to get a lawyer. That, and you have an obligation to correct any misperception the person may have about your role.[50] And then there's the deposition itself.

Is that a problem?

Only from the very beginning. First, when the lawyer on the other side asks the witness if he is represented. And then, when you direct the witness

---

42. RLGL § 132, cmt. i.

43. *Universal City Studios, Inc. v. Reimerdes,* 98 F. Supp. 2d 449 (S.D.N.Y. 2000) (court criticized expert witness's use of the term "accommodation" client).

44. MODEL RULES 1.1–1.8, 1.10–1.17, 2.1–2.4, 3.7; RLGL §§ 14, 16–32, 34–56, 59–97, 104.

45. MODEL RULE 1.18; RLGL § 15.

46. MODEL RULE 1.9; RLGL § 33, 132.

47. MODEL RULES 3.1–3.4, 3.8, 4.1, 4.4; RLGL §§ 98, 105–120.

48. MODEL RULE 4.2; RLGL § 99–102.

49. MODEL RULE 4.3; RLGL § 103.

50. MODEL RULES 1.13(f), 4.3; RLGL § 103, cmt. e.

not to answer, and the lawyer on the other side turns to the witness and asks whether the witness is going to take your advice, will you be acting as lawyer for the witness?

I . . . guess so. It certainly doesn't fit what I see as my role for me to think of this person as unrepresented. Isn't it better to say I am giving advice to my client through a constituent?

That would be so if you were certain that this individual was not in need of independent legal advice and that the individual understood and accepted your view. But that situation may be quite rare,[51] leaving one choice.

I represent this person—at least for this day and trip.

We think so.

What does that mean?

It means, first, that you have a joint representation. But with none of the protections.

How do you mean?

Generally, when you have a multiple representation, the representation of the clients commences at the same time, at the beginning of the representation. That gives the lawyer a chance, at the earliest possible time, to talk about the risks, about how confidential information will be handled, and about what will happen if conflicts develop. Not to mention confirming it all in writing.[52] Here, you, the lawyer, have been representing the company for a long time, you plan to continue representing the company to conclusion, and you view this representation as a punctuation mark in a long paragraph— which doesn't mean you don't have to contend with these matters.

How am I going to do that?

You're going to walk a tight rope, my friend. And explain it to both clients in writing.[53] If you don't, and if the company and the employee are now at loggerheads and unwilling to waive the conflict, your corporate client had better start looking for substitute counsel.

Meaning?

You probably will be forced to withdraw.[54] We hope that the entire time you were in accommodation mode, you were not aware of any conflict,

---

51. MODEL RULE 1.13(f) & cmt. [2].

52. MODEL RULE 1.7(b)(4).

53. MODEL RULE 1.7; RLGL §§ 75, 128, 131.

54. *In re Rite Aid Corp. Sec. Litig.*, 139 F. Supp. 2d 649 (E.D. Pa. 2001) (law firm that represented defendant corporation and defendant former chief executive who resigned during the

because if you were, you might be in trouble for not withdrawing from the constituent's representation at a much earlier time. A lawyer, for sure, can represent the organization and its officers, partners, or directors at the same time. But, as with all joint representations, they may only continue so long as no unwaived conflict arises between or among them.[55]

Again: no good deed goes unpunished.

ℳ The Internal Investigation

Now you've got me worried about how I deal with constituents. Should I have any special concerns if I'm the lawyer conducting an organizational investigation?

Quite a few. The first is to make sure the investigating lawyer knows to whom she will report and the scope of the matter.

Anything else?

If the investigation is to be viewed as independent by some outside body, then that may be the next issue to be addressed.

Well, I'm assuming outside counsel would be involved.

It's true that outside counsel is much preferred if the goal is to convince some third party that the investigation was independent and unbiased. Preferable, but not necessarily enough.

How's that?

Outside counsel may not be viewed as independent simply because she is "outside." If that lawyer regularly does work for the company—even if it's totally unrelated to the present matter—there could be a challenge. Similarly, outside counsel should not have any other relationships—social or

---

litigation not disqualified where former CEO dealt with law firm solely through corporation and was therefore an accommodation client and consented to law firm's subsequent continued representation of corporation after it had ceased representing former CEO because of conflicts); *Miller v. Alagna*, 138 F. Supp. 2d 1252 (C.D. Cal. 2000) (county lawyers disqualified from representing police officers in excessive force and wrongful death claim); *Int'l Bhd. of Teamsters, Chauffeurs, Warehousemen, and Helpers of Am. v. Hoffa*, 242 F. Supp. 246 (D.D.C. 1965) (lawyer who represents union may not also represent union official who is the subject of alleged wrongdoing); *In re Brownstein*, 602 P.2d 655 (Or. 1979) (lawyer who represented small corporation and shareholder where the rights of one client conflicted with the other reprimanded for failing to withdraw from both representations).

55. Lawrence J. Fox, *Defending a Deposition of Your Organizational Client's Employee: An Ethical Minefield Everyone Ignores,* 44 S. TEX. L. REV. 185 (2002).

business—that could be asserted as compromising independence. Having the same country club memberships or prior business affiliations are examples of the kind of challenges to independence that have been unearthed and asserted.

So we get independent outside counsel. Now what?

Now it's time to think through how the investigation will be approached. Counsel needs to be able to affirm that no limitations were placed on documents to be reviewed or individuals interviewed.

We're ready to go?

Not quite so fast. The next item on the agenda is to be clear about how each interviewee is to be approached. Especially with organization employees, it is critical that the lawyer explains whom the lawyer represents and how the information learned will be treated.

There goes the investigation. Read the employees Miranda *warnings, and no one will cooperate.*

It is true that approaching matters this way could have a chilling effect. But the risks of not providing the appropriate disclosures could be far worse. These individuals are unrepresented, and they must be reminded of that fact, and advised to seek their own counsel.[56] The interview is privileged and confidential, but the privilege belongs to the company, and what is said during the interview will be the subject of a report to others in the company—not very confidential from the interviewee's point of view, and a real possibility for confusion if the lawyer simply mumbles.

Let's go back to those Miranda *warnings. Do we have to tell the company employees anything about the attorney-client privilege? Like that the company may choose to waive it later?*

Anytime entity lawyers need to conduct an investigation through entity employees, they are on the horns of a dilemma. To secure as much information as possible, the warnings given to the employees should be minimized. At the same time, however, the lawyer has an obligation to avoid any confusion. If the lawyer does discuss the lawyer-client privilege with an employee during an interview, the lawyer then must make it absolutely clear that, not only is the privilege the entity's, and not the individual's, but also that it may turn out to be in the best interest of the company to waive the privilege and disclose the information to the government, opposing parties, or others.

---

56. MODEL RULES 1.13 (f) & cmts. [10],[11], 4.3.

But the last thing you want is for employees to think that what they tell the lawyer will never be shared with anyone on the outside.[57]

〽 Representing a Constituent in an Unrelated Matter

I understand now that I represent the entity, not the employees, but sometimes these people are my clients.

If you are also representing an organization, taking on such matters raises some important issues. Of course, it depends on what work you are doing and for whom.

Well, you know how it is. I work in-house, surrounded by clients. They know I'm a lawyer. So they ask me to review an agreement of sale for a house or help draft a simple will.

That is certainly the most benign example of a lawyer concurrently representing both an entity and what we technically refer to as constituents of the organization.

So what do I have to worry about?

First, if you are a full-time employee of the company, you have to be sure your employer does not consider your "outside" work with your colleagues to be a breach of your commitment to the company. Some companies might not be thrilled that their full-time employee has a greater interest in growing a cottage industry of other engagements with its employees or for anyone else for that matter.

They don't own me?

The organization client may think so. They may worry about liability, or interferences with your dedication, or the chance that your outside work might generate conflicts of interest, undermining one of the great benefits of having full-time counsel. Whether you are inside counsel or outside counsel, you must find out the organizational client's policy on representing constituents. And if you are inside counsel you must learn the client's policy toward any other representations—of employees or outsiders.

What if I don't charge?

Even then. Free services raise many of the same issues. Do you have malpractice insurance that covers these representations? Are you licensed to

---

57. *See* Chapter 6, Figure 7: Interviewing Organization Employees.

represent individual clients in this jurisdiction? And free services also raise a serious concern simply because they are free.

How could that be?

Well, the organization may view the providing of free legal services to its officers and employees by its lawyer—whether inside or outside—as a compromise of those constituents' independence, particularly if those individuals are the ones who select outside lawyers or set compensation for in-house counsel.[58] The entity may also worry about a perquisite being provided to only some employees as unfair.

That's a lot of baggage for free advice to carry.

True enough, but as you know, sometimes no good deed goes unpunished.

And that's the benign example!

It is indeed.

What's more serious?

✺ The Constituent vs. The Entity

I once had a CEO ask me to transfer some land owned by the company to him. "I'm taking it off the company's hands," he remarked.

What did you do?

I told him I didn't do real estate. Then I wondered whether the deal was legit. Now I'm wondering whether I should tell the company? Do I have to tell the company? It's all so troubling.

The answer turns on what role the CEO was playing when he approached you. If he was the CEO of your client, then your duty to tell the client is clear.[59] If he was a prospective client, then you owe him the same duties of confidentiality you owe any prospective client, and you cannot disclose the information unless it falls within an exception to confidentiality in your jurisdiction.[60] One thing may be certain: the CEO might claim you breached a duty to him if you do disclose.

The truth is, I don't know. The word "client" wasn't mentioned. But we have done personal work for the CEO before.

---

58. MODEL RULES 1.7, 1.13(g); RLGL § 131.

59. MODEL RULE 1.13(b) & cmts. [3]–[5]; RLGL § 96, cmt. e, § 131, cmt. e.

60. MODEL RULE 1.18; RLGL § 15.

It may help you to know that the reasonable expectations of the "client" govern whether a client-lawyer relationship has been established or proposed.[61] In the ordinary situation, most jurisdictions start with a presumption of sorts that the CEO was acting on behalf of the company when he spoke to you.[62] That presumption is problematic here, however, for two reasons. First, your prior personal representation of the CEO may lead him to believe that you would do so again.[63] Second, the CEO in this conversation asked you for personal legal services, the "offer" of a prospective client. If you give him any legal advice at all (except the advice to get his own lawyer) you have "accepted" his "offer." The burden is on you to clarify the situation, and you may have already waited too long to do so.[64]

🐌 Start-Ups

So, I got a call from a client, Joe. We do his taxes, wrote his will. Nothing big. He's got a new idea. Wants to come talk to me. Says he's bringing his partners.

Turns out, they think they're the next Google. Joe's going to be the money guy, the idea is Howard's, and Diane will be the CEO. They want us to form the new entity, partnership, corporation, whatever.

Can I represent them?

Who?

That's my question.

Well, you already represent one of them.

Guess that's right. Hadn't thought about that.

And you certainly would want to represent the next Google.

You can say that again.

In other words, you want your current individual clients to "morph" into an entity. In a few jurisdictions, such a metamorphosis can have

---

61. RLGL § 14.

62. *E.g., Doe v. Poe*, 595 N.Y.S.2d 503 (N.Y. App. Div. 1993).

63. *E.g., Meyer v. Mulligan*, 889 P.2d 509 (Wyo. 1995).

64. RLGL § 14, cmt. f.

retroactive effect.[65] But in most, you represent the individuals as joint clients—at least until the entity is established.[66]

Which means I have to worry about conflicts, confidentiality, and my preexisting relationship to Joe?

Now you get the picture. The lawyer who proceeds without recognizing the client identity problem could easily find herself on the wrong end of a claim by any one (or more) of the clients alleging that the lawyer failed to protect that client's interests.[67] "I didn't get a non-compete." "My royalty's being collected by the bank." "My loan to the company wasn't secured." All such claims will be anything but far-fetched assertions when the honeymoon ends and each former "partner" is looking to minimize losses.[68]

✹ Clients that Morph: The Corporate Family

I love doing work for Fortune 500 companies. Well, some of the time. But they operate under so many difference disguises, I find they conflict me out at every turn. I'm doing a lease for Movies Unlimited, and I can never be adverse to any of the companies in the Colossus family of companies in any matter. That's like 500 different enterprises. And to add insult to injury, what happens if Colossus follows through on a merger with another huge conglomerate?

Before we discuss what the ethics rules provide, we need to address two practical considerations.

First, whatever the rules say, you must abide by any stipulation Movies Unlimited made when it first retained you. So, if Movies Unlimited told you that a condition of the engagement was never being adverse to any Colossus-related company, you cannot change the arrangement just when it starts to bind. Clients are always entitled to ask for greater protections than

---

65. *See Jesse v. Danforth*, 485 N.W.2d 63 (Wis. 1992) (physicians who retain a law firm to organize a medical corporation were not individual clients where attorney's involvement with the physicians was directly related to the corporation and the medical corporation was eventually incorporated because the entity rule applied retroactively); Ariz. State Bar Formal Ethics Op. 02-06.

66. MODEL RULE 1.7, cmt. [28]; RLGL § 130, Illus. 4.

67. *See*, Chapter 7, Joint Clients: The Start-Up and Chapter 10, The Start-Up Fallout.

68. *E.g., Straub Clinic & Hosp. v. Kochi*, 917 P.2d 1284 (Haw. 1996) (law firm that represented two parties in setting up a business venture disqualified from representing one party when a dispute arose over the other's attempt to withdraw from the joint venture).

the rules provide, and the lawyer may take on the matter subject to that condition, drop it, or negotiate a clearly defined and more limited scope of representation.[69] But once you accepted these conditions, you are stuck.

Second, in taking on a matter adverse to a Colossus-related entity—even if you can justify it under the rules—you will have to make the business decision whether you can live with Movies Unlimited's firing your firm as a result. This is because many clients view a lawyer's obligation of loyalty to be seriously breached by being in conflict with any part of a corporate family, even if the lawyer is able to argue that the rules permit the adverse representation.

I hear you. But this lease matter is so small. And the new representation adverse to Colossus is huge. My partners won't think I'm unproductive anymore. So I think I'm willing to incur Movies Unlimited's wrath.

We hope that means your firm is willing to take on the adverse representation.

Oh . . . sure. But can we do it?

Well, that depends.

On what?

On the identity of your client. There is a comment to new Model Rule 1.7 providing that if Movies Unlimited is a separate subsidiary with its own in-house counsel and operates in a different line of business from the business entity you are attacking, and nothing in your retention by Movies Unlimited suggests a special understanding, then your firm may be free to take on the new matter, because you represent Movies Unlimited, not Colossus.[70]

"May be." That sounds like hedging language to me.

Well, you should know that these conflicts within and between corporate families have generated a fair amount of controversy and case law.[71] The view of the Rule 1.7 comment is not universally applauded.[72] Nor are its

---

69. RLGL §§ 16, 18.

70. MODEL RULE 1.7, cmt. [34]; RLGL § 121 cmt. d.

71. Charles W. Wolfram, *Corporate-Family Conflicts*, 2 J. INST. STUD. LEG. ETH. 295 (1999).

72. *Certain Underwriters at Lloyd's, London v. Argonaut Ins. Co.*, 264 F. Supp. 2d 914 (N.D. Cal. 2003) (insurer and subsidiary treated as one entity for conflicts purposes because of relatively direct financial relationship between them and common management of legal affairs); *Discotrade Ltd. v. Wyeth-Ayerst Int'l Inc.*, 200 F. Supp. 2d 355 (S.D.N.Y. 2002) (lawyer who represented a sister subsidiary corporation disqualified from representing another client in an unrelated lawsuit against another sister subsidiary); *J.P. Morgan Chase Bank v.*

applications universally clear. In fact, identifying the corporate family also can be an example of what we call "clients who morph," because organizations can change by merger, acquisition, bankruptcy, and the like.[73]

Some, including one of the authors of this volume, have argued that a position directly adverse to one member of a wholly owned corporate family is directly adverse to every other member. Even though these other members are not clients, this is so simply because in an integrated conglomerate, it is irrelevant to the overall performance of the enterprise where the losses occur, for example, in the Division of Ford or in the subsidiary of the same company.[74] So this is not a risk-free endeavor, but there is more than respectable authority to buttress your argument that the lease representation does not block you from taking on this career-soaring new matter.

What if Movies Unlimited is not wholly owned by Colossus?

Excellent question. As the percentage of ownership declines, the argument that taking a position directly adverse to Colossus is directly adverse to Movies Unlimited declines in weight.[75] This is because when a lawyer represents an organization, the lawyer does not necessarily thereby represent constituents, absent additional facts. The best example would be that a lawyer for General Motors does not represent GM's shareholders. But even on a much smaller scale, this is true. For example, where a homeowner's association is comprised of only twenty-five members, representing the association itself does not preclude the lawyer, as a matter of ethics, from suing

---

Liberty Mut. Ins. Co., 189 F. Supp. 2d 20 (S.D.N.Y. 2002) (law firm that functioned as holding company's outside counsel disqualified from bringing a major lawsuit against primary subsidiary, as well as other defendants, in absence of any good reason to sever subsidiary from other defendants).

73. *Weil Gotshal & Manges L.L.P. v. Fashion Boutique of Short Hills, Inc.*, 780 N.Y.S.2d 593 (N.Y. App. Div. 2004), *subsequent appeal after remand*, 847 N.Y.S.2d 162 (N.Y. App. Div. 2007) (plaintiff whose law firm represented company that acquired the defendant during the litigation has cause of action for malpractice if it can show that conflict of interest led it to pull punches at trial resulting in a lower recovery).

74. ABA Comm. on Ethics and Prof'l Responsibility, Formal Op. 95-390 (1995) (Conflicts of Interest in the Corporate Family Context); *Colorpix Sys. of Am. v. Broan Mfg. Co.*, 131 F. Supp. 2d 331 (D. Conn. 2001) (law firm that represented parent company in prior substantially related matter disqualified from representing subsidiary in a later representation due to identity of interest between parent and subsidiary and confidential information from parent that could be used against it in the subsequent case); *Pennwalt Corp. v Plough, Inc.*, 85 F.R.D. 264 (D. Del. 1980) (lawyer who had previously withdrawn from representing sister corporation permitted to bring suit against affiliate where no relevant confidential information had been disclosed by former client).

75. RLGL § 131, cmt. d.

any individual member of the association, absent special facts that might give rise to an independent lawyer-client relationship.[76] Similarly, a lawyer for a company does not thereby represent the CEO, or the members of the board, or even a 10 percent shareholder of a closely held company.[77]

Of course, the original warning still stands.

What do you mean?

If you are going to sue the CEO of your client or the president of the homeowners' association, you must be prepared for the adverse party to take a broader view of loyalty than the Rules of Professional Conduct might mandate. These might be called business and ethical, as opposed to legal, conflicts. But the wise lawyer ignores them at her peril, because winning the battle now (the disqualification motion) may mean losing the entire representation later, when you're fired.

🦋 Imputation: The Firm Split

What an ugly divorce.

We didn't know you did matrimonial.

We don't. Not the marriage kind anyway. But we've just been through a doozy. As clients. Our firm was going along fine. Then we talked merger with one of those big international firms. The negotiations were endless. Some saw it as our only solution—others as the road to perdition. So when it was all done, we lost sixty lawyers to this other firm. And one hundred of us stayed together. The process was ugly but it's over—except for one thing.

What's that?

We don't know how to divorce our database. Do all of us carry around all of the conflicts of the old firm forever? Frankly, for those of us left behind, it would be best if our former partners had as few conflicts as possible so they can earn enough to pay us their final settlement amount as quickly as possible.

Let's look at it from each side. As to the firm that continues—you guys—all clients that have departed your firm entirely can now be treated

---

76. ABA Comm. on Ethics and Prof'l Responsibility, Formal Op. 92-365 (1992) (Trade Associations as Clients); *Westinghouse Elec. Co. v. Kerr-McGee Corp.*, 580 F.2d 1311 (7th Cir. 1978) (trade association member who shared confidential information with law firm considered client for purposes of disqualification in subsequent substantially related representation).

77. MODEL RULE 1.13 (a) & cmt. [1]; RLGL § 96(1) & cmt. b.

as former clients. As to those former clients your firm—the surviving firm—may take positions directly adverse to those now former clients as long as the new matters are not the same or substantially related to any matters your firm handled before or do not implicate confidential information that current lawyers at the surviving firm are privy to.[78]

No waiting period?

None whatsoever.

And our former colleagues?

They obviously must continue to treat all clients they take with them as present clients of their new firm. As for clients they left behind. . . .

Thank goodness, there are plenty of them.

They must only treat as former clients those clients for whom they worked or as to whom they have confidential information. As to those, they may not take on any matters directly adverse that are substantially related or as to which they have confidential information.[79] With respect to all other clients of the former firm, they can immediately be directly adverse.

Sounds like the lawyers who left are in better shape—only conflict-wise, we hope—than the true believers who stayed behind.

That is true. The Rules really don't contemplate more than one or two lawyers leaving at a time. When the rules are imposed on a firm split they yield a slightly asymmetrical result depending on who is considered remaining at the old farm. But the good news is that your former colleagues have fewer impediments to making those payments.

✐ Quasi Clients: Third-Party Beneficiaries

Sometimes I do the right thing. Sometimes I don't. Take representing my sister-in-law's business. Maybe I shouldn't have taken it on. But my husband begged me. So I did. Now I wince every time she calls, and too often, she's in my over-120-day category. This time, she's borrowing money from the bank. And we're defending her in an employment suit. So the bank wants an opinion letter about the suit. I want to help her out. She says I should make it clear the suit's no big deal. That's what I keep telling her—to calm her down.

---

78. MODEL RULE 1.9; RLGL § 132.

79. *Id.*

You certainly can undertake the assignment. We hope you get paid. But you must remember this letter is not to satisfy your sister-in-law. You are giving an opinion to a bank—an opinion the bank will say it relied on when it made the loan.[80]

But the bank isn't my client.

True enough. But you can take on quasi-client or client-like duties when your client asks you to give an opinion to a third party. You must be competent to give the opinion, and you must use reasonable care and steer clear of misrepresentation in writing it.[81]

I'm in trouble then?

How come?

Because if I write an objective opinion, I'll have to tell the bank that although, in my view, the case is bogus, it did survive a motion to dismiss, the plaintiff is a sympathetic grandma, and, if the plaintiff wins, she'll win big.

Then you'd better tell your sister-in-law that that's what you have to write in your letter to the bank, and let her decide what she wants you to do.[82] That will save you from becoming a guarantor of your sister-in-law's loan—on top of those unpaid bills.[83]

---

80. MODEL RULE 2.3(a); RLGL § 95(1).

81. RLGL §§ 52(2), 95(3).

82. MODEL RULE 2.3(b)(c); RLGL § 95(2).

83. *Greycas, Inc. v. Proud*, 826 F.2d 1560 (7th Cir.1987).

TWO

Fees

"Remember to round each billable hour off to the nearest week."

𝄞 Introduction: Clarify Your Fee

LAWYERS ARE FIDUCIARIES and therefore owe clients certain pre-contractual duties of fairness in bargaining for fees imposed by professional codes and case law.[1] These obligations impose an objective standard of reasonableness on every fee and expense you agree to, charge, or collect.[2] Factors determining reasonableness include the time and difficulty of the matter, the fee customarily charged, the amount involved, results obtained, your experience and ability, and the kind of fee you charge.[3] Contingent fee contracts and fee-splitting arrangements require a written agreement,[4] and some jurisdictions impose a writing requirement for all fee arrangements.[5]

This chapter explores the most common fee agreements (hourly, flat, contingent, statutory, and blended), as well as fee modification, splits, and retainers. Throughout, we will examine the legal requirement of a reasonable fee and the power of this concept before, during, and after a representation.

𝄞 The Billable Hour

It's hard to remember it was clients who were insisting on billable-hour billing on their matters. The organizations hired general counsel, and in order to prove their worth to their CEOs, general counsel decided to hold outside lawyers accountable. We hated it in the beginning, but now I see it as a real plus. Take this example. Our client has agreed to pay us for all time we dedicate to the matter. We say that includes travel time. So I've instructed our lawyers, when they endure those lengthy security lines, to bill the client for when they are traveling, but to work on another client's matters. That way, a six-hour flight to L.A. garners the lawyer twelve billables.

Do you tell the client that's your approach?

---

1. RLGL § 34, cmt. b.

2. MODEL RULE 1.5(a); RLGL § 34; *In re Fordham*, 668 N.E.2d 816 (Mass. 1996) (lawyer disciplined for accurately charging client $50,000 for 227 hours of time to obtain an acquittal on a drunk driving charge, based on expert testimony that a reasonable lawyer would charge no more than 40 billable hours).

3. MODEL RULE 1.5(a); RLGL § 34, cmt. c.

4. MODEL RULE 1.5(c)(e).

5. *E.g.*, D.C. Rule 1.5(b); N.J. Rule 1.5(b).

You must be kidding. But if the client would pay for the lawyer to sleep, watch the movie, or collect those cute little bottles, what's the difference?

It is true that if your client agrees to pay for travel, your lawyer is not required to write lengthy research memos on a laptop to earn the fee, but it is unethical, absent full disclosure, to manufacture hours like some modern day alchemist. So if you are too embarrassed to tell your corporate client of your little scheme to create the 48-hour day, you don't get to bill on that basis.[6]

Same goes for other creative billable-hour billing practices. You go to motion court for three clients, and you're stuck there all day. You are required to allocate your time spent sitting on those hard wooden pews among the three clients, not to triple your hours.[7]

I hear you. But what about this: a client called up and needed some research done. We spent forty hours undertaking virtually the same assignment for a different client two months ago. Takes us forty-five minutes to customize the old memo. Second client should pay us for at least twenty hours, maybe forty. Don't you think?

If you're willing to fully explain to the client that your approach is to calculate hours in this way, you might have a leg to stand on—but only one. In the absence of such disclosure, however, when you tell clients you are billing them on the basis of the time spent on their matter, you'd better mean what you say.[8] If something takes longer than you expected, you are free to bill that time. But if you manage to proceed in a particularly efficient manner—itself your ethical obligation—then you'd better pass on to your client the benefits of that efficiency. This means sometimes your clients will be billed for a mere fifteen minutes of sheer brilliance and insight and on other occasions, hundreds of hours of plodding review of a gazillion documents.

🕮 The Offshore Advantage

Massive discovery, document production a huge problem. Our client needs help, fast. Our firm can't handle it, but we found a cost-effective alternative in India.

---

6. ABA Comm. on Ethics and Professional Responsibility, Formal Op. 93-379 (1993) (Billing for Professional Fees, Disbursements and Other Expenses).

7. *Id.*

8. *Id. See also,* Calif. Formal Op. 1996-147.

They charge us only half of what we'd charge the client. What a windfall! We'll charge the client our regular rate.

There are two issues here. First, can you delegate this important responsibility to a law firm in India? The lawyers there are not admitted to practice in the United States. They are unfamiliar with our procedures, and they certainly don't fully understand our concepts of attorney-client privilege, confidentiality, and attorney work product. So in dealing with the lawyers in India, you will have to supervise their work with the same level of scrutiny that you currently use for in-house, non-lawyer staff, such as paralegals.[9] That, of course, because of the geographical distance, presents its own special problems. Are you going to send lawyers to India? How can you otherwise say you are supervising their work? After all, ultimately, you are going to be responsible to the client and the courts for the proper administration of the discovery process. What appears to be an inexpensive alternative could turn out to be false economy.

You said there are two problems.

Yes. The second problem is how you are going to bill for this work being done in India. Your client will need to know that they are being billed at a rate higher than the usual disbursement rate. That is perfectly okay given the fact that you are taking responsibility for their work. Nonetheless, your firm can charge no more than a reasonable fee for this supervisory responsibility. The reasonableness of this arrangement will be subject to after-the-fact scrutiny if the client believes that it has been overcharged for this paid activity.[10]

𝍫 Contingent Fees

I was talking to a client the other day. He owns a chain of hardware stores. Sells building supplies to contractors. Some don't pay on time . . . or at all. So we do a lot of collection work for him. He was wondering whether instead of paying us an hourly rate, we could take those on a percentage basis. Thing is, he can afford to pay our regular hourly rates, so I don't think he's eligible for a contingent fee arrangement.

---

9. ABA Comm. on Ethics and Professional Responsibility, Formal Op. 08-451 (2008) (Lawyer's Obligation When Outsourcing Legal and Nonlegal Support Services).

10. *Id.* (In the absence of an agreement with the client to the contrary, the lawyer may bill the client only the actual cost of the outsourcing charges, plus a reasonable allocation for overhead.).

It is true contingent fees certainly started on behalf of clients who otherwise could not afford to hire lawyers. The contingent fee has provided keys to the courthouse for legions who otherwise would have had no way of bringing a case. But that does not mean that the wealthiest client is not entitled to be represented by a lawyer working on a contingent fee. Some say, correctly, there is no better way to align the interest of lawyer and client than to have the lawyer only get compensated whether and to the extent the client recovers. Wealthy entities, as well as governments, have been the happy beneficiaries of contingent fee agreements. So charge ahead. Just make sure the percentage you agree on is a reasonable one, and put the entire arrangement in writing.[11]

One more caveat. For those who embrace contingent fee work for the wealthy or the downtrodden, but particularly the former, it is an ethical obligation (even if the lawyer will not take the case on a non-contingent basis) to inform the client of the alternatives that are available to proceeding on a percentage of the recovery basis.[12]

✐ Reverse Contingent Fees

One of our corporate clients has been sued for an alleged antitrust violation by a major customer claiming an illegal tying arrangement—using its monopoly in one product to increase sales of others. The CEO said to me, "If it wasn't for contingent fees, these extortion cases would never be brought. And now," the CEO observed, "your firm,"—that's me—"gets to run its meter and charge us a fortune, regardless of the outcome." He got me to thinking. What if we took on the defense on a contingent fee? He's been sued for $25 million. How 'bout if we charge him 25 percent of everything we save the company under $75 million (damages trebled)? Then, the CEO won't be grousing so much, and plaintiffs' lawyers won't be the only ones buying chalets in Vail.

You are talking about a reverse contingent fee. In that case, your fee is a percentage of what the client saves. That is a perfectly legitimate approach.[13]

---

11. MODEL RULE 1.5(c).

12. RLGL § 35, cmt. c; ABA Comm. on Ethics and Professional Responsibility, Formal Op. 94-389 (1994) (Contingent Fees).

13. ABA Comm. on Ethics and Professional Responsibility, Formal Op. 93-373 (1993) (Contingent Fees in Civil Cases Based on the Amount of Money Saved for the Client).

While they have not caught on generally, such arrangements are ethically appropriate and have been used successfully. But there are two issues you need to be aware of.

There you go again. Qualifying everything.

Well, you don't want to be accused of charging an unreasonable fee.[14] To avoid that, you must first consider what the right benchmark is. Simply because the suit is for $25 million trebled does not mean that you should be rewarded for every dollar saved below that figure. Then the percentage also may be an issue. Even if personal injury lawyers one-third in your jurisdiction, that does not mean such a high number is justified here. A long discussion with the client and, if it doesn't have in-house counsel, a recommendation that it consult other counsel regarding the fee arrangement, will go a long way toward protecting your huge fee when you save this lucky client a fortune.

There's no guarantee.

In the world of lawyer's fees, nothing is an absolute certainty. A client is always free to challenge a fee as unreasonable. Not just contingent fees. The more you can document the process you followed, the discussions you had, and the details of the arrangement you reached, the more likely the fee will withstand a challenge. And remember: although it's always a good idea to put a fee agreement in writing, for contingent fees, it's a requirement.[15]

Well, the one thing I really worry about is a change in the client's point of view from now, at the beginning of the case, until the matter is concluded. Today the corporate client is all excited; any hope they are not allowed to contest the fee based on 20-20 hindsight?

Buyer's remorse is a risk for every lawyer working on a contingent fee. The client likes the idea going in—no fees to be paid until conclusion—then looks at a great result and wonders why the client should share so much of the recovery with the "greedy" lawyer. Many observers in the area of professional responsibility think the reasonableness of any contingent fee should be judged at the time the deal is cut.[16] But there are ethics gurus who argue that the client should be able to have a "look back" on reasonableness.[17]

---

14. MODEL RULE 1.5(a) & (c); RLGL §§ 34, 35.

15. MODEL RULE 1.5(c).

16. ABA Comm. on Ethics and Professional Responsibility, Formal Op. 94-389 (1994) (Contingent Fees).

17. GEOFFREY C. HAZARD, JR. & W. WILLIAM HODES, THE LAW OF LAWYERING § 8.6 (3d ed., Aspen 2002).

So long as that is true, lawyers will be at risk of challenges, and a "look back" could be just as applicable to a reverse contingent fee.

𝄞 Fixed Fees

Our corporate client has been sued in a class action. So have the officers and directors. Frankly, I think the CEO may be liable. And, of course, he and the others insist on their own counsel. In the CEO's case, that's probably obligatory. There may be a conflict. Anyway, the by-laws require we advance their fees. As you'd expect. But what a huge expense. And we'll have no control of these lawyers. Independence of counsel and all that.

Well, you are right about that. The principle is so important that we have it in our rules twice—1.8(f) and 5.4(c). He who pays the piper does not call the tune. The client does.[18]

That's great in principle, but a disaster fiscally. Anyway, we got a call from Sam Griffin at Griffin & Howe. He recognized our problem right away. He offered to represent all the directors for a fixed fee: $500,000. That's it. I say a half a mil ain't chump change. But at least our exposure will be capped.

Your exposure for legal fees.

Right. I know, we are a defendant.

No. That's not what we mean. Your exposure for legal fees for the directors will be capped. But if it turns out it was an unnecessarily high fee, it can be deemed unreasonable.[19] If it turns out to be an unnecessarily low fee—one with too little incentive for the lawyer to give it the attention it deserves, the fixed fee arrangement may be deemed a failure to fulfill the company's agreement to advance fees. Insurance companies who hire lawyers to represent their insureds run into this predicament all the time.[20] When a third party undertakes to pay someone else's legal fees, it cannot do so on a basis that interferes with the professional independence of the hired lawyer, precisely what can occur if the fixed fee is too low. So you might take Sam's deal. Just be aware of the risk.

---

18. Model Rules 1.8(f) & 5.4(c); RLGL § 134.

19. *In re Kutner*, 399 N.E.2d 963 (Ill. 1979) (lawyer disciplined for charging flat fee of $5000 for criminal battery defense when case was dismissed one week after filing).

20. *E.g., American Ins. Ass'n v. Kentucky Bar Ass'n*, 917 S.W.2d 568 (Ky. 1996) (lawyer who agrees to do all of insurer's defense work for a set fee subject to discipline for violations of Rules 1.7(b) and 1.8(f)).

Well, maybe I'll hire him on an hourly basis to avoid that problem. But I'll only do so on one condition.

What's that?

I want to see detailed monthly bills. Make sure he's not running his meter. Damn four-hour conferences of the entire team. Filing frivolous summary judgment motions just to run up the fees.

Slow down, slow down.

Why?

Well, you can take some steps to limit fees. But again, you must be certain that you are not interfering with the lawyer's independence. If the lawyer and client agree that a summary judgment motion is in their best interest, we don't think you get to say much. And as for the bills, you are probably entitled to some information. But typical bills include both attorney-client privileged and attorney work-product information to which you are not entitled, and it could act as a waiver of the directors' privilege if you received it. The path of good intentions is paved with potholes.[21]

✄ Retainers

I can't believe our good fortune. Just got a smart new business-entrepreneur client who agreed to a $50,000, non-refundable retainer to handle all of his corporate business. I'm off to Rome!

Well, we have two different issues here. First, what kind of a "retainer" do you mean? "Retainers" come in two distinct forms: "advance" or "specific" retainers, designed to advance payments for fees and expenses and "general" or "availability" retainers. Lawyers and clients frequently confuse the concept of a "retainer" with the reality of an "advance." Most "retainers" are actually "advances," and advance payments must be placed in your client trust account until earned. They are never nonrefundable.[22]

You said there were two issues?

Yes, the second question is whether you get to spend the $50,000 now? The answer is almost certainly no. Of course, you may ask a client for an

---

21. *E.g., In re Rules of Prof'l Conduct*, 2 P.3d 806, 822 (Mont. 2000) (insurance defense lawyers are prohibited by Rule 1.6 from submitting detailed descriptions of professional services to outside auditors without first obtaining "contemporaneous fully informed consent of insureds").

22. MODEL RULE 1.15(c); *In re Kendall*, 804 N.E.2d 1152 (Ind. 2004).

advance "retainer." There's nothing wrong with that. But you have not earned that advance unless you have either dedicated $50,000 worth of time to the matter or, if you were working on a fixed-fee agreement, you have completed the work. Thus, if the client fires you before you finish, the client is entitled to the refund. Not the whole $50,000, mind you. But the amount that is unearned. So if you put $10,000 worth of time in already, the client gets back $40,000. If you have done half the required work on a fixed fee arrangement, the client gets back $25,000 If not, you have probably run afoul of the applicable rules.[23]

The only retainer arguably earned when paid is an "engagement" or "availability" retainer, designed to compensate a lawyer for being available to perform legal services for a client for a specific time period. This retainer is a flat fee, which guarantees your attention—complete with the Five C's—when the client needs you. These retainers are rare and require agreements that are quite explicit about the ramifications of the client deciding to go elsewhere. You will know this retainer because it provides for additional compensation for actual legal work.[24] If this is what you and your client intend, use a written agreement that specifies "availability"—an agreement that includes a time period, details the basis for your other compensation, and indicates how the client benefits from the arrangement.[25] Some jurisdictions will allow you to designate such a fee "nonrefundable," but others disagree, pointing out that all fees are subject to refund if they are unreasonable or unearned.[26]

彡 Fees in Stock

My good fortune seems to never end. We have been approached by a professor at Princeton. He's patented a gene-splicing technique. He's ready to form a company. And they want us to do it. When we told them it would cost $200,000 in legal fees, there was dead silence. Then they asked would we take stock in lieu of cash? Can you believe it? Getting in on the ground floor. Of course, we said "yes." What a chance!

---

23. MODEL RULE 1.15(c); RLGL § 44(1); *In re Haar*, 698 A.2d 412 (D.C. 1997) (lawyer negligently misappropriated client funds by withdrawing disputed legal fee from client trust account despite lawyer's entitlement to the fee).

24. RLGL § 34, cmt. c.

25. *Ryan v. Butera, Beausang, Cohen & Brennan, P.C.*, 193 F.3d 210 (3d Cir. 1999).

26. *Id.*; *In re Cooperman*, 633 N.E.2d 1069 (N.Y. 1994).

That's the right word: chance.

Oh, I know the stock may not make me a millionaire. So I haven't bought the Ferrari yet.

That's not what I meant.

Then what?

You agree to provide legal services for a start-up. So you launch it. And six months later, the stock plummets. Do you feel any risk?

Not if we did our job right. Stocks are volatile. Particularly recently issued stock.

True enough. But when those disgruntled investors look around for suspects, you—the lawyers—will be in their sights. And for good reason. They will assert you weren't just advisors; you were principals or promoters. You should've forced additional disclosures that would have kept investors away. But, no—your firm had to go along because that was the only way you'd get paid.

I get the point. But we would never compromise our integrity for a fee.

Let's hope not. Even if that risk doesn't slow you down, you should remember that you can get hurt on the upside as well.

How can that be?

Because a lawyer's fee must be reasonable.[27]

Reasonable. This one is bargain basement.

That's how it looks now. But what if the stock soars. What if they go up tenfold. Your $200,000 fee has become a cool two mil.

My dream come true.

Only if no one seeks to challenge it as an unreasonable fee for the work performed.

That would be so unfair. Reasonableness should be judged based on the value at the time of the services.

You'll certainly agree on that.

I already did.

But that won't stop those seeking a fee reduction from asserting that they get a look back—a second judgment on reasonableness—once the stock is issued. In any event, if you are going to take a fee in stock, remember one more thing.

Still more?

---

27. MODEL RULE 1.5(a); RLGL § 33.

Yes. Generally, taking a fee in stock is viewed as doing business with the client. This means you must follow all the heightened conflict-of interest-requirements of Rule 1.8(a). The agreement must be in writing. You should put in writing your recommendation that the client might want to have other counsel to advise it on the fee arrangement. The transaction viewed from the point of view of the client must be entirely fair.[28]

I hope that's it.

Not quite. Because your fee for stock agreement is governed by the very stringent "doing-business-with-clients" rule, courts impose a presumption of undue influence should you seek the stock that your client somehow refused to deliver.[29] Conveniently, however, advice of independent counsel will rebut this presumption, just as it will help you avoid professional discipline under Rule 1.8(a).[30]

🎞 Fee Splits

This opportunity is so amazing. General Counsel for Lowe Depot wants us to bring a class action antitrust claim against copper pipe manufacturers— something about tacit mutual agreements to limit production. This is big. And the only thing he wants in return is our agreement to give him 20 percent of our fee for sending us the work. Between you and me, we would give him 30 percent if he is half right about the case.

Congratulations. Maybe you want to hire us to handle the bribery scandal when this all comes to light.

Bribery? It's a standard referral fee.

We assume that general counsel is a full-time employee of Lowe Depot. You cannot rebate a portion of your fee to him for sending you the business

---

28. *Tabner v. Drake*, 780 S.2d 85 (N.Y. App. Div. 2004) (lawyer's business transaction with client grounds for bona fide defense to lawyer's suit for fees and basis for client's counter-claim for breach of contract and malpractice).

29. *Passante v. McWilliam*, 62 Cal. Rptr. 2d 298 (Cal. Ct. App. 1997) (lawyer who "came through in the clutch" raising money for a client's company and was promised three percent of company stock unable to enforce oral promise because it did not comply with written disclosure and consent requirements and otherwise constituted a mere gratuitous promise).

30. MODEL RULE 1.8, cmt. [4]; RLGL § 126, cmt. f; *Monco v. Janus*, 583 N.E.2d 575 (Ill. App. 1991) (lawyer failed to provide clear and convincing evidence of full and frank disclosure and of adequate consideration to support fifty percent business ownership interest despite client's eventual consultation with another lawyer after business was started).

any more than the copper tube manufacturers can slip extra money into the wallet of Lowe Depot's of buyer plumbing supplies.

What if it's outside counsel?

That's a different story. Every jurisdiction permits a fee division between referring and receiving counsel.[31] That is done to encourage counsel to get the client the very best specialists when that is in the client's best interests. But it can be done only with some stringent safeguards, which vary quite a bit. The most liberal jurisdictions permit a "naked" referral. In that situation, the referring lawyer has no responsibility, the client is informed that there is a referral fee, but is not informed of the basis for the split and the overall fee must be reasonable.[32] The last requirement is easy to meet here since, in a class action, the fee will be set by the court.

We're probably not lucky enough to be in one of those liberated states.

The more demanding jurisdictions only permit a fee split if the lawyers divide the fee in accordance with the amount of work each does or if the referring lawyer agrees to remain financially responsible for the representation, and the client is informed in writing about the basis of the split.[33]

What does that mean?

It means that if there's malpractice, the client may sue the referring lawyer as well.[34]

Even though he only made a referral?

Yes. If he wants to share a percentage without regard to the work he does.

Anything else?

Yes. The client was to be informed of the basis on which the division is made. Ten percent; fifteen percent; whatever, and the total fee must be reasonable.

And the most stringent?

These jurisdictions require full disclosure to the client and permit a division only on the basis of the percentage of the work the referring and receiving lawyers undertake.[35]

That means the lawyers might get into a fight over who does what?

---

31. MODEL RULE 1.5(e); RLGL § 47.

32. *See, e.g.,* Mass. Rule 1.5(e); Mich. Rule 1.5(e); Pa. Rule 1.5(e).

33. *E.g.,* MODEL RULE 1.5(e); D.C. Rule 1.5(e); Ill. Rule 1.5(f)–(i); Iowa Rule 32:1.5(e); N.Y. Rule 1.5(g); Va. Rule 1.5(e).

34. MODEL RULE 1.5, cmt. [7]; RLGL § 47, cmt. d.

35. *E.g.,* Fla. Rule 1.5(d).

Could be. But that's the rule, and, of course, there's always someone there to enforce it.

What do you mean?

The lawyer who thinks he worked harder than his fee allocation.

✏ Statutory Fees

Client company wanted to pursue an environmental action against a former property owner, but didn't want to take on the cost of an hourly fee. So I agreed to a 40 percent contingent fee. We won. The client is receiving $100,000 in damages. We also petitioned for statutory attorney fees, and the court awarded the client $80,000. I say I'm entitled to 40 percent of $100,000, plus the $80,000. The client says I get the $40,000, and that's it. What an ingrate.

Under your fee agreement, which we are sure you crafted, your client could be correct. Let's start with whether your fee is reasonable. In many jurisdictions, this would depend on the Rule 1.5(a) factors, such as the difficulty of the matter, the results achieved, and the customary fee in your locality. But in some places, contingent fees are more specifically regulated. For example, in Florida, your 40 percent contract would subject you to discipline.[36]

Now, assuming you contracted for a reasonable fee, if the fee agreement provides that you will receive 40 percent of your client's recovery, your contract fee is $40,000. If, however, you were smart enough to contract for 40 percent of any money received by the client from the opposing party, including statutory fee awards, you should get 40 percent of your client's total $180,000—or $72,000.[37]

Absent statute, the American (unlike the British) Rule does not provide for fee-shifting to a prevailing party. But fee-shifting statutes, often called private attorneys general provisions, can create a right to a "reasonable attorney's fee" to a "prevailing party."[38] Hundreds of statutes, including

---

36. Fla. Rule 1.5(f).

37. *Gobert v. Williams*, 323 F.3d 1099 (5th Cir. 2003) (upholding validity of fee contract that provided for contingent fee in addition to any statutory fees awarded plaintiff).

38. *Buckhannon Bd. & Care Home, Inc. v. W. Va. Dep't of Health & Human Res.*, 532 U.S. 598 (2001) (parties who receive a judgment on the merits, or a court-ordered consent decree, are "prevailing parties," but a party who recovers because of a defendant's voluntary change in conduct not caused by the underlying lawsuit is not); *Loggerhead Turtle v.*

environmental, securities, civil rights, and consumer provisions, provide for fee-shifting. When this occurs, the statute governs the entitlement.[39] But typically, these provisions pay your client (the prevailing party)—not you. You are free to contract for a reasonable fee, be it contingent, hourly, or flat.[40] Many lawyers blend provisions, providing in the fee contract that any contingent fee owed the lawyer will be offset by the statutory fee award. So we hope you carefully read the statute, and the cases construing it, to create a fee contract that benefits both you and your client.

But the fee award was $80,000. I should at least get that! Otherwise the client keeps my fee.

Not so fast. As we've already explained, statutory fee-shifting provisions provide for a fee to the prevailing party, not the prevailing party's lawyer. Unless your fee agreement with the client contemplated that result, you are limited to your own bargain.

🏛 Class Action Fees

We've been defending our government client against a ridiculous class action suit alleging police brutality. I think we can offer the named plaintiffs a great settlement of their claims. We'll give them minimal injunctive relief if they agree not to seek a court award of fees.

Class action fees are subject to two bodies of law: first, any relevant statutory fee-shifting provision, and second, the court's common law obligation to supervise common fund settlements.[41]

That's just great. You mean I have to justify this settlement to the court?

Yes, and you probably will only get this sweet result for this client once. But, you will be relieved to know that the Supremes have blessed a settlement similar to the one you suggest. Since the suit was no doubt brought pursuant to relevant civil rights statutes, which grant the fee shift to the

---

County Council of Volusia County, 307 F.3d 1318 (11th Cir. 2002) (*Buckhannon* applies only to "prevailing party" statutes, not to "whenever appropriate" fee award statutes such as the Clean Water and Clean Air Act).

39. *City of Burlington v. Dague*, 505 U.S. 557 (1992) (lodestar calculations required under federal fee-shifting statutes).

40. *Gobert v. Williams*, 323 F.3d 1099 (5th Cir. 2003) (fee contract providing for contingent fee in addition to any statutory fees awarded plaintiff upheld).

41. *Nilsen v. York County*, 400 F. Supp. 2d 266 (D. Me. 2005).

"prevailing party," the Court has held that fee waivers by parties can be approved by courts as long as the defendants do not have a policy, practice, or law that requires waiver as a condition of settlement.[42]

※ Fee Modification

So I convinced the CFO of Magna Corporation that our firm would take on Magna's dispute with the engineer who designed the new product line on a contingent fee basis. The case looked like a lay-down. The production line was supposed to produce fifty microchips a minute; current production isn't half that. We've been in discovery for months. The case is costing us a fortune. And we're not close to being finished. We now know there's a good argument that it's not the production line, but the use of inferior raw materials, that caused the problems. I'm ready to either throw in the towel or insist we get paid on an hourly basis, at premium rates.

We sympathize with your plight. But there is a reason they call these fee agreements "contingent." Because there is an element of risk. Will the client recover? If so, how much? Maybe the client will drop the suit. Or settle for non-monetary relief not contemplated by the agreement. Lawyers try to minimize the risk before signing on: by researching as much as possible the strengths, and particularly the weaknesses, of the case. And by rejecting those that carry high levels of risk. Once the contingent fee agreement is signed, the lawyer is on the hook. The client gets to decide whether and when to settle and to force the matter to trial and, unless the contingent fee agreement says otherwise, even to appeal.[43]

I see a theme developing here. The client gets to decide. So I'll have a heart-to-heart with my client. As long as the CFO agrees, I can shift to an hourly fee, right?

Except for one problem.

What's that?

---

42. *Evans v. Jeff D.*, 475 U.S. 717 (1986); *Bernhardt v. County of Los Angeles*, 279 F.3d 862 (9th Cir. 2002) (*Evans* justifies successful challenge to settlement agreement where governmental unit exhibits a pattern or practice of requiring attorney fee waiver, or when such agreements have the effect of deterring lawyers from representing plaintiffs in civil rights cases).

43. ABA Comm. on Ethics and Professional Responsibility, Formal Op. 94-389 (1994) (Contingent Fees).

You may have to convince a court as well. Your client, Magna, may be able to avoid any modification to a fee contract made after the client-lawyer relationship begins even if the modification was made with its ostensible agreement.[44] The courts presume undue influence once your fiduciary duty attaches.[45] That leaves you with the burden of proof to establish that the modification was "fair and reasonable to the client."[46] If the modification results in a larger fee for you, you probably won't be able to keep it. If your client has independent counsel in deciding whether to modify, you're in better shape, but still not home completely free. You will have to show that the modification made sense from the client's perspective when made, and that you properly disclosed the details of both arrangements.[47]

ℳ Fees on Termination

You know our firm. A bunch of stick-in-the-muds. Grinding out the hours. Limited by the fact that our lawyers get exhausted. Then some of our corporate clients pushed back. Asked us if we'd take matters on a contingent fee. They claimed cash flow problems. And getting bleary-eyed reading endless time sheets filled with meaningless entries. We got a little excited. Maybe we'd hit. Get a big pay day. So we took one on as an experiment. A suit against the manufacturer of a new production line. Never worked right, and our client claimed millions in damages. So we sign up for 25 percent. We agree to upfront the costs, too. Not everyone was happy. Such a big case screwed up our billable hours' budget. But the vision of the sugar plums cohort prevailed.

We worked our collective tail off. Hired experts. Depositions galore. And the electronic discovery! Then the client got a new CEO. He didn't know us, but he decided we were too conservative. He had a friend who is, as he said, "A real plaintiffs' lawyer." We were fired. And the new guy is going to trial next week. On our work product.

Now you know yet another reason they call these contingent fees. The client can fire you at any time, and for no reason.[48]

---

44. RLGL §§ 18, 38(2).

45. *Vaughn v. King*, 167 F.3d 347 (7th Cir. 1999).

46. RLGL § 18(1)(a).

47. RLGL § 18, cmt. e.

48. MODEL RULE 1.16 (a)(3); RLGL § 32(1).

So unfair. And you know, we never even thought about that. We've represented the client for 27 years! We still do.

Now you want to know what fee you get?

Exactly. 2700 hours. Disbursements of $200,000 or so. And our client's fate in the hands of someone else.

With your fee. If your client loses, you'll get nothing. Maybe reimbursement of the expenses.

We're not even thinking about that possibility. What happens when the client wins?

You'll be entitled to the lesser of the ratable portion of your contract fee or quantum meruit.[49]

Is that funny words for a few dollars?

Could be. In many jurisdictions, quantum meruit is defined as your hours times a reasonable rate.

But we didn't even keep time records. Our folks loved that.

Well, some courts are kind. Others are not so kind in the absence of time records.[50]

But we should get a percentage. A big percentage. We did all the work.

Some jurisdictions agree. For them, quantum meruit might easily mean that your firm could get a significant percentage. But be prepared for a dog fight with the CEO's high-flying friend who will argue he had to start all over, and, without his formidable trial skills, the company would never have collected a dime.[51]

There goes our firm's contingent fee practice.

At least you learned one lesson.

And that is?

If you're going to do contingent fee cases, you should pursue many of them. Having only one case in the inventory is way too risky a business model.

49. RLGL § 40.

50. *E.g., Badillo v. Playboy Entm't Group, Inc.*, No. 04-00591, 2008 U.S. App. LEXIS 25056 (11th Cir. Dec. 12, 2008).

51. *E.g., Vance v. Gallagher*, No. 02C8249, 2006 U.S. Dist. LEXIS 63211 (N.D. Ill. Aug. 29, 2006).

Fiduciary Duty

𝒲 The Five C's

WHEN YOU ENTER INTO A CLIENT-LAWYER RELATIONSHIP, the law governing lawyers recognizes that you have assumed five core fiduciary obligations (the Five C's):

1 Deference to client Control over the goals of the representation (Chapter 3)[1]
2 Competence (Chapter 4)[2]
3 Communication (Chapter 5)[3]
4 Confidentiality (Chapter 6)[4]
5 Conflict-of-interest resolution (Chapter 7)[5]

These fiduciary duties originated in agency law and are now restated in lawyer codes. They rest on a key agency insight about client-lawyer relationships: client-principals empower lawyer-agents, whose superior knowledge and skill enable them to control or manipulate a client representation for the benefit of themselves or others. To ensure that the client's best interests are respected, fiduciary duty imposes on lawyers affirmative obligations of proper deference to client control, communication, competence, confidentiality, and conflict-of-interest resolution. When these duties are met, clients properly determine their own best interests within the bounds of the law.

---

1. MODEL RULE 1.2

2. MODEL RULES 1.1 & 1.3.

3. MODEL RULE 1.4.

4. MODEL RULES 1.6, 1.8(b), 1.9.

5. MODEL RULES 1.7, 1.8, 1.11, & 1.12.

When they are breached, a lawyer usually has under-identified with a client's interests.

The key to understanding these foundational fiduciary duties is to remember that the law governing lawyers imposes an affirmative obligation on lawyers to initiate all conversations about the Five C's. Failure to do so leaves a lawyer vulnerable to a myriad of remedies including civil liability, fee forfeiture, disqualification, injunctive relief, constructive trusts, and professional discipline.[6]

---

6. RLGL § 6.

THREE

Control

❦ Introduction: Who's in Charge?

LIKE OTHER AGENTS, lawyers have a duty to act on the client's behalf, subject to the client's right to control the objectives of the representation.[1] At the same time, many clients defer to and rely on their lawyers' expertise regarding the means to accomplish client goals. Lawyer codes and the law of agency recognize three spheres of authority between client and lawyer. In the first two, clients and lawyers each retain sole authority to make certain decisions that cannot be overridden by the other.[2] In the third, client and lawyer decision-making authority overlap.[3] The scope of a client's control and the lawyer's authority also impact the client's and the lawyer's relationship with third parties.[4]

In the first sphere, clients retain sole authority to make decisions concerning the goals of the representation, including specifically whether and when to settle or appeal a matter, and in criminal cases, how to plead, whether to waive a jury trial, and whether to testify.[5] Clients may authorize their lawyers to make a particular decision within this sphere, but the ultimate authority of clients to decide may not be completely ceded to their lawyers.[6]

---

1. RLGL § 16; RESTATEMENT (THIRD) OF AGENCY §1.01 (Tentative Draft No. 2, 2001).

2. RLGL §§ 22, 23.

3. RLGL §§ 20, 21.

4. RLGL §§ 25–30.

5. MODEL RULE 1.2(a); RLGL § 22(1).

6. *Abbott v. Kidder Peabody & Co.*, 42 F. Supp. 2d 1046 (D. Colo. 1999) (lawyers representing 200 individual plaintiffs disqualified because of contract that gave settlement authority to a select group of plaintiffs; each individual client's approval is essential); *Mattioni, Mattioni & Mattioni, Ltd. v. Ecological Shipping Corp.*, 530 F. Supp. 910 (E.D. Pa. 1981) (provision in contingent fee contract that required lawyer's consent before settling case invalid and voided entire fee contract; lawyer reduced to quantum meruit recovery for fee).

In the second sphere, lawyers retain sole authority to refuse to perform, counsel, or assist a client's unlawful act.[7] Lawyers also may take actions in tribunals they reasonably believe to be required by the law or by court order, despite client preferences to the contrary.[8]

In all other decisions not reserved exclusively to clients or lawyers, clients and lawyers share authority.[9] You and your clients are free to bargain about any lawful means that will be used to pursue the client's objectives. If you do not want to engage in the scorched earth tactics your client insists upon, you may withdraw from the representation,[10] just as the client may discharge you if the client is unhappy with your approach to the matter.

All three spheres of authority place affirmative duties of communication on lawyers during a representation. Whenever a client decision arises, you must promptly inform and consult with the client about the decision.[11] Whenever a client insists on illegal conduct, you must promptly inform the client that the conduct is not permitted, and must explain why.[12] Once the client has decided on an objective, you must act to implement it,[13] reasonably consulting with your client as to the means by which the objective is to be accomplished.[14]

The outcome of this consultation creates the express terms of the engagement or, in agency terminology, actual authority, which obligates you to obey the client's lawful instructions and empowers you to act on behalf of the client.[15] Actual authority includes implied authority, which encompasses the authority to act in a manner that will further the client's objectives, as long as the lawyer reasonably believes the client desires such action.[16]

---

7. MODEL RULE 1.2(d); RLGL § 23(1).

8. MODEL RULE 3.3; RLGL § 23(2).

9. MODEL RULES 1.2(a), 1.4; RLGL §§ 20, 21.

10. MODEL RULE 1.2, cmt. [2], l.16(b)(4).

11. MODEL RULE 1.2(a), 1.4 (a)(1); RLGL § 20(3).

12. MODEL RULE 1.4(a)(5); RLGL § 20(1).

13. *Vandermay v. Clayton*, 984 P.2d 272 (Or. 1999) (lawyer liable for breach of fiduciary duty without expert testimony for drafting ambiguous indemnity agreement that did not include the protections client insisted upon); *Olfe v. Gordon*, 286 N.W.2d 573 (Wis. 1980) (lawyer liable without expert testimony for failure to effectuate client's instruction to secure a first mortgage in sale of her home).

14. MODEL RULE 1.4(a)(2).

15. RESTATEMENT (THIRD) OF AGENCY § 8.09 (Tentative Draft No. 2, 2001); RLGL § 21, cmt. d.

16. RLGL § 21, cmt. b; RESTATEMENT (THIRD) OF AGENCY § 2.01 (Tentative Draft No. 2, 2001).

Once reasonable consultation has occurred, you are impliedly authorized to take lawful measures to advance the client's objectives.[17] A lawyer agent who acts within this scope legally binds the client- principal.[18] A client also can be bound by a lawyer's apparent authority, that is, authority "traceable to the principal's manifestations" that causes another reasonably to believe the lawyer agent had the requisite authority to act on behalf of the client.[19]

Eliminating Rambo

I'm dealing with a new General Counsel at my old client, Hopewell Industries. It's going to be a culture shock. I gave opposing counsel an extra two weeks to respond to our motion for summary judgment, and when the new GC found out, you would've thought I'd killed his first born. What a string of expletives. I was told in no uncertain terms that from now on, Hopewell Industries gives no extensions. And I was not authorized to make any decisions—any—without consulting GC. Can that be right?

Generally, we think of allocation of responsibility as being divided into threes. (See Table 1) There are those matters where the client is absolutely entitled to decide—generally, the goals of the representation. Whether and on what terms an organization is going to settle is the best example of that.[20] Next are those matters decided by the lawyer in consultation with the client—generally, the means to accomplish the client's goals. Typical of those would be how to conduct discovery, whether to file a motion, and the hiring of experts or consultants.[21] Third are matters that are implicitly delegated to the lawyer—lawyers retain sole authority to refuse involvement in a client's unlawful acts, and may take action in tribunals reasonably required by law or by court order, despite client preferences.[22] Determining what the client must produce in discovery is a good example of that. Typically, so would be whether to grant an extension of time. But if the client wishes to insert itself into such matters, the client might get to decide.

---

17. Model Rule 1.2(a); RLGL § 21(3).

18. RLGL § 26.

19. Restatement (Third) Agency § 2.03 (Tentative Draft No. 2, 2001); RLGL § 27.

20. Model Rule 1.2(a); RLGL § 22.

21. Model Rules 1.2(a), 1.4; RLGL §§ 20, 21.

22. Model Rule 1.2(a), cmt. [2]; RLGL § 23.

TABLE 1 Client-Lawyer Allocation of Authority

Client's Sole Authority	Negotiated Authority; Delegated Discretion	Lawyer's Sole Authority
Objectives, goals, and specific decisions	Means	Refuse unlawful conduct and take action before tribunals
MR 1.2(a) [objectives, decisions to settle; in criminal cases, pleas, jury trial waiver, and whether client will testify] RLGL § 22	MR 1.2(a) [means and implied authorization], MR 1.2(b) [moral views], MR 1.2(c) [scope of the representation], MR 1.4 [initiate communication] RLGL § 20, 21	MR 1.2(d) [criminal or fraudulent activity], MR 1.4(a)(5) [consult about relevant limitations] RLGL § 23, 25

No client's going to tell me when to grant an extension. I live in this community and expect to be a good citizen. Besides, I might need an extension someday. The way I practice law, I'm sure of it. What goes around comes around, as they say.

We admire your approach. Therefore, it is incumbent upon you to persuade your client of the importance of this example of professionalism at work.

And if I cannot?

Then you have two choices. Fulfill your client's demands. Or resign. Rule 1.16 (b)(4) provides that a lawyer has grounds for withdrawal if the client persists in a course of action with which the lawyer has fundamental disagreement or finds repugnant.[23]

That may prove to be the case here.

Pretty harsh remedy.

It is. But life is too short to give in to clients—even important corporate clients—who won't permit you to practice law in a way that makes you proud.

ℳ Dilatory Discovery

So I gave in on the hard ball extension issue. But now we are in a new battle. The other side asked for all documents relating to the drug at issue. The client

---

23. *See also* RLGL § 32(3)(f).

uncovered some very damaging ones. But they were found in the client's Canadian lab in Montreal. General Counsel tells me to object to producing all documents outside the United States. It is too burdensome. I say client cannot assert that in good faith when the documents have already been identified. Do I give in again? It is a big client.

Not this time. This is an area where your duties as an officer of the court trump any client wishes. Just as a client cannot insist your closing argument include references to facts outside the record, you must insist on producing the documents. If the client directs you not to—after your most persuasive arguments (including the chances of litigation sanctions)[24] fall on deaf ears—then resignation is the only proper remedy.[25]

So then they'll hire a new lawyer and not tell that lawyer about the documents?

That is not your problem. Your duty to disclose depends on the relevant procedural rules, such as Federal Rule of Civil Procedure 26. Here, since production is yet to come, and you will withdraw, be sure to check the relevant rules. If they impose no duty, you may withdraw in silence.

⁂ The Limits of the Law

My client has some wonderful employees who just happen to be undocumented workers. She instructs me not to report their income or pay the requisite taxes in preparing the company tax return, adding: "Don't worry about signing the return, just prepare it, and I'll sign it. Then the risk's on me."

Would you bribe a judge for your client too? While it's true that clients determine the goals of the representation, that authority is limited to

---

24. *E.g., In re Anonymous Member of S.C. Bar,* 552 S.E.2d 10 (S.C. 2001) (law firm partners and other lawyers who directly or indirectly supervise other lawyers could be sanctioned and subject to discipline for failing to mitigate known misconduct of another lawyer in discovery and depositions, failing to make reasonable efforts to supervise, even without knowledge of misconduct, or failing to put systematic procedures in place to prevent misconduct); *Qualcomm Inc. v. Broadcom Corp.,* Case No. 05cv1958-B (BLM), 2008 U.S. Dist. LEXIS 911 (S.D. Cal. Jan. 7, 2008) (sanctions of $8.5 million against client for withholding tens of thousands of decisive documents, six lawyers referred to disciplinary counsel, and client and lawyers ordered to create a comprehensive case review and enforcement of discovery obligations protocol); *In re Telxon Corp. Sec. Litig.,* Nos. 5:98CV2876, 1:01CV1078, 2004 U.S. Dist. LEXIS 27296 (N.D. Ohio July 16, 2004) (entry of default judgment appropriate sanction for bad faith refusal to comply with discovery orders).

25. Model Rules 1.16(a), 3.4(d); RLGL §§ 132(2), 118(2).

lawful actions. If you have determined that your client's refusal to report is unlawful, you may not assist her in preparing the tax returns, whether or not you sign. A lawyer has absolute authority and obligation—that may not be overridden by client instruction—to refuse to perform, counsel, or assist unlawful client activity.[26]

✹ Blanket Settlement Authority

That unfortunate answer raises another point. Even my corporate clients show such bad judgment. You'd think with all that money. . . . Anyway, too often they reject my settlement recommendations, pursue a matter to conclusion, then end up so disappointed. My partners and I are thinking of adding a standard clause to our retainer agreement delegating settlement authority to us. What do you think?

If lawyers ruled the world, what a wonderful world it would be. But we don't. We live in a client-centered world where all major decisions are those of the client, and even mere procedural decisions are to be made in consultation with the client. So your proposed delegation of authority is a non-starter.[27] We would even go further.

Give me an example.

Well, suppose your corporate client's general counsel tells you the client would never settle for less than half a million dollars. She's quite adamant. Time passes, and you get an offer for $375,000. Do you turn it down without calling the client?

Sure. You don't want to bother a busy general counsel.

Yes you do. Even with that firm instruction, you should pass the offer along. Even if the instruction was received yesterday. This is because there is no telling how a firm offer might change minds or at least approaches. On Tuesday, your client might've said, "I wouldn't dignify an offer under $500,000

---

26. MODEL RULES 1.2(d), 1.16(a)(1), (b)(3); RLGL §§ 23(1); 32(2)(a), (3)(e), 94, 96, cmt. d.

27. *In re Lansky*, 678 N.E.2d 1114 (Ind. 1997) (retainer agreement that authorized lawyer "to settle for any amount he determines is reasonable without further oral or written authorization" violated MODEL RULE 1.2(a)); *In re Lewis*, 463 S.E.2d 862 (Ga. 1995) (lawyer whose client signed a retainer agreement giving lawyer full authority to take all actions on client's behalf in a personal injury case and then settled her case without her express authority suspended for eighteen months).

with a response." But on Friday, the client might want to counter $375,000 with $600,000. Better to be a nudge than to be second-guessed later.[28]

𝕸 Authority—Apparent or Real?

We have been representing an accounting firm in a malpractice claim brought by their former client. We went to a pretrial conference, and the plaintiff, for reasons I don't understand, said he would accept $1 million. I know this case would cost more than that just for defense costs, so I gladly accepted it. Now I have reported back to the managing partner who angrily rejected the settlement, claiming they would never settle—it's a matter of principle.

Entity clients are like other clients. Settlement authority is allocated to the client exclusively. You may have thought this was the best deal available and that it would disappear if not accepted, but that is no excuse for not getting authority from the client. The really bad news is that the client might have a claim against you for the settlement amount.[29]

What's the good news?

The good news is that you can defend on the ground that the client was not harmed by your seizing the moment. The deal was a great deal. But you also better be prepared to demonstrate that settlements don't hurt reputations—professional reputations.

𝕸 Checking Back

Client had a huge case against a competitor. I had been dealing with the CEO. She asked me to appear before the board to discuss a possible settlement. The board authorized a settlement of $5 million. When the other side made a ridiculous low ball offer, the CEO and I rejected it, and we filed suit. The CEO

---

28. N.Y. State Bar Ass'n Op. 760 (2003) (because unlikely that the necessary disclosures will be possible at the time of retainer, lawyers may not use general powers of attorney to settle matters without obtaining more explicit instructions from the client after the lawyer and client have discussed the merits of the case, the client's willingness to settle, and the settlement terms acceptable to the client).

29. *Moores v. Greenberg*, 834 F.2d 1105 (1st Cir. 1987) (lawyer who failed to relay a $90,000 settlement offer because he believed sums offered by defense were "too niggardly to be relayed" liable for difference between offer and eventual $12,000 jury verdict).

was fired five months ago for other reasons. Now the company is suing my firm. They claim if we had not sued, we could have settled the case for $4 million, and I should have gone back to the board. Am I in trouble?

Changes in management can be hell on lawyers. New management's ability to second-guess old management is not limited to business issues. But you had no obligation to go back to the board. The designated representative of the client, for purposes of this representation, was the CEO. She asked you to get authority from the board to settle, which you received. You were not able to settle for that number and, therefore, the proper approach was to continue to deal with the CEO. The only situations in which you would have been required to return to the board were if the board directed you to do so (the board is the highest authority that can act for the corporation), or if you needed authority to settle for a number lower than the number the board originally authorized.[30] It is unfortunate that new management is taking this action. It does serve as a reminder of just one more difficulty representing an organization of musical chair officers.

A Split of Authority

The corporate client has been pursuing this litigation for years. We told them they should do it on a contingent fee basis, but they insisted on paying our hourly rate. Now the CFO wants us to switch to a contingency. Something about company cash flow. But when the executive vice president heard that, he called me and said, "That's ridiculous. We are so close to trial. This is no time for us to switch the fee arrangement or you lawyers'll make a fortune!" Who should I listen to?

Now is the time to know how governance works in the organization you represent. Sometimes that will be very formal and quite clear; sometimes the organization chart is non-existent. If you think the CFO reports to the executive VP, then you need to confirm your understanding in discussions with both of them and then follow the superior officer's instructions. If you have no idea, you must pick your way up the ladder to someone whose authority is superior to the two combatants, and get that individual to get back to you with an organizational decision on whether you are to change the fee arrangement.

What if I think the final decision of the CFO is stupid?

30. Franklin A. Gevurtz, Corporation Law § 3.1 (West 2000).

In many respects, the answer to that question is the same as it would be for an individual client. Clients get to decide. And they get to make mistakes. Or do things we lawyers think are unwise or worse. So too with our proverbial corporate employee. That person to whom you are assigned is allowed to make stupid decisions. And so long as those decisions are legal, it is not your job to second-guess. So if the general manager decides, for example, to reject a settlement that the GM is empowered to reject, that is the GM's prerogative. Your obligation is to give your best advice, to urge the general manager to the contrary, but if you believe you have satisfied your advice function, then your next job is to abide by the instructions of the General Manager. The General Manager's job performance ultimately will be judged based on this and a hundred other decisions she makes. It is not up to you to substitute your judgment for the judgment of the clearly assigned client representative.[31]

𝍌 Who Has Authority?

I represent this small business. Mom and Pop operation really—though very profitable. They sell cheese for pizza. Seem to control the whole market. Anyway, the boss hired me to handle some tax matters. I asked for a big retainer, which I got in cash. He then decided to go on one of those round-the-world cruises. With the wife. Tells me to deal with his son in his absence. I agree to do so. Then the son calls me up a week later. Wants me to help the company with the purchase of a building. At a foreclosure sale. I ask for another retainer. The son says, "Use the one you have." So I do. Go right through it. Dad returns. Hears what the son did. He's furious. Fires me and demands I pay him back the retainer. I say no way . . . but I am a little scared.

And you should be a little worried. It's true dad left his son in charge and told you to deal with him. But dad also defined the scope of the representation: tax matters. He didn't say anything about other services. And as you say, he's the boss. Analytically, he's the person who represents the highest authority in the company. You can defend his claim on the basis of the son's instructions, but don't count on it as a winner.[32]

---

31. MODEL RULE 1.13, cmt. [3], RLGL § 96, cmt. d.

32. *E.g., Machado v. Statewide Grievance Comm.*, 890 A.2d 622 (Conn. App. Ct. 2006) (lawyer violated Rules 1.2(a) and 1.4(a) by following client's agent's unauthorized request to redirect lawyer's efforts to tax lien instead of bankruptcy).

✄ Hiring an Expert Witness

I know we need an expert witness on damages because the plaintiffs have hired one of the best firms on the topic. They are going to put big numbers on the blackboard. But my client, Colossus Corporation, says no way. We put on our expert, they argue, and we sound like we are conceding liability. I reminded them of what happened in the famous Pennzoil case,[33] but the general counsel remains adamant. Actually, he understands our point, but the CEO is a real swashbuckler. The company is also cheap, with a capital "C." I think I'll go ahead and hire one anyway. I'll bury it in our fees. You said this is one of those shared responsibility deals, right?

Not when the client says no. Then you follow orders . . . or resign.[34] Our suggestion is that you make one more try at it. This time in memo form. If you think the expert is material to the outcome, make that clear to your client. If that doesn't change the mind of Colossus, at least you have a record of your best advice.

And a real chance to break the record for the largest plaintiff's verdict since Pennzoil.

You could resign. But remember, your client is not acting unlawfully, and this is not a decision—hiring an expert—you are entitled to make without client consultation.[35]

✄ Another Lawyer

Just to be super careful, I contacted my law school buddy about a complex matter, and I followed her advice. Now the deal's falling apart. When I told my client I had consulted with the best, he's found another reason to sue me. You never win.

Lawyers consult with each other all the time. You needed help understanding the deal, and you were wise to find out more. But we hope you didn't retain your buddy, on behalf of your client, because you had no authority to do so without your client's consent.[36] If you did, you now have three problems. First, if you are sharing a fee, you needed your client to consent to

---

33. *Texaco, Inc. v. Pennzoil Co.*, 729 S.W.2d 768 (Tex. App. 1987).

34. RLGL § 21(2).

35. RLGL § 23.

36. RLGL § 14, cmt. h.

that arrangement.[37] Second, if you did anything other than discuss the matter in a hypothetical format, you disclosed confidential client information, again, without your client's consent.[38] And third, if your friend's advice was flawed and you followed it, you may have committed malpractice.[39] If it was impossible to get clear help from your friend without disclosing detailed facts, you should have asked your client before doing so. It's always best to let your client know how you are proceeding; that way you can head off any objections before they occur.

ℋ Limiting the Scope of the Representation

Inside counsel asked me to provide a quick legal opinion about a proposed mediated settlement between the company and a fired employee. I did so, relying on their facts. Now the company claims I should have discovered additional facts, facts which would have changed my opinion.

Clients, especially inside counsel on behalf of companies, often hire outside lawyers to handle specific cases or matters. You might prefer the client who wants you to handle all legal matters. But increasingly common is the client who seeks or the lawyer who offers the opposite: "unbundled" legal services that limit the scope of the representation by breaking down legal services into discrete tasks such as drafting, negotiation, or court representation, or by providing service only for a particular legal issue, such as custody or property valuation.[40]

Model Rule 1.2(c) and the Restatement both approve of these contractual bargains, but only if the limitation is reasonable and the client gives informed consent.[41] Here, the reasonableness standard is determined from the viewpoint of the client, not the professional, so consider whether the benefits of the limitation to your client (reduced fee, able lawyer) would outweigh the risks (inadequate or incomplete legal advice).

---

37. MODEL RULE 1.5(e); RLGL § 47.

38. MODEL RULE 1.6(a), cmts. [4]–[5].

39. *E.g., Whalen v. DeGraff, Foy, Conway, Holt-Harris & Mealey,* 863 N.Y.S.2d 100 (N.Y. App. Div. 2008) (lawyer who relied on local counsel without consulting client liable for local counsel's malpractice).

40. Forrest S. Mosten, *Unbundling Legal Services: A Guide to Delivering Legal Services a la Carte* (ABA Law Practice Management, 2000).

41. RLGL § 19.

The bookends are clear: just as you cannot agree to limit your client's right to settle a matter or whether to plead guilty in a criminal case,[42] you cannot agree to conduct a "preliminary" investigation that does not provide an opinion upon which the client can rely.[43] Be especially aware of specialty areas of practice: A bankruptcy court has held that a lawyer representing a Chapter 7 debtor may not limit the scope of representation and must represent the debtor in all aspects of the bankruptcy case.[44] And don't forget lesson number one: identify your client. For example, if you are retained by an insurance company, duties to your primary or sole client (the insured) mean that the insurer may not limit your obligation to the insured by requiring prior approval of depositions, research, and motions.[45]

On the other hand, agreeing to offer short-term legal services via a legal services hotline,[46] to handle a trial but not an appeal,[47] to advise about one transaction or claim but not others,[48] or, as you did, to provide an expeditious legal opinion about a proposed mediated settlement without additional factual investigation[49] all are reasonable as long as your client gives "informed consent" and your written work product clearly reflects any agreed-upon limitations.[50] Informed consent requires that the client understands the alternatives, especially those that other lawyers might include in the same representation.[51] So, for example, a lawyer may be acting reasonably in limiting a representation to a quick opinion without further factual investigation,

---

42. *Jones v. Barnes*, 463 U.S. 745 (1983) (fundamental decisions to plead guilty, waive jury, testify, or appeal are for defendant); *In re Lansky*, 678 N.E.2d 1114 (Ind. 1997) (fee agreement provision that gave up client's right to settle civil matter violated Rule 1.2(a)).

43. MODEL RULE 1.2, cmt. [7].

44. *In re Egwim*, 291 B.R. 559 (Bankr. N.D. Ga. 2003).

45. *In re Rules of Professional Conduct*, 2 P.3d 806 (Mont. 2000) (insurance defense counsel may not abide by agreements to limit the scope of representation that interfere with their duty to insured client).

46. MODEL RULE 6.4.

47. *Young v. Bridwell*, 437 P.2d 686 (Utah 1968).

48. *Delta Equip. & Constr. Co. v. Royal Indem. Co.*, 186 So. 2d 454 (La. Ct. App. 1966).

49. *Lerner v. Laufer*, 819 A.2d 471 (N.J. Super. Ct. App. Div. 2003).

50. MODEL RULE 1.0(e); RLGL § 19.

51. *Barnes v. Turner*, 606 S.E.2d 849 (Ga. 2004) (lawyer who perfected client's securities interests by filing UCC financing statements also undertook duty to renew statements after five years or inform client of need to do so).

but only if the client understands that other lawyers might look into further facts, and that those facts could change the opinion.[52]

𝄞 The Lawyer's External Authority

My client was negotiating a merger agreement with another corporation. The principals were having difficulty dealing with each other, so my client asked me if I would negotiate with the other lawyer. My client told me, "Get the best deal you can, no less than $10 a share. But come back to us before you seal the deal." I started negotiations with the lawyer on the other side, and she gave me a final offer of $12 per share that had to be accepted that day. I could not reach my CEO, but I knew he would love the deal, so I accepted it. Before closing, my client got an offer of $15 a share from another company. They took that deal, and now the company that was negotiating with me has sued my client, claiming I had actual and apparent authority to bind my client. Am I in trouble?

That requires a two-step analysis. First, is your client bound by the deal you struck? That is unlikely. While lawyers in the context of litigation are sometimes deemed to have settlement authority, outside of litigation it is generally understood that the client controls the decision on such a transaction. And, therefore, only when the client ratifies the lawyer-negotiated result will the client be bound.[53]

Second, are you accountable? If the court in your jurisdiction takes a different view and finds by action or deed that your client is bound, unless you believed you were authorized, the client will undoubtedly have a claim against you for failing to follow the client's explicit instructions not to accept any deal until the client approved it.[54] You also might be accountable to the third party, even if your client is not, if you purported to have authority when you knew you did not.[55]

---

52. *Greenwich v. Markhoff*, 650 N.Y.S.2d 704 (N.Y. App. Div. 1996) (lawyer only acts reasonably in limiting representation to worker's compensation claim if client understands that other lawyers are available who could identify and pursue additional tort claims against third parties).

53. RLGL § 21(4); *Sarkes Tarzian, Inc. v. U.S. Trust Co. of Fla. Sav. Bank*, 397 F.3d 577 (7th Cir. 2005).

54. RLGL § 27, cmt. f.

55. *Id.*; RLGL § 30(3).

🦋 Is the Client Responsible?

I am representing a corporate client in a very strange situation. Because of the conduct of the client's previous lawyer in some very important litigation, the court has sanctioned the lawyer, of course, but also the client. I say there is no way the client is responsible. The lawyer acted just like Rambo, thwarting discovery at every turn, making scheduling of depositions an impossibility, and otherwise acting in an obstreperous manner. In my view, just the lawyer should be responsible.

Well, you learn something every day. It is true that the lawyer is responsible for the lawyer's conduct. If the lawyer in fact acted outrageously, the lawyer should pay a price, but the questions will be (a) whether the client was aware of what the lawyer was doing, and (b) did the client ratify that conduct. If, in fact, the courts view the client as being well aware of what was going on and permitting it to continue because it fulfilled the client's purposes at the time, the client will not be allowed to escape responsibility, though placing responsibility on the client won't get the lawyer off the hook. Quite simply, the courts do not condone the conduct of clients in celebrating their lawyer's hardball tactics, and then seeking to escape responsibility for the conduct of their agents when the going gets rough.[56]

---

56. *E.g., Indus. Roofing Servs, Inc. v. Marquardt,* 726 N.W.2d 898 (Wis. 2007) (lawyer's failure to respond to discovery requests resulting in dismissal of action with prejudice could be imputed to client who knew or should have known of lawyer's conduct).

FOUR

Communication

% Introduction: The Foundation of the Five C's

COMMUNICATION IS ESSENTIAL to every aspect of the client-lawyer relationship. It defines the initial terms of the relationship and is required to make each of the Five C's work properly. Clients cannot control the goals of the representation without information about feasible options. Conversation also provides you with the obligation and opportunity to educate clients about the limits of the law. You cannot act competently without understanding what the client hopes to accomplish and how you will assist the client in getting there. You must ask clients before disclosing confidential information. And you must search for and disclose conflicts of interest in order to properly resolve them.

The key to understanding your foundational fiduciary duty of communication is to remember that you must initiate the conversation.[1] When you do, you will be in a position to know what your client wants and expects, when your client is willing to disclose confidences, and whether your client understands and waives conflicts of interest. When you do not, you will breach a basic fiduciary duty designed to protect the client-principal whose interests you have agreed to further. Because the duty to communicate is so fundamental, it is formulated broadly.

In certain well-defined instances, the law governing lawyers requires more than just conversation. Informed consent, which requires specified disclosures and usually a written confirmation of client instructions, is required as a means to enable clients to maintain control and to prevent lawyers from breaching fiduciary duties. The Model Rules of Professional Conduct define the requirement and impose the obligation on lawyers as a precondition to receiving

---

1. MODEL RULE 1.4; RLGL § 20.

instructions from a client,[2] to limiting the scope of a representation,[3] to disclosing or using confidential information,[4] and to resolving conflicts of interest.[5]

Figure 1   Seven Events That Trigger Your Duty to Communicate with Clients

1. Initially, to agree on a fee arrangement and to define the scope of the representation, both of which should be explained in an engagement letter.
2. Initially and throughout the representation, to explain the matter to enable the client to determine the objectives of the representation.
3. Throughout the representation, to keep the client reasonably informed about the status of the matter, including information about important developments in the representation itself, as well as changes in the lawyer's practice, such as a serious illness of the lawyer or a merger with another law firm.[6]
4. When you make a material mistake in the matter.[7]
5. When a client requests information.[8]
6. When the law imposes limits on conduct that a client expects you to undertake.
7. When you must obtain the client's informed consent, including when you seek to:
   - Limit the scope of a representation.[9]
   - Obtain a waiver of a fiduciary obligation owed your client, especially confidentiality and conflicts of interest.[10]
   - Obtain a waiver of a fiduciary obligation to a prospective client.[11]
   - Provide an evaluation for use by a third person that is likely to adversely affect the client's interests.[12]

---

2. MODEL RULES 1.2(a), 1.4.

3. MODEL RULE 1.2(c).

4. MODEL RULES 1.6(a), 1.9(a), 1.18(d).

5. MODEL RULES 1.7(b)(4), 1.8–1.12, 2.3(b).

6. MODEL RULE 1.4 (a)(3); RLGL § 20, cmt. c.

7. MODEL RULE 1.4 (a)(3); RLGL § 20, cmt. c.

8. MODEL RULE 1.4 (a)(4); RLGL § 20, cmt. d.

9. MODEL RULE 1.2(c); RLGL §19.

10. MODEL RULES 1.4(a)(1), 1.6–1.12; RLGL §§ 20, 60–62, 121–135.

11. MODEL RULE 1.18; RLGL § 15.

12. MODEL RULE 2.3; RLGL § 95.

𝕸 An Informal Engagement

I cannot believe our good fortune. Met this guy on the plane. Got a first class upgrade. That's how you meet successful folks. Anyway, he just left Google. Going out on his own. I couldn't even understand what he was saying. But he needs a lawyer to launch the enterprise. The flight went so well, at the end, he told me his name, put out his hand and said, "You're my new lawyer, friend." How do you like that for business development? I replied, "Meet your new General Counsel." And today, believe it or not, he called me up with our first assignment.

Well, it could be good.

Could be? You are a constant little storm raining on my parade.

Just trying to protect you—without squelching your enthusiasm. First, who is your client? From the sound of the conversation on the plane, you may have taken on several out-sized assignments. When you set up the company, are you this guy's personal lawyer? Are there other investors involved? Will you represent them as well? Once you set up the company, what about the scope of your representation? General Counsel for the company. Yet you've never met again. You don't know what the client's needs are. You don't know whether you have the requisite experience and expertise. Yet you have some guy out there thinking you are addressing all his legal concerns. Not to mention your fee. Have you discussed this?[13]

Two pieces of advice. Meet with the client as soon as possible to learn about his business and identify his needs. Then, send a written engagement letter setting forth the scope of the retention[14] and the basis on which you expect to be compensated.[15]

And this letter is no time for business development. It was one thing to call yourself GC after three miniature bottles of vodka and a five-hour plane ride. Here, we want you to list the specific tasks for which you have accepted responsibility and a protocol for expanding your work beyond that, if that becomes necessary.

Retention letters are sometimes mandated,[16] always desirable, and especially important in an organizational setting in which the array of services

---

13. RONALD E. MALLEN & JEFFREY M. SMITH, LEGAL MALPRACTICE § 2.10 (West 2007); GARY A. MUNNEKE & ANTHONY E. DAVIS, THE ESSENTIAL FORMBOOK: COMPREHENSIVE MANAGEMENT TOOLS FOR LAWYERS 141–144 (ABA Law Practice Management 2004).

14. MODEL RULE 1.2(c); RLGL § 19.

15. MODEL RULE 1.5 (b); RLGL § 38.

16. *See, e.g.,* 22 NYCRR §§ 1215.1, 1215.2.

that might be required is particularly vast.[17] And as noted above, some of the work that is required may require special expertise in vastly disparate areas from tax to labor law, from mergers and acquisitions to licensing. Make sure you have the qualifications in your shop to do the work or the way to gain the expertise through others.[18]

✺ I Forgot

The good news is we remembered to counsel our corporate client that in hiring a new CEO, it might want to put a non-compete into the agreement. That was wise advice, and the client, through its board chairman, said that is exactly what they wanted. As broad a non-compete as the law allows. But somehow, that clause never ended up in the agreement that has now been signed. And the new CEO starts next week.

Your first responsibility is to notify the board chairman of your error.[19] We would be shocked if he actually looked at the agreement before he signed it. Once you have made that disclosure, you will just have to deal with the client's response. It could be that the client will be furious, and that is the end of the representation. Or he could ask you to renegotiate with the CEO.

More likely than not, though, the client will respond by biding its time to see if, in fact, the absence of a non-compete ends up hurting the client. It may be that only then will the client come after your firm for the damage caused to the company, on the theory that the claim against your firm did not arise until the CEO left for a competitor and the need for a non-compete arose.[20]

---

17. *See* GARY A. MUNNEKE & ANTHONY E. DAVIS, THE ESSENTIAL FORMBOOK: COMPREHENSIVE MANAGEMENT TOOLS FOR LAWYERS 280 (ABA Law Practice Management 2000).

18. MODEL RULE 1.1, cmt. [1]; RLGL § 48.

19. RLGL § 20, cmt. c; *Leonard v. Dorsey & Whitney LLP,* 553 F.3d 609 (8th Cir. 2009) (lawyer has a duty to disclose potential malpractice claim if claim creates a conflict of interest that would disqualify the lawyer from representing the client such that lawyer's interest in avoiding liability conflicts with client's interest to seek recovery for harm caused by the lawyer's error); *Crean v. Chozick,* 714 S.W.2d 61(Tex. Ct. App. 1986) (failure to disclose malpractice to client tolls the statute of limitations).

20. *E.g., Fedderson v. Garvey,* 427 F.3d 108 (1st Cir. 2005) (discovery rule, that cause of action for legal malpractice does not commence until client should have known all material facts essential to the cause of action, does not toll statute of limitations where client could have reasonably discerned that he suffered some harm caused by the lawyer at an earlier point in time).

Further, most jurisdictions hold that the statute of limitations does not begin to run as long as you continue to represent the company.[21] In any event, the only good news is that it may be very hard for the company to prove any damages it incurred as a result of your lapse.[22]

The good lawyering point here is that your prompt notification to the company and your acknowledgment of your error will go a long way toward maintaining the good will you had with the client when the client thought you were following its instructions after you gave the client such wise counsel.

𝍤 The Nondisclosed Option

I was representing a partnership in a dispute with one of its vendors over some shoddy work. I met with the management group to discuss the case, and they told me they were so dissatisfied that they wouldn't offer anything in settlement. So we tried the case despite my warnings they could lose. And, in fact, the jury came in with a verdict for the vendor. Obviously, my client wasn't pleased, but they did remember my warning to them.

Now, five weeks later, I get a call from my client's managing partner. She tells me she was explaining to a friend about the loss, and the friend, who is a lawyer, said to her, "Why didn't you mediate the matter? That way you would have been able to compromise." The managing partner said to me, "We never even discussed mediation." She thinks the partnership is a victim of bad advice. Frankly, I did not consider mediation because they told me they never wanted to settle, and that is what you attempt to do when you mediate.

Your situation presents a classic problem for lawyers. Is it the obligation of a lawyer always to recommend mediation? Or are there only certain matters where it is appropriate? When and what do lawyers have to communicate to clients?[23] (See Figure B) Under these circumstances, you can be sure that the partnership, if it comes after your law firm, will find someone who opines that mediation is a recommendation every lawyer handling a litigated matter must make. When the ABA Ethics 2000 Commission reviewed the rules, it was importuned to create a mediation recommendation as a black

---

21. *E.g., Shumsky v. Eisenstein,* 750 N.E.2d 67 (N.Y. 2001).

22. *E.g., Hazel & Thomas, P.C. v. Yavari,* 465 S.E.2d 812 (Va. 1996) (client must show that other party would have accepted contractual clause to recover for lawyer's failure to propose it).

23. MODEL RULE 2.1, cmt. [5].

letter obligation. That suggestion was rejected on the theory that the rules cannot be a place to catalogue all wise practices and judgments.[24] But that rejection will not stop former disgruntled clients from making such judgment calls grist for the litigation mill.

✄ Nonlegal Opinions

So I just incurred my client's wrath. I should say the CEO's wrath. I was attending a board meeting. Making a presentation regarding a proposed merger. When I was done, I just should have exited stage left. But I was invited to stay, and you know how valuable for client relations it is to spend time in the inner sanctum. So the discussion turns to the company's export business. They make really high-tech laboratory equipment. The Iranians are very interested in some of their products. I start thinking what a black eye the company might get doing business with a member of the axis of evil. And all the board discussion is focusing on letters of credit and currency fluctuations. So I finally pipe up. I no sooner get the words out of my mouth, than the CEO turns to me, livid, really livid, and announces, "We have you for your legal advice, not public relations. Maybe it would be better if you left right now."

When we are hired as lawyers, we don't cease being human beings. In fact, Model Rule 2.1, counseling clients, provides that in rendering candid advice, a lawyer may, but is not required to, refer to moral, economic, social, and political factors. So you were acting consistently with the rules of professional conduct and in the highest traditions of the profession. This does not mean that your client was required to welcome your views, let alone act on them. Your plight calls to mind when one of the authors, sitting in on a board meeting, shared his views with a client of some new business proposal, only to be not so politely reminded that his firm had been hired for its legal advice and that if he were really an entrepreneur, he would never have practiced law.

✄ Keeping in Touch

Here's the problem with this communication obligation. Let's get specific. Every day, I'm being buffeted about by differences of opinion between the CFO's staff

---

24. *But see* Col. Rule 2.1.

and the CEO's contingent. Sometimes I side with one, sometimes with the other. On occasion, I think they're both misguided.

We sympathize. As you know, an entity's direction ultimately is determined by dozens, or even thousands, of persons acting within the scope of their various employments, which means you must communicate with the appropriate constituents to enable them to determine the organization's best interests. But, if any employee acts or refuses to act in violation of a legal obligation or law, that is, in a way that you know—remember that word—is likely to result in substantial injury to the organization, then it is your obligation—not just your opportunity—to proceed as is reasonably necessary in the best interest of the organization.[25]

𝓂 Up-the-Ladder Obligations

So how do I determine when it's better to speak up and when it's better to back off?

The list of communications required by Rule 1.4 is a good place to begin. But in representing an organization, Rule 1.13 also addresses the issue of communication. It tells us that we take instruction from the assigned individual unless the lawyer knows that a corporate employee is about to take action, or refuse to take action, that is likely to result in substantial monetary harm to the organization.

What do we do then?

Hope that it never happens. Note both the standard of knowledge and the standard of harm the rules require before the lawyer acts. But if it does occur, all states require the lawyer to take some kind of reasonable remedial action.

What does that mean?

The lawyer may remonstrate with the employee, seek a second opinion, try moral suasion.[26]

And if that doesn't work?

One possibility is to go over the head of the individual to the next higher level of the organization.

Go to his boss?

---

25. Model Rule 1.13(b); RLGL § 96(2).

26. Model Rule 1.13, cmt. [4]; RLGL § 96(3) & cmt. f.

Precisely.

That takes guts. This person's probably the one who hired you.

Could well be. But remember, even if you have called this individual your client for a decade, played golf with him, had him to your kid's bar mitzvah, your client is the entity. So you go to the boss.

And if the boss backs the guy up?

Then you are permitted to continue up what is called the corporate ladder.

You use that metaphor 'cause high ladders are dangerous.

And the air is thin, but ultimately, you are free to go to the highest authority authorized to act for the organization.[27]

The board?

That's usually correct.

Sure, I'm going to walk into a board meeting and tell them their CEO has it wrong. I'd rather walk a gang plank.

Courage, my friend. We lawyers have real responsibility to our organizational clients, and if such a situation is triggered, this may be what your fiduciary duty to your client requires. Lawyers often have to undertake unpleasant tasks to provide clients with advice they may not want to, but nonetheless, must hear. When the extraordinary standard of Rule 1.13 gets triggered is one of those times. For some, it is unlikely to earn the love and affection of the client representatives. For others, it may earn you the respect and gratitude of the organization.

ℳ Original Rule 1.13

I've heard there are two versions of Rule 1.13 with different up-the-ladder obligations.

Original Model Rule 1.13, the rule still applicable in most jurisdictions as of this writing,[28] is very sensitive to disruption of the organization. Thus it leaves it very much to the discretion of the lawyer to choose how to act under those special circumstances where the possibility of harm was great.[29]

---

27. MODEL RULE 1.13, cmt. [5]; RLGL § 96(3) & cmt. f.

28. *E.g.*, Del. Rule 1.13, Appendix A.

29. *E.g.*, Alaska Rule 1.13(b); Del. Rule 1.13(b); Fla. Rule 4-1.13(b); Nev. Rule 1.13(b); Va. Rule 1.13(b); RLGL § 96(3).

Under this version of Model Rule 1.13 and the Restatement, the lawyer is offered a number of options. Suggest that the general manager secure another opinion. Remonstrate with the general manager about the proposed course of action. The key here is not to simply pay lip service to the issue, merely check a box, but rather use your best persuasive powers to achieve a change in course, a rethinking of the expressed approach. Think of the counseling you would provide to your troubled best friend or close relative.

What about "know?"

We wanted to emphasize that standard in original Rule 1.13 and Section 96 of the Restatement because the trigger for further action on your part requires that you know something is likely to happen. And "know" is a defined term. It means actual knowledge, though the lawyer cannot blind herself to obvious facts to avoid knowing. So if you think a certain course of action—a disclosure issue, for example, is a very close question on which you and general counsel have a legitimate professional disagreement, the "know" standard is not triggered. On the other hand, if you are convinced that your client's making certain commission payments violating the Foreign Corrupt Practices Act, then you have a duty to act.

What if the CFO persists in following this troubling course of conduct?

If that happens and you are operating in a state that has adopted the original rule, you are provided the option, but not the requirement, to take a special trip we call "up the ladder."

Sure hope that ladder is leaning against something.

Good point. This is a perilous little trip, yet worth it in both the short and long term if the situation should be remedied. If the lawyer chooses to go up the corporate or organizational ladder, what the lawyer does is identify on a chart or otherwise the various levels of authority and contact each one seriatim so long as the lawyer's nerve hangs on and those at each successively higher authority rung persist in the conduct that triggered the lawyer's concern in the first place. The journey continues all the way up to the board of directors or trustees or any other "highest authority in the organization" that is authorized to act in the name of the entity.[30]

Right!

What do you mean?

I'm going to walk into the boardroom of Magna Corporation and tell them about a decision that has been approved by the CFO, the general counsel, the executive vice president, and the CEO. You think I believe in suicide?

---

30. RLGL § 96(3) & cmt. f.

Your point is an excellent one. It is very hard for a lawyer to go up the corporate ladder. Even the first rung takes real nerve. And walking into the boardroom takes real . . . oops, this is a family publication. But such a journey may prevent an organization nightmare or disaster. Original Rule 1.13 and the Restatement make all of this optional, leaving it to your best discretion how to serve the best interests of your client.

Post-Enron Rule 1.13

You mean in some places Rule 1.13 has been amended and removes my discretion?

Yes. If a triggering event occurs, the new rule strips the lawyer of any discretion to decide what the best course is. The lawyer must go up the corporate ladder.[31]

But it might have been enough—and a lot less disruptive—if the lawyer got the general manager to seek another opinion.

The lawyer could do that, and if it changes the manager's opinion, the matter ends. But if that does not occur, the lawyer must go up the ladder and ultimately must go to the board.[32]

What were they thinking? The Rule must have been written by people who had no clue how scary it would be to go over the head of the general counsel, let alone walk into a boardroom.

You are right there. One would think that if another lawyer—general counsel of all people—made a decision for the entity, outside counsel would be off the hook. But no. The proponents of new Rule 1.13 thought that wasn't enough. Outside counsel has the same authority and responsibility as the organization's own full-time "senior vice president and general counsel." But if you live in a state that has adopted present Model Rule 1.13 (and nearly twenty have),[33] then this is the rule you must follow.

---

31. *E.g.*, Ind. Rule 1.13, Appendix A. For public companies, Sarbanes Oxley also imposes up-the-ladder requirements. *See* Chapter 11, Figure 11, and Table 5.

32. Model Rule 1.13(b) & cmts. [3]–[5].

33. *E.g.,* Ark. Rule 1.13; Colo. Rule 1.13; Idaho Rule 1.13; Ind. Rule 1.13; Iowa Rule 1.13; La. Rule 1.13; Md. Rule 1.13; Mich. Rule 1.13; Neb. Rule 1.13; Nev. Rule 1.13; N.H. Rule 1.13; N.J. Rule 1.13; N.D. Rule 1.13; Okla. Rule 1.13; Or. Rule 1.13; R.I. Rule 1.13; S.C. Rule 1.13; Utah Rule 1.13; Wash. Rule 1.13.

𝍶 Up the Ladder: Enough?

But, in a way I'm relieved. The shareholders elect the board; if I go to the board and urge it to act or not act in some way, and the board tells me to pound sand, and they're wrong, the shareholders can complain to the board, even sue 'em for violating the board's fiduciary duties. Am I right?

You should be. But you must keep two things in mind. First, some of the states that have mandated going to the board have also given the lawyer permission to go outside the board—to the SEC or other government regulations, to the shareholders—to disclose what is going on.[34]

You're kidding me, right?

'Fraid not.

The board exercises its authority, and I'm supposed to blow the whistle on my client? Call the constabulary? Visit Carl Ichan? The lawyer gets to trump the judgment of the board, the duly elected highest authority? It makes no sense. I'm just a lawyer. What do I know?

New Post-Enron Model Rule 1.13 does take a different approach. A lawyer's permission to disclose confidential information under new Rule 1.13 gets triggered when the lawyer knows that proposed conduct is clearly a violation of law and reasonably believes that the violation is reasonably certain to result in substantial injury to the organization.[35] It can sound outrageous, but the Rule does force the lawyer to focus on the best interests of the organization. And you should recognize that some states have adopted this rule.[36]

So. You say it's optional, but it looks like someone is just setting lawyers up to be sued when they disagree with the judgment of their organizational client's highest authority and the board turns out wrong. "Why didn't the lawyer call the police?" someone will assert.

Fortunately, it hasn't happened yet. But it is part of a trend that got a big boost from Enron and other debacles of the turn of the century. Which brings us to the second matter to worry about, to keep in mind. Some view with scorn the instrumental role of the lawyer for an organization. Rather than the lawyer implementing the judgment of the duly constituted governing authority of the corporation, they would have the lawyer act as some sort of all-seeing, all-knowing guardian of the enterprise, refusing to implement the

---

34. Model Rule 1.13(c).

35. Model Rule 1.13(c) & cmt. [6].

36. *See supra* note 33.

instructions of employees, officers, and directors of these entities if the lawyer believes they are not acting in the best interests of the shareholders.[37]

But isn't that what the shareholders elected the directors to do? Don't the directors exercise judgment in selecting officers? Don't they all have fiduciary obligations the violation of which can result in their removal and lawsuits for the breach?

One would think so. But anyone operating in this terrain must recognize the drumbeat, resist it at every turn, but not be surprised when a Rule 1.13 gets enacted that places way too much more responsibility on lawyers, or some judge adopts the guardian angel view of how lawyers' obligations should be defined.

I suppose this claptrap comes from the pens of those who have never been in a boardroom or counseled a client on a disclosure obligation?

The idea was the brainchild of several outstanding academics. But it received support from some very talented and well-respected practicing lawyers who got caught up in the frenzy of Enron and thought this change might stem the tide of officious intermeddling by the feds, a hope that went unfulfilled, alas.[38]

But suppose I think one way. Everyone in the organization—even the board—decides contrariwise and I, a mere lawyer, get to override all of them by calling the SEC or the state attorney general or writing the shareholders or calling the Department of Environmental Protection?

In the limited circumstances we've discussed, that is true.

So the ABA, in adopting this crazy new rule, trumped corporate governance rules in every state, gave the lawyer for an entity more power than the board, and set lawyers up for liability for not reporting outside the organization, when we all learned in law school that the board of directors or trustees was the highest authority that could act for an organization?

So it appears to some. One thing is clear: The new Model Rule raises one of the most critical issues of all in representing an organization: when can a lawyer rest on the judgment of an individual or group of entity representatives? When we represent an individual, that client can make any mistake he or she wants so long as it doesn't injure any third parties. Not so with

---

37. *E.g.*, E. Norman Veasey & Christine T. DiGuglielmo, *The Tensions, Stresses, and Professional Responsibilities of the Lawyer for the Corporation*, 62 BUS. LAW. 1 (Nov. 2006).

38. *E.g.*, Robert W. Gordon, *A New Role of Lawyers? The Corporate Counselor After Enron*, 35 CONN. L. REV. 1185 (2003), Susan P. Koniak, *When the Hurlyburly's Done: The Bar's Struggle With the SEC*, 103 COLUM. L. REV. 1236 (2003).

corporate clients, at least under new Model Rule 1.13. As to them, lawyers must continue to pursue the best interests of the entity, becoming either guardian angels or super CEOs, depending on your point of view.

🕮 Searching for Common Ground in Rule 1.13 Variations

Wow! I must admit, I'm still a bit troubled about the two versions of Rule 1.13.

Didn't mean to do that. In the end, the rules are far less important than the good lawyering points.

Organizational clients come in all shapes and sizes, filled with individuals with vastly different levels of sophistication, understanding, and psychological makeup. The good lawyer will recognize this and, in representing the organization and respecting its governance, proceed using good judgment and common sense to minimize the number of instances in which, in the lawyer's view, the organization is jumping off the railroad tracks.

Quite simply it is very rare that a lawyer will know more about the business and mission of the organization than those in control, and therefore for the lawyer to be substituting the lawyer's judgment for the client's on the safety of a new product, the efficacy of a proposed transaction, or the decision to deaccession some paintings is entirely unjustified. A lawyer's gut reaction is no substitute for a chemist's three years of controlled laboratory studies.

The lawyer, perhaps somewhat chastened by the foregoing principles, will feel a need to act, to see the best interests of the organization differently from those expressed by the assigned organizational client contacts. When that occurs, taking into account everything the lawyer knows and acting really without regard to Rule 1.13, the lawyer should adopt a formal strategy to change minds and, if there is a higher authority within the organization, assure that authority is aware of the matter and the lawyer's concerns with the chosen course of conduct. That wise counseling is the least we owe our organizational clients.

🕮 Informed Consent: Confidentiality

I just came in-house to Small Co. My first assignment—a delicate property negotiation—is almost at an end. All I need do is produce some of our internal memos to the other side to document our discussions. I was having copies made of the documents when it suddenly occurred to me whether I better run this document request by someone else at Small Co.

You have to do more than that. The Model Rules require more than a "run-by" to waive an important client right—in this case, confidentiality.[39] Confidentiality[40] and conflicts waivers,[41] along with client instructions about the scope[42] and goals of the representation,[43] are valid only if secured with the client's "informed consent."[44] And that requires lawyers to initiate two communications. First, you must inform, or communicate, "adequate information and explanation about the material risks of and reasonably available alternatives to the proposed course of conduct."[45] Second, you must clarify that your client (through the appropriate agent, of course) actually does agree, or consent.

As you describe it, it would be best if that person were not you. Getting informed consent from yourself gives you nowhere to hide if later your little disclosure triggers some unhappy response from your buyer.

But I'm dealing with a CEO. He really plays it close to the vest. What if he doesn't agree?

That would give you the opportunity to point our how good your deal is, and why it won't fly without the document disclosures. Then, if the CEO decides otherwise, you've fulfilled your obligation, and he has fulfilled his.

✍ Informed Consent: The Settlement Conference

We had a settlement conference coming up—mean judge. My client's executive director and I agreed we would offer $200,000 to settle, and our final offer would be $500,000. I get to the conference, and in response to a demand for my client's bottom line, I tell the judge $200,000; he looks me in the eye and proclaims that $200,000 is a bargaining ploy. He wants to know my client's last final offer. I repeat $200,000, and the judge calls poor executive director into his vast chambers.

---

39. MODEL RULE 1.4(a)(1).

40. MODEL RULES 1.6(a), 1.9(a), 1.18(d).

41. MODEL RULES 1.7(b)(4), 1.8–1.12, 2.3(b).

42. MODEL RULE 1.2(c).

43. MODEL RULE 1.2(a).

44. MODEL RULE 1.0(e).

45. *Id.*

Then, throwing the fear of God into my client, the judge asks the same question. The client blurts out $500,000. Now the judge wants me disbarred.

Of course, you properly consulted with your client before the settlement conference, and you obtained your client's explicit informed consent and proper delegation of specific settlement authority to you. But that delegation did not include a waiver of your client's right to confidentiality.[46] Informed consent is required twice here: first to authorize you to settle, and second to authorize you to share your client's bottom line. This judge had no business overreaching, but that does not justify your big white lie.[47] The next time you deal with a judge at settlement talks, you have two ethical solutions: either make sure that your client's delegation of authority is limited to your client's first offer (or revoked if the judge demands an answer), or decline to answer the judge's request.

⅏ Informed Consent: Prospective Waivers

I'm General Counsel of the next Amazon. I just know it. The company started eighteen months ago. I was their first outside counsel. Six months ago, they lured me inside. So much to do; sales growing fifteen percent per month! Now it looks like we're joining the big leagues. I've been hearing from New York firms. Can you believe it? Little ol' Webstat with a name brand law firm.

Anyway, they convinced me we needed their assistance on some tax stuff. In business a year and a half, and our worry is our tax bill. So I said, "Great." And they sent me a retainer letter. Seven pages, single-spaced. So I started reading it, and buried on page five is the following:

C. Waiver of Conflicts
There is always the possibility that we may be called upon by other present or future clients to act against your interests. At present, we see no such conflict between your interest and the interest of our other clients. However, there may come a time when there are or may be such conflicts. If this occurs, you agree that our law firm will remain free, notwithstanding

---

46. *In re Anonymous*, 654 N.E.2d 1128 (Ind. 1995) (lawyer who revealed information relating to the representation of a prospective client thinking it would not cause harm subject to discipline despite lack of improper motive).

47. ABA Comm. on Ethics and Prof'l Responsibility, Formal Op. 93-370 (1993) (Judicial Participation in Pretrial Settlement Negotiations).

our representation of you and whether or not during the course of our representation of you, to represent any present or future client of our law firm with interest adverse to you in any matter (including representation in litigation, arbitration or mediation in which you and such other client are or may be adverse parties) so long as such matter is (a) not substantially related to matters in which we are currently representing you, and (b) does not require us to utilize confidential information that we have learned from you while working on your behalf.

I figure that can't possibly be enforceable, so I told my CEO to sign it as is. Imagine a lawyer suing his own client.

We can understand your dismay. These prospective waivers are a plague on our profession. The rules require strict loyalty by lawyers to their clients. And those fancy pants New York firms (and others) try to contract out of their obligations. By burying a clause like this one.

Well, they wouldn't try to enforce it, would they? We wouldn't stand for that.

Your last point first. Now you say you wouldn't stand for it. But when the time comes for this new firm to take a position directly adverse to your company, it may not be so easy to fire them. You might have become dependent on them. You might be in the middle of a critical deal. Or about to go to trial in a big case.

Well, we're only hiring them for tax work.

That's now, and that's why prospective waivers like this one should never be enforceable. At the time you sign the waiver, there is one state of affairs. By the time big shot firm tries to enforce it, the firm may be handling a dozen matters, and who knows what confidential information you will have shared with this firm. So, even if you really agreed to this waiver now, that does not mean you would accept it four years from now under the circumstances then prevailing. Anyway, we just want to make sure you recognize how being forced to fire your law firm is not a perfect solution.

But you do agree that I gave good advice? This can't be enforceable.

The Model Rules require "informed consent" for all conflicts waivers, including prospective waivers.[48] But, by definition, in the case of a prospective waiver, the client cannot be fully informed. At the time the prospective waiver is secured, the client may not know: a) when the law firm will try to enforce the waiver; b) what the representation that triggers the invocation of

---

48. MODEL RULE 1.7(b)(4); RLGL § 121.

the waiver entails; c) what representations the law firm will have undertaken between the time the waiver is secured and the time it is invoked, and d) what confidential information of the client the lawyer will have learned in the interim.

But the Model Rules now have a comment that gives the ABA's endorsement to prospective waivers.[49] Not a blanket endorsement, mind you. But the comment does say that waivers that identify the likely adverse representation could be enforceable. If the prospective waiver is narrowly crafted, includes with particularity the likely adverse representations, is enforced within a reasonable time, and the representation of the client has not changed dramatically from what it looked like at the time the prospective waiver was sought, perhaps the prospective waiver will be enforceable. However, whether open-ended waivers like the one here could be enforceable as to sophisticated clients depends on what the parties actually foresaw at the time the waiver was signed.[50]

That's weird. I'm not very sophisticated, as you can easily tell. But, even if I were, being sophisticated does not mean that I'm clairvoyant, that I can tell where the representation's going to go, what we will have told our outside law firm.

Precisely what the detractors of this comment decried. But, alas the comment's the comment. So anyone who signs one of these prospective waivers is in some jeopardy—jeopardy of at least having to litigate the enforceability of the prospective waiver—if the client signs it.

---

49. MODEL RULE 1.7, cmt. [22]; RLGL § 121, cmt. d.

50. *Celegene Corp. v. KV Pharmaceutical Co.,* No. 07-4819, 2008 U.S. Dist. LEXIS 587353 (D.N.J. July 28, 2008) (law firm failed to sustain its burden of proof that it had obtained truly informed consent in advanced waiver from very sophisticated client); *El Camino Res., Ltd. v. Huntington Natl. Bank,* No. 1:07-cv-598, 2007 U.S. Dist. LEXIS 67813 (W.D. Mich. Sept. 13, 2007) (law firm that took on defense of bank in bankruptcy litigation to recover voidable preferences when it already represented two creditors in the same bankruptcy disqualified; advance waiver obtained by law firm was specifically limited to matters not involving bank in adverse actions); *Gen. Cigar Holdings, Inc. v. Altadis, S.A.,* 144 F. Supp. 2d 1334 (S.D. Fla. 2001) (co-party that signed waiver of conflicts to current or future representation against other co-party bound by advance waiver in subsequent suit over unrelated matter between the co-parties); *Worldspan, L.P. v. Sabre Group Holdings, Inc.,* 5 F. Supp. 2d 1356 (N.D. Ga. 1998) (law firm that represented client in tort case against existing client for whom law firm handled tax matters disqualified despite five-year-old waiver); *City of Cleveland v. Cleveland Elec. Illuminating Co.,* 440 F. Supp. 193 (N.D. Ohio 1976) (city's prior general consent to conflicts arising from representation of city in municipal bond issues valid where city had full knowledge of scope and depth of law firm's long-standing representation of defendant utility), *aff'd,* 573 F.2d 1310 (6th Cir. 1977).

Well, they say if we don't sign it, they can't afford to take on our matter.

Funny word: "afford." Last time we checked, that firm's profits per partner were $2,400,000. But maybe you can't afford to hire them as your lawyers. Sure are a lot of outstanding firms that will take these clauses out or, better yet, never ask for such a waiver in the first place.

Competence

"Legal advises finger-pointing."

※ Introduction: Why You Were Hired in the First Place

CLIENTS HIRE LAWYERS for competent service precisely because they are not able to navigate a complex legal system themselves. Agents who breach competence or fiduciary duties may be liable in both contract and tort. The contract remedy usually is reserved for cases where a lawyer disobeys a clear and legal instruction of the client or acts contrary to the client's clear interests.[1] Tort remedies include intentional torts, such as fraud[2] and conversion,[3] and more typically, negligence based on allegations of breach of fiduciary duty [4] or malpractice.[5]

In situations where the client has been deprived of the central protection of the client's interests, such as control, communication, confidentiality, or loyalty, courts identify a breach of fiduciary duty remedy to redress a lawyer's failure to observe a basic fiduciary duty.[6] In these situations, the client has been deprived of a core fiduciary duty, or, as some courts put it, the lawyer

---

1. *E.g., Interclaim Holdings, Ltd. v. Ness, Motley, Loadholt, Richardson & Poole*, 298 F. Supp. 2d 746 (N.D. Ill. 2004) (upholding compensatory damages of $8.3 million and punitive damages of $27.7 million on breach of contract theory against law firm that settled claims and released frozen assets without client's consent).

2. *E.g., Baker v. Dorfman*, 239 F.3d 415 (2d Cir. 2000) (lawyer who lied about the extent of his legal experience to client liable for fraud, including compensatory, emotional distress, and punitive damages).

3. *E.g., Disciplinary Counsel v. McCauley*, 873 N.E.2d 269 (Ohio 2007) (lawyer indefinitely suspended from practice for stealing client's money after agreeing to consent judgment for conversion, fraud, and malpractice); *ERA Realty Co. v. RBS Props.*, 586 N.Y.S.2d 831 (N.Y App. Div. 1992) (lawyer who used invalid legal process liable for conversion); *Barbara A. v. John G.*, 193 Cal. Rptr. 422 (Cal. Ct. App. 1983) (lawyer who told client he "couldn't possibly get anyone pregnant" liable for battery and fraud after client suffered a tubal pregnancy, which resulted in permanent sterility).

4. *E.g., Maritrans GP Inc. v. Pepper, Hamilton & Scheetz*, 602 A.2d 1277 (Pa. 1992) (law firm breached fiduciary duty of loyalty by taking on adverse substantially related representation); *Perez v. Kirk & Carrigan*, 822 S.W.2d 261 (Tex. App. 1991) (lawyer breached fiduciary duty of confidentiality by disclosing client's statement to prosecutor); *Olfe v. Gordon*, 286 N.W.2d 573 (Wis. 1980) (lawyer breached agency duty by negligently disregarding client's instructions to draft a first rather than second mortgage).

5. *E.g., dePape v. Trinity Health Sys., Inc.*, 242 F. Supp. 2d 585 (N.D. Iowa 2003) (law firm breached duty of communication by failing to provide necessary information to client); *Jerry's Enters. v. Larkin, Hoffman, Daly & Lindgren, Ltd.*, 711 N.W.2d 811 (Minn. 2006) (negligent failure to research or raise relevant issue in property transaction); *Ziegelheim v. Apollo*, 607 A.2d 1298 (N.J. 1992) (negligent settlement advice).

6. RLGL § 49; Ray Ryden Anderson & Walter W. Steele, Jr., *Fiduciary Duty, Tort and Contract: A Primer on the Legal Malpractice Puzzle*, 47 SMU. L. REV. 235 (1994).

has acted "outside the scope of authority granted by the client."[7] Other courts describe this cause of action as constructive fraud,[8] or assume that breach of fiduciary duty is a species of malpractice that does not require expert testimony to show duty and breach.[9]

Most of the situations where clients seek a tort remedy do not involve such clear breaches of fiduciary duty. Instead, the client alleges a breach of the duties of care or competence—that the lawyer should have known more, should have had more experience, or should have exercised better judgment or care in accomplishing the client's goals. These situations commonly allege legal malpractice and usually require expert testimony to prove that the lawyer did not "exercise the competence and diligence normally exercised by lawyers in similar circumstances."[10]

Model Rules 1.1 and 1.3 mimic the malpractice standard of care by requiring "reasonable" competence and diligence. Reasonable competence and diligence usually must be established by expert testimony in a disciplinary or malpractice case, as well as in considering whether to reverse a criminal conviction for ineffective assistance of counsel.[11] Incompetence or lack of diligence also can provide the basis for discipline, although disciplinary agencies typically do not proceed against lawyers for isolated instances of incompetence or lack of diligence.[12]

Courts also recognize some limited legal duties to non-clients when doing so will foster the client's intent and not harm the client-lawyer relationship. Clients should receive frank advice untainted by lawyer concerns about liability to others. But at the same time, lawyers cannot escape generally applicable law that creates responsibility to non-clients (such as fraud and

---

7. *Kilpatrick v. Wiley, Rein & Fielding*, 909 P.2d 1283, 1290 (Utah 1996).

8. RLGL § 40, cmt. a; RESTATEMENT (SECOND) TORTS § 551(2)(a).

9. *E.g., Estate of Fleming v. Nicholson*, 724 A.2d 1026 (Vt. 1998) (no expert testimony necessary to establish negligence as a matter of law against lawyer who failed to inform client about a permit violation discovered during a title search on land the client wished to purchase, despite lawyer's claim that state had a nonenforcement policy concerning that type of violation). *See also* Charles W. Wolfram, *A Cautionary Tale: Fiduciary Breach as Legal Malpractice*, 34 HOFSTRA L. REV. 689 (2006).

10. RLGL § 52.

11. *Strickland v. Washington*, 466 U.S. 668, 688 (1984) ("The proper measure of attorney performance remains simply reasonableness under prevailing professional norms.").

12. *E.g., In re Johnson*, 32 P.3d 1132 (Kan. 2001) (lawyer's lack of experience no defense to professional discipline for repeated instances of lack of competence and diligence).

other intentional torts).[13] Courts also find lawyers liable for economic harm on a negligence theory when a client invites third party reliance, creates a third-party beneficiary of the lawyer's services, or when the lawyer engages in a negligent misrepresentation or aids and abets a client's fraud or breach of fiduciary duty.[14]

Figure 2   Legal Malpractice & Breach of Fiduciary Duty

1. Client-lawyer relationship (foreseeable plaintiff)
   a. Offer
   b. Acceptance
   c. Consideration or Detrimental Reliance
2. Duty = Expert Testimony usually required except:
   Common Knowledge
   a. Breach of fiduciary duty (compliance with reasonable client instructions, disclosure, confidentiality, and some conflicts of interest)
   b. Missed deadlines
   c. Failure to research law
3. Breach
4. Cause
   a. Actual = but for = case within a case
   b. Proximate = foreseeable consequences
5. Damages
   a. Economic Loss
   b. Emotional distress
   c. Punitive

✵ The Standard of Care: Forgotten Boilerplate

I was in a hurry and forgot to insert the standard boilerplate in a supply contract I drafted for my manufacturing client. I don't think my client even mentioned it though, so I'm safe, right?

---

13. RLGL § 56, cmt. b.

14. RLGL § 51.

Depends on what you mean by "safe." If your client did mention it and told you to insert the boilerplate, you breached your fiduciary duty to comply with client instructions or deference to client control.[15] But your client paid you not only to obey its instructions, but also to offer it relevant legal options. If you and your client didn't discuss the matter, but the boilerplate you left out is "standard" in these kinds of supply contracts in your jurisdiction, you are just one expert witness away from a legal conclusion that you did not exercise the requisite skill, diligence, and preparation necessary for the representation. This violates Model Rule 1.1, although you are unlikely to be subject to professional discipline for just one slip. It also constitutes a breach in the malpractice standard of care, although your client would have to show that the breach caused harm.[16]

The requirement of Model Rules 1.1 and 1.3 of "reasonable" competence and diligence mean that you don't have to be perfect, but you do have to meet or exceed the standard of practice in your jurisdiction. Reasonable competence and diligence usually must be established by expert testimony in both malpractice (See Figure C) and disciplinary matters.

Let's hope that no dispute develops between your client and the supplier. But remember, if it does, establishing malpractice liability also requires proof of causation and damages.[17]

ℳ The Standard of Care: It Can't Be That Hard

We have been representing this start-up company for a number of years and, believe it or not, it looks like their new software is about to take off. They even have an investment banker who is recommending an initial public offering to finance the next phase of the company's expansion. The client asked us whether we thought that was a good idea and wondered whether we could undertake the matter. I, of course, answered, "Yes. How exciting! We cannot wait to help you become a public company." But the truth is, we have never done an IPO, though I did find one of those checklist outlines from some PLI program which I did not attend.

---

15. *Olfe v. Gordon*, 286 N.W.2d 573 (Wis. 1980) (lawyer liable without expert testimony for failure to effectuate client's instruction to secure a first mortgage in sale of her home).

16. *E.g., Russo v. Griffin*, 510 A.2d 436 (Vt. 1986) (lawyer who failed to offer non-compete option to employer-client subject to malpractice liability).

17. RLGL § 53.

It is your principal obligation to be competent. Everyone has to do every-thing for the first time once. But an IPO is a pretty sophisticated proposition, and, if no one in your shop has IPO experience, this might be a situation where you must affiliate with someone else who has the requisite back-ground and experience.[18]

But, if we do that, we will lose the client.

That may be, but we are not sure that following mere book learning from a PLI checklist is the way to go. We think you should tell your client you will need co-counsel and hope that, because of your long relationship, you'll be able to keep the client who will admire you for your candor and willingness to seek help.[19] And after this transaction is completed, you will have experi-ence in IPOs, or at least in handling one.

%% Diligence: Not to Worry

I'm a new associate. About a month into the job, I finally got to the bottom of a stack of subrogation cases on my desk left by the last disgruntled associate. Turns out the statute of limitations had expired on the claim. My boss told me not to worry, insurers in this county never raise the defense. Should I quit?

We sympathize. Your boss should have given you better guidance. But even if you didn't know the claim was approaching the limitations period, you should have reviewed the files first with that in mind, or asked someone who could help.

Model Rule 1.3 requires that lawyers act with reasonable diligence and promptness. Diligence requires commitment and dedication to the client's interests—something called zealous representation in the ABA's earlier Model Code of Professional Responsibility.[20] Promptness should speak for itself: you must manage the workload imposed by your practice so that you can give rea-sonable and timely attention to each client matter. Simple procrastination in a matter may or may not be serious, depending on the time deadlines imposed and the exigencies of the situation. But anytime "being behind" causes harm to your client, you may face malpractice or disciplinary consequences. If you

---

18. MODEL RULE 1.1, cmt. [1], RLGL § 52, cmt. d.

19. *Horne v. Peckham*, 158 Cal. Rptr. 714 (Cal. Ct. App. 1979) (lawyer had duty to refer client to an expert tax practitioner or comply with specialty standard of care).

20. RLGL § 52, cmt. c.

have supervisory authority in a law firm, you have an obligation to watch the workload of those you supervise. You are responsible for establishing policies and procedures that prod all lawyers in the firm to comply with this obligation.[21]

Both you and your boss are responsible to the client, who could file a grievance. You have no defense of reasonable reliance on your boss, because Model Rule 5.2 only allows that excuse to "subordinate lawyers" where there was no arguable question of professional duty.[22] We think your boss—not you—deserves the discipline, for failure to supervise.[23] As to malpractice, you are both on the hook. Maybe the former disgruntled associate, too.

✐ Obvious Negligence

So I didn't worry, because I believed my boss when he told me the defendant-insurer would not raise the statute defense. But they did, and the trial judge just dismissed my case. And our client is furious. Now am I in trouble?

If you miss a time period and cannot secure an extension, you must tell the client.[24] You also will face a potential malpractice claim, though disciplinary agencies will seldom impose sanctions unless you exhibit a pattern of such behavior. As for malpractice, juries don't need an expert to know that

---

21. MODEL RULE 5.1; RLGL § 11.

22. *Daniels v. Alander*, 844 A.2d 182 (Conn. 2004) (associate who failed to correct supervisory lawyer's false statement to a court made when associate was present reprimanded); *People v. Casey*, 948 P.2d 1014 (Colo. 1997) (lawyer who assisted client in crime of criminal impersonation by not correcting court record of client's name not relieved of responsibility because he consulted with senior partner); Lawrence J. Fox, *I'm Just an Associate . . . at a New York Firm*, 69 FORDHAM L. REV. 939 (2000).

23. *In re Cohen*, 847 A.2d 1162 (D.C. 2004) (partner who had "no system in place to impart rudimentary ethics training to lawyers in the firm" suspended for thirty days because given the discreet nature of the case, extended length of the representation, and small law firm size, he reasonably should have known of associate-son's ethics violations and intervened to mitigate or avoid them); *In re Anonymous Member of S.C. Bar*, 552 S.E.2d 10 (S.C. 2001) (law firm partners and other lawyers who directly or indirectly supervise other lawyers could be sanctioned and subject to discipline for failing to mitigate known misconduct of another lawyer in discovery and depositions, failing to make reasonable efforts to supervise, even without knowledge of misconduct, or failing to put systematic procedures in place to prevent misconduct).

24. *Leonard v. Dorsey & Whitney LLP*, 553 F.3d 609 (8th Cir. 2009) (lawyer has a duty to disclose potential malpractice claim if claim creates a conflict of interest that would disqualify the lawyer from representing the client, such as running of a statute of limitations).

promptness requires you to file a case or appeal on a timely basis.[25] In evidentiary terms, the "common knowledge" exception to the expert testimony requirement applies because deadlines are obvious, and lawyers should know and comply with them on behalf of their clients, all of which translates into your need for an appropriate tickler system to remind you about dates.

𝕸 Legal and Factual Research

I gave my utility client advice based on the relevant environmental statutes, but I missed a recent administrative regulation that changes the result. The difference cost them millions in clean-up costs, and the state agency appears reluctant to allow them to raise rates. Now my client is making noises about our firm covering the difference. That can't be right.

We suggest you notify your malpractice carrier. The failure to do any legal research or investigate relevant facts constitutes a breach of your diligence obligation to make sure both have been completed.[26] In a malpractice case, it also comes within the common knowledge exception to the expert testimony requirement. If you relied on your memory but didn't do the research, your client could get to the jury without an expert witness to prove your breach of the standard of care. If you looked it up but misconstrued it, then an expert would be needed to establish how a reasonable lawyer would have read the new regulation.

𝕸 Breach of Fiduciary Duty

Our medical clinic client asked us to work out the immigration status of a new physician they hired. We sent everyone our standard retainer letters. Next, we learned that the physician wouldn't take the medical licensing boards that offered the best chance of permanent residency. So we did the best we could, but the physician couldn't get across the border. Now he's blaming us.

---

25. *George v. Caton*, 600 P.2d 822 (N.M. 1979).

26. *Smith v. Lewis*, 107 Cal. Rptr. 95 (Cal. Ct. App. 1973) (expert testimony not required to prove lawyer's failure to research applicable law); *Schmidt v. Crotty*, 528 N.W.2d 112 (Iowa 1995) (expert testimony not required to prove lawyer's failure to research facts about property descriptions in valuing estate taxes after lawyer was put on notice of their inaccuracy).

Who told you the physician wouldn't take the exam? Did you tell him about his immigration options or just rely on the clinic to do so? You had two clients here, and the clinic didn't have an immigration problem. If you communicated with the clinic and not the physician, you have a problem.[27] Many courts have held that juries do not need expert testimony to understand basic breaches of fiduciary duty, including the failure of a lawyer to follow a client's instructions, to communicate relevant legal advice and options, and to maintain client confidentiality (see Figure 2). Don't ever assume to know what any of your clients want. Until you hear it clearly from that client, you must communicate to clarify your client's objectives so that you can implement them. So if your client instructs you to deal with him through an agent, clarify the agent's identity and exact scope of authority.[28] If you client directly instructs you to draft an employment agreement or an estate plan or pursue a certain immigration status, make sure the client understands all of the relevant legal options, and make sure you understand which options the client selects. Then draft the documents competently to effectuate the client's wishes.[29]

⚅ The Unprivileged Disclosure

We represent a big beverage distributor. One of their employee truck drivers was involved in a terrible accident with a school bus, killing more than twenty children. We visited the employee in the hospital, told him the employer sent us to represent him, and took his statement, all witnessed by his dad and uncle. Once we learned that the employee failed to follow company policy about checking the truck brakes, we withdrew and got him his own lawyer.

---

27. *dePape v. Trinity Health Sys, Inc.*, 242 F. Supp. 2d 585, 609 (N.D. Iowa 2003) (expert testimony not required to prove lawyers liable for failing to give immigration client any information about visa options, which caused a failed fraudulent entry attempt and lost wages); *Lane v. Oustalet*, 873 So. 2d 92 (Miss. 2004) (expert testimony not required to prove closing lawyer had a duty to provide buyers with copy of termite inspection report at closing).

28. *Machado v. Statewide Grievance Comm.*, 890 A.2d 622 (Conn. App. Ct. 2006) (lawyer reprimanded for mistakenly following the direction of an agent for an incarcerated client outside the scope of agent's authority).

29. *Vandermay v. Clayton*, 984 P.2d 272 (Or. 2000) (lawyer liable for breach of fiduciary duty without expert testimony for drafting ambiguous indemnity agreement that did not include the protections client insisted upon).

You can imagine the pain in our small community caused by this accident. The prosecutor was threatening to subpoena our record of the employee's statement. To be good citizens, we handed it over without a fight. The grand jury indicted the employee for involuntary manslaughter. After he was acquitted three years later—turns out the brakes had nothing to do with the accident. Now he's suing us for turning over that statement. All we did was cooperate in the investigation of a horrible tragedy. And the statement wasn't even privileged, because the dad and uncle's presence waived it. We should be safe, right?

We think not, not by a long shot. First, you should have advised the employee that his dad and uncle's presence would waive the privilege. Second, your fiduciary duty of confidentiality extends to all information relating to the representation, privileged or not. Third, you had a conflict of interest when you turned his statement over to the prosecutor, because you were now favoring the employer's interests. Why didn't you ask his new lawyer whether he would advise consent to the disclosure?

As a matter of civil liability, we advise settlement. You have breached a core fiduciary duty: confidentiality. The fact the driver was "only" a former client at the time you turned the statement over makes no difference.[30] This breach is so obvious that it will not require expert testimony to prove. In terms of harm caused, it cost your former client three years of misery while he waited for the trial. His damages easily can include emotional distress as well as economic loss.[31]

✼ Representing the Competitor

We represented a small business for a number of years and, as a result, really came to learn the industry, particularly the burden of labor costs. We sought out other businesses in the industry to market our newfound skills. Several hired us. We were very happy, until our first client tells us we have no business representing the competitors, especially in labor negotiations. We tried to reason with the client, but to no avail. The company fired us and now threatens to seek an injunction to prohibit us from representing our current clients in the industry.

---

30. MODEL RULE 1.9; RLGL § 132.

31. *Perez v. Kirk & Carrigan*, 822 S.W.2d 261 (Tex. App. 1991) (lawyers who turned over client's statement to prosecutor without client's consent liable for breach of fiduciary duty).

There is no way our former client will be able to show that we caused any harm, because it's still in business, competing just as effectively as ever. What a waste of time. Maybe we should file a Rule 11 motion.

Forget the Rule 11 motion. While it's true that lawyers often represent competing businesses, they cannot use or disclose client confidences contrary to the interests of any current or former client.[32] If labor costs are the central competitive factor in this industry, and if you learned the former client's strategies about labor negotiations, you cannot use that information in representing your current client competitors. We don't see how you can avoid using the information on these specific facts. And if a court agrees with us, they have the inherent power to disqualify you by granting the injunctive relief to prevent your breach of fiduciary duty. At this point, no showing of harm is necessary. Your former client does not have to wait to be put out of business before it has a right to prevent your use of its confidential information.[33]

🦬 Putting it all Together: The Consult

This one qualifies as no good deed goes unpunished. Though the good deed wasn't mine. And in retrospect it wasn't very good either. We decided to take on a patent application for Biolab. Not our specialty, but we had done some.

Well, we didn't think we had enough expertise. So we consulted another law firm where I have a friend. They assured us a Big Pharma patent was not infringed by Biolab's invention. So we went ahead with the filing, Biolab's patent was awarded, and the product went into production. Now Big Pharma has sued Biolab.

You got Biolab someone else to defend?

No. We thought we could do it, being as how we already were familiar.

But wasn't Biolab going to defend the claim of intentional violation based on the advice of counsel?

Actually, we thought we could defend on the invalidity of the Big Pharma patent.

Let's stop right there. Did you discuss this with Biolab?

Not really.

Well you had two problems there. We'll call them problems three and four.

There's a one and two?

---

32. MODEL RULES 1.6, 1.9; RLGL §§ 60, 132.

33. *Maritrans GP Inc. v. Pepper, Hamilton & Scheetz*, 602 A.2d 1277 (Pa. 1992) (law firm enjoined from representing client's competitors because of threatened breach of fiduciary).

We'll get to those. It is true that lawyers handle litigation involving their own work product all the time. But there are some situations in which the role of the lawyer's work product raises a conflict of interest between lawyer and client that must be discussed.[34] Your client Biolab has multiple defenses here. One is advice of counsel—at least to limit any possible treble damages award.

But the Big Pharma patent's invalid.

You think that. The court might agree. But that's still an open question. Obviously, Big Pharma doesn't agree.

True enough. You said there was three and four. What's four?

How are you handling a matter adverse to Big Pharma? Didn't you say they were a client?

Well, this is the patent area. When you start, you have no idea what other entity might be involved. So we took the application part on with a clear path.

But then Big Pharma showed up.

That's true too. But by then, our consulting firm told us their patent was not infringed.

That didn't remove the conflict. It created it, setting your firm up to take a position directly adverse to a present client of the firm.[35]

You know, that's exactly what Biolab's CEO told us the other day. She just found out we represented Big Pharma. If we don't win this patent infringement suit, she warned, she's coming after our firm for a conflict of interest and for giving bad advice.

Let's put the advice issues to the side for a moment. The undisclosed conflict is deeply troubling. Even if you win this suit, Biolab may seek disgorgement of the fees you were paid based on a breach of the fiduciary duty of loyalty.[36] In any event, there's no way *you* are going to win the suit.

What do you know about patents?

Nothing. But without Big Pharma's consent, you cannot continue the representation.[37] Whatever can be said of the earlier pre-filing investigation, you now have a direct conflict, one that's arguably not even waivable. So you'll have to withdraw. Sooner rather than later. Maybe you can get the firm you consulted to take over.

---

34. MODEL RULE 1.7, cmt. [10]; RLGL § 132, cmt. d(ii).

35. MODEL RULE 1.7(a)(1) & cmt. [6].

36. RLGL § 37; *Rice v. Perl*, 320 N.W.2d 407 (Minn. 1982); *Jeffry v. Pounds*, 136 Cal. Rptr. 373 (Cal. Ct. App. 1977).

37. MODEL RULE 1.7; RGLG § 128(2); *Cinema 5, Ltd. v. Cinerama, Inc.*, 528 F.2d 1384 (2d Cir. 1976) (law firm may not bring suit against a current client without the consent of both clients).

I was afraid you'd say that. But Biolab doesn't know about the other firm.

And I was afraid you'd tell us that.

We didn't want the client to know we had to go outside the firm for expertise.

The problem is that you breached another fiduciary duty when you did that.

But we thought the competence rule said you should consult another lawyer when you're in over your head.

Oh, it says that alright. But only with client permission. Your duty of deference to client control requires you to obtain permission from the client to consult another lawyer, and your duty of confidentiality requires you to get the client's informed consent to sharing confidential information.[38] That's problem one.

And problem two?

Biolab may have a malpractice claim against you, depending on the outcome of the Big Pharma litigation.

But we consulted the best and the brightest.

On an undisclosed basis. But even if disclosed, you still had responsibility for the engagement, and you are totally responsible vis-à-vis the client for the malpractice, if any there was.[39] By the way, did this firm do its work gratis?

Of course not. We paid the bill.

Out of your pocket.

No. We just added the amount to our bill by assigning the hours and descriptions of the work to our firm lawyers.

Some questions one should never ask. Now you've added a fifth lapse to this catalogue of horrors.[40]

Let's just hope Big Pharma's patent was not infringed.

Maybe prayer will help. But it won't be a complete solution.

💋 The Mistake

I feel terrible. Sick to my stomach. We represent Grady Hospital in Old City. Have for years. Their development director called us up. Wanted help on structuring a gift from the chief of cardiology. Boy, does that doc have big bucks. Anyway, Doc

---

38. RLGL § 14; ABA Comm. on Ethics and Prof'l Responsibility, Formal Op. 98-411 (1998) (Ethical Issues in Lawyer-to-Lawyer Consultation).

39. *Whalen v. DeGraff, Foy, Conway, Holt-Harris & Mealey*, 863 N.Y.S.2d 100 (N.Y. App. Div. 2008) (law firm that failed to inform client about hiring local counsel liable to client for local counsel's malpractice).

40. *E.g.*, Conn. Ethics Op. 96-20 (billing statements that the lawyer claimed to perform services, when in fact the lawyer did not, contained false and misleading communications about the lawyer and the lawyer's services in violation of MODEL RULE 8.4(c)).

Mason, that's his name, wanted to know how to maximize the tax benefit of his gift. We put him together with our estate tax guru. The whole thing went as smooth as silk. The papers were signed, and the gift was announced at a big news conference. The president of the hospital even gave our firm a plug. Problem is, my colleague came to see me today. Could hardly speak. Turns out he missed a new provision in the Taxpayer Freedom Act of 2007. No one had noticed it. But the effect is to wipe out half the deduction Doc Mason thought he'd receive. The good news is, Mason wasn't our client; he paid us nothing. We just billed the hospital. So I hope we're off the hook, but I'm not sure.

We sure do sympathize. No one knows what all is in these 600-page bills passed at two o'clock in the morning before Easter recess. But there are two points you must address. First, you were doing this work for Grady Hospital. So you must tell someone there. A lawyer's obligation to communicate with clients under Rule 1.4 includes the delivery of bad news.[41] It doesn't mean you have to write a check, but the development director should be told of this missed provision. And, of course, the hospital may decide it should inform the good doctor. He is the donor and on staff.

I guess we can do that. Maybe they'll figure the likelihood the IRS will catch this is quite slim and just let it pass.

Maybe. Though I doubt that's the advice an objective lawyer would give them. In any event, we don't think that ends your obligations. When a lawyer is asked by a client to perform services on which a third person will rely (e.g., give an opinion, file a deed, hold a deposit), the lawyer owes a duty of competence to the third party.[42] Here, at a minimum, that's what occurred. Doc Generous relied on you to steer him straight. In fact, Doc may think you were acting as *his* lawyer. Just because there was no retainer agreement, conflicts check, or fee paid does not mean that the good doctor does not think you were providing him with legal services, paid for by the hospital for their mutual benefit. You probably have what we call an accidental client.[43] As a

---

41. RLGL § 20, cmt. c; *Leonard v. Dorsey & Whitney LLP,* 553 F.3d 609 (8th Cir. 2009) (lawyer has a duty to disclose potential malpractice claim if claim creates a conflict of interest that would disqualify the lawyer from representing the client such that lawyer's interest in avoiding liability conflicts with client's interest to seek recovery for harm caused by the lawyer's error); *Crean v. Chozick,* 714 S.W.2d 61 (Tex. App. 1986) (failure to disclose malpractice to client tolls the statute of limitations).

42. MODEL RULE 2.3; RLGL § 95, *Greycas, Inc. v. Proud,* 826 F.2d 1560 (7th Cir. 1987).

43. RLGL § 14; *Kremser v. Quarles & Brady, L.L.P.,* 36 P.3d 761 (Ariz. Ct. App. 2001) (corporation's lawyers undertook responsibility to perfect non-client creditor's security interest).

result, you would be wise to notify the doctor now. Maybe the matter can be rectified. And maybe no one would consider your conduct malpractice. The sound way to get a good result is to do what you arguably are obliged to do: gain credibility by being forthcoming and spring into action to make things as right as they can be. Maybe the doctor's charity will extend to your firm and maybe there will be ways to correct or mitigate the problem.

Good Idea. I'll explain what happened, and as a gesture of good will, offer the good doctor a cash settlement.

That's a good idea except for the settlement offer. If Doc Mason is a (now former) client, he's protected from your undue influence. Unless you advise him in writing of the desirability of seeking independent counsel and give him time to seek it out, your offer overreaches, and you probably won't be able to enforce it, even if the good doctor agrees.[44]

⅏ The Opinion Boilerplate

My firm gave an opinion to help our farm client, an agriculture co-op, secure a bank line of credit. We inserted the usual boilerplate: "We have conducted a UCC, tax, and judgment search, and all equipment listed below is free and clear of all liens or encumbrances." But the partner working on the opinion trusted a paralegal who forgot to check the UCC records. Turns out some of the combines were already pledged. We figure it's the client's fault; they told us there were no liens. Besides, why did the bank have those lawyers—whose fees the co-op had to pay—if they weren't going to check themselves?

Not so fast. Let's start with malpractice to your client, the co-op. If your partner (or her paralegal) didn't look at the proper records at all, that's a breach of the standard of care, no expert testimony required.[45] If she did, but misread them, expert testimony that no lawyer should delegate this job to a paralegal or that proper supervision would have uncovered the liens could create the same basis for establishing a breach of the standard of care. Once you discovered the correct lien situation, you have breached another fiduciary obligation. You should have consulted with your farm client about the adverse effect of your findings, and not released the letter disclosing the liens

---

44. MODEL RULE 1.8(h)(2); RLGL § 54(3).

45. RLGL § 52, cmt. g; *Schmitz v. Crotty*, 528 N.W.2d 112 (Iowa 1995) (lawyer failed to investigate property descriptions of predecessor counsel in valuing estate taxes).

unless your client gave informed consent to the proper disclosures.[46] Perhaps other collateral was available, or perhaps the bank would have loaned your client less money on the unencumbered property. If the co-op might lose money on the loan due to this breach, you should notify your carrier.

But your troubles don't end there. You also might be liable to the bank. Many courts require privity with the lawyer and reject the idea that lawyers owe duties to undifferentiated third parties in malpractice. Here, however, the bank was the only intended third-party beneficiary, and therefore, you again need to notify your carrier of this exposure.[47]

But I already told you the bank had its own lawyers.

True, but they had no obligation to duplicate your work.[48] And, we're sorry to say, it gets worse. Your partner represented that the property was not otherwise pledged, when in fact some of it was. If she knew that, she intentionally lied. If she honestly believed the paralegal would follow through but failed to supervise, she's negligent. If she deliberately disregarded a high risk of harm, say, by not teaching the paralegal how to perform due diligence, then it may be characterized as reckless. Where the misrepresentation is intentional or reckless, most courts label it as "fraud" and hold that all foreseeable third parties (here, the bank) can recover, even if not in privity, as long as they reasonably relied on a misrepresentation of material fact (see Figure 3).[49] Most jurisdictions do not extend liability for negligent misrepresentation to the group of all those who might foreseeably rely, but only to those "in a limited group of persons for whose benefit and guidance" the speaker intends to supply the information.[50] Some jurisdictions might find a group of lenders or bond holders too large to qualify,[51] but all would extend liability here.[52] And we think you know that many plaintiff's lawyers

---

46. MODEL RULE 2.3; RLGL § 95.

47. RLGL § 51(2).

48. *E.g., Greycas, Inc. v. Proud*, 826 F.2d 1560 (7th Cir. 1987) (lender had no obligation to conduct its own UCC search and acted reasonably in relying on borrower's lawyer to do so).

49. RESTATEMENT (SECOND) OF TORTS § 531; *Ultramares Corp. v. Touche, Niven & Co.*, 174 N.E. 441 (N.Y. 1931).

50. RESTATEMENT (SECOND) OF TORTS § 552(2).

51. RESTATEMENT (SECOND) OF TORTS § 552(2).

52. *Denney v. Deutsche Bank AG*, 443 F.3d 253 (2d Cir. 2006) (law firm's $81 million class action settlement of fraud claims for providing opinion letter used to market tax shelter later disallowed by IRS); *Mehaffy, Rider, Windholz & Wilson v. Cent. Bank Denver, N.A.*, 892 P.2d 230 (Colo. 1995) (lawyer who issued a legal opinion in connection with a municipal bond

will "underplead" fraud so they can trigger your carrier's coverage of negligence.[53] Not to mention professional discipline.[54]

Figure 3   Misrepresentation: RESTATEMENT (SECOND) OF TORTS §§ 525–552C

1. A false representation was made
2. Concerning a presently existing material fact
3. Which the maker knew to be false or made recklessly, knowing that there was insufficient knowledge upon which to base the representation (fraud), or which was made negligently
4. For the purpose of inducing another to act
5. The other party reasonably relied on the representation
6. To his injury or damage.

✺ The Bad Client

I've represented this entrepreneur for years. Set up a number of businesses for him, all of which failed. Just set up another, with two investors I've never met. I notarized their signatures and filed all of the incorporation documents with the Secretary of State. Unbeknownst to me, my client uses the company credit to pay for personal expenses, including a Bermuda vacation. He also uses it to buy me some new office furniture as a bonus. Once again, the business doesn't go anywhere, and the investors want their money back. We have a big meeting with them and their lawyers. My client tells them he's negotiating a sale of the business, and they'll get their money back when the deal goes through. I paper the sale from my client d/b/a a sole proprietor. Only problem, my client doesn't pay back the initial investors, and they're now suing us both.

You never represented the investors, only the business, so you ought not be liable to them individually in malpractice. We also don't detect any misrepresentations you personally made to the investors, so you are probably off

---

offering may be liable to third-party investors under RESTATEMENT (SECOND) TORTS § 552 for negligent misrepresentation).

53. *E.g., Greycas, Inc. v. Proud,* 826 F.2d 1560 (7th Cir.1987).

54. *Id.*; MODEL RULES 4.1(a) & 8.4(c).

the hook in terms of accountability for misrepresentation. However, your client breached fiduciary duties to the investors by using company credit cards for personal expenses, including of all things your desk. Many courts now recognize a cause of action against a lawyer for aiding and abetting a client's breach of fiduciary duty. In addition to the client's breach and the lawyer's knowledge of the client's breach, they require "substantial assistance," by the lawyer, which some courts hold requires something more than everyday legal services or advice, such as fraud, criminal acts, statutory violations, self-dealing, or "malice."[55]

We fear that some of these may be held to apply to your conduct. For starters, you violated the notary statute by notarizing the investor's signatures without them present. That's not only a statutory violation but a crime in many jurisdictions. Even worse, you assisted in the sale of the business you helped incorporate as a sole proprietorship, after your client, in your presence, promised the investors their money back from the sale. What were you thinking? Then there is the office furniture. You gained a benefit beyond your fee in this representation. If you knew you client had no money before this deal where did you think the money was coming from? The fact that you have represented this client for a long time and knew he had never been successful in a business suggests that you were more than a simple scrivener here.

And why did you draft documents selling the business as a sole proprietorship when you helped incorporate it? A court or jury might well conclude that you were in a position to prevent this harm at several points, and instead, you blindly followed your client's instructions, knowing that there might be significant trouble (see Figure E).[56]

Your situation illustrates the limits of client control. You should follow client instructions, but only lawful client instructions. When your client

55. *LeRoy v. Allen, Yurasek & Merklin*, 872 N.E.2d 254 (Ohio 2007) (lawyer may be liable to third party for aiding and abetting if fraud, collusion, or malice were present in preparing a will and stock transfer in close corporation for elderly client; conflict of interest or collusion with beneficiaries presented fact issue); *Reynolds v. Schrock*, 142 P.3d 1062 (Or. 2006) (lawyer privileged to give client legal advice as long as lawyer committed no crime, fraud, or statutory violation).

56. *Chem-Age Indus. v. Glover*, 652 N.W.2d 756 (S.D. 2002) (lawyer may be liable to third-party business investors for assisting client in establishing a business corporation and later selling it as a sole proprietorship when lawyer knew investors were relying on sale to be repaid).

seeks to use your services to commit crimes, frauds, or breaches of fiduciary duty, you need to withdraw.[57] Dishonest clients can drag business lawyers into exposure for serious liability.

Figure 4 Lawyer Tort Liability to Non-Clients

1. Malpractice:
   a. Third-party beneficiaries of clients, RLGL § 51(3),
   b. Those invited to rely by the lawyer (prospective clients, RLGL § 51(1), *Togstad, supra*), and
   c. Those invited by lawyer or client to rely, if not too remote from the lawyer to be entitled to such protection (RLGL §§ 51(2), 95, *Greycas, supra*).
2. Misrepresentation:
   a. Intentional or reckless misstatements = fraud. Lawyer is liable to all those who reasonably relied on the false information.[58]
   b. Negligent misstatements: Lawyer is liable to those in a limited class of persons "for whose benefit and guidance he intends to supply the information or knows the recipient intends to supply it."[59];
3. Aiding and Abetting a Client's Breach of Fiduciary Duty:
   a. Lawyer knows of client's acts
   b. Lawyer knows client's conduct constitutes a breach of fiduciary duty
   c. Lawyer provides substantial assistance to breach, not just the client
      • Statutory violation
      • Crimes
      • Frauds
      • Self-interested or conflict-of-interest act (collusion)
   d. Breach causes harm to third parties

---

57. MODEL RULES 1.2(d), 4.1(b) & 1.16.

58. RESTATEMENT (SECOND) OF TORTS § 531; RLGL § 56, cmt. f and § 98.

59. RESTATEMENT (SECOND) OF TORTS § 552(2); RLGL §§ 56 and 98.

🎞 Ineffective Assistance of Counsel

You know how the feds are. If they can throw the fear of the Lord into corporate targets by threatening criminal prosecution, they will do so. This time my accounting firm clients said "no way." They were not going down the tubes like Arthur Andersen. They told me they would never cop a plea. Could ruin their SEC practice, as small as it was.

Was?

Yeah. I got offered a plea. Didn't call the client. Who wanted to hear a diatribe? So they tried the case. And lost. Found guilty and have to pay a million dollar fine. The plea deal they offered me called for no fine. Our bad luck, the prosecutor says something to our client's managing partner. "You should've taken the plea deal." The MP screams, "What plea deal?" Now they have brought an ineffective assistance of counsel claim challenging the conviction. And a malpractice claim. They say our law firm should foot the bill for the fine. We did the right thing, right?

Not as clear as we'd like it. To establish ineffective assistance, the client will have to prove by a preponderance that (a) your firm's conduct fell below the standard of care and (b) the error prejudiced or caused harm to the defendant.[60] (See Figure 5)

They told me they'd never settle! How could that be?

Your former client is just one expert away. . . .

Who would lie for those ingrates?

Not me. Just say that since entering a plea is an issue solely given over to the client, you should have passed the plea deal along.[61]

So they would win?

Not necessarily. The judge would have to buy that argument and the client would have to prove that it would have accepted the deal.

They told me they never would.

So you say. But that won't stop them from asserting otherwise now. Hindsight is twenty-twenty, and our bet is you have nothing written that indicates they instructed you in that way.[62]

---

60. *Strickland v. Washington*, 466 U.S. 668 (1984).

61. *Roe v. Flores-Ortega*, 528 U.S. 470 (2000).

62. *Flores-Ortega v. Roe*, 39 Fed. Appx. 604 (9th Cir. 2002) (on remand from *Roe, supra* note 61, court found lawyer's note in client's file indicated client expressed interest in filing appeal).

I didn't need to write it. The speech is still indelibly imprinted on my memory.

Of course, but it would help.

And if they establish ineffective assistance, do we lose the malpractice case? Have to pay the partners a mill?

Not necessarily. The malpractice claim would be a separate proceeding. This one you'd be a party to. You could have a jury. And you might win on either point. In fact, in some jurisdictions you won't even have to endure a jury. In those jurisdictions, malpractice claims against lawyers can only be instituted if the client is acquitted.[63] Here, they are only complaining that they didn't have a chance to plead guilty. So unless they have another constitutional challenge to the guilty verdict that gets them a new trial, and they are found not guilty on retrial, they probably have no claim for malpractice.[64]

Let's hope we're in one of those jurisdictions.

Figure 5   Ineffective Assistance of Counsel

1. Counsel's representation fell below an objective standard of reasonableness, measured by prevailing norms of practice reflected in:
   a. ABA standards
   b. Expert testimony
   c. Per se rules; non-strategic choices (breach of fiduciary duty of obedience or loyalty)
2. Counsel's deficient performance prejudiced the defendant (causation):
   a. Actual prejudice: But for counsel's unprofessional errors, the result of the proceeding would have been different, i.e., not harmless error (proceeding presumptively reliable).
   b. Per se rules: Denial of counsel during a critical stage of the proceeding led to a forfeiture of the proceeding itself (proceeding presumptively unreliable or totally nonexistent).

---

63. RLGL § 53, cmt d.

64. *But see Hilario v. Reardon*, 960 A.2d 337 (N.H. 2008) (claim that lawyer failed to disclose plea bargain unrelated to culpability and therefore not governed by normal causation requirements in legal malpractice suits by criminal defendants).

SIX

Confidentiality

҉ Introduction: The Never-Ending Obligation

ALTHOUGH LAWYERS OFTEN USE THE WORDS "confidentiality" and "privilege" interchangeably, they are in fact quite different concepts. Your duty of confidentiality is a fiduciary obligation that arises from agency law and the applicable rules of professional conduct.[1] It protects prospective[2] as well as actual and accidental clients, and never ends.[3] This fiduciary obligation requires you to keep confidential all information learned in the course of a representation, with a few narrow exceptions as to which, depending on which state you are in, you may or must disclose what would otherwise be confidential.

The privilege, on the other hand, is a rule of evidence that governs what you may be forced to disclose if you are called to testify.[4] Like the fiduciary duty, it too lasts forever.[5] The law of evidence also immunizes lawyer work product from discovery, which includes your opinions and mental impressions formed in representing the client in anticipation of litigation.[6]

Privileged information is a subset of the category of confidential information.[7] The evidentiary privilege has never protected all client confidences, and has developed a number of widely accepted exceptions. The fiduciary duty has always protected nearly all client information. (See Table 2)

---

1. MODEL RULE 1.6; RLGL § 60.

2. MODEL RULE 1.18; RLGL § 15.

3. MODEL RULE 1.9; RLGL § 60, cmt. e, § 132.

4. RLGL § 68.

5. RLGL § 77; *Swidler & Berlin v. U.S.*, 524 U.S. 399 (1998).

6. RLGL § 87.

7. MODEL RULE 1.6, cmt. 3; RLGL § 59, cmt. b.

TABLE 2 Client Confidentiality

	Evidentiary Rules	*Ethical/Fiduciary Duty*
Source of Law:	Statute; Common Law of Evidence	Agency Law and MODEL RULES 1.6, 1.8(b), 1.9, 1.18 MODEL CODE OF PROF'L RESPONSIBILITY Canon 4
Definition:	Attorney-Client Privilege: A communication made between privileged persons in confidence for the purpose of obtaining or providing legal assistance. RLGL § 68 Work Product Immunity: Material prepared by a lawyer in reasonable anticipation of litigation. RLGL § 87	MODEL RULE 1.6(a): Information relating to the representation of a client; DR 4-101(A): Confidences and Secrets;

Exceptions have developed less rapidly, and are less uniform, but tend to parallel those in the law of evidence. (See Figure I)

Organizations as well as individuals are protected by both of these doctrines. Organizational clients are protected whenever you speak to a duly authorized constituent, an employee acting in the scope of employment.[8] Confidentiality encourages clients to communicate fully with their lawyers so that they can be effectively represented. Without all the facts, lawyers will not be able to give competent and complete legal advice, which in turn will disserve clients seeking to follow the law and undermine the ability of lawyers to promote compliance with the rule of law. Confidentiality also promotes trust and privacy in the client-lawyer relationship.[9]

Confidential or Privileged?

Our firm just got a big public relations break. We've been asked to act as local counsel for GE in resisting a third-party document subpoena. Now we can list GE as a client on our Web site. Is that impressive, or what?

8. RLGL § 96, cmt. b (confidentiality); § 73 (privilege).

9. MODEL RULE 1.6, cmt. [2]; RLGL § 60, cmt. b.

A few more motions to quash, and you can say you represent half the Fortune 10. But before you go down that road, remember the fact that in representing a client, information relating to the representation that may not be privileged (for example, your client's identity)[10] nevertheless is confidential.[11] If you want to tout your remarkable achievements for GE, we suggest you receive GE's permission to do so, permission that you should confirm in writing.

𝑀 What's Confidential?

We're always looking for ways to get coverage of our firm in the local business weekly. Just got a call from one of their reporters looking for some information on a professor at the local business school. Our client hired the professor as an expert in a recent case to justify a leveraged buyout by the insiders. I know there's great information about this hot shot in his deposition. And it's on file at the courthouse. So it's a public record. I told the reporter I'd do her a favor and tell her where to find good stuff if she'd do one for me. Pretty creative, don't you think?

Creative? Yes. Ethical? No. The existence and content of that deposition are information relating to the representation, that is, client confidential.[12] The fact that someone could go to the courthouse and, with diligence, look it up does not change that. If you are ever to disclose client confidential information, you need your client's permission first.[13] And one must wonder how you would have the temerity to ask, or any reason for the client to agree, to disclose under these circumstances. After all, the business journal article regarding the professor may turn out undermining the very benefits your client secured in retaining him, we bet, at your suggestion. You must remember: everything you learn in the course of a representation—even a public record—is deemed confidential until it becomes generally known, i.e., it has appeared on the front page of *The Wall Street Journal* (see Table 2).[14]

---

10. RLGL § 69, cmt. g.

11. Model Rule 1.6(a), cmt. [3]; RLGL § 59.

12. Model Rule 1.6(a); RLGL § 59.

13. Model Rule 1.6(a); RLGL § 62.

14. Model Rule 1.6(a), cmt. [3]; RLGL § 59, cmt. d.

𝒲 Use of Confidential Information

Imagine my good fortune, after helping our client Sunset locate a good site for a senior village, to learn that the property next door may be coming on the market. I figure I earn a fee helping them buy the property, and even more building a small hotel next door to house relatives when they visit village residents.

Lawyers receive good fortune like that every day. We learn our clients' plans, hopes, and dreams . . . and, yes, their fears. In fact, we encourage them to do so by telling them we'll keep their disclosures confidential.

Well, I am not going to tell anyone.

Of course not. But our rules have two parts. The lawyer cannot disclose.[15] The lawyer cannot use.[16] And that's what you're doing. Using your client's information.

Well, it won't hurt my client.

You may think so. But that's your client's call. You learned about the next-door property on your senior living client's retainer and therefore owe them the information you've found. Maybe they'll be interested; maybe not. And if not, then you can ask them if it's alright with them for you to buy the property.[17] If they are willing to let their lawyer become a part-time real estate entrepreneur, then you can pursue your hotel idea.

𝒲 The Organizational Privileges

Someone told me, because corporations are legal fictions, no attorney-client privilege applies. Just like no right against self-incrimination.

For very good reasons, and quite fortunately, your friend is wrong. Some have argued corporations should not have a privilege. But the Supremes put that issue to rest in *Upjohn v. United States* back in 1981.[18] In that case, the government sought notes of interviews with corporate employees Upjohn lawyers had conducted all around the world in an internal investigation.

---

15. MODEL RULE 1.6(a); RLGL § 60.

16. MODEL RULE 1.8(b); RLGL § 60.

17. *In re Anonymous*, 654 N.E.2d 1128 (Ind. 1995) (lawyer violated Rule 1.8(b) by using information relating to the representation of a prospective client to sue a third party thinking it would not cause harm despite lack of improper motive).

18. 449 U.S. 383 (1981).

The government argued that the conversations with employees not involved in the actual representation were not subject to either the attorney-client privilege or attorney work-product immunity. The Court rejected that argument, concluding that a corporation was entitled to the benefits of the attorney-client privilege in order to secure legal advice and to the work-product privilege to prepare its defense to the government's charges. So in that respect, these privileges apply to representation of any organization.[19]

What do you mean "these privileges?" Aren't they the same thing?

You are not the first lawyer to confuse them. But it is critical to recognize and address the distinctions.[20] The attorney-client privilege applies to all confidential communications between privileged persons[21] (lawyer and client) for the purpose of obtaining or providing legal advice.[22] In the organizational context, this means communications between organizational agents concerning matters within the scope of their duties that are necessary for providing the legal advice.[23] If the lawyer talks to salespeople to determine whether their sales practices conform to law, those conversations are privileged. So are conversations with the higher-ups responsible for corporate compliance who need to be informed about the content of the earlier conversations. One key element to preserving the organizational privilege is to assume that only those with a need to know are in on the communications.[24] Broad scale distributions, particularly in an era of e-mail, to a cast of hundreds, can very well serve to destroy the privilege. Some courts have suggested that the privilege should apply only to what the client communicates to the lawyer and to the lawyer's response only to the extent that it reflects the former.[25] But the better and more commonly adopted view is that the attorney-client privilege applies to both sides of the communication.[26]

And the work-product privilege? This privilege only applies to work undertaken under the direction and control of the lawyer in anticipation

---

19. RLGL § 73.

20. RLGL § 87, cmt. d.

21. RLGL § 70.

22. RLGL § 68.

23. RLGL § 73, cmts. d & h. .

24. RLGL § 73, cmt. g.

25. *E.g.*, *Brinton v. Dep't of State*, 636 F.2d 600 (D.C. Cir. 1980).

26. RLGL § 69, cmt. i.

of litigation.[27] So if it's a transaction or other non-dispute generated work, the work-product privilege cannot apply. In that sense, it is narrower than the attorney-client privilege, which covers all advice. But the work-product privilege is broader in another sense. It applies to conversations between lawyers and clients regarding a lawsuit. But it also applies to any work done by the lawyer, whether it's communications with the client, third-party witnesses, experts, or consultants or simply research at a library or on a database.[28]

Let us give you an example to highlight the difference. If a lawyer meets with a client and investment banker to discuss a possible acquisition by the client, that conversation is not subject to the attorney-client or attorney work-product privileges because (a) a third party is in attendance,[29] and (b) it's not in anticipation of litigation.[30] But, if a similar conversation takes place among a client, an investment banker, and a lawyer regarding a threatened lawsuit over the acquisition, even though not privileged because of the presence of the investment banker, it would be subject to the work-product privilege because it is undertaken by the lawyer in anticipation of litigation.[31]

Sounds confusing to me. What kind of watered-down privilege applies to organizations?

Well, there are some issues. Let's take them one at a time.

※ Privileged? The Internal Audit

Our client was concerned about whether all of its maintenance employees were complying with various EPA regulations. They just wanted to do a compliance check. We suggested that if the lawyers undertook this assignment, it would be subject to the attorney-client privilege (and maybe work product too). So we did the work—interviewed dozens of workers, took copious notes, and presented the board with a report that included our legal advice on how to proceed. At the time we thought, "Isn't this a conscientious client."

---

27. RLGL § 87; *compare* FED. R. CIV. P. 26(b)(3).

28. RLGL § 87, cmt. f.

29. RLGL § 70.

30. RLGL § 87, cmt. h.

31. RLGL § 87, cmt. d.

Now the EPA has subpoenaed documents from our client. They say they are doing an investigation, and their document request would include all of our notes. We say our notes are privileged. The EPA comes back and claims that we cannot hide required corporate conduct from scrutiny by having lawyers undertake the work. Who's right?

The situation presents a very close question. On the one hand, if it was necessary to interview these maintenance workers to provide the company with legal advice, the privilege should apply. Even though these are low-level employees who otherwise do not deal with lawyers, the client is entitled to the privilege so long as the work was required in order for the lawyers to deliver their advice.[32] On the other hand, if this is just a façade, and the company is otherwise required to check on compliance with EPA regulations as part of its business operations, then asking lawyers to do the work that otherwise could and would be done by non-lawyers may weaken the privilege claim.[33]

Well, how about work product?

You certainly would be able to claim work-product privilege once the EPA commenced an investigation. The question would be whether at the time this investigation was conducted there really was any good faith possibility that litigation was anticipated.[34] As you described it, it does not sound like work product would apply.

🏵 Work Product? The Early Investigation

One of my client's employees had a terrible accident with a forklift. A few weeks ago, a company maintenance engineer sent me a report about the cause of the accident: poor maintenance of the bearings. Now the plaintiff is using discovery to seek any reports regarding the accident. Lucky for the client, I was smart enough to claim the report as work product, which means it'll never see the light of day.

You are overreaching, our friend. Work-product immunity only applies to tasks undertaken at the direction and control of the lawyer. This report, as

---

32. RLGL § 73, cmt. d.

33. RLGL § 73, cmt. g.

34. RLGL § 87, cmt. i.

you describe, first came to your attention once it was completed. No good faith claim of work-product exists, sad to say.[35]

But your question raises a very important practice point. Though it has a certain self-serving character, organizational lawyers should warn their clients, well in advance of a catastrophe, that when such an event occurs, any investigation into the cause and how the entity should respond is best conducted under the direction and control of counsel—and, yes, probably outside counsel—so that at the same time the enterprise can respond in a responsible manner, the results themselves are protected from having to be shared with those who do not have the organization's best interests at heart. And this direction and control must be real. The lawyer should interview and select any experts retained. The lawyer should have the experts report directly to the lawyers. The drafts of any report should be sent to the lawyers first. So if the work product immunity claim is challenged, the direction and control is clear.

So if I supervise the investigation into the cause of the bearing problem, my notes will be privileged forever?

Not quite. Remember that work-product protection, like the attorney-client privilege, can be waived by the client. And when you represent an organization, your client can "morph," by changing organizational structure, filing for bankruptcy, or simply by taking on new board members or a new CEO.[36]

Meaning?

Your client remains protected so long as it does not find it in its best interests to disclose the contents for whatever reason.

Why would they ever do that?

Well "they" may not be management forever. "They" may be replaced by an acquirer that takes a different view on disclosure. "They" may be jettisoned by a trustee in bankruptcy.[37] And "they" may simply change their minds. So whatever you write in a report that you think is likely to be subject of any claim of privilege and/or work product should still only contain language and characterizations that you won't mind being scrutinized by less friendly folks than your present clients . . . we mean client representatives.

---

35. RLGL § 87; *compare,* FED. R. CIV. P. 26(b)(4).

36. RLGL §§ 73, cmts. j, k, 91, 92.

37. RLGL § 73, cmts. j, k.

The bottom line: you have the responsibility to maintain the organization's privilege. Here's a set of guidelines that can help.

Figure 6   Guidelines for Preserving the Organizational Privilege and Work Product Immunity

---

1. Everyone within the organization who communicates with the organization's lawyers should be advised on a regular basis of their responsibility to maintain the privileges, the essential elements of the privileges, and the importance of each individual in the organization for conducting himself or herself in a way that maximizes the chance that the privileges will be maintained.

2. All communications from individuals within the organization seeking advice from counsel should be labeled "attorney-client privileged" and "confidential." The body of the communication should indicate that it seeks the advice of counsel.

3. All communications to counsel seeking advice should be sent directly to counsel, and copies should be sent, if at all, only to those who have an absolute need to know.

4. All communications from counsel to others in the organization should only be sent to those who have a need to know, and anyone receiving a communication from counsel should share such communications with other individuals only with the permission of counsel.

5. Those with a need to know are the employees of the organization from whom information is required for counsel to provide advice and those with whom counsel consults with regard to that advice.

6. Any meetings among organization employees that are intended to be privileged must include only those with a need to know and exclude any non-employees, other than outside lawyers, unless those individuals are agents of the organization or agents of the lawyers. Notes or minutes of such meetings should clearly indicate the portion as to which the privilege will be asserted.

7. No one should rely on automatic legends placed on e-mail or fax cover sheets to establish the privileged nature of the communication. If a communication is believed to be privileged, it should be specifically labeled with the privilege or privileges thought to apply.

8. The labeling of an unprivileged document as privileged does not make it privileged and undermines the credibility of the organization's assertions of privilege as to other documents.

9. Work-product immunity should only be claimed and legended when, in fact, litigation is reasonably anticipated.

10. The labeling of communications as attorney work-product may trigger obligations on the part of the organization to put a litigation hold on any regular document destruction policy of the organization and, therefore, should only occur if, in fact, litigation is reasonably anticipated and only after consultation with counsel in charge of the matter in question.

11. The mere sending of a copy of the document between two non-lawyer employees to counsel will not necessarily render that document privileged.

12. When communications between non-lawyers and lawyers address both legal and non-legal issues, the non-legal matters should be addressed in separate communications, to prevent the privilege from being lost as to the entire communication.

13. To the greatest extent possible, lawyers employed by the organization should not have dual titles lest the assertion be made that the lawyer was wearing his or her other hat when the assertedly privileged communication occurred.

14. Everyone in the organization should be ever mindful that the organization will only be asserting the privilege in the context of a litigated matter in which a highly motivated adversary will challenge every such assertion as somehow deviating from the precise requirements of the privilege or work product doctrine, either of which, in fact, may be disfavored and narrowly construed. To say that the organization must treat the privilege and work product as protecting the crown jewels of the organization captures the care with which all must proceed in this area.

15. Whenever it is discovered that a privileged document has been inadvertently sent or produced to a person whose receipt will undermine the privilege, timely and conscientious attempts should commence to notify the recipients and to recover the document.

🎔 Insiders: Who Is Privileged?

If an organization is simply a legal construct that works through individuals, then any conversation I have with any employee is privileged and covered by work product as well?

No, not really. The conversation has to either relate to giving the organization advice or be in anticipation of litigation. There are plenty of conversations—mostly trivial—but not necessarily so, that wouldn't fall into either category.

🎔 Privileged? Insiders Who Seek Information

Well, assume an employee is suing the organization for employment discrimination. Should that employee be able to learn what advice counsel gave the HR vice president?

"No" should be the right answer. The privilege belongs to the company, and should protect communications between the company's personnel who are dealing with the defense of the company and the lawyer. And that will be true so long as the employee cannot mount an argument that the employee had a lawyer-client relationship with the lawyer at the same time.

How could that happen?

For starters, lawyers, particularly in-house lawyers, often refer to client's employees as "clients." Moreover, it is not unusual for employees to think the lawyer for the organization also represents the employee.[38] Think of filing a patent application on which one of the company's research scientist is named as an inventor, taking an employee to a deposition, or a case where employer and employee are both named as defendants and in fact are jointly represented. Any one of these circumstances might permit the employee adverse to the organizational client to assert an entitlement to privileged information.[39]

---

38. RLGL §§ 14, 73, cmt. f, 96.

39. RLGL § 75.

✎ Privileged? Advice from In-House Counsel

Inside counsel aren't second-class citizens, are they?

No. In-house lawyers are full-fledged counsel.[40] The problem is that so often they have hyphenated titles. Vice president and general counsel; assistant secretary and associate general counsel.

What's wrong with that?

Well, if one wishes to cause an organization fits, one might seek the testimony of one of these hyphens.

Can't do that. What they have to say is privileged.

That's true if the deponent was acting as a lawyer in receiving inquiries or giving legal advice.

That's what I'll tell her to say.

And the other side would come back and argue, "No, the person was being consulted as a business person or was giving business advice in her vice-presidential capacity."

But that's true of outside counsel too.

It is true that if outside counsel gives business advice, that may not be privileged either. But outside counsel doesn't carry a dual title, and, as a practical matter, in-house counsel's conversations are challenged as not subject to the privilege far more often and with some success, for example when in-house counsel has been the sole representative of her company in negotiations and then reports back to others at the client.[41]

So in-house counsel better travel with another officer?

If she does so, that will give her a better argument that her conversations are privileged.

That gives me a great idea. We'll have every top manager in the company run all their e-mails through legal so that we can later claim privilege.

Sounds like a great idea, but, in fact, such a protocol would likely not succeed. Claims of privilege, particularly those involving in-house counsel, will be scrutinized quite carefully to determine (a) whether the in-house counsel was in fact wearing his or her lawyer hat when the in-house lawyer participated in the e-mail conversations, and (b) whether the copying or

---

40. RLGL § 73, cmt. i.

41. RLGL § 72, cmt. c; *Georgia-Pacific Corp. v. GAF Roofing Mfg. Corp.*, No. 93 Civ. 5125, 1996 U.S. Dist. LEXIS 671 (S.D.N.Y. Jan. 25, 1996).

sending of e-mails to legal is simply a façade or, in fact, a good faith effort to seek and receive legal advice.[42] Obviously, the more an entity client is regulated, the more legal advice is essential to every aspect of the client's areas of endeavor, down to sales practices, advertising, product safety, and the like. But this need for regulatory guidance from lawyers does not necessarily translate into a broad view of the privilege for the heavily regulated client. The hostility of the courts to the privilege in this context rests on the theory that such clients cannot foreclose inquiry into the operations of the business simply because lawyers must participate in the decision-making process.

⅞ Privileged? Shareholder Derivative Suits

I hope we're done?

Not quite. There's a potentially big chink in the organizational privilege when it comes to shareholder derivative cases.

How's that?

When a shareholder brings a derivative claim, it is brought in the name and for the benefit of the organization.

Balderdash. Everyone knows it's so some greedy plaintiffs' lawyer can collect a big fee.

That may be true in substance, but the principle still stands. And if the plaintiff shareholder represents the best interests of the company . . .

I beg your pardon.

. . . then some have argued successfully that the organization's privilege can be set aside by what I know you view as an officious intermeddler but who is, as a matter of law, a volunteer on behalf of the company.[43] This doctrine is by no means universal, but if applicable, it can render the corporate privilege pretty much a nullity, at least for purposes of the lawsuit. The minority shareholders get the information because they are part of the corporate family, but the information remains privileged against outsiders.

---

42. *In re Vioxx Prods. Liab. Litig.*, 501 F. Supp. 2d 789, 809 (E. D. La. 2007) (structure of corporation's enterprise, which delegated broad powers to its legal department, does not by itself privilege all 30,000 documents circulated to legal department; corporation must establish that in-house lawyers were "primarily involved in rendering legal advice").

43. RLGL § 85; *Garner v. Wolfinbarger*, 430 F.2d 1093 (5th Cir. 1970).

Who's Got the Privilege?

I'll tell you it makes no sense.

What?

The idea that I cannot represent my ongoing client because the buyer of my client's business can conflict me out.

Tell us more.

I represented John Mills and his company Mills Electronics, actually a start-up internet service provider. So we sold the business to a competitor, Interwatt, for a great price, John walked away with a small fortune, and we received a nice fee plus a bonus.

Then what happened?

Interwatt sued. I know we shouldn't trust those guys. Claiming fraud and misrepresentation.

More business for you.

That's what I thought. I could represent John. Defend his honor. And his money. So I entered my appearance.

And then bad things happened?

Precisely. The new Mills Electronics moves to disqualify me. Claims I am their former lawyer. On substantially related matters. I did represent the Old Mills, but that one disappeared in the merger they did for tax reasons. They even claim they own the privilege. These are the same folks I have been adverse to all the time.

How can they disqualify me? How can they claim John's privilege? They even want to stop me from sharing with John information regarding Mills from the time when I represented both John and the company. A frontal assault on the very idea of privilege. Wasn't it supposed to encourage John to confide in me?

The requested relief is troubling. But it also could well be granted. If the court concludes that the new business is simply just a continuation of the old one there is authority, controversial as it may seem, that the successor must be treated as the same client, that it controls the entity's privilege and that it can disqualify seller's now former counsel from taking positions directly adverse to the new incarnation.[44] And the successor controls the privilege at least as to the operations of the business, if not the legal services

---

44. *Tekni-Plex, Inc., v. Meyner & Landis,* 674 N.E.2d 663 (N.Y. 1996) (long-time counsel for seller company and its sole shareholder cannot continue to represent the shareholder in a dispute with the buyer).

the former counsel provided during the actual transaction.[45] What's more, to the surprise of some, the doctrine seems to apply regardless of whether the deal was a stock sale, an asset sale, or a merger. And arguably most surprising is that it seems to permit the buyer to get an injunction against you sharing information with John *after* the deal that you could have disclosed to him with impunity *before* the deal.

How can you tell them apart?

That is a difficult question. It demonstrates the problems with the doctrine. But everyone representing an entity client must remember that entity clients can morph, they can be purchased, they can go bankrupt, they can be merged and any one of those transformations can trigger a reassessment of who is the client or former client and who controls the privilege. Which is a good trigger to remind lawyers that not everything they want to say—even if privileged—has to be put in writing, perhaps to appear in the *Wall Street Journal* above the fold.

𝑾 Waiver

You said that confidentiality belongs to the organization. Does that mean that the organization also controls disclosure?

Yes, and for starters, the first exception (see Table 3, *infra*) is really important.

What's that?

The privilege belongs to the client, not the lawyer.[46]

I know that!

But that means the client could decide to waive the privilege, and your candid legal advice, perhaps written in anger or haste, might end up on the front page of the *Wall Street Journal*.[47]

Why would they do that?

Well they might do it—that is, the same people with whom you dealt—because they decided it was in the best interests of the company to defend

---

45. *Id.* at 670 (To the extent that business operations of seller continued under new managers, control of attorney-client privilege passed to management of the buyer).

46. RLGL § 86 cmt. b.

47. RLGL § 73, cmt. j, §§ 78, 79, 91, 92.

TABLE 3 Confidentiality Exceptions

	Evidentiary Rules	Ethical/Fiduciary Duty
Client Consent	Waiver: RLGL §§ 78-79	Client consent, express, or implied: MODEL RULE 1.6(a)
Physical Harm	Future and continuing crimeor fraud: RLGL § 82	Future serious bodily harm (crime): MODEL RULE 1.6(b)(1)
Financial Harm/ Client Crime or Fraud	Future and continuing crime or fraud: RLGL § 82	Future crime, prevent, rectify, mitigate substantial financial loss: MODEL RULE 1.6(b)(2)(3)
Seeking Advice	None	MODEL RULE 1.6(b)(4)
Lawyer Self- Defense	Lawyer self-protection: RLGL § 83	Lawyer self-defense: MODEL RULE 1.6(b)(5)
Required by Law or Court Order	Invoking the privilege: RLGL § 86	Required by law or court order: MODEL RULE 1.6(b)(6)

itself based on your advice,[48] or because they claimed privilege and the claim was rejected,[49] or because the government, conducting an investigation, gave them no choice.

Anything else?

Management may change; new management may want to disparage old; or the company may get purchased. Or the company may be the subject of a bankruptcy proceeding and suddenly there's a trustee who couldn't care less about asserting the privilege, who wants to hold prior management—yes even prior counsel—up to ridicule and scorn.[50]

⁂ Waiver under Federal Rule of Evidence 502

I've been so worried about our document production for Colossus. The case involves, what with electronic discovery, over a million documents, though I know many are duplicates. Anyway, I keep telling my associates that we've got to be careful, very careful so we don't produce any privileged documents. But I am always worrying. They stare at computer screens all day. Numbing work. Today one of my associates barges in, a broad smile on his face. What's got him so pleased, I ask. He says the President just signed new Federal Rule of

---

48. RLGL § 80.

49. RLGL § 78.

50. RLGL § 73, cmt. d.

Evidence 502 into law. "Now we don't have to worry about producing privileged documents," he announces.

Would that it were that simple. There is a new evidence rule. And it's a good one. But its scope is rather narrow. It says that if you inadvertently produce privileged documents, that production does not act as a subject matter waiver of all related privileged documents.[51]

That's good.

It is. But this rule will not stop your worries. First, it only applies to "inadvertent" production. Most courts use a balancing test to determine whether your quality assurance was good enough. You don't have to do privilege reviews perfectly, but you'd better come reasonably close.[52]

I hope that's it?

Not yet. The rule doesn't say anything about whether the receiving lawyer must notify you of the receipt of privileged documents. To find the answer to that question, you have to look to the Rules of Professional Conduct. If your jurisdiction has adopted Rule 4.4(b), that rule requires notification. If not, it depends on the common law.[53]

Anything else?

You bet. Federal Rule of Evidence 502 does not tell you whether the receiving lawyer has to return the documents. Nor does Model Rule 4.4. There are some court opinions that require return. Some do not.[54]

---

51. FED. R. EVID. 502(b) (2009).

52. *Rhoads Indus. v. Bldg. Materials Corp. of Am.*, No. 07-4756, 2008 U.S. Dist. LEXIS 93333 (E.D. Pa. Nov. 14, 2008) (proper quality assurance is a factor considered in determining whether precautions taken to prevent inadvertent disclosure of documents was reasonable under Rule 502); *Sitterson v. Evergreen Sch. Dist. No. 114*, 196 P.3d 735 (Wash. Ct. App. 2008) (adopting balancing test to determine whether inadvertent document disclosure waives the attorney-client privilege); *Rambus, Inc. v. Infineon Tech. AG*, 220 F.R.D. 264 (E.D. Va. 2004) (filing of an incomplete privilege log waives privilege as to inadequately described documents); *Amgen Inc. v. Hoechst Marion Roussel, Inc.*, 190 F.R.D. 287 (D. Mass. 2000) (lawyer who failed to take reasonable precautions to protect and recover over 3800 pages of privileged documents inadvertently disclosed in discovery waived client's privilege; motion to compel return of documents denied).

53. *Elkton Care Ctr. Assocs. LP v. Quality Care Mgmt., Inc.*, 805 A.2d 1177 (Md. Ct. Spec. App. 2002) (privilege waived on documents inadvertently included in half-full box of documents, opposing counsel properly tabbed document to be copied, and disclosure went unnoticed until trial); *In re South East Banking Corp. Loan Sec. and Loan Loss Reserves Litig.*, 212 B.R. 386 (Bankr. S.D. Fla. 1997) (lawyer who failed to notify opposing counsel and copied inadvertently disclosed privileged documents lost pro hoc vice status and subject to monetary sanctions for attorney's fees and costs).

54. *In re Kagan*, 351 F.3d 1157 (D.C. Cir. 2003) (lawyer who learned of inadvertently disclosed document acted reasonably under the circumstances when he immediately took steps to

And use them?

And use them. Not everywhere and not under all circumstances. There are certainly cases out there that say you can be disqualified from continuing a representation—and from even talking to successor counsel—if you review and use privileged documents of the other side,[55] but—should you ever be lucky enough to be on the receiving end—other cases take the position that the receipt of privileged documents is an invitation to keep the receipt secret and use them at anytime in anyway.[56]

So now you've parsed the rule and the common law. We're done?

Not quite. The last thing you have to worry about is your client.

My client?

Yes. If your production of privileged documents is found to be a violation of the standard of care you owed your client, you may be liable to the client if the client can demonstrate causation and damages flowing from the disclosure.

Like losing the case?

Precisely.

I guess that's four good reasons to hector my colleagues and resist all efforts to outsource document production to India.

That's another topic we address elsewhere,[57] but you are correct.

---

determine what to do, including consulting outside counsel and by agreeing to stipulate to the confidential information in exchange for return of the document; law unclear about proper course of action); *Transp. Equip. Sales Corp. v. BMY Wheeled Vehicles*, 930 F. Supp. 1187 (N.D. Ohio 1996) (lawyer must return original and all copies of inadvertently disclosed document; recipients also ordered to refrain from using or disclosing contents of document).

55. *Rico v. Mitsubishi Motors Corp.*, 171 P.3d 1092 (Cal. 2007) (lawyer who inadvertently received opposing counsel's notes and used them to impeach defense witness disqualified; lawyer should not have read document any more closely than necessary to determine it was privileged work product and should have immediately notified opposing counsel to try to resolve the situation); *Cunningham v. Appel*, 831 So. 2d 214 (Fla. Dist. Ct. App. 2002) (lawyer who obtained copies of four documents inadvertently disclosed by opposing counsel should not have been disqualified where lawyer had no informational advantage and had not deliberately and surreptitiously obtained the documents).

56. *E.g., Amgen Inc. v. Hoechst Marion Roussel, Inc.*, 190 F.R.D. 287 (D. Mass. 2000) (waiver where lawyer failed to take reasonable precautions to protect and recover over 3800 pages of inadvertently disclosed privileged documents; motion to compel return of documents denied).

57. *See supra* Chapter 2, The Offshore Advantage.

%% Organizational Waiver and Government Investigations

You mentioned earlier that the government can force a corporation to give up the privilege. Sounds unconstitutional to me. What gives?

Your instincts are right on this one. The Justice Department, starting in the Clinton administration and continuing under Bush II, instructed United States Attorneys and their staffs, as well as main Justice lawyers, that they can measure cooperation by organizations for purposes of whether and what to charge them criminally by assessing the willingness of the putative corporate defendant to share privileged—attorney-client and attorney work-product—material with the government.[58]

How can that be? A waiver of the privilege must be knowing, informed, and voluntary, and the last time I studied the matter, that which is done with a gun to one's head is rarely viewed as voluntary.

True enough. And only recently has Justice taken a slightly different view, measuring "cooperation" by voluntary disclosure of "relevant facts and evidence.[59] This still leaves lawyers and clients in a difficult position. The SEC joined the gun-toting crowd as well, but has now backed off somewhat.[60] If you are conducting a corporate investigation you must always consider whether your client will be forced to make this Hobson's choice of "voluntary disclosure" or being charged or charged more seriously, and waiver, as involuntary as it is, could follow quickly.

What can be done about it?

The organized bar has been joined by organizations ranging from the Chamber of Commerce to the ACLU to convince the government to change its ways. A recent breakthrough was agreement with the Sentencing Commission that waiver of the privilege should play no role in determining the level of cooperation for determining the proper sentence,[61] followed by the DOJ's decision to disengage cooperation credit from privilege waivers.[62] Perhaps most influential has been the Second Circuit's affirmation of Judge Kaplan's third *Stein* opinion, which attributes some of the coercion on some

---

58. *See U.S. v. Stein*, 435 F. Supp. 2d 330 (S.D.N.Y. 2006).

59. 24 Law. Man. Prof. Conduct 493 (ABA/BNA 2008).

60. 24 Law. Man. Prof. Conduct 597 (ABA/BNA 2008).

61. 22 Law. Man. Prof. Conduct 193 (ABA/BNA 2006).

62. 24 Law. Man. Prof. Conduct 473 (ABA/BNA 2008).

employees to the government and dismisses the employees' indictments as a result.[63] But until the charging decision is similarly insulated from any effect based on waiver of the privilege, companies and their lawyers—particularly lawyers conducting internal investigations—will have to conduct themselves accordingly.

It is so sad.

That it is. But it illustrates how the organization's interests can diverge from those of its constituents, even its loyal constituents.

Figure 7   Interviewing Organization Employees

Initial Disclosures[64]

1. I represent _____ organization, not you or any other employee.
2. I am gaining information to provide legal advice to the organization about _____.
3. I will disclose the content of this interview to the organization's management.
4. This interview is privileged, but
5. The privilege belongs to the organization, not to you or any other employee, and
6. The organization can decide to release any information, privileged or not, to outsiders, such as opposing parties or the government.

Additional Warnings When Lawyer Reasonably Anticipates Employee's Acts May Bind the Organization[65]

1. What you have done, your acts or omissions, may create liability for your employer.
2. You may face personal legal accountability (civil or criminal).

---

63. *U.S. v. Stein*, 541 F.3d 130 (2d Cir. 2008), *affirming U.S. v. Stein*, 440 F. Supp. 2d 315 (S.D.N.Y. 2006).

64. MODEL RULES 1.13(f), 4.3.

65. MODEL RULES 1.7, 1.13(f), 4.3.

3. Your interests and those of your employer may not be the same.

4. You cannot control if or when your employer may decide to disclose information, or to whom it decides to disclose.

5. I represent only your employer.

6. You should consider separate counsel for personal legal advice.

🖋 Preventing Physical Harm: Toxic Waste

While I was out visiting our corporate client to discuss an employee discrimination lawsuit, my conversation with the plant superintendent, who is my contact, was interrupted by a maintenance foreman who declared that he had just discovered some old arsenic drums in a maintenance cabin not far from our town's major lake. The plant superintendent dismissed the employee, observing that there was nothing extra in the super's plant budget for cleanup this year. "They must have been there so long, another year won't make any difference," he declared. Since I am representing the client in employee matters, I figure, I have no responsibility for this interchange I just happened to overhear.

Without looking at the rules, let's first address the good lawyering point. At a minimum, you should have discussed with the plant superintendent what we take to be your view that something should be done here, even if it is only further investigation. Arsenic is serious stuff, and the location of these drums so close to the lake may or may not present a serious problem. So your job was not to sit in silence but to say something to the superintendent.[66] Any further course of action will depend on how he responds. If he remains dismissive, you certainly are free, but not required, to talk to somebody above the plant superintendent about the situation.

Is this one of those up-the-ladder deals?

No, because you simply do not know enough. But your worry that it's "toxic" raises another concern. If, in fact, you later learn information that leads you to believe that serious physical harm may be threatened by these drums, then our rules of confidentiality may give you permission to go outside the company if the company refuses to act.[67] But, obviously, the best

---

66. MODEL RULE 2.1; RLGL § 94.

67. MODEL RULE 1.6(b)(1); RLGL § 66, Illus. 3.

solution is to solve the problem within the company and the company's zone of confidentiality.

ℳ Preventing Physical Harm: The Undisclosed Discovery

Damndest thing. I'm handling a routine automobile accident case for my corporate client. Actually was hired by my client's insurance company. The insurance company instructs me to send plaintiff to our doc for a physical. Our doc tells us the plaintiff's expert has it all wrong. The plaintiff's injuries are much worse. The young kid has an aneurysm—a dangerous weakening of an artery. It might've been caused by the accident. So I called the insurance company. They say, whatever we do, we should not tell the kid's lawyer about the problem. It would turn a $10,000 case into a damage disaster. I gotta tell you, I'm worried about that kid.

For good reason. And adding to your humanitarian instinct, consider that if the aneurysm ever ruptures, your client may end up owing millions—or punitives. So maybe you want to appeal to their pocketbook as well as to their humanity.

Filthy lucre aside, maybe the call to the insurance company was the wrong call to make. Your client is the insured and its driver. Maybe they'll have a different view about telling the kid's lawyer. The defense lawyer in *Spaulding v. Zimmerman* made the same mistake.[68]

But even if no one will give you permission to disclose, you probably can anyway. The rules permit disclosure of confidential information to prevent reasonably certain death or serious bodily harm.[69] We don't know how certain it is, but aneurysms are not the kind of things people trifle with. We cannot imagine anyone would second-guess your decision to disclose on these facts.[70]

---

68. 116 N.W.2d 704 (Minn.1962). *See also* Timothy W. Floyd & John Gallagher, *Legal Ethics, Narrative and Professional Identity: The Story of David Spaulding*, 59 MERCER L. REV. 941 (2008); Roger C. Cramton & Lori P. Knowles, *Professional Secrecy and its Exceptions: Spaulding v. Zimmerman Revisited*, 83 MINN. L. REV. 63 (1998).

69. MODEL RULE 1.6(b)(1); RLGL § 66.

70. RLGL § 66 Illus. 1.

🎚 Lawyer Self-Defense: Collecting a Fee

We've given Pharmacorp the best of service. Battling antitrust claims that they went too far in protecting their patents. Claims of overcharging Medicare. You name it. Now they've fallen way behind. We know they've got cash. They're spending a billion to buy back their stock just this year. I'm fed up. I think we should threaten to disclose how they ignored our advice on Algyrol if they don't pay in thirty days.

You don't want to go there. Trust us. It is true that lawyers are free to disclose client confidential information to defend or assert a claim or collect a fee.[71] That is an exception for which the profession has often been criticized as totally self-serving—lawyers can disclose to help themselves—but there are some major limitations on this right of disclosure. First, a lawyer may only disclose information relevant to the claim or defense. That's not clear here, but unless the fees you seek to collect are from the Algyrol matter, you may not threaten or actually disclose that information simply to pressure the client into paying.[72] Second, even if you do disclose confidential information, you are required to take all available steps to make sure the information is not generally available. Pleadings should be filed under seal. Depositions should be subject to protective orders. The idea is that the lawyer should only be allowed to use the confidential information in the most limited way, just to prevent your extortionate ideas.[73]

🎚 Lawyer Self-Defense: Malpractice

I guess we blew it. It turns out the tax advice we gave our partnership client was wrong. The partners, individually, were not entitled to one of the major

---

71. MODEL RULE 1.6(b)(5); RLGL §§ 64, 65.

72. *Lawyer Disciplinary Bd. v. Farber*, 488 S.E.2d 460 (W. Va. 1997) (lawyer who had legitimate reasons to withdraw from client representation suspended for four months because he added an affidavit to his motion that disclosed client confidences unnecessary to support the motion).

73. *State ex rel. Counsel for Discipline of Neb. Supreme Court v. Wilson*, 634 N.W.2d 467 (Neb. 2001) (lawyer who threatened to disclose confidential information to INS and reopen client's divorce unless client paid disputed fee created after client began a relationship with lawyer's estranged wife suspended for two years); *In re Boelter*, 985 P.2d 328, 331 (Wash. 1999) (lawyer who warned client that firm would sue for unpaid fees and added that, in suit, lawyer "would be forced to reveal that you lied on your statement to the IRS and to the bank" suspended for six months).

deductions on the K-1s our firm prepared for them. Though they are threatening to sue us for malpractice, I actually think we warned them that this was problematic. But the real point is that I think their threat is no more than blowing off steam. That is because we know about some serious environmental problems they have on one of their Brownfield developments. I have told them if they sue us for malpractice, then we are going right to the EPA to disclose these environmental issues.

Not so fast. It certainly is true that one of the exceptions to Rule 1.6 governing confidentiality is that a lawyer can disclose confidential information to defend a claim. That, for example, would permit you to defend the claim on the tax issue by disclosing the content of your otherwise confidential warning to this client. But here you are talking about confidential information totally unrelated to the claim or your defense. You are absolutely prohibited from using that information and, in fact, you should never have threatened to use it.[74] Our advice to you is to immediately apologize to the client and assure the client that you will never disclose the Brownfield information unless compelled to do so.

※ Lawyer Self-Defense: Third-Person Claims

Our firm represented our corporate client on a major loan from Big Bank—tough negotiations, lots of reps and warranties, complicated transaction. Client has defaulted on the loan, and now Big Bank is suing our firm, claiming that we aided and abetted our client's fraud. We have lots of information in our files that will help us defend ourselves. The problem is, it is not only confidential, but it is labeled attorney-client privilege, and I am worried because some of it is labeled attorney work-product privilege.

You have two different issues there. You are free to disclose confidential information to defend yourself against a claim by a third party just as much as you may do so on a claim from the client itself. And that same exception to confidentiality applies to privileged information as well, so you are free to use the information in your defense.[75] But we are a little worried about

---

74. *In re Frost*, 863 P.2d 843 (Alaska 1993) (lawyer who informed former client that filing a claim against lawyer would result in waiver of all attorney-client privileges publicly censured for impliedly threatening to use client's information for lawyer's own advantage).

75. RLGL § 80.

the attorney work-product information. Once you start using privileged information to defend yourself, the bank is going to see the attorney work-product designation and ask you the basis on which someone at your firm placed that legend on these documents. They are going to want to know what litigation you were anticipating when you were, in fact, working on a transaction. You just may want to ask yourself whether the embarrassment that will arise from that work-product designation is not so damaging that you are better off not using those memoranda in your defense. Remember, once you start using privileged documents, you do not get to pick and choose which ones get shared. Waiver as to a lone document waives the privilege as to every other document relating to the same subject matter.[76]

◊ Seeking Advice

This one is so difficult. I've had this client for decades. Who knew when my high school classmate started getting involved in something called "web-based shared software" that he would be CEO of a billion dollar public company, and I would end up with a highly profitable client that presents a potpourri of difficult legal questions?

So who do you represent?

Oh, I know what you're getting at. I represent the company, but I also represent my lifetime friend. We did his estate planning. So our firm has two clients. And that may be the problem.

Because?

Well, I just met with Matt—my guy—and he started talking about his stock options. Sounded to me like it's possible some of them were backdated. You know what the SEC is thinking about that issue.

We guess you have a responsibility.

Responsibilities. That's the problem. So I met with my partners to discuss the matter, and we decided we'd better consult someone outside our firm to help us sort this out.

Good idea.

That may be true. But how do I share my clients' confidential information with another lawyer? Maintaining client confidentiality is a paramount fiduciary duty.

---

76. RLGL § 79, cmt. f.

You learned your lessons well. The good news is that the Model Rules—as well as many state rules that adopted the Ethics 2000 changes—provide a specific new exception that permits a lawyer to share confidential information with an outside lawyer to secure legal advice on the lawyer's conformance with his or her obligations.[77] But there are a couple of special requirements.

And they are?

First, you must make sure the lawyer you consult doesn't have a conflict of interest. Second, you should only share as much information as is needed to secure the advice.

There are some who thought this right to consult was already an implicit exception. But this rule was adopted both to make the exception explicit and to encourage lawyers to seek legal counsel when they face difficult issues. We find that lawyers who identify issues and conscientiously consider the situation are far less likely to get in trouble—with their clients or the disciplinary authorities—than lawyers who simply run through the intersection.

And what if my state doesn't have the new exception in its code?

Fortunately, most have. But if yours has not, you can consult an outside lawyer and assert either that you were implicitly authorized,[78] or that you were sharing confidential information to defend a claim,[79] but the consultation does carry some risk that either argument will be unavailing. In any event you should use hypotheticals and other similar devices to minimize the confidential disclosures.

✎ Client Fraud

I represent a family company in the sale of some commercial real estate. Last week, the buyer asked my CEO about zoning, and the CEO replied it was heavy industrial. Today, the CEO told me that in fact, the zoning is only light industrial. We both know that the buyer wants to build a manufacturing plant on the land that will require the heavy industrial zoning. The deal closes tomorrow. What should I do?

---

77. MODEL RULE 1.6(b)(4).

78. MODEL RULE 1.6, cmt. [4]; RLGL § 61.

79. MODEL RULE 1.6(b)(5); RLGL § 64.

Both contract and tort law create an obligation to correct previous misstatements of material fact believed to have been true, to avoid a "fraud."[80] If your client closes this deal without disclosing, your client will commit a fraud, and you will run afoul of the prohibition against counseling or assisting client crimes or frauds.[81] You have two choices: withdraw to avoid assisting,[82] or stay in, disclose, and renegotiate.

⚉ Client Fraud: The Late Discovery

No good deed goes unpunished. An old college buddy who now heads an up-and-coming electrical contractor called me to paper a loan with the bank to allow them to expand their highway lighting contracts with state government. I examined the loan documents and opined that the deal was consistent with state law. A year later, I learn that a rogue employee had cut side deals with government employees and otherwise acted illegally. If the state finds out, they'll cancel the contracts. My buddy's firm has drawn down about half of the bank's line of credit and needs the other half in the next sixty days. Help!

The opinion you gave was valid when given, as far as you knew. You weren't expected to investigate into possible impropriety by some of your client's overzealous employees. But now your opinion is out there. Arguably, the bank is relying on it. The entire loan proceeds have not yet been paid out. And you know that your opinion is wrong. The contracts are the product of old-fashioned American bribery. To make matters worse, your buddy needs the rest of the money.

The answer to the question again will depend on your jurisdiction's rules. First you look to Rule 4.1. That governs your obligation to be truthful and also to avoid aiding and abetting a client fraud. Here, withdrawal may not be enough to avoid assisting your client's continuing fraud.[83] It is a fraud on the bank that the contracts upon which it relied were procured improperly and therefore do not represent the kind of security for repayment the bank thought it had. And you provided assistance, albeit unknowing assistance, to your client's fraud. As a result, Rule 4.1(b) would require you to make the

---

80. RLGL § 98, cmt. d.

81. Model Rule 1.2(d); RLGL §94.

82. Model Rule 1.16(a).

83. Model Rule 4.1, cmt. [3].

minimum disclosure necessary to extricate your client from the fraud. That could probably be accomplished if you inform the bank that it may no longer rely on your opinion. If that doesn't work, disclosure of the fraud will be required. Except Rule 4.1 contains its own caveat. It provides that the lawyer is required to disclose *unless* disclosure is prohibited by Rule 1.6. So you must look at your jurisdiction's Rule 1.6. Most permit, but do not require, disclosure to prevent client fraud.[84] But a few have a version of Rule 1.6 that does not contain such an exception.[85] Even without the exception, there is still some authority in Rule 4.1's comments that would permit you, not to disclose the fraud, but to at least tell the bank it may no longer rely on your opinion when you notify them you have withdrawn.[86]

℀ Crime-Fraud Privilege Exception

I counseled a corporation a few years back about its corporate tax obligations. Specifically, I told the CFO his scheme to undervalue certain assets wouldn't fly and why. Now the government is investigating, and I've been subpoenaed to appear before the grand jury. I already told 'em that anything they ask me is protected by the privilege. Don't waste my time (and yours). I claim it's privileged, but they say crime-fraud applies. Who's right?

That's the government for you. No respect for the privilege. Turning lawyers into witnesses gets them plenty of information. But of course, it stops clients from talking to their lawyers.

Anyway, your claim should hold up. So long as you merely gave advice but played no role in preparing tax returns or documenting the transactions—all you did was give your best advice—then the conversation retains its privileged character.[87] If it were otherwise—say you signed the return as a tax advisor—then even if you were an innocent dupe of your client, the privilege would not attach because you were an instrumentality of your client's crime.[88]

That's probably the case with the lawyer they consulted after they consulted us!

---

84. MODEL RULE 1.6(b)(2); RLGL § 67.

85. *E.g.*, Mont. Rule 1.6(b); Or. Rule 1.6(b).

86. MODEL RULE 4.1, cmt. [3]; N.Y. Rule 1.6(b)(3).

87. RLGL § 82; *U.S. v. Bauer*, 132 F.3d 504 (9th Cir. 1997); *Purcell v. Dist. Attorney for the Suffolk Dist.*, 676 N.E.2d 436 (Mass. 1997).

88. *E.g.*, *U.S. v. Chen*, 99 F.3d 1495 (9th Cir. 1996).

🎗 Law or Court Order

My client's chief engineer in a superfund case inflated his credentials in a deposition. Since I didn't know the actual facts until later, I'm safe in maintaining confidentiality, right?

Don't think so. First, what do you mean by "inflated his credentials?"

Well, he said he had a master's degree, but in fact he hasn't finished college.

And what role has he played in the superfund?

He's in charge of the cleanup.

And what are the issues surrounding the deposition?

You know, the usual. Whether our method of cleanup is reasonable enough to require others to contribute to the fund.

So, his testimony is central to the main issue in the case, and his credentials are central to his credibility regarding that issue?

That's about it.

Then you are wrong. This is a lie about a material fact. Failure to correct the lie would constitute a fraud on the court. The fact that it occurred in a deposition doesn't matter, because it's sworn testimony in a court proceeding. You have to take "reasonable remedial measures" to correct the record. If you can correct his answer to the deposition, fine. If you cannot, then you must inform opposing counsel about the actual facts.[89]

But I wasn't aware he was lying when he testified.

You duty is triggered when you "know" he lied. You now know, so you must correct the record.[90]

🎗 Other Law

I'm outside counsel to a company that has uncovered some problems with a new medical device. The product engineers say the problem is serious, but the board of directors followed the CEO's advice that it wasn't so bad and decided not to disclose to the FDA. As I read the regs, the company must disclose, even if no one has yet been harmed. What can I do now?

If you gave them your best advice and the client rejected it, you are not required to act further. If you think the failure to report is a crime or

---

89. MODEL RULE 3.3(b); RLGL § 120.

90. *U.S. v. Shaffer Equip. Co.*, 11 F.3d 450 (4th Cir. 1993).

fraud likely to result in serious financial loss to third parties—banks, shareholders—you are free to disclose the confidential information outside the company if your jurisdiction has adopted an exception to permit disclosure to prevent a client future crime or fraud.[91] If your jurisdiction has adopted the "to comply with other law or a court order" exception, you may disclose if *you* are required by that other law to do so, and you have taken appropriate steps to protect the privilege.[92] If the client is a public company and you think the failure to report is a violation of law likely to result in serious injury to the issuer or investors, you also may report out under the Sarbanes-Oxley regulations adopted by the SEC.[93] Finally, if you live in one of the twenty-plus jurisdictions that have adopted a provision similar to Model Rule 1.13(c), and you know this failure to report will substantially injure the client, you also may breach confidentiality and report the information.[94]

That's a pretty heavy burden to put on the lawyer.

It sure is. If the highest authority of the organization reaches one conclusion, and you reach another, you can trump the judgment of the client acting through its duly constituted authority. At least, so far, it is rare that this breach of confidentiality is required except in the precious few states that mandate disclosure.

🕮 Rule Conflicts

You keep talking about variations of professional rules, especially confidentiality exceptions, but my company has offices in twenty-five states, and I'm admitted in three. What rules should I read and abide by?

Conflicts of rules problems are as uncertain of confident resolution as conflicts of other law, perhaps even more so. The lawyer, at a minimum, must abide by the rules of her state of admission. If the rules of the forum are more stringent, then those must be followed.[95] Even if not, since confidentiality rules are designed to protect the client, a great argument can be made that the opposing party is entitled to the benefit of the rules of its

---

91. MODEL RULE 1.6(b)(2); RLGL § 67.

92. MODEL RULE 1.6(b)(6); RLGL § 63.

93. 15 U.S.C. § 7245 (2008); 17 C.F.R. pt. 205 (2008).

94. *See supra* Chapter 4, note 33.

95. MODEL RULE 8.5.

home jurisdiction and perhaps the rules of the state where it is doing business as well.

Maybe I can avoid this dilemma by putting a paragraph in our engagement letters that promises that our lawyers will never exercise discretion to disclose?

A great question, one for which we do not yet have a definitive answer. Of course, your engagement letter cannot override a mandatory disclosure obligation such as required under Rule 3.3 or 4.1(b).[96] But apart from these obligations, can a lawyer, in advance of knowing the circumstances that might give rise to an opportunity to disclose, agree not to do so? Or must discretion be exercised one matter at a time? The debate on this point rages on.[97] No one has yet been disciplined for writing such a clause into every engagement letter or running ads in the *Wall Street Journal* proclaiming, "Hire Martyn & Fox: we promise confidentiality," so stay tuned.

96. *See also* Ill. Rule 1.6(b) (mandatory obligation to disclose to the extent necessary to prevent client acts that would result in serious bodily harm or death); N.J. Rule 1.6(b)(1) (mandatory obligation to disclose reasonably certain future crimes, frauds, or other illegal acts likely to result in serious bodily harm, death, or substantial financial harm).

97. *E.g.*, David McGowan, *Why Not Try the Carrot? A Modest Proposal to Grant Immunity to Lawyers Who Disclose Client Financial Misconduct*, 92 CAL. L. REV. 1825 (2004); Samuel J. Levine, *Taking Ethical Discretion Seriously: Ethical Deliberation as Ethical Obligation*, 37 IND. L. REV. 21 (2003).

SEVEN

Conflicts of Interest

✺ Introduction: Your Loyalty Obligation

THIS CHAPTER EXPLORES another core fiduciary duty—loyalty—which can be traced back several centuries in the law of agency.[1] Agency law recognizes that lawyers derive power from clients, but at the same time, also have the superior knowledge and skill to overpower client interests.[2] The loyalty obligation ensures effective client representation by obligating lawyers to avoid harm to clients. You accomplish this by recognizing and responding to any influences (conflicts of interest) that may interfere with your obligation to act in the client's best interests.

The law governing lawyers first requires that you properly identify conflicts of interest created by your own interest, the interest of a third person, or the interest of another current or former client of your law firm that may arise or change throughout a representation.[3] Once identified, all conflicts must be disclosed to clients. Many, but not all, conflicts are consentable, and modern law requires an "informed consent confirmed in writing" to properly waive a conflict.[4]

Failure to properly identify and resolve conflicts can mean overlapping remedies for clients. The client can seek tort relief for harm caused[5] and

---

1. RLGL Chapter 8, Introductory Note.

2. RESTATEMENT (THIRD) OF AGENCY § 1.01 (Tentative Draft No. 2, 2001).

3. MODEL RULE 1.7, cmt. [1]; RLGL §121, cmt. b.

4. *Compare* MODEL RULES 1.0(b), 1.7(b) *with* RLGL § 122.

5. *E.g., Anderson v. O'Brien*, CV044003913, 2005 Conn. Super. Lexis 3365 (Conn. Super. Ct. Dec. 8, 2005) (client stated cause of action for legal malpractice, recklessness, and violation of state unfair trade practices act for failure to protect seller's interests while simultaneously representing buyers in a real estate transaction); *Ellis v. Davidson*, 595 S.E.2d 817 (S.C. Ct. App. 2004) (client stated cause of action for breach of fiduciary duty and legal malpractice against lawyer who took sixty percent interest in client company that lawyer set up).

injunctive or disqualification relief when harm is threatened.[6] Proceeding with a representation without disclosing a conflict also can result in fee disgorgement[7] or a constructive trust of other property.[8]

Figure 8   Four Steps to Resolving Conflicts of Interest

1. **Identify the client(s): RLGL §§ 14, 96.**
2. **Determine whether a conflict of interest exists. Six categories:**
   A. Personal Interests of a Lawyer
   General Rule: 1.7
   Specific Rules: 1.8(a) Business transactions with clients
                        1.8(b) Use of client information
                        1.8(c) Client gifts to lawyer
                        1.8(d) Literary rights
                        1.8(e) Financial assistance to client
                        1.8(h) Limitation of liability to client
                        1.8(i) Proprietary interest in litigation
                        1.8(j) Lawyer/client sexual relationship
                        3.7 Lawyer as witness
   B. Interests of Another Current Client:
   General Rule: 1.7
   Specific Rules: 1.8(g), 1.13(g)
   C. Interests of a Third Person:
   General Rule: 1.7
   Specific Rules: 1.8(f), 5.4(c), 1.13(a)
   D. Interests of a Former Client:
   General Rule: 1.9
   E. Government Lawyers:
   General Rule: 1.11
   Specific Rule: 1.12
   F. Imputed Conflicts:
   General Rule: 1.10
   Specific Rules: 1.8(k), 1.11, 1.12

---

6. *E.g., Maritrans GP Inc. v. Pepper, Hamilton & Scheetz*, 602 A.2d 1277 (Pa. 1992).

7. *E.g., Burrow v. Arce*, 997 S.W.2d 229 (Tex. 1999).

8. *E.g., Monco v. Janus*, 583 N.E.2d 575 (Ill. App. Ct. 1991).

> 3. **Decide whether the conflict is consentable: 1.7(b)(1)-(3).**
> 4. **If it is, consult with affected clients and obtain informed consent, confirmed in writing: (1.7(b)(4).**

⁄⁄ The Deed

The CEO of Mega Corp. asked me to draft a deed transferring vacant land owned by Mega to the CEO. "It's just a liability for Mega," the CEO explained. What should I do?

What are you worried about?

Plenty.

Please explain.

First, we represent Mega Corp. So, is the CEO asking me to do this on behalf of the company or on his own behalf?

Well, as you say, you represent Mega Corp.

It's not that simple. We've done work for the CEO, too.

And you call him your client?

Of course I do. You think I should call him my client representative?

Oh, you should. But nobody does. Everyone refers to entity client reps as "clients." No ethics preaching will change that. What else worries you?

How do I know the transaction is legitimate? Maybe the CEO is doing the company a favor. But maybe not. And he should be the last person who gets to decide that question.

So you recognize two problems. Each requires you to consult someone else at the company.

Easy enough for you to say. But I didn't want to upset the CEO. Up until now, he's been our meal ticket. Besides, don't I owe him a duty of confidentiality?

You very well might. If he reasonably believes he's your client,[9] then you may be limited in sharing the information with anyone at the company unless you have a prior understanding that will occur. . . .[10]

Trust me. No prior understanding.

---

9. RLGL §§ 14, 131.

10. MODEL RULE 1.7, cmts. [30], [31]; RLGL § 60, cmt. i.

Or an exception to the rules permits it. The latter would require knowledge on your part that the CEO is engaged in fraud. . . .

No way. I'm just suspicious.

Or a finding under Rule 1.13 that you know a constituent of the organization is acting in violation of law or duties owed the organization that is likely to result in substantial injury to the organization.

No way again.

Then you would get back to the CEO. See what you can learn from him about the transaction, whom he thinks you are representing, who else at the company knows about the proposed transaction, etc. Then you can determine how much risk you might be running if you did not tell anyone . . . or if you did.[11] But to the extent it appears that the interests of the company and CEO are adverse, you should at the very least politely decline to undertake the transfer.[12]

✄ Personal Conflicts: The Lawyer as Director

How lucky can I be? We've got this new client. They are developing the next iPod. They want to go public as soon as possible. And even before that happens, they want me on the board. What a coup for Caldwell & Moore! And for me! Talk about getting close to the client. To say nothing of the stock options.

You are one lucky lawyer. Maybe.

Maybe? This is the break of my career.

If all goes well, that might be true. But we want you to think long and hard before you take advantage of your good fortune.

You ethics guys! First you tell us when we can't represent clients who want to hire us. Now you tell me I can't take advantage of this great offer to serve. Isn't that why I went to law school? To help my clients?

True enough. But are you really helping your client when you go on its board?

They get my wise counsel. I get to vote on all the important matters that come before the board. Maybe I get some business from the other companies represented on the board—Big Bank, Colossus Corporation.

---

11. *In re Silva*, 636 A.2d 316 (R.I. 1994) (lawyer for financial institution who warned CEO/ friend that his conduct in diverting funds from the financial institution was criminal disciplined for failure to disclose CEO's wrongdoing to the financial institution's board even when CEO refused consent to the disclosure).

12. RLGL § 96, cmt. e, § 131.

Let's talk about your wise counsel.

I didn't mean to sound conceited.

Of course not. That's not what we were addressing. When you sit in that boardroom, are you giving legal advice?

Of course; I'm their lawyer.

All the time?

All the time.

How'bout when you approve the CEO's stock options? Or a merger?

Well, I hope our firm wrote the stock option plan. And our firm, of course, will be doing all the company's M&A.

That would be a plus. But what about your vote as a director?

I guess you're right. That's not legal advice; that's me exercising my business judgment as to what's in the best interests of the company.

So that's not legal advice?

I guess not.

And therefore not privileged?[13]

I thought I was supposed to ask the questions. Get answers from you. But no, not privileged.

So some of what you do as a lawyer director is privileged? And some is not?

You'd have to concede that.

No *you'd* have to concede that. And how would your fellow directors know?

When I give legal advice—its privileged. Otherwise not.

And what do you think happens when, as a director of the company, you get deposed in some lawsuit?

There won't be much I can testify about. We'll claim privilege.

And what do you suppose the other side will do?

Argue that I was acting as a director, not a lawyer, and that there is no privilege for the conversations.

Precisely! And how will the judge side?

I hope our way.

Exactly the right answer. You hope. But you don't know. In fact, it'll be a crap shoot. Particularly given the open hostility some courts have to assertions of privilege. Interfering with the search for the truth and all that. And that's the problem.

---

13. RLGL §§ 72, 73.

How do you mean?

The privilege is only valuable if you can predict for your clients with a high degree of certainty when it will apply. That way, the client has the confidence necessary to share its innermost secrets with you for purposes of getting your privileged advice. But if you choose to don a director's hat, every conversation you ever have will be subject to challenge as a director conversation.

I'll be careful. I promise.

You might be careful. But even if you literally change the color of your hat every time you think you are changing roles, that won't solve the problem.

Okay, okay. I'll warn the client that's a risk. But suppose they conclude it's worth it?

Watch out that they might be doing the right thing for the wrong reason.

How can that be?

All too easy. Too often clients decide they want to put their lawyer on the board to lend gravitas to an otherwise shaky operation. If Fly-by-Night can say so-and-so, a senior partner at Caldwell & Moore is on its board, the good name of Caldwell & Moore and so-and-so's exemplary reputation might lend some dignity to Fly-by-Night.

And what's wrong with that?

Nothing. Nothing at all. With two big "ifs."

They are?

First, if in fact Fly-by-Night is a worthy recipient of Caldwell & Moore's trust. Second, if the association with Fly-by-Night doesn't end up tarnishing Caldwell & Moore. Reputations take years to earn and just moments to lose.

But this is a great business opportunity. The company's going to do swell. And in that boardroom, I'll cement the relationship. No "we hire lawyers, not law firms" here.

There is another problem.

Uh, oh. I hate to hear this.

Well, the question is, how are you going to reconcile your role as a director with your role as a lawyer?

Reconcile? No problem at all. Lawyers are fiduciaries. Directors are fiduciaries. We both have the best interests of the company in mind.

You don't see the contradiction?

Sorry, I don't.

Well, there's a proposal on the table. A new venture. The entrepreneur in you says go for it. The lawyer in you says way too risky, way too close to the edge. Which advice do you give? How do you vote?

That might happen once in a blue moon. But otherwise, I am sure my advice and vote would be consistent.

And then there'll be the times you'll have to recuse yourself.

Why would that be?

When the board decides who should act as counsel, review counsel's performance, worry about legal fees.

So I'll leave the room.

That might help, but it won't stop disgruntled shareholders from claiming that this related party transaction—hiring Caldwell & Moore, paying your outrageous hourly rate—wasn't fairly reached. It's no different from leasing office space from a director, don't you see?

I guess I get the point. But it'll be worth it to get the company's business.

If you can keep it with you as a director, that is.

That's the real reason to do it.

But that's the point. Just when the company most needs your firm's services, just when the bet-the-ranch class action is launched or the derivative claim is brought, because you are a director, your firm may have an impossible conflict of interest.[14] Caldwell & Moore may be a defendant. And even if the firm isn't sued, you may be. Or your role may be the centerpiece of the matter. And instead of choosing your firm, the client will have to search elsewhere. For a firm that could swoop in and replace yours. All because you were a director.

Then how come everyone does it?

Everyone doesn't. Many reject serving on the boards of clients. But some accept. And as long as all goes smoothly, no harm, no foul. But before you go on that client board, at least sit down with your client and discuss the downsides. Then discuss the downsides with your professional colleagues. And only then, confirm your client's informed consent in writing.[15] That way, if you should go on the board, at least you will have done so, and your client will have done so, with eyes wide open.[16]

---

14. MODEL RULE 1.7(b); RLGL § 131, cmt. g.

15. Susan R. Martyn, *Lawyers As Directors: Who Serves and Why?* 1996 Symposium, The Professional Lawyer 107, *reprinted in The Lawyer-Director: Implications for Independence; Report of the Task Force on the Independent Lawyer* (ABA Litigation 1998).

16. MODEL RULE 1.7, cmt. [35]; RLGL § 135, cmt. d.

🐾 Personal Conflicts: Business Transactions

Our corporate client hit a rough patch. Real cash flow problems. Line of credit cancelled. So we stepped into the breach. Loaned them $200,000. At twelve percent. That's how high the credit squeeze sent interest rates. And we got an option on 100,000 shares. So the company survived. Even thrived. But they still haven't paid back the money. And when we asked to exercise the option; they turned us down flat. What can we do?

Well, we know you acted out of the best of intentions. But you may be disappointed with the result. What you did was enter into a business transaction with a client. That will be judged under Model Rule 1.8(a). This Rule requires your deal to be in writing, to include advice to the client to seek other counsel in connection with the transaction, and to be entirely fair to the client.[17]

Well we didn't follow the first two. But it sure was fair. They were desperate.

That was then, and this is now. If the first two omissions aren't fatal to your claim—and they may be—the third could be. The interest rate seems quite high and the option quite a giveaway. You might litigate your entitlement, but a presumption of undue influence would probably prevent your recovery of any interest.[18] If it were us in this predicament, we would insist on our money back and hope for some interest and leave it at that.

🐾 Personal Conflicts: The Gift

The IPO was a huge success. Are we heroes? So much so that when we went to the closing dinner, the CEO, a little inebriated by the libations and his newfound wealth, offered me a personal bonus, just for me. I thought nothing of it, but he just asked me to draft a deed of gift to transfer 1000 shares. "No need to bother the board," he said. "Just between you and I."

Grammar aside, we assume you said no.

---

17. *See also* RLGL § 126.

18. *Buechel v. Bain*, 766 N.E.2d 914 (N.Y. 2001) (fee agreement giving lawyers an interest in client's patent void; even if fee agreement complies with federal law authorizing such arrangements, lawyers must comply with Rule regarding business transactions with clients); *Passante v. McWilliam*, 62 Cal. Rptr. 2d 298 (Cal. Ct. App. 1997) (lawyer who "came through in the clutch" raising money for a client's company and was promised three percent of the firm's stock unable to prevail for breach of oral contract because, if promise was bargained for, it violated the lawyer's ethical duty, which should have included a written waiver and advice to seek outside counsel and, if gratuitous, not legally enforceable).

Are you kidding? The shares are already trading at $47. A college fund for my oldest.

No joke here. Two things. First, you are a partner at your firm, and we are certain such a magnificent gift must be shared. This is no personal token.

But the firm got its full fee. The client said this was just for me.

The client cannot rewrite your partnership agreement. No matter how much he loves you. Second, if there is some legal work to be done in connection with the gift, neither you nor anyone else in your firm can do it. Rule 1.8(c) prohibits lawyers' drafting documents for clients to make gifts to lawyers. Your client can use in-house counsel or another firm, but not you.[19]

He's really not the client. In your words, just a constituent.

That may be so, but your defense to a disciplinary action should not depend on such sophistry.[20]

🎞 Personal Conflicts: Media Rights

I have a new idea. The CEO of Big Bank is in real trouble. What was he thinking, selling stock ahead of the bank's write-down of its CDOs? Now his bank accounts have been frozen, but he says he'll pay me by assigning the story rights to my firm. Talk about the perfect example of recent corporate excesses. The movie'll make a fortune.

Sorry. This one is prohibited. Until the matter is concluded, only Steven Spielberg can get the rights. Your career as the next Scott Turow will have to be put on hold.

Can he assign me his house or his bank accounts?

The house, but not the bank accounts, is a possibility. The house qualifies as a business transaction with a client that will be judged by its entire fairness, whether you put everything in writing, and whether you advised your client that he should seek the advice of independent counsel as to the terms of the deal.[21] And what's he going to pay that guy with? Not the movie rights.

---

19. RLGL § 127.

20. *McRentals Inc., v. Barber*, 62 S.W.3d 684 (Mo. Ct. App. 2001) (lawyer met burden of proving no undue advantage in business transaction with client; lawyer repeatedly told client that lawyer would not represent client in the transaction, and client in fact consulted with another lawyer); *Comm. on Prof'l Ethics v. Randall*, 285 N.W.2d 161 (Iowa 1979) (lawyer who named himself sole beneficiary in drafting client's will disbarred).

21. MODEL RULE 1.8(a); RLGL § 126.

You also should be warned that if you take the house, the government, if it seeks civil forfeiture, may claim you're not entitled to it.[22] Moreover, should your client go bankrupt, the assignment of the house might be challenged by other creditors.

The bank accounts are an entirely different matter, because they may well be the subject matter of the litigation. And lawyers cannot acquire proprietary interests in litigation beyond the lawyer's interest in a reasonable contingent fee.[23]

⁂ Personal Conflicts: Limiting Liability

I shouldn't be skeptical, but I am. My good buddy, Ian, at Caldwell & Moore has been representing the leasing company OPM for years. Paid for his beach house on that client. I guess Ian got too greedy. OPM—I should say its CEO—came to see me last week. Said Caldwell & Moore was taking the company for granted. Looking for someone new who would value the business.

You called Ian, we hope?

First thing I did. He didn't seem surprised. But he surprised me. When I asked him if there was anything I should know, he said that his client and he had mutually agreed to part company. Couldn't tell me anymore. I thought there was an umbrella of confidentiality because he represents the same client we were thinking of taking on.

And you found out that was wrong?[24]

Yep. Who knew? Predecessor counsel, Ian told me, cannot disclose confidences to successor counsel without client permission. So I was a little worried.

We can see why.

But I think I've solved the problem. We'll get a huge retainer, bill monthly, and if he falls behind one month, we'll withdraw.

That should help. But don't forget to put that in your retainer letter. Make it clear that is an obligation of the client within the meaning of Rule 1.16(b)(5).

---

22. 21 U.S.C. §§ 848, 853 (2006); *U.S. v. McCorkle*, 321 F.3d 1292 (11th Cir. 2003) (burden of proof on lawyer to identify portion of fee not subject to forfeiture because collected as bona fide purchaser for value).

23. MODEL RULE 1.8(i).

24. MODEL RULE 1.6(a); RLGL § 60, cmts. d, e.

And I have one more idea. We'll get OPM to agree that they won't sue us for malpractice. And indemnify us for any claims by third parties.

A great idea! Except for one thing. Model Rule 1.8(h)(1) prohibits a lawyer from prospectively limiting the lawyer's liability to the client.[25] You can't seek such a waiver from the client. And, by the way, if you're this worried, maybe this is one where you should just say "no." Beware clients switching counsel, especially leaving someone you admire and respect. You could be the next former counsel, and you have no idea, right now, why that might occur.

✐ Personal Conflicts: Proprietary Interests in Litigation

Our client, a limited real estate partnership, claims that it was a joint venture partner with a vulture fund that bought an interest in three marginal shopping centers in Boston. Its putative partner has responded that our client was only a partner in two centers in Providence, Rhode Island. Problem is, the client has no money and, in this climate, is hesitant to make a capital call. So they asked if we will agree to take it on a contingency. If we win and the client gets its rightful share in the shopping centers, they will give us their interest in one of the three. Our choice. Sounds great to us.

Sounds great to us too, unless the Rhode Island argument prevails, that is. But it may be too good.

You repeat that mantra too often for our money.

Well, the problem is twofold. Taking an interest in the shopping center is not unlike being paid in stock. So you would have to comply with Rule 1.8(a), doing business with clients. That rule requires the arrangement to be reduced to writing, the client must be advised in writing to consult other counsel in connection with the arrangement, and the transaction is reviewable for its entire fairness to the client.[26]

We can certainly do all that.

So we've taken care of one. The other issue is whether someone will assert that you took a proprietary interest in the litigation, a practice that is prohibited.[27]

---

25. RLGL § 54(2).

26. RLGL § 126.

27. MODEL RULE 1.8(i); RLGL § 36(1).

This is just like a one-third contingent fee. They get the interest in two shopping centers; we get one.

You make a great argument.[28] Just beware that one could make the counter-argument after the fact. That one might turn out to be your very own client, whose generosity abounds as it lures you into the engagement with visions of sugar plums but, after your advocacy is successful, decides one shopping center is one strip mall too many.[29]

✄ Personal Conflicts: Sex with Clients

First I was appalled, then delighted. We just learned our prized corporate associate, Sarah Reynolds, has been involved with the CFO of Big Bank, one of our very best clients. The guy's so dull. And I'm sure he's married. Twenty years older than Sarah, at least. But then I thought, what a great way to cement our relationship. You know, with this romance in full bloom, if work can be sent our way, it will be.

So long as the affair continues.

There is that. But in the short term. . . . And Sarah seems so happy. Even if she hasn't gone public. One of our secretaries saw them together at a hotel in New York. Holding hands.

But there is this little ethical problem.

What's that?

Lawyers are prohibited from having sex with clients.[30]

Well, we don't know there's any sex involved. Maybe they are just good friends. Besides, that's obviously a rule to stop those male divorce lawyers from taking advantage of their vulnerable domestic relations clients. No one was thinking of the lawyer being a woman!

That may be so, but the rule is gender neutral, and it applies to all lawyers.

---

28. ABA Comm. on Ethics and Prof'l Responsibility (2002), Formal Op. 02-427 (Contractual Security Interest Obtained by a Lawyer to Secure Payment of a Fee).

29. *Ankerman v. Mancuso*, 860 A.2d 244 (Conn. 2004) (client's promissory note secured by mortgage on property subject to litigation gives lawyer no interest in client's property or cause of action); *In re Mason*, 938 P.2d 133 (Colo. 1997) (en banc) (lawyer who acquired property from client as payment for legal fees knowing that ownership of certain property was in dispute and likely to become subject of litigation suspended for six months).

30. MODEL RULE 1.8(j) & cmts. [17]–[19].

You can't be serious. This is an organizational client. Surely they are not covered by this rule.

In most jurisdictions, they are. The rule prohibits lawyers for organizations (inside and outside counsel) from engaging in sexual relationships with constituents who supervise, direct, or regularly consult with the lawyer.[31]

But poor Sarah. The way we work her, this may be her only chance to develop a personal relationship, even if the guy's married. The rule simply makes no sense.

Maybe yes; maybe no.

How can you say that?

Let's assume you're counting on Sarah at some point in her dealings with the bank to just say "no" or tell the bank a proposed course of action is foolhardy. How independent do you suppose Sarah can be, given her secret relationship with the CFO? It's that little doubt that just crossed your mind that demonstrates one sound policy reason behind the rule.

🎇 Third-Person Influence

I don't know what to do. I was retained by Big Bank to represent its CFO in a huge SEC investigation into insider trading. They've been paying my bills like clockwork. Now they tell me I have to tell them if I am negotiating a deal for the CFO, or they'll stop paying the CFO's bills.

You recognize how unethical that would be. Whenever a lawyer is paid by a third party, the lawyer must, nonetheless, maintain the client's confidences and not let the third party interfere with the lawyer's professional judgment. Even when it is dad paying irresponsible son's legal bills, dad gets a cold shoulder from you as to confidential information regarding son.[32]

Tell Big Bank there can be no conditions to your service. If that means they stop paying your fees, that is a result you and your client must live with. We don't have to tell you that the bylaws or employment contract of Big Bank with the CFO may require Big Bank to pay your client's fees, and, if they do, a condition of fulfilling that corporate obligation cannot be a requirement that you breach the confidentiality of the client.

---

31. Model Rule 1.8, cmt. [19].

32. Model Rule 1.8(f), 5.4(c); RLGL § 134.

✻ Aggregate Settlements

I represent this large group of beer distributors. In big markets and small. They have been sued for antitrust violations, and we are lucky enough to get the representation of clients whose product we simply love. They have agreed that if a majority of the members approve a settlement, they will each be bound by it. I got them this great settlement, or at least I thought it was. But the vote was very, very close. Now the dissenters want to fire me and continue the litigation. I am trying to keep peace, but it's not looking good.

Well, you face one very big problem. What you received from the members when they signed onto the representation was a prospective agreement to be bound by the vote of the majority. But they did that at a time when they had no idea what the settlement would be, or, for that matter, how the case would unfold. As you know, under our rules, the decision to settle a case is exclusively that of the client. The fact is, each client gets to decide, and they get to decide at the time the settlement is presented to them.[33] As a result, the courts refuse to enforce agreements like this, and, in fact, you may be in trouble for recommending that they proceed in this fashion.[34]

✻ Joint Clients: The Start-Up

So I understand that business start-ups are usually joint representations. But this happens all the time. I get a call from a client who brings others into my office for advice about setting up a new business. I assume I'm free to proceed.

Proceed, yes. But free, no. Suppose you want to represent the idea guy and the CEO. How can you do it?

You tell me. They've already agreed that the company'll pay a royalty of ten percent of sales revenues. And the CEO gets $100,000 per year for three years. So maybe I can do it?

Think non-compete. Have they agreed whether the CEO signs a non-compete? Or the nature of the license from the idea guy. Is it exclusive?

Oh, they didn't mention either of those matters. Though I did think about both.

---

33. MODEL RULE 1.8(g); RLGL § 128, cmt. d(i).

34. *E.g., Burrow v. Arce,* 997 S.W.2d 229 (Tex. 1999) (violation of aggregate settlement rule grounds for fee forfeiture).

Glad to know you're still alive. But you get the point. The parties may have thought they have struck a deal. But you know probably dozens of items—like non-competes and the nature of the license—that they haven't considered. And if you're representing the company, it's certainly in its best interest to get a non-compete from the CEO and an exclusive license from the idea guy. But if you are representing either of them, maybe those are not very good ideas. And if you think you are representing all of them—Tom, Frank, Joyce, the company in formation—what do you do when a thought about a non-compete pops into your head?

Wish I hadn't thought of it?

Right! But now you have, and now you've demonstrated why you cannot possibly represent all of them. And that would be true even if you didn't already represent Tom. But you do. So I'm afraid you're going to have to send Frank and Joyce off to get their own lawyers.

There are two reasons that's gotta be wrong. First, this is a start-up. Tom's only putting up $200,000. They don't have money to burn on lawyers. They want to spend their money on R&D.

And the second?

I send them to other lawyers, and my chance of representing the next Google walks right into someone else's office! You can talk about the subtleties of some fancy conflict-of-interest rules, but I live in the real world. And so do these clients.

I know, I know. But the beginning of your salvation is clear recognition that this situation is fraught with conflicts. Sure enough, all three are figuratively holding hands to launch the next big thing. But the lawyer who concurrently represents the three of them clearly triggers Model Rule 1.7(a)(2) because in advising each, the lawyer has a material limitation on the advice he or she gives due to the lawyer's loyalty to the others or to the future enterprise. So at a minimum, the lawyer must advise them of the conflict and urge them to get other counsel, as painful as that might be.

And if they plead poverty, practicability?

Then you have to determine whether you can get them from where they are today to the actual start of the company with their ordering their own issues where they have conflicts, while you undertake the conflict-free tasks of offering legal options, documenting their decisions, and otherwise taking steps to implement their common interests in implementing the best structure for the enterprise going forward. Going down that road will require real care.[35]

---

35. MODEL RULE 1.7, cmt. [28]; RLGL § 130, cmt. c.

How do you mean?

Well, you are going to have to discuss the implications of this approach. Fully explain the conflicts. Remind them again of the desirability of each having individual representation. Get their agreement to waive any conflict. Explain and obtain their understanding about confidentiality. Essentially, you can advise them about their legal options, but you cannot advise them about which options to select.[36]

So, explain your plan to give them a checklist of issues they need to address among themselves. Explain the scope limitation on your role as a lawyer. Make sure you advise them about confidentiality.[37] And then confirm the arrangement in a clearly written letter to each, seeking confirmation in writing that they understand how you plan to proceed.

Very elaborate for something that happens every day.

Maybe. But the commonality of the situation does not diminish the ethical difficulty the situation presents.

𝍎 Joint Clients: The Entity and a Constituent

What about if the company asks me to represent both an employee or officer and the company? For example, we represent this small public company. The SEC is investigating insider trading and alleges two employees bought ahead of some good news. General counsel says it's a bogus claim. Wants us to represent the company and the two employees. That way, the company won't incur too big of an expense since it's liable to advance the employees' legal fees.

This, of course, happens all the time. For instance, any employee being sued for some action in the course of employment, such as being in an accident with a company vehicle.[38] The injured sue the company and the driver of the company car. But this has to be handled like any joint representation. Your first obligation is to determine whether there is any possible conflict of interest between your entity client and the individual seeking the advice. To do this, begin by looking at the facts. Did the employee or the management of the company do anything legally wrong? Is there any chance the company will fire or penalize the employee for her conduct? Then consult

---

36. MODEL RULE 1.7, cmt. [8], [32].

37. MODEL RULE 1.7, cmt. [31].

38. *E.g., Perez v. Kirk & Carrigan*, 822 S.W.2d 261 (Tex. App. 1991).

the law that governs the matter. Are the defenses the same? Does the company or the employee have rights against each other? Is this a civil or criminal case? Finally, check out the relationship of the parties. Does insurance cover the claim? Might your preexisting relationship with the company or one of its employees create an impediment to your representation of both?

If you see a potential conflict in the representation, you still may proceed only if you determine it is reasonable to seek a waiver, you tell the prospective individual client you need to seek a waiver, you get his or her permission to do so, and you obtain informed consent from someone at the organization other than the person seeking the legal services (even if that person is the CEO) who has authority in the organization to grant a waiver. This last issue—getting a waiver from the organization from an independent person with authority—is an explicit requirement of Model Rule 1.13 (g).[39]

Further, you must explain to each client the benefits of being separately represented, and that the SEC may balk at the joint representation. Then, you must reach an understanding with both clients about how the lawyer is to handle confidential information learned from each, discuss what happens if a conflict arises later that prohibits the lawyer from representing both, and explain to the company that by proceeding in this way, the company is at risk of losing the services of its longtime lawyer, even if the parties now agree that should a conflict arise, the lawyer would plan to drop the individual and keep the company. This latter result occurs because the waiver from the employee that the lawyer, in the face of a conflict, will get to represent the company is a prospective waiver that can always be challenged later as not sufficiently well informed.[40]

Whew! I never thought about confidentiality in a conflicts waiver. What am I supposed to say?

This is really important. In any joint representation, you want to establish ground rules for the handling of confidential information received from just one of the clients. If you don't, Model Rule 1.6 will provide the default rule and your client might not know or want that. So your clients should decide, up front, will the lawyer keep information from one client confidential, no matter how much the other client(s) would love to know it? Or will the lawyer promise to share it, no matter how embarrassing it is to the

---

39. *See also* RLGL § 131, cmt. e.

40. MODEL RULE 1.7, cmt. [22].

secret-revealing client? At least in the latter situation, the blabbing client will have been forewarned about the lawyer's commitment to disclose.

So you tell each client that they have a choice: either agree to share all confidential information from any source, or not share certain well-defined information if given by one client to the lawyer confidentially.[41] And add an explanation of the joint representation privilege that confidential matters will be privileged against outsiders, but will not be privileged between the clients in subsequent litigation.[42]

Even if the lawyer doesn't disclose, the lawyer is obliged to withdraw from one or both representations if the information itself creates a conflict or if the information, if undisclosed, achieves the same result.[43]

The worst situation in a joint representation is when no ground rules have been established, and you learn a troubling fact from one client. Then you must try to determine what the default rule is in the applicable jurisdiction and act.[44] Either way the lawyer goes (disclose; don't disclose; just withdraw), the lawyer's conduct will be subject to second-guessing by the unhappy client who either had her information disclosed or did not learn a critical piece of information known to her lawyer.

Figure 9   Joint Representation Disclosures to Employees

1. I represent _____ organization, not you or any other employee.
2. I can only represent you if you have not violated the law.
3. If you do not believe you have violated the law, but subsequent events disclose this is likely, I will not be able to continue representing you, but will continue to represent the organization.

---

41. MODEL RULE 1.7, cmt. [31]; RLGL § 60, cmt. l.

42. MODEL RULE 1.7, cmt. [30]; RLGL § 75.

43. MODEL RULE 1.7, cmt. [29].

44. The default rule will be that jurisdiction's version of confidentiality exceptions. *See A. v. B.*, 726 A.2d 924 (N.J. 1999) (in absence of explicit understanding in retainer agreement, lawyer who learns material facts from one joint client may tell the other only if the facts fall within a specific confidentiality exception.)

4. If this occurs, I will be free to disclose to the corporation anything you told me while you were my client and the corporation has the power to decide whether to disclose any information to outsiders.

5. If I cannot continue representing you, you will have to hire new counsel.

6. If you decide that I should represent both you and your employer, what either of you tell me will be disclosed to the other, and can be used against the other in subsequent litigation.

🎐 Joint Clients: Representing Everyone?

Company's subject of an enforcement proceeding by the SEC. And they're rattling sabers about a DOJ referral. Serious stuff. But we know what the company did was legit. And the accountants knew about the special purpose entities and blessed the company's not including these debts as liabilities on our balance sheet. So it's time to man the ramparts. We're going to represent the company and its officers.

Throw down the gauntlet ever so carefully. Representing the company and its officers is a high-stakes game fraught with peril.[45]

But all my clients are on the same page.

That's true now, but how long will that last?

I met with the individuals, and we all agreed to defend this to the hilt. I looked each one in the eye.

But you cannot predict the future. Let's consider the possibilities. First, who in the company will be asked to waive any conflicts?[46]

Hadn't thought about that. I guess it can't be the officers who we will represent as individuals?

Right. Next, you start interviewing each officer individually. You find some were more involved than others. Any problems?

Of course not. I told you of the joint pledge.

But you didn't tell me how your advice to each might differ. Maybe those more involved might have more to worry about as individuals.

---

45. MODEL RULES 1.7, cmt. [34], 1.13, cmt. [10]; RLGL § 131.

46. MODEL RULE 1.13 (g); RLGL § 131, cmt. e.

You're right there.

And, therefore, need advice at least to consider cooperating against the company. To cut a deal.

But I have the pledge.

As we noted, the pledge was good when given. Now—just hypothetically, of course—you know more. The person who invented these SPEs may be in more trouble than the general counsel or the VP for marketing. That person needs advice on cutting a deal. But that deal would hurt the company. If you represent the company, you can't give the advice.

You got me there.

And the reverse is true as well. You represent the company, and you've got to do everything in your power to avoid an indictment. For the employees, it might be a fine or even a jail term. For the company, an indictment could be a death sentence. So the company might want to cooperate, even volunteer to waive the privilege. This could mean sending your investigation reports, your notes to the constabulary. But when you took those notes, you assured the individuals you represent that you would maintain confidentiality. You assured them everything was privileged. You feeling uncomfortable yet?

I'm beginning to get your drift. Can I never represent the company and its constituents?

Oh. There are probably cases where it would be okay, at least initially. Think about a lawsuit against a company and its truck driver for an accident on the highway.[47] But as soon as either the company or one or more of the employees has an incentive (staying out of jail, avoiding a suspension, whatever) to protect itself at the expense of another of your clients, then that representation should be rejected from the beginning or terminated as soon as the conflict becomes clear.[48]

So I guess we have to get them their own lawyers?

You certainly should.

Well at least if we have to hire them lawyers, we can buy some loyalty for our money?

Loyalty?

You know. Cooperate with the company's defense; no deals; get our approval if they're going to file any motions or take any useless depositions.

---

47. *E.g., Perez v. Kirk & Carrigan*, 822 S.W.2d 261 (Tex. App. 1991).

48. RLGL § 131, cmt. e.

Dream on, our friend. You can pay their fees. You may even have to. But no matter, you cannot interfere with the independence of your officer's lawyers. They get to decide these matters without interference from the company.[49]

Well at least if we agree to pay the bills of the officer's lawyers, the detail we require on invoices will give us insight into what they are up to.

Wrong again. You can ask for anything. But you should keep in mind two things. First, sharing too much information might act as a waiver of the privilege for these individuals.[50] Remember, they are your kin, and it's unlikely you would like that result to befall them. Second, you are not entitled to that information if it would interfere with the professional independence of their lawyers. So don't be surprised if those lawyers simply refuse to give you real detail, yet still claim—correctly—that their clients are entitled to have their fees advanced.

Can't we solve that waiver problem with a joint defense agreement? We use those all the time in "big" multi-defendant cases.

If there truly is a joint interest, such an agreement can protect the sharing of privileged information among parties on the same side of the "v;" but using that device creates another warning.[51]

Enemies everywhere.

So it would seem. The Justice Department has asserted that a measure of a company's lack of cooperation is its willingness to enter into joint defense agreements with individual evil-doers.

Outrageous. Besides, we believe everyone acted properly.

That's your view. And it should be enough to satisfy entering into a totally reasonable joint defense agreement. Just keep in mind that DOJ often convicts before anyone is indicted, and if your company client enters into these agreements—or even advances fees as its bylaws or state corporate law requires—DOJ may announce that your company is not cooperating. The Sentencing Commission has determined that cooperation should not be measured in this way,[52] and Judge Kaplan, in the KPMG case, rejected such DOJ tactics.[53] The McNulty memorandum from whence all this mischief

---

49. MODEL RULES 1.8(f), 5.4(c); RLGL § 134.

50. *E.g., In re Rules of Prof'l Conduct,* 2 P.3d 806 (Mont. 2000).

51. RLGL § 76.

52. 22 LAW. MAN. PROF. CONDUCT 193 (ABA/BNA 2006).

53. *See U.S. v. Stein,* 440 F. Supp. 2d 315 (S.D.N.Y. 2006), *affirmed,* 541 F.3d 130 (2d Cir. 2008); *U.S. v. Stein,* 435 F. Supp. 2d 330 (S.D.N.Y. 2006).

springs has only recently been dropped as the DOJ's practice.[54] The SEC has followed suit, but both continue to allow "voluntary" privilege waivers.[55]

✅ Joint Clients: Competing for a Scarce Resource

Business development doesn't get any better than this. Two of our present clients are competing for a license for a new television broadcast channel allocated to Chicago. We debated which client asked us first (that is our usual rule) when someone got the bright idea we should represent both of them. After all, these are sophisticated clients. We are the best in the business. We will form two different teams. And think what the clients will save in messenger fees.

Another bright idea! You guys sure are imaginative. The problem is, there is only one channel, so only one client can win, and the other client is bound to lose. Starting off two representations knowing the best you can bat is .500 is not a very bright idea. Moreover, inevitably, in order to move your one client forward, that client's team is going to have to be free to disparage the other client. And, if that's not bad enough, think of what happens when Team A decides Team B is doing a bad job for its client. Will they celebrate or will they worry about malpractice liability?[56] In our view, this conflict is very real, and therefore very difficult to waive.[57]

Okay, okay, so we won't represent both, but we can represent one of them, can't we?

Well, you can . . . but only if the other client consents.

Don't tell me that. We're not taking a position directly adverse to one of our clients. I know that.

You could make that argument, although it is a hard one to accept. There's no "v," for sure, but that is not always required to be directly adverse. Think buyer and seller. In any event, you certainly will be laboring under a "material limitation" as you go forward for the same reasons described above. If you are seeking a new channel for Client A, you must be in a position to be free to

---

54. 24 Law. Man. Prof. Conduct 473(ABA/BNA 2008).

55. 24 Law. Man. Prof. Conduct 473, 597(ABA/BNA 2008).

56. *Kilpatrick v. Wiley, Rein & Fielding*, 909 P.2d 1283 (Utah Ct. App. 1996) (breach of fiduciary duty claim against lawyers who represented multiple clients interested in acquiring a television station).

57. Model Rule 1.7(b)(1); RLGL § 122(2)(c).

disparage Client B. And even if B is only a client in other matters, an objective view is that situation would force you to pull your punches. So, only with a very specific waiver, upon informed consent, can you represent either of the prospective new channel owners.[58]

🎐 Thrust-Upon Conflicts

Clients! Love 'em and hate 'em. Listen to this one. We're representing Big Bank in a huge loan to Acme Incorporated, the miniconglomerate. It's a revolving line of credit, and Big Bank has already syndicated the facility. Yesterday we learn our client—Grant Communications—is buying Acme. My partner says we have a conflict. We'll be representing our client Big Bank in lending money to our client Grant Communications.

Your colleague is right. Though there are arguments about subs and parents that can be made, in the final analysis, you have clients adverse to each other. On a big transaction.

But Acme is separately represented.

Of course they are, but Acme is still your client or will be as soon as Grant buys them.

But Big Bank (and we) are totally innocent. Isn't Big Bank entitled to our continuing services?

There is a new comment to the Model Rules that may come to your half-rescue.[59]

Half-rescue?

Yes. This comment says that when a conflict develops in the middle of a representation, and the lawyer and the lawyer's client had nothing to do with that development, then the lawyer faces a "thrust-upon" conflict. And when presented with such a conflict, the lawyer may have the option of withdrawing from the representation of one client and continuing the representation of the other, in this case, Big Bank. But that permission comes at a cost. Unless Grant is willing to waive the conflict that its purchase has created, you have to drop Grant as a client. If you don't drop Grant, then you have to withdraw from the representation of Big Bank.

---

58. MODEL RULE 1.7(b)(4); RLGL § 122(1).

59. MODEL RULE 1.7, cmt. [5].

Uh oh. I can see a big fight coming. Which client should we drop? That won't be a pleasant discussion at our shop.

% The Hot Potato Doctrine

I like the idea of dropping the client—not that I want to be in that business, you understand. But we had a situation a little while ago. One of our partners had a chance to take on a huge matter adverse to Colossus. He was drooling 'til he found out a new partner in our Myrtle Beach office was handling a storefront lease for a sub of Colossus. And you guessed it, the South Carolina partner agreed in his engagement letter to treat all affiliates as a single client.

Prospective client would not let us seek a waiver. So I came up with the bright idea that we drop the new partner. He wasn't performing all that well anyway. Vastly overstated his portables. But our otherwise avaricious firm CEO suddenly got all soft about this guy being a partner. So then I thought, let's just fire the client. The fees were peanuts, and the new matter was big, real big. Make 'em a former client, and I figured we were home free.

Say it isn't so. Rule 1.16 permits you to withdraw from a representation for no reason at all so long as there's no material adverse effect on the client. But dropping a client to take on another client has been universally condemned by the courts.[60]

Well, how 'bout this thrust-upon stuff? Does that change the rule?

The thrust-upon exception is strictly limited to its facts, that is, that the client's business activity—not the lawyer's—caused the conflict. But the hot potato doctrine remains otherwise intact.[61]

I knew we should've never hired the South Carolina fella.

% Rely-on-Your-Memory Conflicts Check

Okay, I admit it. We didn't do the conflict check that was required. Everything happened so quickly. Excelsior needed an injunction to prevent the lift-out of an entire department by its largest competitor in violation of Excelsior's standard

---

60. *See, e.g., Universal City Studios, Inc. v. Reimerdes,* 98 F. Supp. 2d 449 (S.D.N.Y. 2000).

61. *Eastman Kodak Co. v. Sony Corp.,* Nos. 04-CV-6095, 04-CV-6098, 2004 U.S. Dist. LEXIS 29883 (W.D.N.Y. Dec. 27, 2004)

non-compete. And I was sure we had sued the competition last year in a patent infringement suit. So I didn't send around a memo, though I did check the box that said I did. Well, it turns out, a) we got the injunction; b) the patent infringement suit was four years ago; c) our corporate partners had helped the defendant/competitor get a loan from Big Bank at the same time we were handling the Excelsior matter.

How'd Excelsior find out?

That's just it. The CEO of competitor made some remarks to Excelsior's CEO as they left the courtroom. Something about how happy competitor was with our firm's services.

Then what happened?

Nothing—until Excelsior's CEO told his general counsel about the other CEO's remark. Then GC decides he's going to be a hero. So we get a letter from CEO demanding a return of the fees he paid us because we had a conflict. Some conflict. We won didn't we? If someone might complain, you'd think it would be competitor.

That's what you might think. But the truth is they can both complain.

Wait! We got them everything they wanted.

So they can't sue you for malpractice. But that doesn't mean Excelsior can't seek fee disgorgement even if it cannot prove a dollar of damages for a breach of fiduciary duty. You admit you didn't check. You just relied on your memory.

How unfair!

If it's really unfair, you can argue that they should get some but not all of the fee disgorged. But you will have the burden to show you conferred a benefit on the client apart from your misconduct.[62]

✍ Issue Conflicts

We followed your advice. Twice. But I think we still might be in trouble.

We misled you?

Let me explain. You told us to be zealous advocates for our clients. So when we found out our client's adversary shared some documents with the SEC relevant to our proceeding, we raced into court arguing waiver. And the court agreed.

---

62. RLGL § 37, cmt. e; *Burrow v. Arce*, 997 S.W.2d 229 (Tex. 1999).

Ordered our adversary to turn over all privileged documents the SEC had received, plus any other privileged docs on the same topic.

I was so excited to be able to get our hands on these docs, I didn't think about another client, Innovent, the high-tech conglomerate we were representing at the same time. Innovent is facing a class action suit by shareholders. Great case for our firm to be handling. Problem is, those darn class action lawyers claim Innovent waived privilege when it shared docs with its auditors. That's absurd. You taught us to defend the corporate privilege at all costs, and we were doing just that. But now I'm afraid the plaintiffs' lawyers will use our victory—arguing waiver by sharing with the SEC—against us. Two federal cases, both in the Northern District. The issues are completely different, but should I be worried?

Issue conflicts are real.[63] Here, you may have an argument that the sharing with the accountants raises different issues from sharing with law enforcement. But the question is whether "there is a significant risk that a lawyer's action on behalf of one client will materially limit the lawyer's effectiveness in representing another client in a different case; for example, when a decision favoring one client will create a precedent likely to seriously weaken the position taken on behalf of the other client."[64]

It is true that you could win both cases. But let's hope you don't lose the second case and have the judge's opinion in the first cited against you.

In the meanwhile, do I have to do anything?

If you think the rule standard has been triggered, you should notify Innovent, inform Innovent of the possible conflict, and give the client a chance to retain separate counsel that might be able to take a more aggressive approach, particularly in attacking your successful waiver argument in the first case.[65]

✌ Former Clients: Keeping It in the Family

How's this for keeping it in the family? We used to do the tax returns for wife's business. Now husband gave us a call. He wants us to represent him in a divorce proceeding.

---

63. *Williams v. State*, 805 A.2d 880 (Del. 2002) (lawyer making contradictory arguments in appeal of two capital cases allowed to withdraw from one representation to avoid conflict).

64. MODEL RULE 1.7, cmt. [24].

65. ABA Comm. on Ethics and Prof'l Responsibility, Formal Op. 93-377 (1993) (Positional Conflicts).

One big happy family. The question will be whether there is a substantial relationship between the work you did for wife and the divorce matter. That turns on a couple of questions. How long ago did you do the tax return? And could the confidential information you discovered about wife's business play some role in the divorce proceeding? Maybe the only issue between them is child custody. On the other hand if your work for wife's business was recent and the estranged couple is feuding about division of property, you should decline husband's invitation, because if you don't, wife can have you disqualified.[66] Or disciplined.[67]

ℳ Former Inside Counsel

We want to hire Melinda Jones, the GC of Capitol Hospital. What a boost for our healthcare practice. And we can get her cheap. But the question is, will she hurt more than she helps?

What do you mean?

Well, we don't want to lose business because of her conflicts. We met her as an adversary, you see.

The analysis goes two ways. If she brings Capitol with her, then the firm has to treat Capitol as a present client and recognize all concurrent client conflicts.

So we could never be directly adverse to Capitol.

Not without the consent of all affected clients.

What if Capitol doesn't follow her?

We won't ask why you would hire her, then. We're sure she is a wonderful lawyer. In any event, then Ms. Jones would treat Capitol as a former client under Rule 1.9, and any conflict Ms. Jones had would be imputed to your firm under Rule 1.10. As a result your firm could undertake no matters adverse to Capitol that are the same or substantially related to matters handled by Ms. Jones for Capitol.[68]

---

66. *Ennis v. Ennis*, 276 N.W.2d 341 (Wis. Ct. App. 1979) (lawyer who represented husband in divorce and four years later represented former wife to reopen divorce on grounds of fraud should have been disqualified by the trial court on the opposing party's motion).

67. *In re Conway*, 301 N.W.2d 253 (Wis. 1981) (same lawyer, same facts as *Ennis, supra* note 67, publicly reprimanded for taking the second case without the former client's consent).

68. RLGL § 132.

She was GC. That makes her responsible for everything. With her on board, we can never take on anything related to Capitol.

That's certainly not true. New matters will arise that occurred after she left.

So we can sue Capitol for malpractice?

Certainly not as to cases that arose before she departed. Or claims that arise from events when she was still around. But as to new claims, perhaps. It would depend on whether the hospital has a reasonable substantial relationship argument. If the new case involves the same botched procedure as an earlier case, maybe not. And Capitol might argue a substantial relationship exists because Mrs. Jones knows the hospital's playbook. Some courts are receptive to that argument.[69] Others have rejected it.[70]

How about lobbying on behalf of Small Hospital—a competitor of Capitol on Medicaid reimbursement rates?

That would depend on whether, in representing Small, you would be in a position to use Capitol's confidential information to enhance Small's plea. We would need to know more facts.

---

69. *In re N. Am. Deed Co.*, 334 B.R. 443 (Bankr. D. Nev. 2005) (the presence of playbook information overcomes any doubt and confirms existence of a substantial relationship between prior representation of debtor in a wide array of matters and current adversarial representation of debtor's individual officers); *Jessen v. Hartford Cas. Ins. Co.*, 3 Cal. Rptr. 3d 877 (Cal. Ct. App. 2003) (substantial relationship exists if playbook information is relevant to the subject matter of an action if the information might reasonably assist a party in evaluating the case, preparing for trial, or facilitating settlement); *In re Carey*, 89 S.W.3d 477 (Mo. 2002) (en banc) (lawyers who billed Chrysler over 500 hours on products liability and consumer fraud matters and later formed a new law firm that took on plaintiffs in a national products liability class action against Chrysler violated Model Rule 1.9 and were indefinitely suspended, with leave to reapply for admission after one year because: (1) the subsequent matters involved the same former client and the same type of case; (2) the lawyers deposed several of Chrysler's expert witnesses in the past; (3) the lawyers knew Chrysler's roadmap in defending and settling similar products liability cases; and (4) the lawyers had access to detailed confidential information about a government investigation that was the subject of the litigation).

70. *Guzewicz v. Eberle*, 953 F. Supp. 108 (E.D. Pa. 1997) (lawyer who was general counsel to corporations not disqualified in subsequent representation of minority shareholders against majority shareholders and corporations because corporations were nominal defendants); ABA Comm. on Ethics and Prof'l Responsibility, Formal Op. 99-415 (1999) (Representation Adverse to Organization by Former In-House Lawyer) ("[F]act that the lawyer had represented his former employer in similar types of matters or that the lawyer had gained a general knowledge of the strategies, policies, or personnel of the former employer is not sufficient by itself to establish a substantial relationship," but courts have diverged on the question; "whether the lawyer has protected information depends on the facts and circumstances of each particular case.").

What if we need to give antitrust advice to Lexington Hospital about buying up a rehab center in Collier County? Assume Jones gave Capitol antitrust advice regarding the same market.

Again, the analysis will turn on the substantial relationship. If Capitol can assert in good faith that the earlier advice is germane to the Lexington representation, your firm can't undertake the representation. GCs raise special problems. As you know, the general rule is that when a lawyer leaves a practice setting, the lawyer only takes with her the conflicts arising from the matters on which she worked and as to which she has confidential information. But the GC supervises all, so hiring Ms. Jones certainly arms Capitol with many arguments if it wants to create mischief.[71] Maybe you are better off turning Capitol into the centerpiece—with Ms. Jones—of the firm's healthcare practice.[72]

⅏ Imputation: The Lateral Hire

The trial's next week. And my best associate just told me she's leaving this Friday to go to work for those blankety-blank lawyers on the other side. I've lost my right arm. My left, too. Help!

The rules of professional conduct apply to all lawyers. Even associates. And Model Rule 1.16 provides that, without cause, a lawyer may only withdraw from a representation if it will not have an adverse effect on the client. Obviously, that is not the case here. Tell her she may only leave after the case is over.

But who wants her now? If she's already lined up a job, that means she's been talking to the other side for a while. What a turncoat.

You are right there. You were entitled, as was the client, to know about these employment discussions well before now.[73] In the words of an ABA

---

71. ABA Comm. on Ethics and Prof'l Responsibility, Formal Op. 99-415 (1999) (Representation Adverse to Organization by Former In-House Lawyer).

72. *E.g., Jamaica Pub. Serv. Co. v. AIU Ins. Co.*, 707 N.E.2d 414 (N.Y. 1998) (former inside counsel for insurer on Canadian professional liability insurance matters not disqualified in subsequent representation of insured against insurer in coverage dispute not involving same or similar matters); *Haagen-Dazs Co. v. Perche No! Gelato, Inc.*, 639 F. Supp. 282 (N.D. Cal. 1986) (former inside counsel/senior attorney disqualified based on substantial relationship and the unique role of "access to business thinking").

73. ABA Comm. on Ethics and Prof'l Responsibility, Formal Op. 96-400 (1996) (Job Negotiations with Adverse Firm or Party).

opinion, you were entitled to know "no later than the commencement of serious discussions with the new firm."[74] But that doesn't solve the present problem.

Correct. What do I do now?

In most jurisdictions, you may now move to disqualify the law firm on the other side.[75]

But my associate says she is being screened.

That may be so, but there is almost no authority for screening as a solution to side-switching, even in jurisdictions that otherwise recognize screens.[76] Your associate's representation of your client and the confidential information she possesses is imputed to her entire new law firm. That imputation rule says that if one lawyer in a firm is disqualified, then all lawyers are disqualified. So one thing seems reasonably certain. The trial may not be next week after all—that is, once your associate's new firm is barred from continuing the representation.

𝄪 Imputation: The Joint Defense

These multi-defendant cases seem appealing until you actually litigate them. All that shared responsibility. Committees for everything. Then you have to rely on a guy you don't think is all that impressive to make the argument for the group. Personally, I prefer playing one-on-one. Know what I mean?

---

74. ABA Comm. on Ethics and Prof'l Responsibility, Op. 99-414 (Ethical Obligations When a Lawyer Changes Firms).

75. *Kala v. Aluminum Smelting & Ref. Co.*, 688 N.E.2d 258 (Ohio 1998); *City Nat'l Bank v. Adams*, 117 Cal. Rptr. 2d 125 (Cal. Ct. App. 2002).

76. *Kala, supra* note 75. *See also Intelli-Check, Inc. v. Tricom Card Technologies*, 2008 U.S. Dist. Lexis 84435 (E.D.N.Y.) [screen upheld despite lateral lawyer's prior role two years earlier in same matter where motion to disqualify not timely made]; *Lucent Technologies Inc. v. Gateways, Inc.*, 2007 U.S. Dist. Lexis 35502 (S.D. Cal.) [firm disqualified because lateral lawyer worked personally on the same case]; *CSX Transp. Inc. v. Gilkison, Peirce, Raimond & Coulter, P.C.*, No. 5:05CV202, 2006 U.S. Dist LEXIS 81019 (N.D. W. Va. Nov. 3, 2006) (overlap in parties, potential witnesses, and facts and circumstances from which alleged physical injuries or lack thereof arose created substantial relationship and warrant disqualification which cannot be cured by screening); *In re: Gabapentin Patent Litigation*, 407 F. Supp. 2d 607 (D. N.J. 2005) [primary responsibility in same matter, screen not sufficient to prevent disqualification]; *Harvey v. Allstate Ins. Co.*, 2004 U.S. Dist. Lexis 30138 (W. D. Tenn.) [firm disqualified due to lateral's direct prior involvement in same case, which "can be justly regarded as a changing sides in the matter in question"].

We understand your dismay. And what you've identified is not the only downside to these joint defense cases.

What do you mean?

Well, you know better than we that the only way these arrangements work is if you enter into a joint defense agreement.

It protects information right?

Precisely. If lawyer for defendant A talks to lawyer for defendant B, absent a joint defense agreement, the conversation would not be privileged. Both lawyer for A and lawyer for B could be deposed about the conversation.

So we need an agreement, right?

The agreement does not create the joint defense privilege, which arises under the appropriate circumstances simply by operation of law,[77] but it does formalize it and gives the parties proof positive that when they started cooperating, they expected each party's lawyer to maintain confidentiality as to what was shared and raise the joint defense privilege if testimony were sought.

That's why it feels so much better entering into these arrangements, as much as I despair at the way those cases unfold.

Well, you do receive real protection, at least so long as the parties remain part of the agreement.

I thought the parties and their lawyers were bound by these agreements forever.

They are, but only as to the information shared up until the time any party decides to withdraw. As to that information, every party to the agreement must waive the privilege before any party can be permitted to disclose any information subject to the joint interest privilege.

We went off on a tangent, and you never described the other downside.

Right. This is a slight risk, but one that carries huge implications. You enter into a joint defense agreement. You operate under it enthusiastically, working together. Then, one of the law firm participants is disqualified from its representation.[78]

Too bad, but that's their problem.

---

77. RLGL § 76; *Hanover Ins. Co. v. Rapo & Jepsen Ins. Servs., Inc.*, 870 N.E.2d 1105 (Mass. 2007) (recognizing common interest doctrine of RLGL § 76 for separately represented defendants with joint defense agreements).

78. ABA Comm. on Ethics and Prof'l Responsibility, Formal Op. 95-395 (1995) (Obligations of a Lawyer who Formerly Represented a Client in Connection with a Joint Defense Consortium).

It could be yours, too, if the entity that was successful on the DQ motion can persuade a court that you learned its confidential information from its now-former lawyer. It's even possible every law firm that was part of a joint defense agreement could be disqualified. The risk may not be great, but these agreements do carry some downsides.[79]

Besides boredom.

ℳ Of Joint Defense Agreements, Prospective Waivers, and Screens

These darn conflicts rules. Sometimes it seems as if we can't go through a day without getting in trouble.

No one promised you it would be easy being a professional. But how proud would you be of your role as a lawyer if we weren't held to a higher standard?

I love the idea in the abstract. But serving the ethics committee of my firm makes me feel like we should rename it the "No Business Committee." We get in trouble even when we take precautions. Wait until you hear the latest.

We're all ears.

So here's the tale. We just merged with a small antitrust boutique. One less competitor. And we're handling four individual antitrust actions against the same software vendor, Silkysoft. When we did the merger, the new guys ran Silkysoft through their database. Nothing came up. They had represented an officer of Silkysoft, but they assured us that wouldn't create a problem.

Now we've been hit with a motion by Silkysoft to disqualify us from the four cases.

So there are some more facts you need to share.

You got it. Turns out our new partners represented this officer in a DOJ investigation regarding the same issues that arise in our four civil actions.

Uh oh!

---

79. *In re Gabapentin Patent Litig.*, 407 F. Supp. 2d 607 (D.N.J. 2005) (joint defense agreement created client-lawyer relationship between each defendant and each lawyer; one lawyer's new firm needed consent of each joint defendant to represent plaintiff in same matter); *Associated Wholesale Grocers, Inc. v. Americold Corp.*, 975 P.2d 231 (Kan. 1999) (lawyer who represented co-party under an agreement not disqualified where agreement provided for sharing of information but did not address use of confidential information and movant was unable to show that information was actually shared).

Why do you say that?

Because you can be disqualified by a non-client under certain circumstances. And this might just be one of them.[80]

That's what Silkysoft asserts. Our new partners represented the officer. But Silkysoft was also the object of DOJ's attention. Silkysoft and the officer entered into a joint defense agreement permitting them to share confidential information. And our new partners admit they did. But it still seems farfetched.

Not really. The case law is clear. A lawyer whose client is party to a joint interest may be disqualified by another party to the agreement if the lawyer learned confidential information of the non-client that could be used in the subsequent representation adverse to the non-client.[81] We always advise lawyers that this is one of the risks of entering into such agreements. But what we don't understand is why your new colleagues were so confident that you didn't have to worry about their prior representation of this Silkysoft officer.

You can be sure that was my first question after I learned the details of the DQ motion.

And what did they say?

They had two excuses.

Let's take them one at a time.

They had Silkysoft sign a waiver in the joint defense agreement. They agreed to waive any conflict that might arise out of the sharing of information under the agreement.

No limit as to time?

None.

No limit as to who the adverse party might be?

Only the identity of the law firms; not who their clients might be.

No limit as to the nature of the adverse matter?

None. Isn't that perfect?

Well, actually all of that renders the prospective waiver far less likely to be enforceable.[82]

---

80. RLGL § 132, cmt. g(ii).

81. *Wilson P. Abraham Constr. Corp. v. Armco Steel Corp.*, 559 F.2d 250 (5th Cir. 1977) (lawyer who represented co-defendant in prior criminal investigation disqualified to protect non-client's shared confidences in joint defense arrangement); *Analytica, Inc. v. NPD Research, Inc.*, 708 F.2d 1263 (7th Cir. 1983) (law firm disqualified where co-counsel relationship gave it access to potentially relevant confidential data).

82. MODEL RULE 1.7, cmt. [22]; RLGL § 122, cmt. d.

But Silkysoft is so sophisticated.

Sophisticated perhaps, but not clairvoyant. While some observers of the ethics scene believe a sophisticated client can somehow give informed consent to an unknown conflict, the courts have not been so tolerant of their use, striking them down as too open-ended or unlimited as to time to be the equivalent of informed consent, even for corporate clients.[83] So we doubt that argument will save you from disqualification.

Well, there is one more reason they told us not to worry.

Let's hope this one is better.

They assumed that if a problem ever arose, our firm would simply screen our new partners. One of those, how you call'em, ethical walls.

Did you screen these lawyers when they came over?

Of course not. We were told it was no problem. But we screened them when the motion to disqualify was filed. Right away.

That may be a real problem. Courts, in situations in which they endorse screens, require they be timely erected, which means right away.[84]

Well, we didn't do that. Do we still have an argument?

Very interesting. These lawyers—your new best friends—were intimately involved with the earlier matter. The rules of more than thirty jurisdictions do not permit involuntary screens to be erected to cure imputation to the entire firm of transferring-in lawyers' conflicts of interest.[85] And another ten only permit them when involvement was quite limited and the confidential information to be protected was not material.[86] That is not the case here.

So we are going to be disqualified because of the relationship between lawyers who were not even here at the time and some folks who were not even their clients?

Just remember, as the court observed in a very similar situation, though disqualification is not to be favored, "The paramount concern, though,

---

83. *E.g., All American Semiconductor, Inc. v. Hynix Semiconductor, Inc.*, Case No C 07-1200, 2008 U.S. Dist. LEXIS 106619 (N.D. Cal. Dec. 18, 2008), *affirmed*, 2009 U.S. Dist. LEXIS 12315 (because conflict which developed was not specifically mentioned in advance waiver, law firm subsequently disqualified despite screen).

84. MODEL RULE 1.0(k) and cmt. [10]; RLGL § 124, cmt. d(iii); *LaSalle Nat'l Bank v. Lake County*, 703 F.2d 252 (7th Cir. 1983) (court applied substantial relationship test to disqualify former government lawyer's firm where screen not timely established).

85. MODEL RULE 1.10, RLGL § 124.

86. *E.g.*, Mass. Rule 1.10, Minn. Rule 1.10.

must be the preservation of public trust in the scrupulous administration of justice and the integrity of the bar."[87]

※ The Joy of Screening

I've heard about screening. Is that just a made-up idea?

Not at all. Screens originated as a condition of client consent to a conflict, which is, of course, the client's prerogative.[88] Today, the rules of all jurisdictions further permit the screening, without client consent, of government lawyers who leave public service.[89] Those lawyers are barred from being involved in any matter in which they were substantially and personally involved, but their new firms can handle such matters if they screen the former government lawyer from any participation in the matter. This special rule was adopted to encourage lawyers to undertake government service and not render these individuals unemployable by the very firms most likely to want to have them because those firms deal regularly with those agencies.[90]

A similar exception for screening—without client consent—involves judges, arbitrators, and mediators who join a firm.[91] The fact that the judge, arbitrator, or mediator presided over a matter does not prohibit the firm from taking a substantially related matter so long as the judge, arbitrator, or mediator is screened from the matter.[92]

And the last exception for screening without client consent involves prospective clients, but only if the lawyer took reasonable steps to avoid learning any more information than necessary to do a conflicts check.[93]

---

87. *All American Semiconductor, supra* note 83, at 14–15.

88. MODEL RULES 1.9, 1.10; RLGL § 122.

89. MODEL RULE 1.11; RLGL § 124(3).

90. MODEL RULE 1.11, Comment [4].

91. MODEL RULE 1.12.

92. *E.g., Monument Builders of Pa., Inc. v. Catholic Cemeteries Ass'n,* 190 F.R.D. 164 (E.D. Pa. 1999) (allowing screening of former judicial clerk).

93. MODEL RULE 1.18(d); RLGL § 15; *Poly Software Int'l Inc. v. Su,* 880 F. Supp. 1487 (D. Utah 1995). New York adds another requirement: that "a reasonable lawyer would conclude that the law firm will be able to provide competent and diligent representation in the matter." N.Y. Rule 1.18(d)(3).

What is a screen?

A great question. The word "screen" is used casually, but rarely are the requirements for an "effective" screen the subject of serious consideration. A screen should keep the individual with confidential information away from anyone on the other side of the screen. That really means the integrity of everyone involved is the only real safeguard for confidential information. Beyond that, a screen might include memos reminding all lawyers of its existence, legending files to limit access, and establishing computer firewalls regarding these same matters. But those efforts are much more form than substance; substance comes from being able to trust everyone involved not to learn what the screened lawyers know.[94]

How come I hear people talk about screens so often?

Because oftentimes law firms, in order to induce a client or former client to consent to a conflicting representation, will offer to screen the lawyers working for the client from the lawyers working on the matter that created the conflict. These are voluntary screens.[95] The client knows the nature of the matter and the identity of the lawyers involved and is totally free to make a case-by-case decision whether this screen is likely to be effective and whether its likelihood of effectiveness is enough incentive to cause the client to consent. Compare that with a rule, adopted in some jurisdictions, which would simply inform the affected client that a conflict has arisen but that the problem has been solved by the institution of a screen.[96] Although complying with such a rule will avoid discipline, courts may nevertheless decide to disqualify the firm. This is why former client consent to screens is always the best response.

𝍖 Involuntary Screens

I am a wreck. As general counsel of my company I retained Caldwell & Moore to handle this really important negotiation for us. It's a potential acquisition of a competitor. This is huge. The partner, Sam Lane, put the day-to-day responsibility in the hands of one of his young partners, Sarah Cromwell. Turns out she was really a contract partner. That is, she was. She left Caldwell & Moore a week ago.

---

94. MODEL RULES 1.0 (k), 1.11(b), (c), 1.12(c), 1.18(d).

95. *E.g.,* MODEL RULE 1.10; N.Y. Rule 1.10.

96. *E.g.,* Pa. Rule 1.10(b); Or. Rule 1.10(c).

Sam is putting on a brave face, but I can tell how upset, how at sea he is. Like he lost his right arm.

She should never have quit. Didn't she realize you can't just leave a client in the lurch. Rule 1.16 demands no less. Younger lawyers may not think this way, but the fact that they are supervised by senior lawyers does not mean the withdrawal rule doesn't apply to them.

Well, you've identified one problem. But there's a bigger one.

How's that?

Sarah went to work for our competitor's law firm. The S.O.B.'s that have been giving us such a hard time. And you know how we found out?

Sarah called you?

Not at all. The other law firm sent me a letter telling us Sarah was being screened. Just like that. No request that we approve a screen. I thought if she went to work for the other side, that firm would be disqualified unless my client consented. That's the way it has always been since I became General Counsel here.

That is correct. Sarah switches sides. Her conflicts get imputed to her new firm. If the new firm wants to avoid the conflict, you get a call, you know what Sara knows, Sara's integrity, and the character of her new firm. You consider those and you get to decide. Complete client autonomy.

So what's with this announcement I received?

Well, several jurisdictions have adopted a rule that allows screening of any lawyer without client consent, and the American Bar Association just changed Rule 1.10—dramatically.[97] If a lawyer leaves a firm and goes to work for the opposing team, there is no imputation. The lateral moving lawyer can be screened whether the former client likes it . . . or not, as long as appropriate written notice is given.

That's what I thought. I told my client that Sarah would be screened. My client's CEO asked what does that mean. So I told him about screens.

And what did he say?

He went berserk. "How do we know," he asked. " She's the one who told me the competitor's law firm was not trustworthy, that we had to get it all in writing. And now I'm supposed to feel all warm and fuzzy about Sara working for those sleazy lawyers. Outrageous!" How can I calm my client down?

Why bother? Your client is right. This is the biggest assault on client loyalty since the ABA approved suing your client's subsidiary. However, we do have

---

97. 25 LAW. MAN. PROF. CONDUCT (ABA/BNA 2009).

several suggestions to protect your client. First, consider which jurisdiction's rules govern this screen.[98] Many do not allow involuntary screens without the former client's consent, and some allow it, but only for lawyers whose involvement was minimal.

So we could file a disciplinary complaint?

Yes, but you also could seek disqualification, if you're in litigation, or if not, injunctive relief to prevent Sarah's new firm from continuing with the matter.[99] The same remedies would be available to your client if the screening itself is defective. Consider, for example, the content of Sarah's notice. Did it include a description of the screening procedures? Did it state that Sarah will receive no part of the fee in the matter? Did it affirm that Sarah and her new firm had complied with all of these requirements? Did it give your client notice that review may be available from a tribunal? Did Sarah's new firm agree to respond to any inquires by Sarah's former client?[100] If not, the screen may not in fact be adequate, and if not adequate, the only other ground to screen is your client's consent.[101]

⚅ The Ethics of Mediation

Are we ever in trouble. With our biggest client. Public Service Illuminating. We fell prey to this alternative dispute resolution stuff. The advocates of ADR told us how happy it would make our clients. So we convinced the Light Company, that's what we call them, to mediate its endless disputes with the gas company over the annual renewal for the Second Bay plant. That's what we did last year. Mediated away. You ask me, it took longer than trying the case, but it was all very polite. Retired Judge Jamison—he's now of counsel at Berry & Berry— presided. And on the fifth day, we got a settlement for 2005. But now its 2006,

---

98. MODEL RULE 8.5.

99. *Maritrans GP Inc. v. Pepper, Hamilton & Scheetz*, 602 A.2d 1277 (Pa. 1992) (law firm enjoined from representing client's competitors because of threatened breach of fiduciary).

100. *Norfolk Southern Railway Co., v. Reading Blue Mountain & Northern Co.*, 397 F. Supp. 2d 551 (M.D. PA. 2005) (Firm whose disqualification is sought bears the burden of demonstrating compliance with screening provisions of applicable rule, including former client is assured that the principle of loyalty is not compromised by side-switching. To be effective, screens must be timely, prohibit discussion of the matter, restrict circulation of documents and access to files, and evidence a strong firm policy against breach, including sanctions, physical and/or geographic separation and assurances that screened lawyer will receive no part of the fee from the screened matter.)

101. MODEL RULE 1.10(c); RLGL § 123.

and before we get around to deciding whether to mediate again, the Light Company gets sued by the gas company. If that weren't bad enough, guess who's representing the gas company? Berry & Berry. You can imagine how our client feels. Judge Jamison promised us confidentiality. Lord knows what all they told him in our caucuses. And now his firm is suing us. How can we let this clear conflict of interest continue, our client wants to know. I have the same question.

We guess your state has adopted amended Model Rule 1.12. That rule permits law firms to take on matters from which the firm would otherwise be disqualified by the firm's employment of a former judge, arbitrator, or mediator so long as the former neutral is screened from participation in the matter. Formerly, the rule applied to judges and arbitrators, but not mediators. When the ABA amended the rules, the mediation community asked that the rule be amended to include mediators. The goal was to encourage practicing lawyers to also act as mediators without significant conflict of interest concerns.[102]

But mediators are different. Judges and arbitrators rarely learn confidential information. They never meet with parties ex parte. They never gain access to your client's innermost secrets on a pledge that they will never reveal them.

That is true. But those arguments did not carry the day (although not all courts agree).[103] And now your client is justifiably upset. It must rely on Judge Jamison's pledge that he is screened and won't share the Light Company's secrets with his colleagues; but given the dubious reputation of Berry & Berry (why the good judge went there escapes us), we can understand their dismay. The only way around this little difficulty is to privately order more protection than the rule allows when you hire a mediator the next time.

If there is a next time!

---

102. *See, e.g.,* Carrie Menkel-Meadow, *The Lawyer as Consensus Builder: Ethics for a New Practice,* 70 TENN. L. REV. 63 (2002).

103. *E.g., Matluck v. Matluck,* 825 So. 2d 1071 (Fla. Dist. Ct. App. 2002) (law firm whose lawyer acted as mediator for the parties in the same action disqualified from subsequently representing one of the parties, in order to preserve the confidences of parties to the mediation and to protect the integrity of the mediation process itself); *Poly Software Int'l Inc. v. Su,* 880 F. Supp. 1487 (D. Utah 1995) (screen not allowed in a subsequent matter substantially related to prior mediation).

EIGHT

Limits of the Law

"Do you think now that we're doing fewer illegal things
we can scale back the legal department?"

🕮 Introduction: When You Must Say "No"

UP TO THIS POINT, we have examined the contours of fiduciary duty, or the Five C's: control, communication, competence, confidentiality, and conflict of interest resolution. Put another way, we have been exploring what it means to say "yes" to your clients.

At the same time, every agency relationship is subject to one significant limitation: neither your client's power of control nor your obligation of loyalty allows either of you to violate the limits or bounds of the law.[1] Both of you remain responsible for the consequences of your conduct as autonomous legal persons.[2] We explore these legal limits in this chapter—when you must say "no" to clients. This is not an unfamiliar role, as lawyers have always been in the business of advising clients to avoid illegality.[3]

The limits of the law include several familiar bodies of law, such as crime, fraud, and procedural rules, which are explicitly incorporated into lawyer code provisions. This extends the reach of general law into the scope of professional discipline. As a result, lawyers can face legal and equitable remedies, such as procedural sanctions, civil and criminal accountability, and equitable relief, as well as professional discipline for the same conduct.

🕮 Supervisory and Subordinate Lawyers

It just doesn't seem right. I was asked to supervise a document production. The search yielded a few unfortunate e-mails, to say nothing of a memorandum written by the CFO. I brought the offending documents to the attention of the partner in charge. He tells me that I'll have to produce the e-mails, but I can withhold the memo on the ground of privilege. I agreed, but as I started thinking about it, I wondered how could that memo be privileged? I got up enough nerve to ask, and the partner replied that responsibility for making such determinations is why he is paid the big bucks. No reasoning, but he did take responsibility.

---

1. MODEL RULE 1.2(d); RLGL § 23(1).

2. RESTATEMENT (THIRD) OF AGENCY §1.01 cmt. f(1) (Tentative Draft No. 2, 2001).

3. MODEL RULES 1.2(d), 2.1; RLGL § 94. Former ABA President Elihu Root famously said: "About half the practice of a decent lawyer consists in telling would-be clients that they are damn fools and should stop." PHILIP C. JESSUP, 1 ELIHU ROOT 133 (1930).

TABLE 4 Sources of Legal Limits and Corresponding Model Rules

Law	Legal Penalties	Corresponding Model Rule(s)(Professional Discipline)
Crime (Approx. 4000 Federal and 1000 State provisions)	Fines, imprisonment	1.2(d), 8.4(b)
Tort (e.g., fraud)	Damages, Loss of a Contractual Bargain	1.2(d), 3.3, 4.1, 8.4(c)
Evidence (privileges)	Contempt, Sanctions	3.4
Court Orders (inherent power of the court)	Disqualification, injunctive relief, court-ordered counsel	3.4(c)
Procedural Rules (e.g., Fed. R. Civ. P. 11, 26, 37, 60)	Sanctions, injunctive relief	3.1, 3.4
ADR Rules (arbitration or mediation codes or procedures)	Disqualification	1.12, 2.4
Administrative Regulations (e.g., Sarbanes Oxley)	Disbarment	1.6(b)(6), 1.13
Federal and State Conflict-of-Interest Provisions	Criminal penalties	1.11, 1.12

Can you simply leave the decision to the partner? Let's hope not. You are a lawyer, albeit one of lower rank in your firm. But that does not absolve you of responsibility. You may accept a decision with which you disagree from a supervising lawyer if it is a reasonable resolution of an arguable question.[4] For example, you might think it is not privileged because a copy was sent to a third party; but the partner might assert that the client can claim the third party was an agent for the purpose of the representation, and therefore, sending the copy to that individual did not break the privilege.[5] But here, it sounds like there is no arguable point. And if that is your view, then this is one of those occasions when you must seek further consultation. Perhaps you should consult someone in your practice setting. Does your firm have a designated ethics counsel or an ombudsman with whom you could chat? Whatever the possibilities, this is no time to resolve the question yourself, even if it means going outside your firm to counsel with a former professor or a lawyer who specializes in advising lawyers.

---

4. MODEL RULE 5.2; RLGL § 12.

5. MODEL RULE 3.4(d); RLGL §§ 70, cmt. e & 105.

Partners, it is true, are more experienced. They also might have a different perspective. But pressures from the client may distort that perspective. Even the most objective of lawyers sometimes succumb to these forces. And partners don't have a monopoly on wisdom. So as difficult as it may be, you must now take responsibility.[6]

✀ Withdrawal: Non-payment

I've sent out three reminders. Received one promise from the CFO and another from the CEO that we'll be paid promptly. Yet they're 120 days past due, and as we gear up for next month's trial, I know the meter will be running faster and faster. I say we cut our losses and send them a letter of withdrawal.

Do you have grounds?

Of course we do. They haven't paid us for four months. What more do we need?

You need to comply with Rule 1.16.

Doesn't it permit lawyers to fire deadbeats?

Not exactly. It provides that you may withdraw if the client fails to fulfill an obligation of the representation, but only if you have given the client reasonable warning that you will withdraw.[7]

Surely that's what this is. We sent our bills. They're not paid. There you go.

Not so fast. Many lawyers have relied on that language to claim an entitlement to withdraw when the receivables start smelling like aged Gouda. But the courts do not always buy the argument.[8] Consistent with another provision of the rule, they also refuse to allow lawyers to withdraw for no reason at all unless the withdrawal "can be accomplished without material adverse effect on the interests of the client."[9] Some courts have concluded that failure to pay can be considered an unfilled obligation of the representation

---

6. *E.g., Daniels v. Alander,* 844 A.2d 182 (Conn. 2004) (associate who failed to correct supervisory lawyer's false statement to a court made when associate was present reprimanded), *People v. Casey,* 948 P.2d 1014 (Colo. 1997) (associate who failed to correct client's lie to the court subject to discipline despite consulting with senior lawyer because duty not "arguable.").

7. MODEL RULE 1.16(b)(5); RLGL § 32(3)(g).

8. *E.g., Gilles v. Wiley, Malehorn & Sirota,* 783 A.2d 756 (N.J. Super. Ct. App. Div. 2001).

9. MODEL RULE 1.16(b)(1); RLGL § 32(3)(a).

within the meaning of the rule only if the retainer letter so states.[10] What's yours say?

I don't think it says that. But it does set forth the hourly rates, and it states that bills are due upon presentation.

Then you might add a clause in the future that explicitly states that failure to pay invoices when they come due will constitute a failure to fulfill an obligation of the representation and will provide you grounds for withdrawal. That should solve your first problem, but not your second.

I have a second problem?

You certainly do. Rule 1.16(c) provides that, even if you have grounds for withdrawal (as you might here and certainly would under your new improved retainer letter), you still must get the permission of the court to withdraw, hardly a certain proposition here.[11]

But Judge Jones was a private lawyer. He wouldn't want to see us go further into the hole.

If we're talking about the same Judge Jones, he might recognize your plight, but we also know what a stickler he is for moving cases and protecting his docket. So don't be surprised if he doesn't permit you to withdraw from a case where trial is imminent. Oh, and one more thing.

What could that be?

Your problems with your client are confidential. You should do everything in your power to get the issue of your withdrawal decided by Judge Jones without sharing your client's bad habits with the other side. Try filing ex parte or couching your publicly stated grounds for withdrawal in the most general terms.[12]

Withdrawal: Time to Leave

You instructed me well. I am free, you said, to counsel my clients on non-legal issues. This client manufactures baby food. As you would expect, the FDA requires dating of the product. Past the date on the label, it cannot be sold, and that is the case for a warehouse full of mashed carrots, strained green beans, whatever. Then the CEO got this great idea. We'll sell it in Africa where they don't

---

10. *E.g., Kriegsman v. Kriegsman*, 375 A.2d 1253 (N.J. Super. Ct. App. Div. 1977).

11. MODEL RULE 1.16(c); RLGL § 32(5).

12. MODEL RULE 1.6(b)(5), cmt. [14]; RLGL § 65, cmt. d.

have such laws, he announced. A "humanitarian" gesture that will turn a disaster into a huge profit. I advised them not to do it. The gain is not worth the discomfort of foisting stale food on the poor of our most impoverished continent. To say nothing of the possible bad publicity. The CEO turned to me and reminded me he got his sermons at St. Clements. Was it illegal? It wasn't, and I told him so. But I think its time for me to resign. Can I do it?

You're certainly not required to. Rule 1.16(a) tells lawyers when such drastic action is required. That is not the case here. The sale is not illegal, and you're not participating in it anyway.[13] But Rule 1.16(b) tells you when you may withdraw, even if doing so would have an adverse effect on the client. One of the grounds is when the client pursues a course of conduct that you find repugnant. That is certainly your present view and, we might add, for good reason.

❦ Inside Counsel Whistleblowers

I'm inside counsel to a bank. Management hates the banking department's community lending requirements. "We're a bank, not a charity," the CEO complains. As a result, it's my view that their required disclosures to bank regulators vastly overstate what they're doing. I've argued with management to no avail, and I'm tired of their cover-ups. Yesterday, I threatened to disclose to the regulators unless they changed their policy. Today, I was escorted out of my office and fired. Can I sue for wrongful discharge and bring out all the facts?

The only answer we can give you is that it depends on where you are located. The general proposition is that a client can fire a lawyer at any time for any reason, for no reason, or for the entirely wrong reason, and the lawyer has no recourse. The question is whether that doctrine gets modified when the lawyer is a full-time employee of the organization in a situation in which non-lawyer employees are free to bring wrongful discharge suits. Are the lawyers considered to be lawyers first or employees first? Some states have allowed a claim,[14] others have not.[15] And most haven't decided.

---

13. MODEL RULE 1.2(d); RLGL § 94.

14. *E.g., Tartaglia v. UBS Paine Webber, Inc.*, No. A-107/108-06, 2008 N.J. LEXIS 1797 (N.J. Dec. 16, 2008); *Crews v. Buckman Labs. Int'l, Inc.*, 78 S.W.3d 852 (Tenn. 2002).

15. *E.g., Balla v. Gambro, Inc.*, 584 N.E.2d 104 (Ill. 1991).

If you are free to bring such a suit, you would be free to use the confidential information you learned about the community development laws in the litigation. But you would also be required to maintain the confidentiality of the information, nonetheless, to the greatest extent possible by filing your complaint under seal and otherwise seeking protective orders to keep the ugly dispute from the prying eyes of your former client's regulators.[16]

✵ Crimes

We represent a meat-processing plant. They asked us to audit their immigration compliance, and we found massive numbers of undocumented workers. I suspect they even recruit them in Guatemala. Now they want us to represent them in negotiations with the INS. What should we do?

Depends on what they are asking you to do. Clients in trouble, clients who might have committed crimes in the past, are entitled to representation.[17] So embrace the opportunity to negotiate with the INS. Just keep in mind the limits you must respect.

I thought you were big proponents of zealous representation.

We certainly are. And you can bring all the zeal you can muster to the enterprise. Just make sure of a couple of principles. You don't want to do anything that can be viewed as aiding and abetting an ongoing criminal operation. So it's fine to defend past conduct, but once it continues along with your representation, you cannot counsel or assist.[18] In other words, tell them to desist, or you will withdraw.[19]

Nor do you want to make any false or misleading statements to the INS. In this context, your obligations under Rule 3.3 or 3.9 are not triggered. The INS is not acting as a tribunal. But the INS is a third party, and under Rule 4.1, you certainly are obliged to avoid making any misrepresentations. This means there may be many questions you cannot answer.

---

16. ABA Comm. on Ethics and Prof'l Responsibility, Formal Op. 01-424 (2004) (A Former In-House Lawyer May Pursue a Wrongful Discharge Claim Against Her Former Employer and Client As Long As Client Information Is Protected).

17. MODEL RULE 1.6, cmt. [8]; RLGL § 67, cmt. b.

18. MODEL RULE 1.2(d); RLGL § 94.

19. MODEL RULE 1.16(a); RLGL § 32(2)(a).

𝕸 Politics? Greasing the Way

What a quandary. Our client, the Illuminating Company, does a lot of business with the Commonwealth of Virginia. Means lobbyists galore, bundling political contributions. You get the idea. Now there's a big tribute dinner to fund the next campaign. They say if they can buy two tables, they are sure their application for a new facility will be looked upon with favor. But the company has maxed out. So they want our firm to buy a table. Ten thousand bucks. For the Local People's Party. We would certainly earn the undying affection of Illuminating.

Clients lean on lawyers all the time. Chamber of Commerce dinners, Boys Club testimonials honoring the CEO, galas for the orchestra. And lawyers certainly succumb to client imprecations. They have no choice. But here, the question is the legality of the "contribution." If Illuminating were reimbursing you for the cost ("charge us what you wish"), it would be illegal, probably criminal.[20] If the contribution were a bribe, a quid pro quo, that too would be criminal. And lawyers may not engage in criminal conduct.[21] On the other hand, simply currying the favor of politicians is an ancient and hoary American tradition. Your assignment is to spend a little time assuring yourself that your firm's ten grand is the latter, not the former. If not, you'll have to find a different excuse for not succumbing to your client's urgent pleas.

𝕸 The Ponzi Scheme

The other lawyer's client. What a crook. I mean that literally. The guy is running a Ponzi scheme. All my client wants is his money back. Can we threaten that we'll report the client to the U.S. Attorney unless we're paid in ten days? Maybe that'll get their undivided attention.

---

20. *Fla. Bar v. Brown*, 790 So. 2d 1081 (Fla. 2001) (lawyer suspended ninety days for assisting client in violating campaign finance laws).

21. *Disciplinary Counsel v. Conese*, 812 N.E.2d 944 (Ohio 2004) (lawyer Board of Elections member who threatened to fire a Board of Elections employee unless the employee agreed to contribute one hundred percent of his salary to the county Democratic party convicted of misdemeanor and suspended for two years); *In re Convery*, 765 A.2d 724 (N.J. 2001) (lawyer who pled guilty to a federal misdemeanor of promising employment in return for political activity, when he was discovered to have used his local political position and influence to pressure a local zoning board to grant a variance for his client, suspended for six months).

That you can do. The old Model Code prohibited it.[22] But when the Model Rules were adopted, that provision was dropped. So long as the threat of criminal prosecution relates to the underlying civil claim, and does not constitute extortion, you are free to threaten away.[23] Of course, you had better have a good faith basis for the allegation. And make sure you direct publication of your complaint to the authorities. No courthouse press conferences. You don't want to buy a libel or slander counterclaim.

🕮 Lawyer Fraud: The Tester

My client wants me to send one of my paralegals into the Burger Chef commissary posing as a food writer to see if they are using beef tallow to flavor the fries. What a great idea.

Not so fast. A lawyer may not engage in a misrepresentation.[24] Nor may a lawyer do, through the acts of another, what the lawyer is prohibited from doing herself.[25] As much as some may claim that only good can come from such undercover inspections (somehow, your view depends on whether you are the tester or the testee), lawyers run afoul of these rules if they send their paralegals into the plant.[26] The interesting question is whether the client is

---

22. MODEL CODE OF PROF'L RESPONSIBILITY DR 7-105 (1983).

23. ABA Comm. on Ethics and Prof'l Responsibility, Formal Op. 92-363 (1992) (Use of Threats of Prosecution in Connection With a Civil Matter); ABA Comm. on Ethics and Prof'l Responsibility, Formal Op. 94-383 (1994) (Use of Threatened Disciplinary Complaint Against Opposing Counsel) (threatening disciplinary complaint against opposing counsel to gain advantage in a civil case may not be done where the lawyer is otherwise obligated to report misconduct, and is improper if unrelated to civil claim or not well founded in fact or law).

24. MODEL RULES 4.1(a), 8.4(c); RLGL § 98. *E.g., Siegel v. Williams*, 818 N.E.2d 510 (Ind. Ct. App. 2004) (lawyer who told former client who sued him for legal malpractice that he had only $25,000 to settle the claim because his wife had gotten all of his money in a divorce and who stated that if the jury awarded more than $25,000 he would declare bankruptcy committed fraud; expert testimony about jury value of case admissible to show damages); *In re Pautler*, 47 P.3d 1175 (Colo. 2002) (prosecutor who impersonated a public defender over the telephone in order to get a suspect to surrender to law enforcement officers violated Model Rules 8.4 and 4.3. The suspect later refused to trust anyone in the public defender's office, appeared pro se, was convicted of the murders, and given the death penalty); *In re Gatti*, 8 P.3d 966 (Or. 2000) (lawyer who falsely represented himself as a medical professional to gain information publicly reprimanded).

25. MODEL RULES 5.3, 8.4(a).

26. *In re Pyle*, 156 P.3d 1231 (Kan. 2007) (lawyer disciplined for violating Rule 4.2 by drafting affidavit and encouraging client to give it directly to opposing party); *In re Ositis*, 40 P.3d 500

free to undertake such conduct. If it is not unlawful for the client, then the question arises whether and to what extent, beyond telling the client of the possibility,[27] the lawyer may participate in the enterprise. It should be noted that there is nothing wrong with a lawyer engaging in surveillance in a public place.[28] It is the misrepresentation of the identity and purpose of the operation that runs afoul of Model Rules 4.1 and 8.4(c).

⅋ Mediation Candor

We're in a mediation. The mediator has decided to let each side strut its best stuff to the other. Venting, she calls it, and claims it's cathartic. And she insists that the principals of the warring companies take the lead. Enough of lawyer talk, she declaims. So my CEO goes first. Uses a Power Point. Not doing a bad job, when out of the blue, he asserts that we've lined up a world-renowned engineering firm as our expert. At a break, I take him aside and ask him what the hell he's doing. He assures me we could get that firm if we needed to. And he's certainly not going to correct the record—to the mediator or to the other side. Is this one of those candor-to-the-tribunal deals where I have to disclose this lie to the mediator?

Certainly not for that reason. Rule 3.3's duty of candor only applies to actual adjudications. Courts, of course. Arbitrations as well. And court-annexed mediations. But private mediation is simply viewed as a very sophisticated form of negotiation. So Rule 3.3 doesn't apply. Rule 4.1 does. That rule addresses a lawyer's duty to be truthful to third parties. You did not make the statement. Nor do you have to reveal the lie, unless your continuing to represent the client in any iteration of the mediation process would constitute aiding and abetting client fraud.[29] It's unlikely in our view that

---

(Or. 2002) (lawyer who suggested line of inquiry for private investigator to use in posing as a reporter to interview client's neighbor and potential adversary publicly reprimanded for having made misrepresentations through the act of another).

27. *Fair Employment Council of Greater Washington, Inc. v. BMC Mktg. Corp.*, 28 F.3d 1268 (D.C. Cir. 1994) (tester-plaintiffs asserting racial discrimination against an employment agency had no standing to seek relief because they deceived the agency about their intentions and their credentials).

28. *Apple Corps Ltd. v. Int'l Collectors Soc'y*, 15 F. Supp. 2d 456 (D.N.J. 1998) (contact with sales representatives by lawyer's undercover investigators to detect violations of consent decree proper); *Gidatex v. Campaniello Imports, Ltd.*, 82 F. Supp. 2d 119 (S.D.N.Y. 1999).

29. MODEL RULES 1.2(d), 4.1(b); RLGL § 98.

that's what this is. We hope no one's relying on your client's boasting about the strength of the company's case to decide whether to settle. So your participation in further negotiations hardly constitutes aiding and abetting. Of course, you'd better hope your client is right that, if the case doesn't settle, you really can hire the engineering firm your client disclosed to the assembled group.

My real worry is that the other side has already hired them.

🖎 Negotiation Ethics

Representing companies, we're always in negotiation. Selling property. Employment agreements. New borrowings. What have you. You know how these things go. Back and forth. Conversations with the other side's lawyer. Meetings between clients and lawyer. Phone calls. E-mails. Faxes. It's endless.

That's what I get paid for. And I'm good. What worries me is when mistakes are made. By our side. When do we have to correct? When can we leave well enough alone?

Let's start first from principles, not rules, of good, ethical lawyering. Any misstatement of fact by lawyer or client has the potential for causing mischief. It might not be deemed a misrepresentation.[30] And the other side may not have relied on it. But if it is recognized before the deal is signed or the transaction closes, there are excellent reasons the record should be corrected. For if the other side is disgruntled with the deal and discovers the error later, the risk that the mistake will form the basis for some claims is very high. So regardless of duty, the conscientious lawyer will at least suggest that for good business reasons it pays to make full disclosure up front.

I take your wise counsel. But what's the law, what do the rules require?

Let's take 'em one at a time. Suppose you tell the other side the property's zoned commercial. That's what your client told you. But you then learn it's still residential. You ask your client to correct the record, but she refuses. Says it'll kill the deal. What must you do?

You must consult Rule 4.1. You certainly did not violate Rule 4.1(a) when you spoke. Your misstatement was made totally unknowingly. But your subsequent failure to correct what you now know to be a misstatement of

---

30. RESTATEMENT (SECOND) OF CONTRACTS, § 159 ff; RESTATEMENT (SECOND) OF TORTS § 525 ff.

material fact probably fits within the tort of misrepresentation, which means that your failure to correct the previous misstatement violates Rule 8.4(c).[31] Disclosure, being required by (tort) law, also creates an exception to client confidentiality under Rule 1.6(b)(6).

Now suppose the same facts. What if my client makes the statement about zoning in my presence? It turns out my client was wrong, but she didn't know it at the time. I recommend the client correct and she refuses.

If the client makes the disclosure, you are in a different position. You have not yet misspoken, but your client has the same obligation to correct her misstatement that you did. For you, this inquiry is governed by Rule 4.1(b). It requires you to ask many questions. The first is whether your failure to correct the misstatement is essential to avoiding assisting a criminal or fraudulent act by the client. That in turn requires an inquiry into whether your client was simply mistakenly or affirmatively misled you. But it also requires a determination whether, even if your client knew she was supplying you with misinformation, the conduct is fraudulent—a question which then requires you to be familiar with the law of fraud. Did your client intend for the other side to rely on the misstatement? And even if the client did, was it reasonable for the other side to rely on that statement. Wouldn't a reasonable purchaser, particularly of commercial property, check on the applicable zoning? Of course, by now you recognize that it is likely only after the fact that definitive answers to some of these questions will be forthcoming. Which might lead you to the view that you should disclose.

But that conclusion does not end the matter either. Rule 4.1(b)'s obligations to disclose to avoid assisting a criminal or fraudulent act by the client can only be evaluated in light of the applicable version of Rule 1.6 in your jurisdiction. If that rule, like the Model Rule, permits disclosure to prevent, rectify, or mitigate a fraud in which the lawyer's services have been used, then you must disclose. But if your jurisdiction prohibits disclosure with respect to client fraud, then you would be barred from making any disclosure, absent client consent. Back to remonstrating.

And if my client won't allow me to speak?

Even if you don't disclose, you are certainly required to withdraw from the representation, even if the closing is scheduled for the day after you learn of

---

31. RLGL § 98, cmt. d; ABA Comm. on Ethics and Prof'l Responsibility, Formal Op. 92-366 (1992) (Withdrawal When a Lawyer's Services Will Otherwise be Used to Perpetrate a Fraud).

the error.[32] And if the other side draws some inference from the fact that you are no longer on the scene, that is an acceptable result so long as all you disclose is the withdrawal itself.

For example, suppose your client intentionally tells the other side the wrong information. It's the only way we'll get our price, he announces. You hit the ceiling, demand a correction, but your client refuses and reminds you what you said regarding confidentiality.

Here, the client fraud is clear. The misstatement is not only intentional but is designed to be relied upon by the other side. If the other side finds out, it will back out of the deal. After unsuccessful remonstration, you must withdraw from the representation.

🕮 Healthy Skepticism

We represent the general partner of a whole string of limited partnerships. All based offshore. We work with Cayman Islands counsel on some. Isle of Man on others. Keeping them offshore is a tax dodge, but one that is perfectly legal. An affiliate of GP buys real estate—mostly apartments—then packages them into these investment vehicles. Bills paid on time. Work for our tax guys, real estate guys, corporate guys. I'm a hero around here. Except one thing.

What's that?

I just worry. The partnerships are all said to be thriving. The money flows in. And the officers of the general partners are living the high life.

That's bad?

Only in that I remain suspicious. We're the GP's third law firm. And frankly number two had more expertise than we do.

Well, it's smart to keep your antennae up. Particularly when everything seems to be going perfectly. The key for the diligent lawyer is to maintain your independence, keep your eyes wide open, and be prepared to raise questions at the first red flag. Your present mood may just reflect your black Irish gene. Then again, you might be right.

We all want to provide top-notch, enthusiastic service for an ever-growing list of expanding enterprises. We all want to be cheerleaders for our clients' endeavors. And pausing seems so disloyal and counterproductive. But pause we must and act just a little bit like the accountants, not by

---

32. MODEL RULES 1.2(d), 1.16(a), 4.1, cmt. [3]; RLGL §§ 32, 94.

compromising our loyalty or undertaking duties to the public, but by adopting an attitude of healthy skepticism. Maybe everything is totally legitimate. Maybe your client is the next Microsoft. And, even if not, there may be nothing of concern. The plea here is simply not to get caught up in the wave of enthusiasm without stepping back and placing your own work for this client in a larger context so that you do not find yourself a participant (and some may say later an aider and abettor) in a fraudulent scheme. Two things can help: your careful due diligence in papering your client's transactions, and the simple process of sharing with another lawyer what you know and why you feel uneasy could serve as a great reality check.

✠ Continuing Client Illegality

For a long time, I've had a great job as inside counsel to a chain of nursing homes. I've consistently counseled them to clean up their act in understaffing some of the homes, and management has just as consistently refused to spend the money, even though I've told them that criminal penalties are a real possibility. Last week, a friend suggested that I have an ethical obligation to quit if they won't make the staffing changes. That can't be right.

Your job is to give them the right advice. And when we say "them," we mean the proper constituents of the organization. And we hope that's what you meant as well. Who have you counseled?

First I talked to the VP for operations. Then I talked to the CEO. The latter shut me down.

So you haven't talked to the board?

Of course not. Can you imagine how furious the CEO would be? This isn't one of those public companies, y'know.

That makes no difference. If we are talking about any organization, Rule 1.13 comes into play. And potential criminal liability is clearly a trigger for going, at a minimum, to the highest authority able to act for the organization. Here that would be the board, and we're afraid to say that is your next stop.

Then I don't have to resign?

Certainly not yet. That's an issue to revisit after you've been to the board.

If I still am employed.

Of course. And if they correct the staffing, you are off the hook.

And if they don't?

Then you are free to resign.

I can do that anytime, right?

That's right, but now you'll have grounds.

'Cause of the staffing?

Precisely. The client is pursuing a course of conduct that you find repugnant. You also have a substantial disagreement on the course the client should follow.[33]

But do I have to?

We don't think so. That would be the case if you were counseling or assisting your client's criminal acts.[34] But you haven't counseled them—quite the contrary—you've consistently advised them to stop. As for assisting, you aren't furthering their crimes, as long as none of your legal work aids their continuing criminal activity.[35] You've given them your best advice contrary to their current conduct. Gave it to the highest authority within the organization. We suggest you put that advice in writing if you haven't already done so. Any further steps by you—including disclosure outside the organization if permitted in your jurisdiction—are voluntary.[36]

🖋 Procedural Rules: Frivolous Lawsuits

Our client manufactures vaccines for children. It's a sin, really. They end up saving hundreds of thousands of kids from the scourge of some of the worst diseases. But there are the inevitable lawsuits. It's like our client for a year thereafter is the guarantor of the health of every kid who receives a vaccine.

You are a passionate defender of your client's business.

But this one's got me more than most. Law firm sued our client claiming kid contracted asthma from taking our newest four-way vaccine. Totally absurd. They filed a day before the statute ran. Didn't even have an expert. Then, last week, they tell us they are withdrawing the complaint 'cause they couldn't find—in this entire country—an expert who agreed with their theory. But not until it cost our client almost a million bucks for the electronic discovery. I say we should go after the lawyers. Their clients are indigent, but those lawyers should pay.

---

33. MODEL RULE 1.16(b)(4); RLGL § 32(3)(f).

34. MODEL RULES 1.2(d), 1.16(a), 4.1, cmt. [3]; RLGL §§ 32, 94.

35. *In re Sharp*, 802 So. 2d 588 (La. 2001) (lawyer who prepared receipt and release that assisted client's attempts to encourage noncompliance by key witness in criminal trial suspended for one year).

36. MODEL RULES 1.6(b), 1.13(c).

We can understand your client's frustration. Even anger. But if the lawyers did not have enough time to find an expert before they filed suit as the statute was about to run, and they then conducted a conscientious search for one, only to come up empty, it's going to be hard—not impossible—to prove that the lawyers' conduct was actionable.[37]

𝒲 Procedural Rules: The Damaging Documents

The bad news is, my client unearthed some very damaging documents. They really will hurt my client's case. The good news is, I think I've found the perfect defense to producing them. These documents came out of the warehouse of my client's subsidiary in Puerto Rico. We'll just respond that it's too burdensome for us to search for documents at any subsidiary and far too burdensome to search outside the mainland United States. No judge is going to let them go on such a fishing expedition.

You would be misstating to the court and the other side the burden of producing *these* documents. You've already identified them. A similar ploy was tried on the *Fisons* case. Somehow the documents came out. And then the wrath of the court fell on the lawyers. Interposing such an objection was viewed harshly. And a very expensive sanction ($325,000) followed.[38]

When it comes to the discovery process, good lawyering often trumps clever objections. Even if you can assert some basis for delaying production of certain information, the question we lawyers must always ask is whether the approach is best for the client in the long run. How will the judge view the objection? What if the documents otherwise surface? Pyrrhic victories are rarely touted on law firm Web sites.

𝒲 Court Orders and Contempt

You know how difficult it is to get judges to understand the scope of the organizational privilege. Now we are defending a partnership. A claim by its

---

37. *E.g., Jandrt ex rel. Brueggeman v. Jerome Foods, Inc.*, 597 N.W.2d 744 (Wis. 1999) (complaint was not frivolous when filed close to statute of limitations, but became so when a lawyer reasonably should have discovered the lack of causation by consulting an expert witness).

38. *Wash. State Physicians Inc. Exch. & Ass'n v. Fisons Corp.*, 858 P.2d 1064 (Wash. 1993).

*disgruntled limited partners. Anyway, we did a pre-suit investigation. Talked to
a dozen partnership employees—salespeople who peddled the limited partnerships. The plaintiffs demanded the interview notes. We claimed both privilege
and work product, citing Upjohn. This wrong-headed judge rejected the claim.
Was she nasty. If they are limited partners, she wrote, they are entitled to see all.
We tried a mandamus. With no success. The documents are due tomorrow, and
we sure don't want to produce them.*

Well, you now have a way to get appellate review. But it'll be powerful. You
can refuse to turn them over. Argue irreparable injury and an entitlement to
judicial review. But don't be surprised when the other side moves for
contempt. And succeeds in getting such a finding.[39] But think of it this way:
you'll join a long line of courageous lawyers who fell on their respective
swords to defend important principles.[40] If you lose at the next level, we think
it will be time for you to cure the contempt and turn the documents over, as
painful as that might be. We don't want any lawyers in civil prison defending
the privilege, no matter how wrong the judiciary gets it.

🕮 Candor to the Tribunal: Legal Authority

*Representing a small boarding school. Not-for-profit. Well regarded. Very presti-
gious. Wish my kids could go there. Anyway, all beside the point. They have this
difficult case. Hints of sexual misconduct by a long-time teacher. We got the case
dismissed on summary judgment. Now we're on appeal. Other side filed its brief
two weeks ago. Ours is due in another two weeks. A new case was just decided.
In another court. Not a controlling jurisdiction. Besides, we think it's dicta.
I thought we should cite it. Client—oops, client's board chairman, who is a
lawyer, says no way. What do you think?*

You've raised a number of issues. First, you have it right that you are only
required to cite authority, even if ignored by the other side, in the controlling

---

39. RLGL § 105, cmt. d, e.

40. *E.g., Maness v. Meyers*, 419 U.S. 449 (1975) (lawyer who advised a client to refuse to obey a
court order to testify in order to trigger immediate appellate review of the issue and to
protect the client's Fifth Amendment rights could not be punished where procedural
rules provided no other means to test the validity of the trial court's ruling and the lawyer
believed in good faith that disclosure of the information tended to incriminate the
client).

jurisdiction.[41] If you are right, that this is dicta—are you?—then there is no requirement that you cite to the case. Even if not dicta, if not in the controlling jurisdiction you are off the hook for that reason.

So that's it?

No. Second, you said you thought you should cite it. We do not know whether your should was a "must" or just a desirable thing to do. Since it looks like Rule 3.3 does not require citation, this question becomes who, between client and lawyer, gets to decide whether to cite. In our view, this is one where the lawyer certainly may consult the client, but in the end, the lawyer should decide. If you find the chairman persuasive, follow his direction. If not, use your judgment. That's why you were hired.

You said there were three points.

Precisely. The last is the good lawyering one, a consideration that you may have already addressed. Even if you do not have to cite a case under the rules, there are so many reasons to do so. The other side may get around to citing it. Or the judge's law clerk may unearth it. And if either of those events occurs, you certainly want the judge to have in hand why the bad language is dicta, why that case is distinguishable from your case, or why that case was wrongly decided. And none of those pearls of wisdom will be available to Her Honor unless you address the new case head-on. Not a rules point, but certainly a good lawyering one.

🕮 Candor to the Tribunal: The Undiscovered Witness

Next thing you know, you'll tell me I have to tell the other side that the witness they've been trying to track down is sitting outside the courtroom.

We don't go that far. Unlike legal authority, this is confidential information. And you have no obligation to help the other side. As long as you avoid any misrepresentation about mystery man's whereabouts, you may remain silent and start your prayers that the mystery man's identity remains your secret until the trial is over (unless you're a prosecutor).[42]

---

41. MODEL RULE 3.3(a)(2); RLGL § 111.

42. *Office of Disciplinary Counsel v. Wrenn*, 790 N.E.2d 1195 (Ohio 2003) (prosecutor who failed to disclose relevant, exculpatory, and unprivileged information when asked by both defense counsel and the court suspended for six months, stayed, despite the fact that defendant's eventual conviction and sentence did not change as a result).

𝍫 Bias

She tells us that the lawyer on the other side was oppressive, kept referring to her as a "girl lawyer," and commented on her clothing, while the judge just seemed to enjoy this conduct, and certainly didn't do anything about it. What can we do about our colleague? She is really upset.

Bias in the courtroom is a lingering problem. Many courts have established task forces to identify and ameliorate such conduct, and some have specifically amended their professional codes to prohibit various forms of discriminatory conduct.[43] There is no excuse for such behavior. It diminishes the system of justice to have lawyers disparage their colleagues, and it is up to the judge, if the conduct occurs in the courtroom, to correct the situation.

You can help the court by pointing out that lawyers have been sanctioned, lost fees, and been professionally disciplined for such conduct.[44] We suggest that your colleague ask the court, on the record, to instruct such oppressive opponents to call her by her name, repeatedly if necessary. Perhaps it is time for this particular court to take a more institutional approach to the problem. You might be most helpful by citing the Code of Judicial Conduct, which explicitly prohibits judges from manifesting bias or prejudice and requires them not to permit others subject to the judge's direction to do so.[45]

---

43. Cal. Rule 2-400; D.C. Rule 9.1; Mich. Rule 6.5; Ill. Rule 8.4 (a)(9)(A); Minn. Rule 8.4(g); N.Y. Rule 8.4(g); Tex. Rule 5.08; RLGL §106, cmt. d.

44. *Thomas v. Tenneco Packaging Co.*, 293 F.3d 1306 (11th Cir. 2002) (lawyer who, in a race *discrimination case submitted documents containing ad hominem attacks on opposing counsel*, including references to the "racism" of opposing counsel, "the little man spewing venom," and the lawyer who was part of "the white law firm," subject to sanctions pursuant to the court's inherent powers); *In re Panel Case No 15976*, 653 N.W.2d 452 (Minn. 2002) (lawyer disciplined for disability discrimination against court's law clerk); *In re Monaghan*, 743 N.Y.S.2d 519 (N.Y. App. Div. 2002) (lawyer disciplined for race-based abuse of opposing counsel at a deposition and unlawful discrimination); *Fla. Bar v. Martocci*, 791 So. 2d 1074 (Fla. 2001) (lawyer disciplined for sexist, racial, and ethnic insults in a divorce case); *In re Vincenti*, 704 A.2d 927 (N.J. 1998) (lawyer disbarred for making insinuations about a witness's sexual orientation and harassing and intimidating her); *In re Plaza Hotel Corp.*, 111 B.R. 882 (Bankr. E.D. Cal. 1990) (lawyer who, inter alia, made sexist comments to opposing counsel disqualified).

45. MODEL CODE OF JUD. CONDUCT R. 2.9(A)(4).

⅏ Ex Parte Communication: The Wandering Expert

I cannot believe it. Working for a big manufacturer. Farm equipment. Lots of product liability suits. You can only imagine the injuries I've seen. Anyway, the other side just told us the name of their design expert. It's the former head of our QC lab. My God, the fellow used to be my best witness. But he left disgruntled. And he had nothing to do with the design of this harvester. Maybe I can invite him out for a drink. If I remember right, he loves martinis. Persuade him to give up the engagement. We can pay him to go away. That's what my GC tells me we should do.

Think again. Rule 4.2 may not apply to him. He is not the opposing party. But he has been retained by the other side. Many jurisdictions take the position that once the expert's been hired, the only approach you may make is through the formal discovery process. Interrogatories? Fine. Demand for report? Of course. Deposition? If authorized. But no ex parte contacts. Unless you can assure yourself your jurisdiction allows them.[46]

⅏ Ex Parte Communication: Contacts with Your Entity's Employees

I'm representing a company, and I'm worried about the lawyer on the other side talking to my clients without going though me. What I think I'll do is tell the gal that I represent all the employees. That way she won't be able to contact anyone, right?

There you go again, referring to your client's employees as clients. We know you call them that to earn their love and respect, but remember: they are not clients, and you don't want to make them clients. It's hard enough to represent two clients at the same time—can you imagine the difficulty in representing a hundred, a thousand, or ten thousand? All these people may work for the same company, but that doesn't mean there aren't

---

46. RLGL § 102; ABA Comm. on Ethics and Prof'l Responsibility, Formal Op. 93-378 (1993) (Ex Parte Contacts with Expert Witnesses); *Camden v. Md.*, 910 F. Supp. 1115 (D. Md. 1996) (lawyer who had extensive contact with former affirmative action specialist of lawyer's client disqualified and evidence suppressed); *In re Firestorm 1991*, 916 P.2d 411 (Wash. 1996) (lawyer who spoke to, but did not initiate contact with, opposing party's expert witness violated discovery rules but not disqualified in the absence of a showing that expert disclosed privileged information or trial strategy).

conflicts—conflicts you would have to worry about if you tried to represent them all! The interests of directors are one thing; the interests of the officers perhaps another; the interests of the employees are all over the place. So, it is no solution to say to the lawyer on the other side, "I represent GM and all its employees."

So, where does that leave me? I know when I represent an individual, the lawyer on the other side can't contact that person without my permission. Isn't an organization client entitled to the same protection?

Model Rule 4.2, the Rule that protects clients from such contacts,[47] does provide some protection for organizations. But the Rule, by the terms of its Comment [7], which restates decades of case law, only protects certain employees of the entity.[48] The first protected group are those individuals in the organization with whom the lawyer deals in receiving instruction on how to handle the matter. This could include a plant superintendent, it could be general counsel, it could be the CEO, or it could be a large group. In some cases, it's the entire board of directors. Quite simply, the lawyer on the other side cannot contact those people.

Is that all?

No, in addition, those individuals within the organization whose conduct may be imputed to the organization with respect to the matter are protected as well. So, for example, if the organization's truck were involved in an automobile accident, the truck driver would be protected from contact; but if there were an employee-passenger in the truck who was a witness to the events, that person could be contacted. If the issue is a claim for a defective product by a company, there may be a whole series of employees who could not be contacted—including those who undertook research and development, those who worked on the manufacturing, and even those who were responsible for marketing.

Well, if I were adverse to an organization, how would I ever know who was in these two groups?

You raise a good point. There is an intentional, or at least, not unintentional, aspect to the Rule as it applies to organizations, that creates a disincentive for lawyers trying to contact represented organizational employees. A lawyer in this context proceeds at her own peril, but you are always free to

---

47. *See also* RLGL § 99.

48. *E.g., Messing, Rudavsky & Weliky, P.C. v. President & Fellows of Harvard College*, 764 N.E.2d 825 (Mass. 2002); *Niesig v. Team I*, 558 N.E.2d 1030 (N.Y. 1990).

contact someone to determine whether certain employees are in one of these two protected categories. And if you aren't sure, you can seek a court order for a determination.[49]

🎞 Ex Parte Communication: Former Employees

Rule 4.2 plays both ways. Now I have a corporate dispute. Two competitors duking it out. Patent infringement. I know I can't talk to present employees of Apex. But my client knows their old R&D guy, who retired early. And the rumor is, it was not exactly voluntary. Can we talk to him?

The Model Rules are clear. You can talk to former employees if your jurisdiction has adopted the Model Rule comment. But you gotta know the rule in the relevant jurisdiction. Some protect former employees in the comment to the rule. Some do it by case law.

How do I know which jurisdiction's rules apply. Apex is in New Jersey. My client is in Delaware. The case is pending in Pennsylvania.

In that case, the forum state's rules should apply. But of course a Pennsylvania court might say that Apex, being a New Jersey company, is entitled to the protection of New Jersey's prohibition on contacting former employees.

So if any possible applicable state's rules protect former employees, I could be in trouble contacting Apex's former employees?

That's correct. Again, Rule 4.2 can have a slightly over-inclusive effect. You won't know whether you're violating Rule 4.2 by contacting former employees until after the fact. So you proceed at your own risk knowing one important fact.

What's that?

If you contact former employees, on the other side there's going to be a highly motivated lawyer to challenge you. Two more caveats as to former employees: when you contact one, make sure the "retired" employee does not have some ongoing contractual relationship that the other side might rely upon to challenge your conversation as unethical.

What a minefield!

And the other caveat. Even if you're allowed to talk with the former employee, that does not mean you can ever seek privileged information

---

49. MODEL RULE 4.2, cmt. [6]; RLGL § 99, cmt. m.

from them. That is always forbidden, and, if received, could lead to your disqualification, or worse.[50]

✎ Ex Parte Communication: Interviewing the Disgruntled Former Employee

What good fortune. We've been in litigation with a company we sold a subsidiary to. The sub was in, shall we call them discussions, with the IRS over some tax issues when the sale took place. Then, unbeknownst to us, the new owners expanded those discussions to include new claims for refunds from years when we owned the company. We found out 'cause the sub's in-house CPA quit her job when the sub wouldn't give her a bonus for her work with outside counsel in securing the huge refund. So we've hired her. On a contingency. She gets twenty percent of what we collect from the new owners. We advised her it was okay to tell us all because that outside counsel was really representing us when he advised the sub about the fund issue. She's going to be our star witness.

Where to begin? Did you check whether she was subject to a confidentiality agreement?

Of course we did. You think we're stupid?

What did she tell you?

We asked her to sign an agreement that said she wasn't subject to any such arrangement.

Did she sign it?

No. She couldn't remember. But we figured that was her problem.

Hardly. You start talking to former employees of an adverse party, and you're entering very risky terrain.

That's why we asked.

But that interchange wasn't enough. First, it is clear that she was the person at the sub who principally dealt with outside counsel.

That's why she was so valuable.

And precisely why you may have run through a number of red lights. First, she is clearly an employee who is considered protected by Rule 4.2.[51] If the

---

50. RLGL § 102; *In re Wisehart*, 721 N.Y.S.2d 356 (N.Y. App. Div. 2001) (lawyer who condoned the use of privileged documents by his client by not informing adversary that client possessed stolen documents and by using them to try to extract a settlement suspended for two years because his conduct involved dishonesty, deceit, or misrepresentation).

51. MODEL RULE 4.2, cmt. [7]; RLGL § 100.

buyer is the adverse party, it is represented, and you cannot speak with those who dealt with counsel on the matter at issue.

But she is a former employee.

True enough. But in some states, lawyers are barred from having contacts with former employees who fit into the protected categories.[52] And even if your state has adopted the Model Rule that generally excludes former employees,[53] you still have serious problems. This employee likely has a confidentiality agreement with her former employer. And you were required to honor that in this context. Take her deposition, you might get a ruling that she must testify. But in talking to her ex parte, Rule 4.4 bars you from allowing her to breach her undertaking.[54] It also may be that she was an officer of the company.

Oh. She definitely was. Senior VP.

Then she owed her former employer fiduciary duties as well. Your conversations with her might have caused a breach of Rule 4.4 for that reason.[55]

Is that it?

'Fraid not. Whether she is protected under 4.2, had a confidentiality agreement with her former employer, or owed her former employer fiduciary duties, you could not inquire of her regarding attorney-client communications with the sub's outside counsel. Rule 4.4 clearly bars that.

She was worried about that, but we assured her that as to these refunds, the sub's counsel was acting for us as well. After all, we too wanted the refund to be huge. Just like our buyer. So it's like we were co-clients.

That may be an argument you can make with a straight face, though we doubt it. But you had no right to decide the privilege question in an ex parte discussion with this former employee. Your adversary was entitled to assert its privilege and have a court decide whether the claim of privilege was a valid one. Or whether your joint-client argument was correct. And there's one more thing.

What now?

It sounds to me like you were giving legal advice to this former employee. Telling her it was alright to share the discussions with counsel with you.

---

52. RLGL § 100, cmt. g , § 102 cmt. d.

53. MODEL RULE 4.2, cmt. [7]; RLGL § 100(2).

54. MODEL RULE 4.4, cmt. [1]; RLGL § 102.

55. *Id.*

But as to you, she was an unrepresented party. Just like when you deal with a current corporate client's employees. And unrepresented persons can only be given one piece of advice by a lawyer for another party.

What's that? We may as well hear it all.

The advice to get a lawyer.[56]

But then we would never have learned how we've been defrauded by our buyer.

That's true. But once this comes out, you may end up with no client in the matter.

Look. If we did something wrong, we'll just ignore what she told us. No harm, no foul.

Sorry. The ink is already in the milk. And the sanctions could be painful. Disqualification.[57] Dismissal of the case.[58] Striking of pleadings or suppression of evidence.[59]

Ouch!

That's right. Which is precisely why we say lawyers have to be so careful when a gift horse turns out to be a Trojan horse, laying waste to all in its path. Interviewing disgruntled former employees is tricky business. And you compounded it here with one more potential transgression.

Too much, already.

No. You must learn this lesson, too. It is totally improper to compensate a potential witness on a contingent fee basis.[60] Then you are not paying for the person's time; you are paying for the testimony. It not only destroys the person's credibility, it might be considered a bribe.[61]

But that's why she wanted to talk to us.

That may be so. But it's no excuse for you to agree. Lawyers, above all, must recognize the limits on their conduct.

---

56. MODEL RULE 4.3; RLGL § 103.

57. *E.g., MMR/Wallace Power & Indus. v. Thames Assocs.*, 764 F. Supp 712 (D. Conn. 1991); *Gregori v. Bank of Am.*, 254 Cal. Rptr. 853 (Cal. Ct. App. 1989).

58. *E.g., Ackerman v. Nat'l Prop. Analysts, Inc.*, 887 F. Supp. 510 (S.D.N.Y. 1993).

59. *E.g., Cooke v. Superior Court*, 147 Cal. Rptr. 915 (Cal. Ct. App. 1978).

60. RLGL § 117.

61. MODEL RULE 3.4(b); RLGL § 117, cmt. d.

✐ Ex Parte Communication: Government Investigations

The damn government. They aren't powerful enough? The EPA is investigating my corporate client's compliance with new water quality regs. Pain in the. . . . Anyway, we get hired to handle the matter. Call the EPA lawyer. Make all nice. Tell her how we'll cooperate. They should go through me. We produce some documents. They ask for more. So far, so good. Then, out of the blue, on a Sunday morning, five EPA lawyers visit five of our employees, flash a badge, interview them. I didn't find out about it until Monday morning. One of the targeted employees said something to his supervisor. Otherwise, we might never have found out. Can they do that?

Well, they did. The government lawyers, particularly the United States government's lawyers, take a rather cramped view of the reach of Rule 4.2, aggressively limiting its protection for the corporate client.[62]

The heart of the free enterprise system—a second class citizen yet again.

Well, as already noted, Rule 4.2 is much more difficult to administer when it comes to organizations, even not-for-profit.

So is what they did okay?

I take it you would assert the contacted employees should have been protected by Rule 4.2?

Absolutely. They talked to the chief environmental officer, the head of the testing lab, the maintenance man in the outflow building, even the guy who empties the trash.

Well, all of them arguably came under 4.2.

For sure. The environmental officer is my contact. All of the others are employees whose conduct could be at issue. They had no business. . . .

You're right. What you are sitting on top of has been a legendary struggle. And a bipartisan one, too.

What do you mean?

Well, the Republicans started it. Dick Thornburg, when he was Attorney General, issued a memorandum that exempted DOJ lawyers from Rule 4.2.

How could he do that?

---

62. *U.S. v. Frass*, 239 F. Supp. 2d 535 (M.D. Pa. 2003) (non-custodial pre-indictment communications by undercover agents with represented persons, which occur in the course of legitimate criminal investigations, are "authorized by law").

Great question. He took the position that Congress's delegation of authority for law enforcement gave the federal government the power to trump state ethics codes governing lawyers. Then the Democrats took up the baton. Janet Reno issued regulations to the same effect, claiming federal law meant her lawyers could contact any client or client representative pre-complaint or indictment on the theory that Rule 4.2 did not lock in until the Constitutional Sixth Amendment right to counsel arose.

But that's ridiculous. Every client has a right to counsel of their choosing at any time. The Sixth Amendment only applies to the right to appointed counsel. Besides, the really important lawyering takes place to prevent the bringing of a criminal charge or the institution of an enforcement action.

That's precisely what the critics argued. And thank goodness for the McDonnell-Douglas Company.

They aren't even in business anymore.

But they were when the Reno regs were issued. And they challenged them . . . successfully. The Eighth Circuit ruled that Congress had not authorized DOJ to issue such regs. Mere delegation of the law enforcement function was not enough.[63] Then we defenders of Rule 4.2 got another gift.

What's that?

DOJ prosecuted Congressmen McDade of Pennsylvania. You know the old saying: if you shoot a king, you better kill him. Well, McDade was acquitted. DOJ became the object of his wrath. And he was so beloved in Congress that, even after he retired, Congress passed what is known as the McDade Amendment, requiring all federal government lawyers to abide by the rules of professional conduct of the state in which they are admitted or practicing.[64]

So what the EPA lawyers did is a rule violation?

It should be. The rules in some states have taken a more liberal view of law enforcement activities, carving out some as within the "authorized by law" exception.[65] And the rules in still other states permit an ex parte application to the courts to violate Rule 4.2, though we doubt very many of

---

63. *U.S. ex rel O'Keefe v. McDonnell Douglas Corp.*, 132 F.3d 1252 (8th Cir. 1998).

64. 28 U.S.C. § 530(B) (2006).

65. *U.S. v. Brown*, 356 F. Supp. 2d 470 (M.D. Pa. 2005) (McDade amendment does not change the fact that many courts have decided that the use of informants by government prosecutors in a pre-indictment, non-custodial situation will generally fall within the "authorized by law" exception); *U.S. v. Grass*, 239 F. Supp. 2d 535 (M.D. Pa. 2003) (non-custodial pre-indictment communications by undercover agents with represented persons, which occur in the course of legitimate criminal investigations, are "authorized by law").

them have been granted. But as a general proposition, it looks like a Rule 4.2 violation.

What can I do now?

Well, of course, since Rule 4.2 is a rule of discipline, you can report the EPA lawyers.

That might not help my client.

That's correct. You could move to disqualify the EPA lawyers from these proceedings.[66] Or seek the dismissal of any complaint they file on the ground of the misconduct. At a minimum, you should be able to preclude the EPA from using the interviews and any fruits of the interviews in the case.[67]

But they know it already.

Which is why you should try to get the lawyers disqualified and prohibited from talking to any successor counsel.

The government is relentless.

It is a sin. As they assert, Rule 4.2 makes their job more difficult. But that's a small price to pay to maintain the important lawyer-client values protections established by Rule 4.2. Clients should never be forced to have direct contact with the other side's lawyers, especially when it is the all-powerful government.[68]

ℳ Instructing Employees

Listening to you, I just know I should have listened to one of my partners early on. He said you can't trust the feds. We should send each employee an e-mail instructing everyone not to talk to anyone.

Glad you didn't do that.[69]

---

66. *Kaiser v. AT&T*, No. CIV 00-724, 2002 U.S. Dist. LEXIS 25768 (D. Ariz. Apr. 5, 2002) (lawyer who engaged in ex parte contacts with a high-ranking former manager who was a critical witness in the case disqualified); *Faison v. Thornton*, 863 F. Supp. 1204 (D. Nev. 1993) (lawyers who engaged in ex parte communications disqualified and ordered to pay $46,000 in fees as sanction; evidence also excluded).

67. *Parker v. Pepsi-Cola Gen. Bottlers, Inc.*, 249 F. Supp. 2d 1006 (N.D. Ill. 2003).

68. *U.S. v. Lopez*, 106 F.3d 309 (9th Cir. 1997) (government's improper ex parte contact with defendant created prejudice sufficient to take case out of the heartland of the sentencing guidelines); *In re Howes*, 940 P.2d 159 (N.M. 1997) (AUSA publicly censured for speaking to a represented defendant who initiated contact).

69. *Terra Int'l Inc. v. Miss. Chem. Corp.*, 913 F. Supp. 1306, 1317 (N.D. Iowa 1996) ("[A]n employer cannot unilaterally create or impose representation of employees by corporate counsel.

But it would've stopped these damn interviews.

Maybe, maybe not. There is something powerful about being visited by a gal with a badge. But such an approach might've gotten you into trouble.

By protecting my poor client.

Yep. DOJ takes the position that such an instruction is obstruction of justice. And they are serious. There is a totally benign alternative, however.

What's that?

You could instruct your client's employees that they are not required to cooperate with any government investigator, that the choice is theirs, that they have the right to be represented by counsel at an interview, and that the company will provide one for them. You could also urge them to call one of your lawyers if they are approached. All of this is totally permissible.

Wish I had thought of that.

Well, let's just say you never thought EPA would not go through you. After all, you were wearing your cooperation face.

✵ The Separately Represented Employee

I'm caught in a cross-fire. The GC on the other side made it quite clear that all contacts with his company employees must be arranged through GC.

And you're not going to listen?

No, I listened alright. But then I got a call from another lawyer. He says he represents the CFO of our opponent. Wants to meet with me. Something about cooperation for a release. I told him I'd get back to him. Who's in charge here?

If this lawyer really represents the CFO individually (something you can confirm with the CFO), then you are free to meet with him without corporate counsel present so long as the CFO's individual counsel gives you permission. We'd get it from the CFO's lawyer in writing. But a clear exception to Rule 4.2 in the organizational context is the permission of the individual counsel for an employee who otherwise would be off limits.[70]

Such an automatic representation rule would serve no useful purpose, but would instead impede the course of investigation leading to or following the filing of a lawsuit."); ABA Comm. on Ethics and Prof'l Responsibility, Formal Op. 95-396 (1995) (Communications with Represented Persons) (general counsel cannot assert blanket representation of all employees).

70. Model Rule 4.2 cmt. [7]; RLGL § 100 cmt. f.

⁒ Make Him Go Away

My corporate client has had nothing but a barrage of lawsuits. All from the same plaintiff's lawyer. He's just running a mill with these products liability claims. So they say to me, "why don't we just give his latest fraudulent claimant an extra $100,000 on the condition that the damn lawyer never sues us again?" Good idea?

So many of our corporate clients have the same gripe. Once a lawyer develops a following as an expert on a certain kind of claim, clients beat a bath to his door, or he starts advertising, or he gets a union to send him a bunch of clients. All opposing clients want is to make him go away. But alas, that is not one of the possibilities. The Rules make it quite clear that you may not offer, nor may opposing counsel accept, a limitation on the right of that lawyer to practice.[71] The reasons for the Rule are pretty clear. First, we don't want to deny clients the opportunity to hire the best lawyer in a particular field. Second, we don't want to put a lawyer in conflict with his client.[72] If your client offers the lawyer $100,000 for this agreement never to sue again, it is clearly in the client's best interest to take the money, but it is not in the lawyer's.

How about if we give the money to the lawyer?

We're afraid that's no better. Now you are basically paying the lawyer a bribe, and that is clearly impermissible. It also puts the lawyer in conflict with his client because what you may be giving the lawyer is money to which the client is entitled. And, in any event, you are restricting the right of the lawyer to practice, in clear violation of the Model Rule.

There is one thing you can do, though.

What's that?

After the case is over, settled or tried, there is nothing stopping your client from trying to hire plaintiff's counsel. If he accepts, then he cannot sue your client, because that would violate the conflict-of-interest rules. That would solve one problem, but then you would have to decide what services he could provide to your corporate client.

---

71. MODEL RULE 5.6. *E.g., In re Hager,* 812 A.2d 904 (D.C. 2002) (lawyer who, inter alia, agreed not to represent any clients against settling defendant suspended for one year).

72. ABA Comm. on Ethics and Prof'l Responsibility, Formal Ops. 94-381 (Restrictions on Right to Practice) and 93-371 (1993) (Restrictions on the Right to Represent Clients in the Future).

But be sure to warn your client that if it is going to make an offer to the plaintiff's lawyer, it cannot breathe a word about this (no winks, no hints) until after the case is completed.[73] Because if you do so, then the proposed contract to hire the lawyer becomes an unethical part of the bargain to settle the lawsuit and creates an expectation in the opposing lawyer that creates a conflict between that lawyer and her client.

𝕸 The Uncertified Class

The power of a class action! I have a client who has been terminated in clear violation of the age discrimination laws. From what he told me, there were dozens in his position. So I brought it as a class action just last week. Now the company's lawyer has called me up. Offered an extra $100,000 to my client if we settle now, and the only condition is that I have to promise not to sue 'em again. When I asked whether they thought the court would approve this deal, they told me the best news of all: the settlement doesn't require court approval. Who knew?

It is true that recent changes to Rule 23 of the Federal Rules of Civil Procedure only require court approval of a settlement after the class is certified.[74] Obviously, your worthy opponent is relying on this change. The problem is, you'll be sorry to learn, the rules of civil procedure do not have the ability to change the rules of professional conduct. You filed a lawsuit as a class action. When you did so, you undertook to represent the class. At that moment, you accepted a fiduciary duty to the class that you cannot so easily jettison simply because suddenly you wish to put the interests of your initial individual client or your own interests in the driver's seat.[75]

Making the offer contingent on your agreeing never to sue the company again, as just noted, is another ethics violation. Lawyers are barred from

---

73. ABA Comm. on Ethics and Prof'l Responsibility, Formal Op. 99-414 (1999) (Ethical Obligations When a Lawyer Changes Firms).

74. FED. R. CIV. P. 23 (e).

75. *E.g., Schick v. Berg*, No. 1:03-cv-05513-LBS, 2004 U.S. Dist. LEXIS 6842 (S.D.N.Y. Apr. 20, 2004), *aff'd*, 430 F.3d 112 (2d Cir. 2005). *See also Janik v. Rudy, Exelrod & Zieff*, 14 Cal. Rptr. 3d 751 (Cal Ct. App. 2004) (class member could allege legal malpractice for failure to pursue cause of action not specifically approved in class certification order as long as cause of action arose out of the same facts and class members would reasonably expect it to be considered).

offering or accepting, as part of a settlement, any restriction on their right to practice law. The Rule, Model Rule 5.6, is designed to save lawyers from the trap that would be created by it being in the best interests of the present client to accept the limitation, even though the lawyer and, more important. the public would want the lawyer experienced in these matters to be able to take on new representations against the company. If the company wants to prevent the lawyer from suing it again, it may do so by hiring the lawyer to represent the company; any such engagement, however, must come after the first matter is settled and not even be hinted at as part of the settlement process.

⚜ Lawyer as Witness

Our firm handled a big transaction for Odyssey. This was huge. Bought out by one of those private equity funds. Everyone at Odyssey got a big payday, but some of it was in the fund's stock. Turns out the fund didn't disclose how lever-aged they were. When credit seized up, the fund couldn't refinance, and now the stock is worthless. I know we were assured about their level of debt.

You do?

Sure, I made the phone call. Even have a memo in my file.

So, if your client sues, you'll be the key witness.[76]

We already sued. We were as outraged as the client because our due dili-gence was so careful.

Does your client agree?

Well, they did remind us they relied on us.

And your firm brought the client's suit?

Of course. Who better to bring it?

But you're going to be a witness.[77]

I know, I know. But I don't think what I have to say will be controversial. I have a memo.

So you plan to try the case?

Not if you tell me I can't—I guess.

---

76. MODEL RULE 3.7; RLGL § 108.

77. *Compare Caplan v. Braverman*, 876 F. Supp. 710 (E.D. Pa. 1995) (lawyer who was part of a conversation where party allegedly made an admission not "necessary" witness) *with World Youth Day, Inc. v. Famous Artists Merch. Exch., Inc.*, 866 F. Supp. 1297 (D. Colo. 1994) (lawyer who was sole negotiator for party was a "necessary" witness).

Even if you step aside, Rule 3.7 allows your colleagues to handle it, but that's subject to a conflict-of-interest analysis. Maybe you should hand the matter off to someone new.

And lose all those fees? This could be really big.

Have you discussed the conflicts with your client?

There's no conflict. We're both determined to make these private equity guys pay.

How's it going to look to a jury when your partner puts you on the stand?

A little weird, I suppose.

And in closing argument, you think your partner's invocation of your testimony will go well?

That will be a little odd too.

No one has discussed this with the client?

I don't think so.

Well, someone better. And they better go further than that. Your firm's role in the transaction—even if you weren't going to be a key witness—raises all kinds of concerns whether your client is best served with your lawyers' handling the litigation. Who's advising your client about any rights they may have against you? The client might go along with it, but that agreement should only be secured after a long and awkward meeting in which the benefits of bringing in new counsel should be thoroughly explored.

🎗 The Referral Club

I've joined a business referral club. For only $350 per year, I get to be the only lawyer member of the group along with one each of various other professionals and business people. All I have to do is attend weekly meetings, give sixty-second "commercials" to the group, and provide referrals to other members. The club's website announces:

> *Joining us is like having dozens of sales people working for you because all of our members carry several copies of your business card around with them. When they meet someone who could use your products or services, they hand out your card and recommend you. It's as simple as that!*

What a business-generating idea.

You are engaging in a very sophisticated version of what can be a totally legitimate activity that is enshrined in the history of our profession.

Lawyers have sent clients to banks, and banks have sent customers to lawyers since time immemorial. I'll scratch your back; you scratch mine. But you need to proceed cautiously or you will run afoul of your obligation to your clients.[78]

First, if you have an informal or formal mutual arrangement of cross-referrals, your clients are entitled to know that. Second, you cannot engage in an exclusive reciprocal referral agreement, so you should remind the client that it may wish to choose a different vendor from the one you recommend. Third, if you are recommending a cross-referred vendor, you must be convinced that vendor is the best available for the client under the circumstances. Fourth, you may accept no money from a vendor for recommending that vendor's services, and you may pay nothing of value to a non-lawyer vendor for making a recommendation that the vendor's clients use your services. You should know that referral rules vary considerably among different jurisdictions. Some state bar associations, for example, have opined that your $350 yearly fee clearly crosses the line.[79]

✌ Multidisciplinary Practice

This one may be an even better financial opportunity for our firm. We represent mortgagees in lending transactions. We were approached by a group of investors who want to set up a new business, make our firm a minority shareholder, and enter into a ten-year contract with us that provides that our firm will have the new enterprise undertake all of the non-legal aspects of our practice (title searches, service of process, advertising foreclosure sales, filing papers, photo-copying, messenger services). "Your clients won't even have to know," our future partners told us.

This arrangement is far more problematic. First, the arrangement you envision must be disclosed to your clients. You can't be recommending that your clients use a vendor in which your firm has a direct financial interest

---

78. MODEL RULE 7.2(b)(4).

79. N.Y. Op 791 (2006) (lawyer may not participate in an organization that requires the lawyer to refer potential clients or customers to other lawyers or to non-lawyer members in exchange for legal business); Md. Op 05-11 (lawyers should not participate in for-profit networking clubs that require members to exchange referrals because referrals could create conflicts, compromise a lawyer's independent professional judgment, and possibly violate advertising rules).

without telling them that,[80] and then, if they choose to hire that enterprise, the client's arrangement with the enterprise must meet all the requirements of the client business transaction Rule 1.8(a). This means not only disclosure, but also that the deal is reduced to writing, the client is informed in writing of the advisability of getting an opinion from another lawyer regarding the transaction, and the entire arrangement passes a test of entire fairness to the client.[81]

Our new business partners won't like that. They want us to commit to an exclusive arrangement.

That's not surprising. And there's probably nothing wrong with their asking. Your accepting is another thing. Lawyers may never enter into exclusive referral arrangements with other lawyers or any other vendor of services.[82] The lawyer must remain free to select another vendor when the lawyer is of the view that the client will be better served with an alternative. One size cannot fit all.

✳ Multijurisdictional Practice

We represent a Norwegian company that has subsidiaries in two distant states. Our lawyers travel to both states to negotiate collective bargaining agreements. Some suggested we were engaging in unauthorized practice. Can that be right? Everyone does it. The Norwegian company has an office in our state.

You raise a question that has bedeviled multistate corporate enterprises in their desire to hire national counsel to coordinate corporate matters in a large number of states in which they have been sued or otherwise need legal services. Think of employment discrimination claims or negotiations with dealers.

Precisely. We're lucky enough to have been recognized for our expertise.

---

80. MODEL RULE 5.7.

81. *In re Edens*, 544 S.E.2d 627 (S.C. 2001) (lawyer who allowed office manager to conduct refinancing closings publicly reprimanded for violating Model Rules 5.3 and 5.5); Az. Op 05-01 (lawyers may refer client to an investment advisor that pays referral fees provided lawyer meets heavy burden of complying with rules on concurrent conflicts of interest and business transactions with clients); Oh. Op. 2004-9 (lawyer may send a letter to a chiropractor asking for a meeting to provide information about the lawyer's services, but the lawyer may not solicit, offer, or reward referrals).

82. MODEL RULE 7.2(b)(4).

The litigation matters are no problem. Almost all courts will entertain pro hac vice petitions that will admit the out-of-state lawyer for one matter. Just be sure to retain local counsel that can fill you in on the quirks and requirements of such admissions, from the judge's foibles, to the requirement that you pay taxes on the income you earn in the jurisdiction, to establishing a local IOLTA account.[83]

And these collective bargaining agreements?

Outside of court, the issue becomes dicier. The case that sent shivers through the profession involved New York lawyers representing a California company in California.[84] That in turn prompted the ABA to look into the topic of multijurisdictional practice. The result was new Model Rule 5.5 that, if adopted in your jurisdiction, provides a safe harbor for out-of-state lawyers to provide certain legal services to clients in jurisdictions in which the lawyers are not admitted. The rule requires some special nexus between the client and the lawyer that would justify an exception to what otherwise would be the unauthorized practice of law. Your nexus might be services provided for clients domiciled in the jurisdiction where you are admitted to practice.[85] Another is services reasonably related to those authorized by federal (labor) law.[86] If you meet the test of Rule 5.5 of the jurisdiction in which you are not admitted, you should be fine. If that jurisdiction has not recognized multijurisdictional practice in this way, tread very carefully. In any event, it is always helpful, if not dispositive of the UPL issue, if you retain local counsel to assist you in the out-of-state representation.

---

83. MODEL RULE 5.5(c).

84. *Birbrower, Montalbano, Condon & Frank, P.C. v. Superior Court*, 949 P.2d 1 (Cal. 1998) (New York lawyers' representation of California business in contract dispute in California was unauthorized practice of law which rendered fee contract unenforceable).

85. *Estate of Condon*, 76 Cal. Rptr. 2d 922 (Cal. Ct. App. 1998) (Colorado lawyer who assisted Colorado client in selling a business in California entitled to attorney's fees).

86. MODEL RULE 5.5(c)(4) & (d)(2).

NINE

Remedies

*// Introduction: So What Can Happen?

LAWYERS WHO BREACH agency-based fiduciary duties to clients trigger equitable and legal remedies[1] as well as the potential for professional discipline.[2] Lawyers who fail to recognize or understand a legal limit imposed on unrestrained legal advocacy also may be accountable to third-party non-clients.[3]

Client legal remedies include breach of contract,[4] malpractice,[5] and breach of fiduciary duty.[6] Equitable remedies for breach of fiduciary duty allow clients to seek a constructive trust,[7] disqualification[8] or injunctive relief,[9] fee forfeiture,[10] or restoration of pre-breach contractual rights.[11]

Non-clients can seek relief against you if they are identified third-party beneficiaries, invited by you or your client to rely on your legal services,[12]

---

1. RLGL § 6.
2. MODEL RULE 8.4(a); RLGL § 5.
3. RLGL §§ 51, 56.
4. RLGL § 55(1).
5. RLGL § 48.
6. RLGL § 49.
7. RLGL § 6, cmt. a, § 44, cmt. h.
8. RLGL § 6(8).
9. RLGL § 6(2).
10. RLGL § 37.
11. RLGL § 6(3)–(5).
12. RLGL § 51(2)–(3).

or if you commit crimes or intentional torts against them.[13] In an increasing number of situations, non-clients also seek relief for negligent misrepresentation[14] or aiding and abetting a client's breach of fiduciary duty.[15]

Many of these client and non-client duties also have become part of lawyer code provisions, so that lawyers who violate them may be subject to both professional discipline as well as legal and equitable remedies for the same conduct.[16]

All of these remedies have been created to support lawyer fiduciary duty or the limits on advocacy imposed by other law. If you understand and observe your Five C fiduciary duties, you should not create grounds for client relief. Identifying and staying within the limits of the law also should keep you out of third-party trouble.

✌ Professional Discipline

In retrospect, I should have stood up to the board. But when they wanted me, in-house counsel, to backdate some agreements, it seemed so benign. Corporate lawyers do this all the time. The backdated date was the date when the board agreed to go forward. But, unbeknownst to me, the board was bent on deliberate fraud—one I knew nothing about. Parking corporate liabilities with a special purpose entity. Somehow, the word got out, and the feds came knocking.

The AUSA promised me a plea bargain to a misdemeanor if I would cooperate. Testify against my former bosses. I agreed, they were convicted, and I got community service and the accolades of the AUSA. But now, the disciplinary counsel thinks I should be disbarred. Even though, without my testimony, the truly bad guys would never have been convicted.

We sympathize, and we are glad you were helpful to the constabulary. However, you also were convicted of a crime: backdating corporate documents.

---

13. RLGL § 56.

14. RLGL §§ 51(2), 95, cmt. c.

15. RLGL §§ 51(4), 56, cmt. h.

16. *E.g.,* MODEL RULES 1.1 (competence obligation); 1.2(a), 1.4, 1.6, 1.7, 1.8, 1.9, 1.10 (control, communication, confidentiality, and conflict of interest resolution obligations); 1.2(d), 3.3, 4.1 and 8.4(c) (duty to avoid fraud, dishonesty, deceit, and misrepresentation); 3.4 (procedural obligations in tribunals); 1.2(d) and 8.4(b) (crimes).

Goes right to your honesty, trustworthiness, and fitness as a lawyer.[17] Your cooperation with the feds may be seen as mitigation in your disciplinary case, but you knew you were lying when you backdated the documents. It doesn't matter if everyone lies or helps clients lie. Lawyers can't do it.[18]

Criminal Accountability

Our client is a big real estate developer in a few towns in Exeter County. I can't tell you how many fundraisers he asks us to attend. You pay a thousand bucks, the food is lousy, and you rub elbows with a bunch of politicians. Ugh! But now our client has gone over the top. He's trying to raise $50,000 for some guy running for county executive. With our campaign finance laws, his company's executives can only contribute $25,000. He wants our partner to bundle the other $25,000. Tell the party chairman it's "inspired" by our client. With all the new work we'll get from his company if this guy gets to be county executive, the developer says we'll earn the $25,000 back in no time. Can we do it?

It's perfectly legal to give political contributions. It is also perfectly legal to encourage others to do so. And as long as it's clear that your firm is not being reimbursed by the client for the contributions he is "encouraging" you to make, everything should be copasetic. But you must be very careful of two things. One, these must be your contributions. No extra charges to clients for services in order to "earn" the contributions back.[19] Two, you must assure yourself that your client is not engaged in bribery of public officials to receive business on either zoning approvals or leasing opportunities.[20] The last thing your firm wants to confront is the charge that you aided and abetted illegal

---

17. MODEL RULE 8.4(b); RLGL § 5, cmt. g.

18. MODEL RULES 1.2(d), 4.1(a), 8.4(c); *In re Palmer,* 835 So. 2d 410 (La. 2002) (lawyer who furthered entity client's sham transactions by backdating documents was convicted of conspiracy to defraud and disbarred, despite testimony of U.S. Attorney that convictions of principals would not have been possible without lawyer's cooperation).

19. *E.g., In re Am. Cont'l Corp./Lincoln Sav. & Loan Sec. Litig.,* 794 F. Supp. 1424, 1451 (D. Ariz. 1992).

20. *E.g., In re Breslin,* 793 A.2d 645 (N.J. 2002) (lawyer whose client attempted to bribe the police commissioner censured because he should have advised client that lawyer could not participate in illegal activity).

conduct by your client.[21] That not only violates Model Rule 1.2(d); it could also have you facing criminal charges.[22]

✻ Misrepresentation

I'm working to settle a substantial case before we have to notify our carrier. Our clients own two pizza parlors. Seems one of their speedy delivery guys injured a pedestrian. Serious injuries. I told the plaintiff's lawyer that she should accept policy limits. That we have no umbrella coverage. She agreed, and we closed the deal for $250,000. Then I checked our policies and discovered I was wrong. We had a big umbrella policy. I'm sure glad I didn't know about it until I settled the case.

You may not be so smart after all. If the plaintiff discovers this information, a suit based on fraud may be the next event. The argument will be that the policies were in your file, and therefore you must have known about them, or were reckless in not checking. That's fraud—grounds to rescind the settlement and for tort recovery. The alternative argument will be that, having spoken before about a material fact, once you found out the actual facts, you had an obligation to correct your prior misstatement. Either way, we don't think you will like the outcome.[23]

---

21. *Fla. Bar v. Brown*, 790 So. 2d 1081 (Fla. 2001) (lawyer suspended ninety days for assisting client in violating campaign finance laws); *In re Sharp*, 802 So. 2d 588 (La. 2001) (lawyer who assisted client in attempting to bribe a witness to drop the charges in client's criminal case suspended for one year).

22. *In re Convery*, 765 A.2d 724 (N.J. 2001) (lawyer who pled guilty to a federal misdemeanor of promising employment in return for political activity, when he was discovered to have used his local political position and influence to pressure a local zoning board to grant a variance for his client, suspended for six months); *Sands v. State Bar*, 782 P.2d 595 (Cal. 1989) (lawyer who was convicted of bribery of a public official disbarred, even though official solicited the bribe).

23. *Slotkin v. Citizens Cas. Co. of N.Y.*, 614 F.2d 301 (2d Cir. 1979) (insurance defense lawyer who settled medical malpractice case after stating that "to the best of my knowledge" there was no excess insurance coverage, when lawyer's file indicted otherwise, liable for fraud); *In re McGrath*, 468 N.Y.S.2d 349 (N.Y. App. Div. 1983) (insurance defense lawyer in *Slotkin* suspended from practice for six months for his misrepresentation); *Siegel v. Williams*, 818 N.E.2d 510 (Ind. Ct. App. 2004) (lawyer committed fraud when he told former client who sued him for legal malpractice that he had only $25,000 to settle the claim because his wife had gotten all of his money in a divorce and that if the jury awarded more than $25,000 he would declare bankruptcy); *Fire Ins. Exch. v. Bell*, 643 N.E.2d 310 (Ind. 1994) (plaintiff's counsel had right to rely on insurance defense counsel's representation of

But that's only if the information gets discovered. How will they ever find out?

Because as best as we can tell, you have a duty to correct the record. You represented a material fact and subsequently discovered it to be untrue. That's fraud, which is ongoing until fixed.[24]

✇ Aiding and Abetting Liability

Partners get into a dispute over partnership real estate. I agree to represent one of them. We finally get a deal. The other partner agrees to transfer his interest to my guy. My guy agrees to pay him 300K upon the sale. My guy has twelve months to sell or find 300K. My guy can't raise the money, so he sells the property. Meanwhile, my client tells me of another dispute he has with his partner. So when the sale goes through, I advise my client to keep the money to partially satisfy this other obligation. It was good advice. Client has a great claim for a set-off. But now my client's been sued. For 300K and punitives. No surprise there. I warned him. What is a surprise is that I've been sued too. Aiding and abetting my client's fraud. And a claim I represented the partnership and therefore could not advise my client adverse to this other partner by giving this advice.

All kinds of issues flying around here. Your client was a partner of this other fellow. At the time of the deal. I take it this was not a social partnership but a legal one. So your client owed this partner certain fiduciary duties. You don't tell us whether they were also formal partners on the other matter, but assuming not, the partnership relationship may have put your client in a special legal place. Not free to assert another claim as an offset. If your client breached fiduciary duties, then you could be in trouble for aiding and abetting a breach of those duties.[25] On the other hand, all you did was tell

---

policy limits, even though plaintiff's lawyer could have used discovery to ascertain limits).

24. RLGL § 98, cmt. d; *Hansen v. Anderson, Wilmarth & Van der Maaten*, 630 N.W.2d 818 (Iowa 2001) (once a lawyer responds to a request for information in an arm's-length transaction, lawyer had a duty to the lawyer requesting the information to give it truthfully; breach of the duty gives rise to a claim for equitable indemnity by the defrauded lawyer against the defrauding lawyer).

25. *E.g., LeRoy v. Allen, Yurasek & Merklin*, 872 N.E.2d 254 (Ohio 2007) (lawyer may be liable to third party for aiding and abetting if fraud, collusion, or malice were present in preparing a will and stock transfer in close corporation for elderly client; conflict of interest or

your client of the client's rights. You gave your client sound advice. You should be privileged to do that.[26] The problem is that the line between good lawyering and aiding and abetting can be a close one.

𝄞 Tort Liability to Clients

We have a specialized tax practice. High end. Corporate. We've saved our clients hundreds of millions. This bank comes along. Bought a troubled S&L. Induced to do so by the FDIC. All kinds of tax benefits. Then Congress changed the rules. Our group, along with dozens of others, sue the FDIC, claiming breach of contract. When the FDIC offered to settle, this bank asked us to consider the tax implications of the settlement so they could determine the real value of the proposed $11 million settlement. We did that. Gave them damn good advice, I say. But now they are threatening to sue our firm. They claim the $11 million represents just ten cents on the dollar. And a bank that took the case to trial got a hundred cents. We should've told them not to settle.

Time to get out your retainer agreement. Our hope is that you didn't use the letter as a sales device and made it clear you were only reviewing the tax aspects. Failing that, we take it some other firm handled the FDIC negotiations.

Right. A great firm with a mediocre tax practice.

So you have that defense. And a hope that when the representation began, whoever handled it for your firm at least had the right scope of representation discussion with the client.

If he remembers.

Exactly. One thing we know. The former client is likely to misremember. And we know what deference the courts and juries give to clients' "mismemories," all of which emphasizes how important it is for lawyers to clearly define the scope of the representation—particularly when the client is a vast consumer of legal services—so there is no dispute about the lawyer's responsibilities—and potential liabilities—at a later date.[27]

---

collusion with beneficiaries presented fact issue); *Chem-Age Indus. v. Glover*, 652 N.W.2d 756 (S.D. 2002) (lawyer may be liable to third-party business investors for assisting client in establishing a business corporation and later selling it as a sole proprietorship when lawyer knew investors were relying on sale to be repaid).

26. *Reynolds v. Schrock*, 142 P.3d 1062 (Or. 2006) (lawyer privileged to give client legal advice as long as lawyer committed no crime, fraud, or statutory violation).

27. *E.g., Barnes v. Turner*, 606 S.E.2d 849 (Ga. 2004) (lawyer who perfected client's securities interests by filing UCC financing statements also undertook duty to renew statements

What if we can't prove we limited our representation to tax advice? It can't be the case that lawyers are liable for settlement advice.

Au contraire. Although a few jurisdictions have agreed with you,[28] the modern trend subjects all of the lawyer's practice, including settlement advice, to the expert judgment of similarly situated professionals.[29]

⑮ Disqualification: Looking for Bigger Fish to Fry

What an opportunity. A possible lawsuit against Apex. Huge. Treble damages. RICO. Can't wait to take this one on. Only one problem. Our Milwaukee office does work for a third-tier Apex subsidiary. Just some leasing. I say we drop the Apex subsidiary—oh so politely—and grab the new matter with gusto. Risking disqualification is well worth it.

Tread carefully, our friend. So much to consider at the outset. You must discuss this with the prospective client. It must know that it is risking losing its lawyer right from the start. Don't tell them, and you may have everyone attacking you. Next, the risk of disqualification is real. And who will pay for your services in defending the disqualification motion?[30] You recognize the argument that you can't sue the parent of your own corporate client.[31]

---

after five years or inform client of need to do so); *Lerner v. Laufer*, 819 A.2d 471 (N.J. Super. Ct. App. Div. 2003) (lawyer who expressly limited his services to reviewing a property settlement agreement did not breach any duty by failing to conduct additional discovery to evaluate the merits of the underlying agreement); *Kates v. Robinson*, 786 So. 2d 61 (Fla. Dist. Ct. App. 2001) (lawyer hired to execute a judgment not responsible for failing to recognize other potential defendants).

28. *Muhammad v. Strassburger, McKenna, Messer, Shilobod & Gutnick*, 587 A.2d 1346 (Pa. 1991) (dissatisfied litigants may not recover for malpractice against their lawyers for negotiating settlements accepted by clients absent fraud).

29. *Ziegelheim v. Apollo*, 607 A.2d 1298 (N.J. 1992).

30. Susan R. Martyn, *Developing the Judicial Role in Controlling Litigation Conflicts: Response to Green*, 65 FORDHAM L. REV. 131 (1996).

31. *Certain Underwriters at Lloyd's, London v. Argonaut Ins. Co.*, 264 F. Supp. 2d 914 (N.D. Cal. 2003) (insurer and subsidiary treated as one entity for conflicts purposes because of relatively direct financial relationship between them and common management of legal affairs); *Discotrade Ltd. v. Wyeth-Ayerst Int'l Inc.*, 200 F. Supp. 2d 355 (S.D.N.Y. 2002) (lawyer who represented a sister subsidiary corporation disqualified from representing another client in an unrelated lawsuit against another sister subsidiary); *J.P. Morgan Chase Bank v. Liberty Mut. Ins. Co.*, 189 F. Supp. 2d 20 (S.D.N.Y. 2002) (law firm that functioned as holding company's outside counsel disqualified from bringing a major lawsuit against primary subsidiary, as well as other defendants, in absence of any good reason to sever subsidiary from other defendants); *Colorpix Sys. of Am. v. Broan Mfg. Co.*, 131 F. Supp. 2d 331 (D. Conn.

And dropping that corporate client to avoid the problem violates the "hot potato doctrine"[32] and may look worse than simply continuing to represent the Apex subsidiary and argue that the representation of Apex does not create a corporate family conflict of interest.[33] Moreover, while disqualification motions are the predominant remedy for most Rule 1.7 violations, disciplinary counsel is certainly free to come after you for what may be, after all, a violation of the rules of professional conduct.[34]

Finally, step back and pause. Life is too short. Do you really want to be known in the community as a firm that would drop a client to take on a more lucrative engagement? For some, such swashbuckling techniques are a badge of honor; but for us, they bring disrespect to the profession and cast all lawyers as unethical in the eyes of the public. The fiduciary duty of loyalty should translate into more than testing the limits of our black letter rules.

⚅ Disqualification: The Peripherally Involved Lateral Hire

We try so hard to be conscientious about conflicts when we hire new lawyers. But this proves you can never be conscientious enough. We hired a third-year associate from a New York law firm. The associate told us everything she had worked on. We're clear. So we hire her, and, and, boom, a motion to disqualify us is filed in one of our really big cases. Seems, or so they claim, she worked on this case where we are on the other side. She'd forgotten the whole thing, but now she vaguely recalls

---

2001) (law firm that represented parent company in prior substantially related matter disqualified from representing subsidiary in a later representation due to identity of interest between parent and subsidiary and confidential information from parent that could be used against it in the subsequent case).

32. *El Camino Res., Ltd. v. Huntington Nat'l Bank*, No. 1:07-cv-598, 2007 U.S. Dist. LEXIS 67813 (W.D. Mich. Sept. 13, 2007) (law firm that took on defense of bank in bankruptcy litigation to recover voidable preferences when it already represented two creditors in the same bankruptcy disqualified; advance waiver obtained by law firm was specifically limited to matters not involving bank in adverse actions); *Santacroce v. Neff*, 134 F. Supp. 2d 366 (D.N.J. 2001) (law firm that dropped one client like a hot potato to avoid conflict with another, more remunerative client disqualified).

33. MODEL RULE 1.7 cmt. [34]; RLGL § 14 cmt. f.

34. *Universal City Studios, Inc. v. Reimerdes*, 98 F. Supp. 2d 449 (S.D.N.Y. 2000) (law firm that took on representation of defendant after it represented plaintiff in an unrelated matter not entitled to drop least favored client like a "hot potato," but plaintiff's failure to timely raise issue would prejudice defendant and prevents disqualification).

doing a research memo in her second week at the firm on—of all things—a motion to disqualify that was denied. She claims she spent less than two hours on the research, which was strictly related to the legal question of how long can you delay filing a motion to disqualify. On the basis of that, we are going to be disqualified?

We can understand your dismay; you were careful. You correctly recognized that the only conflicts the associate brought with her from her old firm are those arising from matters on which she worked and matters as to which she actually acquired "confidential information." The associate didn't remember the assignment, even though her work, whatever it was, was client confidential. Under these circumstances, you certainly can resist a motion to disqualify in good faith.[35] There are a fair number of cases that label your associate's participation "peripheral" and refuse to disqualify a law firm in circumstances similar to these, on the grounds that the associate never "represented" the former client.[36] This just goes to demonstrate that every time a technical violation of the professional rules occurs, the aggrieved party will not necessarily succeed in convincing a court to grant the ultimate sanction.

✳ Injunctive Relief: Cut 'Em Off at the Pass

I'm general counsel of the biggest shopping center developer in the Northeast. Used to be a great job 'til malls went out of fashion. Anyway, that's neither here nor there. Problem is, we hired the best zoning lawyers in Cherry Dale for a new development, we call it a Town Center. Another name for a mall-less shopping center with cutesy storefronts. The firm got us the zoning we wanted. Took years, but we got to build exactly what we had hoped.

Now construction's underway. We have room for two anchors. Looking for a grocery store. And who shows up representing Natures Foods, one of those trendy organic stores, but one of the lawyers from the old zoning law firm. We can't have that. They sat in on our board meetings. Where we talked about everything.

---

35. MODEL RULE 1.9(b); RLGL § 124(1).

36. *E.g., Jamaica Pub. Serv. Co. v. AUI Ins. Co.*, 707 N.E.2d 414 (N.Y. 1998) (generalized allegations that lawyer had access to confidences and secrets not sufficient to create substantial relationship in the absence of a showing that the lawyer worked in a capacity related to the entities and issues raised in the current matter); *Silver Chrysler Plymouth, Inc. v. Chrysler Motors Corp.*, 518 F.2d 751 (2d Cir. 1975).

*Not just the chances of getting zoning and which Lincoln Day Dinners we had to
attend. But the financing. And the projections. They know how desperate we are
to get a grocery. So I thought we could get them disqualified. But then I realized,
there's no proceeding. All they're doing is coming to meetings. Guess we're
screwed.*

Not at all. One thing you can do is tell Natures Foods you don't want to
deal with them unless they get another law firm. If they refuse, the fact that
this is a transaction does not leave you without a remedy. While disqualification is a typical remedy for conflicts of interest in litigation, you can bring an
action seeking injunctive relief.[37] Against the law firm. Breach of fiduciary
duty. Irreparable harm. Just two things.

I know. There are always caveats.

First, you might try a letter reminding them of their continuing duties to
your mutual client. Before you spend a lot on a bazooka. Second, you'll have
to be prepared to demonstrate a violation of Rule 1.9. The substantial relationship between getting zoning and leasing is not immediately apparent.
Just because both representations involve the same shopping center may not
be enough. But the fact that these lawyers were given confidential information about the planned leasing program should be dispositive.[38]

⚊ Undue Influence

*I've got this client. Loves me. How rare is that? Now he wants to give me some
shares of stock in his company because I did such a great job on the last piece of
litigation. I'm talking a real gift.*

Client gifts are suspect. If they are large, they are presumptively void
because of the law of undue influence.[39] If your client *really* wants to do this,
and you think he is capable of making that judgment, then the last thing you

---

37. RLGL § 6(2); *Maritrans GP Inc. v. Pepper, Hamilton & Scheetz*, 602 A.2d 1277 (Pa. 1992) (law
firm enjoined from taking on adverse substantially related representation).

38. Model Rule 1.9, cmt. [3]; RLGL § 132, cmt. d.

39. *Passante v. McWilliam*, 62 Cal. Rptr. 2d 298 (Cal. Ct. App. 1997) (lawyer who "came through
in the clutch" raising money for a client's company and was promised three percent of the
firm's stock unable to prevail for breach of oral contract because, if promise was bargained for, it violated the lawyer's ethical duty, which should have included a written
waiver and advice to seek outside counsel and, if gratuitous, not legally enforceable due
to presumption of undue influence).

want is for you, or anyone in your firm, to draft the documents. Send him to another lawyer.[40]

Then maybe that lawyer will end up with the gift.

That could be, but if your firm drafts it, you have no chance of getting the gift without violating the rules.

𝓂 Constructive Trusts

Our good fortune sometimes seems endless. Our client, Disney, wants to assemble 25,000 acres in the middle of Virginia for a new theme park. This will be a multi-year project. We are supposed to go by stealth, use straw parties to make the purchases, and take our time, lest word gets out and the property value soars. But Disney has told us exactly the boundaries of the property it wants to acquire. It was just last week I was out for a Sunday drive to inspect that area when I noticed a large tract, maybe fifty or more acres, across from what will become the Disney land. I told my partners this morning we should buy that up. Once the Disney plan is announced, the value of this land will soar, and either we'll sell it or maybe we'll joint venture with a hotel operator to put a well-positioned property right across from Disney's new park.

Well, you are right about everything, except your ability to do this. You have confidential information from your client. Without your client's permission, it is totally improper to act on this. The rules not only bar disclosure of confidential information, but also its use.[41] So if you go forward with this, you may very well learn that you are buying the property in a constructive trust for Disney, not your entrepreneurial law firm.[42]

Is there nothing we can do to act on this opportunity?

Oh, you can act on it, but the first thing you must do is disclose the availability of this plot of land to see if Disney is interested. Even though they gave you boundaries to the land they wanted, when they hear this is available, they may change their minds. Even if they are not interested, you should

---

40. MODEL RULE 1.8(c); RLGL § 127.

41. MODEL RULE 1.8(b); RLGL § 60.

42. RLGL § 6, cmt. a; *David Welch Co. v. Erskine & Tulley*, 250 Cal. Rptr. 339 (Cal. Ct. App. 1988) (law firm that used client's confidences to set up a competing business breached fiduciary duty; firm was required to "disgorge their illicit gains" in a constructive trust). *See also Meinhard v. Salmon*, 164 N.E. 545 (N.Y. 1928) (agent who used principal's confidential information to purchase adjacent property held property in constructive trust).

disclose your plans for the property to them. It may be that they do not want their lawyers going into competition with them in the hotel business. Or being distracted by this other endeavor. Or skewing your advice to Disney because you now own this land. Our clients are entitled to our independent advice, something that might not be possible if you are joint venture partner of Hyatt.

🕮 Fee Forfeiture

We did a great job for Colossus. It was hard negotiating that loan. The credit markets froze just as we were about to close. And we were supposed to get paid from the proceeds. I sent the client wiring instructions. But no fee was forthcoming. I finally called the CFO. He laughed. But it was not a humorous moment. The CFO said he just learned that we were doing work for the bank. Some employment discrimination cases. Seems he called the lending officer to smooth some ruffled feathers and rebuild the relationship. The lending officer congratulated him, then he said, "You can thank your lawyers. Now you know why we use them all the time." But instead of thanking us for our superb services, he says the company owes us nothing. That's what his GC tells him is the result for an undisclosed conflict of interest . . . even when the services are superb. Can he be right?

He could be. While it's by no means certain, there are cases that conclude that an undisclosed conflict can form the basis for a fee disgorgement claim.[43] Seems unfair. But it is a way of giving lawyers a real incentive to uncover and disclose conflicts of interest in a timely way.[44]

🕮 Procedural Sanctions

This electronic discovery can drive you nuts. I thought it would be a windfall for lawyers. All that work. But it turns out, lawyers play a secondary role to the geeks our clients need to hire to lead them through the megabit thicket. It does give

---

43. *E.g., Burrow v. Arce,* 997 S.W.2d 229 (Tex. 1999) (lawyers allegedly violated aggregate settlement rule); *Hendry v. Pelland,* 73 F.3d 397 (D.C. Cir. 1996) (lawyers represented property owners with conflicting interests); *In re Eastern Sugar Antitrust Litig.,* 697 F.2d 524 (3d Cir. 1982) (law firm failed to disclose merger negotiations with opposing party's firm).

44. RLGL § 37.

us a lot of documents to review, that is, if the client doesn't send them to India for processing.

We know what you mean.

But get this one. Big case. IP fight. We produce millions of docs. So does the other side. And the deps. They're endless. So we're preparing this key witness for hers. Start showing her some docs. One document in a series seems to be missing. "Maybe it's on my home computer," she advises. "Then, why don't we have it?" we ask. "No one asked me for it" is the reply.

Turns out there are dozens of docs on her home computer. We've seen none of them. So we promptly call the other side, explain the screw-up, they thank us, and we deliver the package the next day.

Five days later, there's a motion to compel all personal PCs of 185 employees. And a motion for sanctions. Against us! We asked for all documents ten times, ten different ways. And our diligence gets rewarded with this sanctions motion. Now we have to respond, blaming our corporate client.

What a mess. But remember that old adage: when it comes to a choice between lawyer and client, the lawyer's job is to make sure it is the client that goes to jail! The issue of responsibility between client and lawyer in discovery is a vexing one, to say the least. The lawyer has the responsibility to the court. The lawyer also has the responsibility to explain fully to the client the scope of the client's responsibility to gather the information. But particularly with respect to the large entity client, there is no way the lawyer can handle the mechanics, the nuts and bolts, of the search. Just the ability to communicate with the necessary personnel, to identify hard drives, to handle the logistics of the gathering process is far beyond the ken of a mere lawyer, even one backed up with a cadre of smart young associates and paralegals.[45]

But sanctions? This was completely inadvertent on our part.

It is your responsibility, now that a sanctions motion has been filed, to decide whether the facts here create such a serious conflict between your firm and your client that you may have to terminate (or suspend) your representation while this is pending. Then, you'll have to decide whether your firm should retain counsel to represent your firm. While you don't want to dignify what we know you consider a frivolous motion, getting a new set of objective eyes to help you through this minefield may be a wise choice.

---

45. *E.g., Qualcomm Inc. v. Broadcom Corp.*, No. 05cv1958-B, 2008 U.S. Dist. Lexis 91104 (S.D. Cal. Jan. 7, 2008).

In any event, you must take whatever steps you can to explain to the court the mechanics and magnitude of your search, how your instructions to the client made the scope of the search clear, how you supervised the client's work in that regard, how you emphasized the importance of conducting a diligent search, and how you were required by the daunting nature of the task to delegate the actual work to the client. Then, you should present an explanation as to how these documents came to be located on a somewhat tardy basis, but that your firm acted as promptly as possible to expedite production once the oversight was discovered. Finally, you should be prepared to assert, if possible, that there was no particular advantage to your client's cause in withholding the late arriving documents from the other side. If you do that, the court should absolve you of responsibility, let alone sanctions for this discovery lapse.

Can't we just go in there and blame the clients? We clearly told them personal PDAs and PCs had to be searched. A couple of times.

You could, of course. In defending yourselves from a sanction motion, you should be entitled to use both confidential and privileged information. If you do so, you owe it to your client to alert them so that they can take whatever steps they might have available to them—from persuasion to motion practice—to prevent the disclosure.[46]

We'll do that, for sure.

But before you go down that road, you really have a good lawyering point to consider.

What's that?

Do you really need to use that kind of information to protect yourself? Is there really such a different defense to this sanctions motion available to you from the client? Is it possible you could defend yourself *and* the client against this motion, which may be no more than a tactical maneuver to drive you out of the case? The answers to these questions may be yes, yes, and no. But certainly, you have an obligation to consider the least drastic and damaging solution to this uncomfortable situation before you go down a more radical road.

---

46. MODEL RULE 1.6(b)(5); RLGL §§ 64, 83.

PART TWO

Representing Specific Legal Fictions

*"I'm not against public service. I just think I can
do more damage in the private sector."*

TEN

Privately Held Businesses

※ Introduction: Knowing Your Client

IN THIS CHAPTER, we focus on a wide realm of legal fictions: businesses without public ownership. Privately held businesses can range in size from sole proprietorships, to small and large joint ventures or partnerships, to family and large corporations. Often, but not always, these businesses will be owned by a small group, perhaps family or friends who know each other well. Some can be characterized by little or no separation of management from ownership. Others are organized and managed much like public companies. Privately held businesses are subject to a myriad of state and federal laws, which offer a variety of legal structures such as general and limited partnerships (with or without limited liability partnership registration), limited liability companies, business trusts, and corporations.[1]

Your ethical obligations to privately held businesses depend on both their legal structure and an equally clear understanding of the law governing lawyers. We explore here issues related to identifying your client, your Five C fiduciary obligations in the context of representing private businesses, and the limits of the law that may have special application in this context.

We will see throughout the chapter that the size of the entity you represent as well as the relationships among its owners shape both their expectations of you and your obligations to them. Although these private relationships can complicate your representation, they also provide you with the opportunity to cement a long-term client-lawyer relationship. Special care must be taken when you represent both the entity and individual constituents. If they feud, you can find yourself in an impossible situation.

---

1. For a chart that compares these business forms, *see* ALAN R. BROMBERG & LARRY E. RIBSTEIN, LIMITED LIABILITY PARTNERSHIPS, THE REVISED UNIFORM PARTNERSHIP ACT AND THE UNIFORM LIMITED PARTNERSHIP ACT (2001), 41 (Aspen 2008).

If you side with one over the others, the disadvantaged will claim you as lawyer and may allege that you either breached your own or your favored client's fiduciary duty to them.

🕮 Representing Close Corporations

I helped three friends form Innonet, Incorporated, but the conflicts don't seem to end. How do I know which clients to listen to?

How many clients do you have?

Only one. We stopped representing Tom, our original client. Now we just represent Innonet.

So how come you referred to clients?

Oh, that. I'm referring to the original three. I guess I shouldn't call them clients.

But everyone does. When lawyers represent organizations—corporations, partnerships, not-for-profits—they always refer to the individuals with whom they deal as clients. It's the natural way of speaking, even dignifies and cements the relationship with these client representatives. But, of course, even if these are the people who hired you, who decide whether you are going to get the next engagement, who review and then authorize the company to pay your bills, they are not the client.

So who is the client?

The client is the entity. It is to that legal construct that you owe all your lawyer duties.[2]

But that's an abstraction. I can't call up an art museum.

Precisely. And our rules recognize that. They tell you that your duties are owed to the client. But you take direction from individuals.

But which one? Innonet is tiny, ten employees. But we do work for Colossus, and it has 27,000 employees.

Great question. One that the rules answer. Generally, a lawyer shall take instructions from the person or persons who are assigned for that purpose.[3] Sometimes it will be the board of directors. Sometimes it will be an officer or

---

2. Model Rule 1.13(a); RLGL § 96(1); *Marchman v. NCNB Tex. Nat'l Bank*, 898 P.2d 709 (N.M. 1995) (even a sole shareholder of a corporation has no individual right of action against a third party for injury to the entity).

3. Model Rule 1.13, cmt. 3; RLGL § 96(1)(b), cmt. d.

general counsel. Sometimes it will be the plant superintendent or the head of the lab whom you go to in the normal course for instructions.

And if it's more than one person, and I get conflicting signals?

It's your responsibility to address the problem. See if you cannot effect a reconciliation of differing points of view. If not, you should follow form.

What do you mean by that?

You take your instructions from the person who has the higher authority within the organization. So if it's a battle between the plant superintendent and the CFO, the officer's view prevails.

𝄢 Representing Partnerships

I understand Rule 1.13 as it applies to corporations. The corporation is my client. I deal with the person I'm instructed to deal with, and if things get really sticky, I can work my way up the ladder. But I've just been asked to represent an accounting firm. It is a partnership of ten partners, or at least that's what the letterhead lists. So who's my client?

Rule 1.13 applies. The partnership is your client; you represent the entity.[4]

That makes no sense.

You're telling us the Rule is flawed?

Well, I was thinking about what we discussed regarding communication. Under Rule 1.13, in the corporate setting, I suppose it's fine if I communicate with my assigned contact. But if someone were representing our law firm, I would want to know what's happening. Unlike shareholders, partners, you might recall, may have unlimited liability depending on the structure selected.

We take your point. But we ought to sort out a number of different concepts.

It's getting complicated.

Not really. First, there is the question with whom you have to communicate. That should be determined when you begin the representation. In a small partnership, it might be everyone; in larger partnerships, that might be impractical.

Who gets to decide that?

---

4. ABA Comm. on Ethics and Prof'l Responsibility, Formal Op. 91-361 (1991) (Representation of a Partnership); RLGL § 96, cmt. c.

The partnership.

If I'm a partner, they don't have to consult me?

It is up to you to know how your partnership is run and to make sure your partner who contacts the lawyer tells the lawyer how your partnership expects to be informed, directly or through one of your colleagues.

So, as the lawyer for this accounting firm, I don't have to worry?

No. You do. It is your job to clarify how the client expects you to deal with its partners. But you can accept the word of the person who calls you.[5]

Then the entity theory does really work with partnerships?

Let's put it this way. It's a start. But there is a lot of positive law regarding partnerships that varies jurisdiction from jurisdiction that you must know, particularly in the area of who is your client.

I thought you said the partnership was the client.

The partnership definitely is. But that's not the end of it.

I have more clients?

In some jurisdictions when you represent a partnership, you also represent all of the partners.[6] In others, you do not.[7]

I have to clear conflicts for all of them? To take a new matter on?

You would.

Even limited partners?

Not usually the case,[8] but in a few jurisdictions, yes.[9]

So what does that mean for me if the partnership wants me to sue one of its partners?

Great question. Under the entity theory, your client is the partnership, and you can take positions directly adverse to any of its partners as long as that individual is not independently your client.[10]

I'm confused.

---

5. MODEL RULE 1.13, cmt. [3]; RLGL § 96, cmt. d.

6. *Rice v. Strunk*, 670 N.E.2d 1280 (Ind. 1996) (lawyer has separate attorney-client relationship with each general partner under Uniform Partnership Act).

7. *Kopka v. Kamensky & Rubenstein*, 821 N.E. 2d 719 (Ill. App. Ct. 2004) (lawyer for partnership does not represent individual partners).

8. *Hopper v. Frank*, 16 F.3d 92 (5th Cir. 1994) (limited partners lacked attorney-client relationship necessary to sue partnership's lawyer for malpractice).

9. *Arpadi v. First MSP Corp.*, 628 N.E.2d 1335 (Ohio 1994); *Wortham & Van Liew v. Superior Court*, 233 Cal. Rptr. 725 (Cal. Ct. App. 1987).

10. *Thruway Invs. v. O'Connell & Aronowitz, P.C.*, 772 N.Y.S.2d 716 (N.Y. App. Div. 2004) (law firm represented limited partnership but not individual partners or subsequently formed corporation).

It's the same as with any organization. Two things. First, it may be that you did some personal legal work for one of the partners. That would make that partner a client for those matters. Second, you may have dealt with one of the partners regarding the business in a way that that person came to consider you the person's lawyer.[11] Calling her "your client." Spending a lot of time together. Having that partner confide in you. In that situation, the partner's reasonable perception might trump your technical view that you only represented the partnership.[12] So you'd be banned from representing the partnership vis-à-vis this partner. Then there's the Rule 1.7(a)(2) issue.

You and your rule numbers. What's that?

Even if the partner can't be deemed to be your client, bringing a claim adverse to a partner of the partnership could trigger a material limitation. You just might pull your punches because you have known the person for so long.

You're telling me I might not be able to take the matter, but neither will anyone else?

Sure they can. A fresh face won't have a history.

But if the lawyer for a partnership is viewed as representing all the partners, how can the partnership find a way to sue a partner in its name? Isn't the partnership's lawyer automatically suing a client?

You have a great point. We suppose in that instance that the lawyer who is consulted by a partnership to bring a claim against one of the partnership's partners, by definition, cannot be deemed to have formed a lawyer-client relationship with the putative adverse partner.[13]

※ The Bad Decision

What happens if I am unhappy with the conduct of the general partner who is my contact? Do I then have a duty to communicate with the other partners?

---

11. *Steinfeld v. Marks*, 96 Civ. 0552, 1997 U.S. Dist. Lexis 13569 (S.D.N.Y. Sept. 8, 1997) (lawyer hired by one of two joint venturers may be lawyer of entity as well as joint venturers); *Responsible Citizens v. Superior Court*, 20 Cal. Rptr. 2d 756 (Cal. Ct. App. 1993) (factors to consider in determining whether partnership's lawyer is also lawyer for individual partners include nature and scope of lawyer's engagement, size and type of partnership, nature and extent of contacts between partners and lawyer, and lawyer's access to confidential information of individual partners).

12. *E.g.*, *Meyer v. Mulligan*, 889 P.2d 509 (Wyo. 1995) (question of fact whether incorporators of business were co-clients in business with standing to sue lawyer for malpractice).

13. MODEL RULE 1.13, cmt. [10]; RLGL § 131, cmt. f.

The case law is split. Certainly, if a Rule 1.13 standard is violated, you must take reasonable remedial action, including going up the organizational ladder.[14]

But who's higher than a partner?

No one. But you would go to one or more other partners or, if the partnership has a governing board, you could go to that body.

What if the problem is short of that? I don't "know" something bad is happening, but I am worried.

Now you have hit upon an important issue. The rules tell you normally you deal with the individual to whom you are assigned. If you know a catastrophe is about to occur, you must follow the Rule 1.13 line of attack. But what about the middle situation? There's a cause for concern far short of a Rule 1.13 triggering event. Then you still owe duties to the partnership, not the individual partner, and you should act like the competent lawyer you are and take steps necessary to fulfill the best interests of the partnership.[15] You may not get disciplined if you don't; but you may violate the standard of care nonetheless.[16]

🎙 The Internal Split

I work for a small green energy start-up. Last week, oldest son, who is general manager, told me to settle a case with a distributor; and the controller daughter said to file a motion for summary judgment.

Now it is the time to know how governance works in the organization you represent. Sometimes that will be very formal and quite clear; but in closely held businesses, the organization chart may be nonexistent. If you think the general manager reports to the controller, then you need to confirm your understanding in discussions with both of them, and then follow the superior officer's instructions. If you have no idea, you must pick your way up the ladder to someone, maybe dad, whose authority is decidedly superior to the

---

14. MODEL RULE 1.13(b); RLGL § 96(2).

15. RLGL § 96, cmt. e.

16. *E.g., Johnson v. Superior Court,* 45 Cal. Rptr. 2d 312 (Cal. Ct. App. 1995) (mere representation of partnership does not constitute representation of partners, but limited partners can sue for breach of obligation to partnership).

two combatants, and get that individual to get back to you with an organizational decision on whether you are to make peace or war.[17]

What if I think the decision of the son is stupid?

In many respects, the answer to that question is the same as it would be for an individual client. Clients get to decide. And they get to make mistakes. Or do things we lawyers think are unwise or worse. So, too, with our proverbial corporate employee. That person to whom you are assigned is allowed to make stupid decisions. And as long as they are legal decisions, it is not your job to second-guess. So if son decides, for example, to reject a settlement, that is his prerogative as general manager.[18] Your obligation is to give your best advice, to urge son to the contrary, but if you believe you have satisfied your advice function, then your next job is to abide by the instructions of the general manager. Son's job performance ultimately will be judged based on this and a hundred other decisions he makes. It is not up to you to substitute your judgment for the judgment of the clearly assigned client representative.

☕ The Start-Up Fallout

The clients—oops, the organizers—came to me asking to form the next Google. Problem was, each of the four of them could not afford to hire his or her own lawyer. So I told them I could get them to the end, but because of conflicts among them—one was investing money; another had the brilliant idea; the third would run the lab; the fourth was the salesman—I would have to give them a checklist, and they would negotiate among themselves. So far so good. They agree. But now there's been a falling out. And the idea guy is suing us. He admits we warned him about the conflicts. But he claims our checklist did not include the possibility that he could simply license his patent. As a result, he assigned it to the corporation, which is now bankrupt. And the patent is about to become the property of the secured creditors. With no residuals to our brilliant software engineer. Are we in trouble?

---

17. MODEL RULE 1.13, cmt. [4]; RLGL § 96, cmt. e.

18. *Burger v. Brookhaven Med. Arts Bldg., Inc.*, 516 N.Y.S.2d 705 (N.Y. App. Div. 1987) (lawyer not responsible for client's alleged breach of contract negotiated by lawyer within scope of lawyer's authority).

Well, we are sure you attempted to limit your representation to the entity to be formed.[19] And you made it clear you did not represent the four individuals. But then you did undertake to provide a checklist of options. And in taking on this limited "representation," it could be found that all four were clients for this very narrow purpose.[20] If our genius can find a lawyer who will assert that the standard of care should have included this option, he may be able to establish negligence. Worse, if your conflict blinded you to presenting the option, he may be able to assert breach of fiduciary duty. But, of course, that won't establish a claim. He'll still have to prove the other three would have gone forward with no more than a license. Otherwise, your non-client will never be able to prove causation.[21] He will also have to prove that the patent had value. Fee disgorgement, however, might be a different story.[22]

𝓜 The Amended UPA

This one has really got me scratching my head. We successfully got three partners through the process of forming a business entity, and ever since, we have been representing the partnership, which has been very successful in developing small strip-shopping centers in the area. The law in effect at the time we formed the partnership provided, and we explained to each of the partners, that the withdrawal of any of them from the partnership would result in its liquidation and dissolution. The partners were fine with that. But now, our state has amended its Uniform Partnership Act, and, under its terms, the withdrawal of one partner would permit the partnership to continue if the two remaining partners were prepared to buy out the third. From what we know about the partners, one will be thrilled by that development (he's wanted out for two years), and the others might be quite dismayed. How do we proceed?

Your client is the partnership, and you ought to continue to stand on that very high ground. Unless there is some reason that one or more of the

---

19. MODEL RULE 1.2(c); RLGL § 19.

20. MODEL RULE 1.7, cmt. [28]; RLGL § 130, cmt. c.

21. *MacFarlane v. Nelson*, No. 03-04-00488-CV, 2005 Tex. App. LEXIS 7681 (Tex. App. Sept. 15, 2005) (client must offer probative evidence of damages caused by lawyer's admitted breach of duty); *Milbank, Tweed, Hadley & McCloy v. Boon*, 13 F.3d 537 (2d Cir. 1994) (in breach of fiduciary duty suits, client required to prove only that breach was a substantial factor in preventing client from obtaining benefit; but for causation not required).

22. RLGL § 37; *Hendry v. Pelland*, 73 F.3d 397 (D.C. Cir. 1996) (client seeking fee disgorgement need not prove that breach of fiduciary duty caused harm).

partners will also think that you are that partner's lawyer, you ought to bring the partners in, explain the development, and tell them that you can only proceed to amend the partnership agreement on their behalf if all three agree. If there is any division among them, you will have to suggest they get other counsel for this purpose.[23] And even in the case where your represent the partnership and one partner, you probably are better off sending all three partners to other lawyers to work this out. You are fulfilling your duty to the partnership by explaining the change of law,[24] but going further than that, under these circumstances, risks a malpractice claim or a charge that you are violating the rules.

So I followed your advice. I brought all three in. They clearly don't agree, and I sent them on their way. Now the lawyer for one of the partners is threatening to sue me for malpractice, claiming I should never have left the partnership dissolution provisions subject to the vagaries of statutory law. In short, she claims I should have insisted they cover this matter in their partnership agreement.

Unfortunately, the claim could have some merit—at least insofar as an expert might testify that the standard of care required you to explain to the partners in the beginning that this was one of the alternatives.[25] So all that stands between you and a malpractice claim may be finding the expert to so testify.

But, that is what everybody did back then.

If that is so, then your expert will respond accordingly. In any event, your failure to include the clause regarding dissolution is not the end of the story. This partner will have to prove both causation and damages, both of which could present fairly insurmountable barriers in our view.[26]

✍ A Partner Complains

We were handling a major lawsuit against a big-shot Hollywood director who failed to honor his contract to direct a film this partnership was producing. After months of wrangling, the partnership decided to settle. So we did. But now, one

---

23. MODEL RULE 1.7, cmt. [7], RLGL § 130.

24. MODEL RULE 1.4, RLGL § 20.

25. *E.g., Russo v. Griffin,* 510 A.2d 436 (Vt. 1986).

26. *Viner v. Sweet,* 70 P.3d 1046 (Cal. 2003) (plaintiff who alleges malpractice in transaction must prove that but for lawyer's malpractice, plaintiff would have obtained a better result).

of the disgruntled partners plans to sue our firm for malpractice. He says we failed to tell the client about mediation as an option. I called the managing general partner who says she's perfectly happy. Can he do this?

Probably not. Only clients can sue lawyers for malpractice.[27] But three factors could make a difference. First, which jurisdiction you're in. Most adopt the entity theory of partnerships, agreeing with the Restatement that you represented the partnership, not any of the individual partners.[28] Second, the partnership agreement itself. Even jurisdictions that rely on the aggregate rather than the entity theory hold that the partnership can designate its own managers, thereby relieving the lawyer of the obligation to consult with all.[29] Here you dealt with a managing partner, so we assume, and hope, that's the authorized constituent you took direction from. Third, what does your retainer letter say? This issue should be clarified from the start of the representation for just this reason. Fourth, assuming you represented the entity alone, you could have taken on an accidental client-lawyer relationship to an individual partner as well, but only if that person reasonably relied on your legal services. Here, any personal reliance would not be reasonable unless, perhaps, you had represented that person independently from the partnership representation.[30]

𝕎 Sharing the Research

Got a call from one of the partners of my client, this accounting firm. Insisted I send him my research file on a case we're handling for her firm. I told her I wouldn't do it. The firm is my client, I explained, and I deal with the CFO of the firm.

What are you worried about?

---

27. *E.g., Barry v. Liddle, O'Connor, Finkelstein & Robinson*, 98 F.3d 36 (2d Cir. 1996).

28. RLGL § 96, cmt. c; *Rice, supra* note 6; *Kopka, supra* note 7.

29. *Richter v. Van Amberg*, 97 F. Supp. 2d 1255 (D.N.M. 2000) (lawyer represented partnership, not individual partners, because partnership agreement designated managing partner); *Rice v. Strunk*, 670 N.E.2d 1280 (Ind. 1996) (lawyer has separate attorney-client relationship with each general partner under Uniform Partnership Act, but relationship may be modified by the way the partnership agreement allocates partnership management).

30. *Zimmerman v. Dan Kamphausen Co.*, 971 P.2d 236 (Colo. App. 1998) (law firm created no attorney-client relationship between individual partner based on representation of the partnership).

First, I don't want to breach my duty of confidentiality. If I represent the partnership, I can't be communicating sensitive information to twenty-three different partners.

Good start.[31] Anything else?

Sure. Won't this waive the privilege? I know when I represent a corporation, to preserve privilege, I have to monitor which employees receive my communication, or there might be a waiver. Is a partnership different?

It could be. If all partners are general partners with unlimited liability, you could make a good argument that you are free to communicate with them generally. But remember, the entity determines its agents for purposes of the privilege. Limited partners, on the other hand, are more like shareholders, and the corporate rules should apply.[32]

🕊 The Partners Settle

I represent the partners in a partnership. It's an architectural firm. The firm got sued for malpractice, and, unfortunately, it looks as if they have no insurance for this particular claim. The insurance company asserts that it only insured projects in the U.S., and this one was in Toronto. So now we have a chance to settle. I have been dealing with the senior managing partner. He tells me to accept the deal, and he will handle allocating the damages to each partner. But my clients are each of the partners. It doesn't feel right to me.

Your concerns are quite legitimate. Your clients, the partners, have been presented with what is an aggregate settlement, just payment of a lump sum. In order for you to fulfill your obligations to them, the aggregate settlement rule—Rule 1.8(g)—requires you to obtain informed consent from each client in writing, and only after each is informed of the amount of the total settlement and the amount each partner will be paying toward the settlement. This is not a duty you can delegate to the managing partner of the firm.[33] You must communicate and receive the informed consent of each partner.[34]

---

31. MODEL RULE 1.13, cmt. [2]; RLGL § 73, cmt. d.

32. RLGL § 73; *Montgomery v. eTreppid Techs., LLC*, 548 F. Supp. 2d 1175 (D. Nev. 2008) (federal common law treats limited partnerships as corporations for purposes of the attorney-client privilege).

33. RLGL § 22, cmt. c.

34. MODEL RULE 1.8(g); ABA Comm. on Ethics and Prof'l Responsibility, Formal Op. 06-438 (2006) (Lawyer Proposing to Make or Accept an Aggregate Settlement or Aggregated Agreement).

✍ Papering the Loan

These close corporations really drive you crazy. Here we have a company with four shareholders. They run a restaurant supply business. We do all their corporate work, contracts, some employee discrimination cases, you name it. They wanted to borrow money from Big Bank and asked us to help them. Actually, the company wanted to borrow money, so I negotiated with the bank, which decided that it would lend the money. But, in this climate, the bank wanted guarantees from the four principals. I explained that to them and also reviewed the guarantee documents the bank needed to be signed.

Six months later, there was a falling out. Turns out one of the shareholders was getting some kickbacks on the side. Nasty stuff. So the company CEO fired him, and we were asked to sue this vice president for damages to the company. Now, however, the defendant has moved to disqualify us based on the advice we gave this individual regarding the guarantees. What do you think?

You certainly have an argument that this person was never a client of your firm. It was really as part of your role as company counsel that you gave the brief advice regarding the guarantees. But we're afraid the better view on these facts is that, in fact, you took on each of these shareholders as clients for this limited purpose. But limited or unlimited, a client is a client.[35]

This, however, is not dispositive because it appears, as you describe it, that the kickback king is a former client.[36] The only advice you gave him related to these guarantees, and then that representation ended. And, unless it turns out that someone can make the argument with a straight face that the guarantees are substantially related to the underhanded conduct, we think the better view is that you can proceed with the lawsuit.[37] Of course, unfortunately, it will be some judge, and not we, who gets to decide. But we certainly think you have a meritorious position.

---

35. *Schnabel v. Sullivan*, 04-CV-5076, 2008 U.S. Dist. LEXIS 79048 (E.D.N.Y.).

36. MODEL RULE 1.9; RLGL § 132.

37. *Richter v. Van Amberg*, 97 F. Supp. 2d 1255 (D.N.M. 2000) (lawyer's previous representation involving a different partnership and different real estate not substantially related to new business); *Jesse v. Danforth*, 485 N.W.2d 63 (Wis. 1992) (lawyer's assistance in creating corporation for twenty-three physicians did not bar subsequent suit against one physician for medical malpractice; corporation, not physician, was client and all communications between physician and lawyer were directly related to organizing the business).

✎ Family Businesses

I represent this family. Actually their business. Quite successful. Dad and mom and their three kids. All was going fine. Typical family business. Everyone makes a good salary. Even some who don't exactly show up for work every day. And the business pays for perks within the aggressive range. Believe me, we do no one's tax returns. All was lovely until the youngest—the only daughter—went to law school. Learned about shareholder rights. Started resenting her dad being so aggressive at the trough. And since dad has given each of the kids a significant number of shares over the years—part of his estate planning—the daughter hired counsel and brought a derivative claim. Against her entire family in the name of the company. Now we've got a tough case to defend.

Not so fast. Can you really take on this case?

Well, we've represented the company from its founding.

That's interesting, but not helpful. In a derivative claim, the company is simply a nominal defendant.

How's that?

Derivative claims are fascinating both as a matter of jurisprudence and ethics. The shareholder "volunteers" to bring a claim that the corporation won't bring.[38]

Well, that's for sure. This corporation is controlled by dad, even if he gave away his stock to the kids.

But the persons who need real representation are dad, mom, and the other kids. They are the defendants. And they are being asked to return the value of benefits they received from the company.

So we'll represent them. After all, we've done all kinds of things for all of them over the years. Dad's will; number one son's DUI; number two son's annulment. You name it.

And daughter?

Oh, that's true. We've represented her, too. Well, not really. She is head of company sales. She got in a dispute with an ad agency over some billboards. We got her out of that pickle. But we really represented the company in that case. Oh, and we did write her will four years ago. But that only makes her a former client.

What does she think?

You are right. She probably thinks we're her lawyer too.

---

38. MODEL RULE 1.13, cmts. [13] & [14]; RLGL §§ 85, 131, cmt. g.

Undoubtedly. So you may have to sit this one out.[39]

Maybe that is just as well.

𝕸 The Ouster

I represent a closely held corporation with two brothers. Each owns half of the shares, and the business is a vineyard. Quite good wine, I might add. I represented the business for twenty years. Now I've been approached by one of the brothers, asking me whether I can assist him in ousting the other brother from the company. I did not even bother to find out the basis so that I could talk to you.

Once again, there is no doubt that the entity is your client. But it is very hard to divorce yourself from the two shareholders of the client when each owns so many shares and, we take it, is actively involved in the business. Even if technically the other brother is not a client, it will be very hard to argue that the other brother doesn't have client-like expectations of loyalty from you, starting with the fact that you almost invariably refer to this person as your client.[40]

I sure do that.

And you have probably given this person advice on legal matters based on time charges paid by the company over the years. As a result, we don't see any basis on which you can commence a representation of Jacob against Esau.[41]

---

39. MODEL RULE 1.13, cmt. [14]; RLGL § 131, cmt. g; *Bell Atl. Corp. v. Bolger*, 2 F.3d 1304 (3d Cir. 1993) (same lawyer cannot represent directors and corporation in derivative suit where fraud alleged).

40. *In re Banks*, 584 P.2d 284(Ore. 1978) (lawyer represented both majority shareholder and corporation when providing legal services and could not thereafter represent either client when their interests were in opposition).

41. *LeRoy v. Allen, Yurasek & Merklin*, 872 N.E.2d 254 (Ohio 2007) (lawyer may be liable to third party for aiding and abetting if fraud, collusion, or malice were present in preparing a will and stock transfer in close corporation for elderly client; conflict of interest or collusion with beneficiaries presented fact issue); *Cacciola v. Nellhaus*, 733 N.E.2d 133 (Mass. App. Ct. 2000) (partnership lawyer may be liable for aiding and abetting partner's breach of fiduciary duty by acting as partner's lawyer in transaction that conflicted with lawyer's duty to partnership); *Fassihi v. Sommers, Schwartz, Silver, Schwartz & Tyler, P.C.*, 309 N.W.2d 645 (Mich. 1981) (plaintiff fifty percent shareholder in close corporation may have cause of action against corporation's lawyer for assisting breach of fiduciary duty of other shareholder in ousting plaintiff from company).

ELEVEN

Publicly Held Businesses

% Introduction: Separating Ownership from Control

PUBLICLY HELD BUSINESSES separate ownership from management and because of their size, can produce tremendous gain or blame in their activities. The law that governs them is intended to address this separation, by assuring stockholder rights. Public disclosure is required for many activities, but, as with other organizations, does not exhaust the fiduciary obligations by of those who act on behalf of the entity.

As with private businesses, your ethical obligations to publicly held businesses depend on both their legal structure and your awareness of the law governing lawyers. We explore in this chapter issues that should now be familiar: identifying your client, the Five C fiduciary obligations in the context of public businesses, and the limits of the law that may have special application in this context.

Federal and state securities laws impose some of these additional obligations, and often require you, as the entity's lawyer, to certify your due diligence in preparing SEC or other regulatory filings. Regulations adopted by the SEC pursuant to Sarbanes-Oxley impose both up-the-ladder obligations similar but not identical to those imposed by Model Rule 1.13. When a public company succeeds, it has nearly always been assisted by its lawyers. If it fails, lawyers and others are often under scrutiny for failing to prevent, or even aiding, in its demise.

% Corporate Authority

I've been handling a major environmental matter for Excelsior Corporation. The EPA has come after them for remediation of a number of Excelsior locations. In this matter, Excelsior has me dealing with the plant superintendent in Pittsburgh. Great fellow, knowledgeable and reliable. The EPA has offered him a plan. It is *really expensive. After I told the plant superintendent I thought this was the best we could do, he said, "We'll accept the deal." So I did, but now I'm worried. It's true that the plant superintendent was the corporate representative assigned to this matter, but I wonder if he has authority to commit Excelsior to a $27 million clean-up. Should I be concerned?*

Generally, lawyers should deal with the constituent of the organization to whom they are assigned. An organization can only deal through constituents, and once the client decides who that person or persons shall be, as a general proposition, the lawyer should be free to accept that person's instructions.[1] There have to be two exceptions, however. The first, of course, is something we have discussed elsewhere. That is, what the lawyer does when the lawyer knows that the constituent is acting contrary to the interests of the organization.[2] The other is when it is not clear the individual or individuals with whom one is dealing really have authority to take whatever the necessary steps are. That is your present situation. The wise lawyer, without ruffling feathers, should first seek assurances from the plant superintendent that he or she has authority to commit Excelsior to the EPA's plan. And if there is then any doubt, the wise lawyer will run the risk of incurring plant superintendent's wrath and seek confirmation of the plant superintendent's authority from someone higher up in the organization.[3]

✏ IPO Fees Paid in Shares

Talk about lucky. We've been asked to do this new IPO. For a stem cell research start-up. We met with them last week. Brought our A Team. They told us they wanted the very best firm, but because of their cash problems, they were hoping the firm they select will take its fee in insider stock. Can you believe it? So much better than just billing hours.

How many shares?

That's just it. Because they're not sure this thing will fly, the fee will only be payable if the IPO occurs; but if it does, they'll give us $5 million in stock. That's probably triple what our normal fees would be. My partners are going to love me.

---

1. MODEL RULE 1.13(a) & cmt. [3]; RLGL § 96(1).

2. *See also supra,* Chapter 4: "Up-the Ladder Obligations" through "Up-the-Ladder: Enough?."

3. RLGL § 96, cmt. e.

They might. Then again, they might not. It sure is true that lawyers have taken stock for fees since time immemorial. But it's not a risk-free endeavor, especially when it's an IPO.

Of course, maybe the deal won't happen. And then we'll have wasted a lot of time.

That's one risk.

There's more?

Two off the top of my head. Let's take 'em one at a time. What happens if the stock crashes?

We'll warn investors properly in the prospectus. We're great at writing bullet-proof "risk factors." We know this will be a volatile stock. That's how come we get such a big upside.

But you know what happens when an IPO goes south. Stock prices plummet; recriminations all around; and disappointed investors and those craven plaintiffs' lawyers look to hold someone responsible.

That's management's problem.

Not if they can argue disclosure in the prospectus was false and misleading.

You know how careful we're going to be.

But you can't know everything, and you've already built into the deal one very bad fact.

We haven't even started our due diligence.

But you have agreed to get paid in a contingent deal in stock. Which means you will be accused of letting a bad deal come to market—instead of just saying no—because that was the only way you would get compensated. Sold the stock to unsuspecting widows and orphans so you guys could unload your shares and get your unreasonable fee for tainted advice.[4]

You don't sound like my lawyer.

No. I'm your Dutch Uncle.

You said there were two problems. Is the second worse?

You be the judge. Taking a fee in stock is said to be the equivalent of doing business with your client.[5]

It's doing business with my client to get paid?

Only if you get paid in stock.

What difference does that make anyway?

---

4. *See, e.g., Prousalis v. U.S.*, 06 Civ. 12946, 2007 U.S. Dist. LEXIS 63025 (S.D.N.Y. Aug. 24, 2007).

5. MODEL RULE 1.8(a); RLGL § 126; ABA Comm. on Ethics and Prof'l Responsibility, Formal Op. 00-418 (2000) (Acquiring Ownership in a Client in Connection with Performing Legal Services).

Well, in addition to the possible need to disclose the transaction in the offering circular, there is a special rule that governs such a transaction. Rule 1.8(a) says that when doing business with your client, you must put the arrangement in writing, advise the client to get another lawyer's advice, and the transaction will be judged by its entire fairness to the client.

Look. We'll do all that. Besides, it was the client who suggested the $5 mil. We didn't bargain at all.

That makes no difference. If in retrospect the fee looks too pricey, there is a chance that someone will challenge it.

But it's so risky. How could anyone ever claim it's unfair?

Hindsight is 20-20. Just don't be surprised if after the fact someone asserts that, upon reflection, the fee is unreasonable, and the deal is not entirely fair to the client.[6]

How unfair to us!

And expensive, too. So if you want to proceed with accepting the shares for your fee, you will at least be doing so with your collective eyes wide open.

✸ Clients Everywhere but Who Can You Represent?

I handled this great engagement. My client, Black Knight, the buyout firm, purchased a majority of the shares of Blender Industries for cash and Black Knight stock. After the deal closes, I am asked to handle many matters for Blender. What a business development opportunity. Blender generates a lot of legal work. But now Blender is in a battle with Black Knight's key shareholders over some very troubling stuff. Blender is wrong, in my humble opinion. And the Black Knight shareholders want me to represent them.

You think you can do it?

Sure hope so. After all, my real clients are the shareholders. They are my buddies.

So what bothers you?

Technically, I would be adverse to my present client, Blender.

Technically?

Sure, it's not a real conflict since Black Knight's folks are right on this one.

But we are afraid it is more than technical. No matter how you got there, Blender is a client.[7] And no matter how right the Black Knight side is, Blender,

---

6. *E.g., Passante v. McWilliam*, 62 Cal. Rptr. 2d 298 (Cal. Ct. App. 1997).

7. RLGL § 14.

through its present governance structure, gets to decide what is in its best interests.[8] And if Black Knight cannot figure a way of exerting control and the dispute continues, you cannot take on the matter adverse to Blender. Can't represent Blender either. If for no other reason than your desire to work for the other side.[9]

🎔 Corporate Employees

Our company bought a new biotech subsidiary. Gene-splicing. Now the SEC is investigating our procedures for keeping that information secret prior to the public announcement. The suspicion is that one or more of our employees bought the new sub's shares ahead of the news. So the board asked us to handle the defense and conduct an investigation.

And you did so?

We did. It really went well. We met with the employees. Told them how our investigation was confidential and privileged. One had no idea about the transaction. Bought because he read a favorable write-up in a professional magazine. The other insists he didn't buy. Doesn't know why he's been singled out. You'd be amazed the precautions the company took. But then there's this little problem.

What's that?

The second guy called me up. Said he just remembered. He might have mentioned the target company to his brother-in-law.

That means he did.

I'm sure you're right. But then he told me not to tell anyone. He reminded me how I told him our conversation was privileged. I meant it was privileged for the client, but I am worried.

And for good reason. These corporate investigations have to be handled so carefully.

That's why I warned him.

But that warning could have confused him. Mentioning the words "confidential" or "privileged" to a corporate employee might lead the employee to think you won't tell anybody at the company, when the reverse is true. You planned to share what you learned with your corporate client.

But if I told him that, he'd never have talked. What did you want me to do? Read him Miranda warnings?

---

8. RLGL § 96 (1).

9. MODEL RULE 1.13, cmt. [14].

Not quite that scary. But something close. (See Figure 10) You had to make it clear whom you represented, that you were undertaking an investigation, and that you were obliged to report the results to the company officials.[10]

Before you know it, these employees will ask if they need a lawyer.

And, if they do, there is only one piece of advice you may—but are not required to—give to your corporate employees. If, in fact, you think the employee should get a lawyer, it is the authors' view that you should say so.

Figure 10   Disclosures to Employee Witnesses in Conducting a Board of Directors Investigation

As you may know, litigation has been instituted against the Company claiming that the Company_____.

The Board of Directors has decided to conduct an investigation of this matter to determine whether those in positions of responsibility properly fulfilled their duties. The Board of course, recognizes that activity undertaken in good faith and involving no actionable conduct may appear incorrect with the benefit of hindsight. On the other hand, it is the responsibility of the Board to determine whether all concerned acted in a manner consistent with their duties to the corporation and its shareholders. It is in that context that we plan to interview you.

It is important that you understand that our firm represents the Company generally. We do not represent you. Our only client is the Board of Directors to whom we shall report the results of this interview, as well as our other interviews, so that the Board can fulfill its important responsibilities. This interview is confidential and privileged, but the privilege belongs to our client, the Board, not to you. This means that the Board can decide to release any information, privileged or not, to outsiders, such as opposing parties or the government.

If you need any legal advice, you are free to contact your own lawyer now or at any time during the interview.

---

10. MODEL RULES 1.13(f) & 4.3; RLGL § 131, cmt. e.

🏛 Conflicts in the Corporate Family

We've got a difficult one. One of my colleagues, older fella (we thought he was well past his prime), gets a call from Lord Silversmith, the British takeover tycoon. Wants Peter, the ol' guy, to represent him in a takeover of Target; not the trendy discount department store, the giant conglomerate. And even better, the deal is just not corporate stuff. We will be filing a complaint in the Delaware County Court to force Target to redeem their poison pill. Work for half of the firm!

So Peter circulates a conflicts memo. No e-mail on this one. He puts a memo in individual envelopes sealed with a blue "confidential" sticker. It's looking good when Peter gets a call from a new lateral in our Miami office. Seems he's working on a small lease in a Coral Gables shopping center for Target B Cosmetics, a wholly-owned subsidiary of Target. The new partner hopes it's not a problem. Peter says drop the lease deal. They're arguing over $500 per month in rent.

You know you can't do that.

Why not? Target B would probably be better off without that foot-dragging new partner of ours trying to make something of a mole-hill representation.

Lawyers can withdraw from a representation for the reasons provided in Model Rule 1.16. They can do so for no reason at all as long as it doesn't have a material adverse affect on the client.[11] But the one thing you can't do is withdraw from a representation in order to turn a present client into a former client, escape the current conflict under Rule 1.7, and get Rule 1.9, the former client rule, to apply.

Why not?

Because of the "hot potato" doctrine. Courts will not allow you to drop the least favored client like a hot potato, but will require that you keep the first client in time.[12]

But if I can do it for no reason, this is a good reason.

---

11. MODEL RULE 1.16(b)(1); RLGL § 32(3)(1).

12. *See, e.g., Santacroce v. Neff*, 134 F. Supp. 2d 366 (D.N.J. 2001) (law firm that dropped one client like a hot potato to avoid conflict with another, more remunerative client disqualified); *Universal City Studios, Inc. v. Reimerdes*, 98 F. Supp. 2d 449 (S.D.N.Y. 2000) (law firm that took on representation of defendant after it represented plaintiff in an unrelated matter not entitled to drop least favored client like a "hot potato," but plaintiff's failure to timely raise issue would prejudice defendant and prevents disqualification); *In re Dresser Indus.*, 972 F.2d 540 (5th Cir. 1992) (national standards of lawyer conduct forbid a lawyer from bringing a suit against a current client without the consent of both clients; disqualification granted).

Good for your firm; not for your client, which did nothing wrong.

Then maybe we could get rid of the partner. He's turned out to have much less business than he claimed, just as I predicted.

That would be ugly, but it could work. If he is the only one with confidential information and he leaves, there would be no imputation back to the firm, and you could take it on as long as there is no substantial relationship between the matters. But I'm not sure you could do that fast enough for Lord Silversmith.

You're right there. But to get to the real point, why do we have to worry about this lease deal at all? How can it be a conflict if we go against Target? Our client is Target B. My lazy Miami partner didn't even know Target B was owned by Target.

Well. . . .

In fact, my Florida guy is sure Target B would be well served if it were owned by Lord Silversmith. The good Lord is a great turnaround artist.

Well, let's slow down. It is certainly true that Target is not your client. And that's who you would be directly adverse to. So far, no violation of Rule 1.7(a).

So far?

Target B is your client. What's the effect on that company?

I already told you it would be better off.

That would be a great conclusion if Target B reached it. But as nice as it would be for you to decide as the lawyer that some action you are about to take is in the best interest of the party creating the conflict, Target B gets to decide whether that is so.

But in any event, the takeover is not directly adverse to Target B. It's merely a sub of Target.

Now you've put your finger on part of the required analysis. Some—including the authors—assert that any time you take action directly against one member of a wholly-owned corporate family—parent, subsidiary, sibling—you are taking a position directly adverse to all. We argue that if you represent Ford, Ford doesn't anymore relish a suit against its Mercury Division than one against its Volvo subsidiary. Either way, they view it as directly adverse to Ford.[13]

---

13. ABA Comm. on Ethics and Prof'l Responsibility, Formal Op. 95-390 (1995) (Conflicts of Interest in the Corporate Family Context) (Lawrence J. Fox, dissenting).

But the Model Rules reject that reasoning. Rule 1.7 has comment [34] which provides that taking a position adverse to a corporate affiliate is not necessarily adverse to the client.[14]

There you go again. Not necessarily?

Yes. You need to know more.

Like what?

Is the affiliate in a different business? Who are its officers? Does it have the same general counsel? How large or significant is the matter in controversy? If the affiliate is conducting business in a sufficiently independent manner, or the legal matter's effect on the parent is very small, then the comment suggests you might proceed with the adverse representation. Of course, if you do so, you know the consequences.

Yeah. No one will think Peter is unproductive anymore.

No, no. Target B will undoubtedly fire you if you sue its parent. So doing this isn't just a question of what the rules permit. There are likely business consequences as well.

I guess you're right, but here—who cares? Stupid lease. Big deal. So is that it?

Not really. Even if it's not deemed directly adverse to your client, you still have to ask whether your firm's representation of Target B would place a material limitation on your firm's ability to represent Lord Silversmith. You guys going to pull your punches?

You're kidding, right? No way.

Well that may be true here on these narrow facts. But you can see how a more important representation of Target B could have such effect. And remember, in retrospect, your decision to proceed will be judged on an objective standard.

Trust me, we're being objective.

You missed my point. You will be asked whether a reasonable lawyer would have considered this a material limitation.[15] Not whether Peter subjectively thought it wouldn't affect his ardor for the cause to save his career. And even if that's okay, there's still one more thing.

Enough already.

---

14. *See also* RLGL § 14, cmt. f, § 131, cmt. d.

15. MODEL RULE 1.7(b)(1); RLGL § 121, cmt. c(iv).

No. This is important. Your firm could be disqualified from proceeding for Lord Silversmith if you learned any confidential information from Target B that could be used in the takeover.[16]

Can't we just solve this whole problem by getting a waiver from Target B?

It certainly is true that a waiver by the affected former or present client can cure a conflict of interest if the conflict is waivable.

I thought all conflicts could be waived?

Not quite. Conflicts arising from law firms being on both sides of the "v" are non-waivable.[17] Some conflicts—conflicts affecting certain public bodies—are non-waivable by statute or common law.[18] Last, Rule 1.7 provides that a conflict is not waivable if no reasonable lawyer would seek a waiver under those circumstances.[19] For example, the authors believe it is hard to imagine how any lawyer can seek a waiver to sue a present client, except perhaps an obligatory cross-claim in a giant environmental case with a hundred defendants. In any event, you'd better determine whether you have a reasonable belief that you will be able to provide competent and diligent representation to each affected client before you ever seek a waiver. Of course, this has been an interesting excursion, but you can't seek a waiver here.

Why not? I had already rationalized that we could.

Because you may never seek a waiver—which by definition requires the disclosure of a prospective client's information—without getting the prospective client's permission to so proceed.[20] And what do you think Lord Silversmith will say when you ask?

Hadn't thought of that.

But, of course, he won't let you get a waiver of the conflict. Lord Silversmith strikes at night by stealth, by surprise. You call Target B to get a waiver, and Target will be alerted of his plans.

Well, can't we just conclude it's no conflict and have Peter call Lord Silversmith up and accept the engagement?

If you can so conclude. But you're bypassing one step.

What's that?

---

16. MODEL RULE 1.9(a); RLGL § 132; *Eastman Kodak Co. v. Sony Corp.*, Nos. 04-CV-6095, 04-CV-6098, 2004 U.S. Dist. LEXIS 29883 (W.D.N.Y. Dec. 27, 2004).

17. MODEL RULE 1.7(b)(3); RLGL § 122(2)(b).

18. MODEL RULE 1.7(b)(4); RLGL § 122(2)(a), cmt. g (ii).

19. MODEL RULE 1.7(b)(1); RLGL § 122(2)(c).

20. MODEL RULES 1.7, cmt. [19], 1.18(b); RLGL § 122, cmt. c(i).

Even if you believe there is no conflict, you have to communicate to Lord Silversmith the real possibility that Target will take a different view and move to disqualify poor Peter. Lord Silversmith is entitled to know that his swashbuckling adventure might get sidetracked by a motion to disqualify in the poison pill litigation, even one unlikely to succeed.[21] Lord Silversmith might, just might, prefer to proceed with a law firm that doesn't carry the potential for a takeover delaying tactic.

I guess Peter's dream may be no more than that.

That will be up to Lord Silversmith and, even if he goes along, then up to some court of law.

✄ Corporate Family Redux

We're in big trouble. Two ways. We were asked to bring a RICO claim against a local stockbroker who invested his client's money with that guy Madoff. We ran a conflicts check. Nothing showed up. So we fired away. Ten days later, we get a nasty-gram from the lawyer for the broker. In the form of a motion to disqualify. He tells us the broker is a third-tier subsidiary of Your Trust Bank. We do employment discrimination cases for the bank. Have for years. But we had no idea. Besides, representing the bank doesn't make the broker our client. How could it?

Let's take it one step at a time. Today, in our consolidating corporate world, we think the standard of care is for you to know. You can buy a service from D&B, maybe others, that will tell you your client's affiliates. Even if not required, having this information will avoid incidents like this.[22]

But why do we care? Our client is Your Trust Bank. Isn't that all we have to worry about?

Not really. Some think that should be the case. Others think quite the opposite. If an entity is a wholly-owned part of a corporate family that includes your client, they believe there is no basis for suing your client's parent, subsidiary, or sibling. The Model Rules adopt a middle ground. A comment to Rule 1.7 requires a fact-specific inquiry that looks into such factors as common line of business, common location, common offices, and common in-house counsel to determine whether you have to treat the

---

21. RLGL § 37; *Hendry v. Pelland,* 73 F.3d 397 (D.C. Cir. 1996) (failure to disclose conflicts of interest grounds for fee forfeiture despite lack of actual harm).

22. MODEL RULE 5.1, cmt. [2]; RLGL § 11, cmt. g.

non-client affiliate as a client for conflict-of-interest purposes.[23] You haven't told us enough facts yet to permit us to advise you whether you can thread the Model Rule needle. They are in two different, albeit related, businesses, i.e., the bank and the broker, but we need to know more.[24] One thing you should also check is whether this topic was addressed. Did you try to address this issue in your engagement letter? Such provisions though viewed with some dismay by the authors have been enforced. When the bank retained you, did it give you instructions on how to treat its affiliates? Many of the more sophisticated corporate clients do. They say they might grant a conflict waiver, but don't go suing our affiliates without asking first. You said you were in trouble two ways?

Oh, yeah. Our client suing the broker is really upset. She signed a contingent fee agreement with us. Now she's making noises about holding us responsible for her losses.

Well, that is a bit much. But if you withdraw or choose to litigate and lose the motion to disqualify, and then your client cannot find alternative counsel on the same basis, you may find yourself underwriting the lawyer.[25]

Well, at least we can get a share of the new firm's fee—for our effort.

We don't think so. If you cannot handle the case because of a conflict of interest, it is impermissible for you to collect a fee.[26]

Damn bank!

⌘ The Corporate Buyout

I'm in a real pickle. I sued a realtor on behalf of a disgruntled buyer. Suit's been ongoing for two years. Now I learn the realtor was just purchased by my client, the Title Company.

---

23. MODEL RULE 1.7, cmt. [34]; RLGL §§ 14, cmt. f, § 131, cmt. d.

24. *E.g., Certain Underwriters at Lloyd's, London v. Argonaut Ins. Co.*, 264 F. Supp. 2d 914 (N.D. Cal. 2003) (parent corporation and its subsidiary, even if wholly owned, are generally regarded as separate entities for conflicts purposes, unless an exception applies—where the relationship between the entities is such that they have a "unity of interests," such as relatively direct financial relationship or common management, including supervision, over the legal affairs of both entities).

25. RLGL § 37, cmt. d.

26. *Silbiger v. Prudence Bonds Corp.*, 180 F.2d 917 (2d Cir. 1950); *Crawford & Lewis v. Boatmen's Trust Co.*, 1 S.W.3d 417 (Ark. 1999).

That is called a "thrust-upon" conflict. You didn't do anything to create it. Neither did your buyer client. It doesn't seem fair that you would have to stop representing the buyer. On the other hand, if you proceed without consent, this is a clear violation of the rules of professional conduct. Maybe your title company client will give you a waiver. If not, you could proceed, and, if the title company moves to disqualify you, you could urge the judge to use her discretion to let you continue. Some courts have done that.[27] The ABA has promulgated a new comment to Model Rule 1.7 that would permit you to choose to continue to represent one client or the other.[28] If it were applied, you would still have to choose which of your clients you wish to abandon. It's better than losing both, but hardly the kind of choice that is designed to generate warm and fuzzy feelings.

✎ The IPO

We've been working on a new public offering for Big Pharma. Raising additional capital to fund their acquisition of Geneben. The deal is set to go, we attend the celebration the night before the deal goes effective, when CFO, perhaps fueled by too much of the Dom, blurts out, "Sure am glad we didn't have to disclose that damn e-mail." My gentle questioning reveals a threatening communication from Genetech received two weeks ago, challenging a Geneben patent. "This might be important," I declaim, to which the CFO responds, "It's totally frivolous; designed to ruin our latest stock sale." Now what do we do? Among other things, we were going to cash out our firm shares as part of the offering. One of us had already ordered a pool for his backyard.

This situation is an opportunity to explore the difference between a lawyer's Rule 1.13 obligations and those imposed on the lawyer by the SEC's rules under Section 307 of Sarbanes-Oxley[29] (See Figure 11 and Table 5). We can also explore a good lawyering point along the way.

I knew SOX would come to haunt us someday. Anytime Congress acts unanimously, you can be sure we're facing bad legislation.

Well, the SEC's Sarbanes-Oxley rules, which were either required or authorized by the Act itself, really added another layer of law to the ethics rules for

---

27. *E.g., Gould, Inc. v. Mitsui Mining & Smelting Co.*, 738 F. Supp. 1121 (N.D. Ohio 1990).

28. MODEL RULE 1.7, cmt. [5]; RLGL § 132, cmt. j.

29. 15 U.S.C. § 7245 (2006); 17 C.F.R. Part 205.

lawyers who represent any public company. Moreover, the rules apply not just to lawyers like you, who actually do SEC work. They apply to any lawyer whose advice for a public company affects its disclosure obligations. So lawyers who never thought about the SEC—lawyers handling tax matters, defending antitrust claims, dealing with vendor contracts—can come within its ambit if the matter they are handling is described, or should have been described, in any filing by the client with the SEC.[30]

But what does it require here?

Well, you really know very little.

No more than what I've been told.

So under Rule 1.13, you undoubtedly have no obligation to act. Rule 1.13 speaks of what the lawyer knows, although you must keep in mind that the rules define "knows" as a state that can be inferred from the circumstances.[31] But right now the situation is really ambiguous.

You can say that again. I am just suspicious. The CFO, fueled with champagne, was very relieved that the e-mail never got disclosed, yet he maintains it was a frivolous threat.

Well, under Rule 1.13, it would be hard to argue that your up-the-ladder reporting requirement was triggered at this point. Which does not mean good lawyering does not suggest that you should pursue this further. You don't know anything about patents. Maybe the CFO doesn't either. But you should determine, at a minimum, that the proper authority at the company at the right level of expertise has addressed this issue.

Under Sarbanes-Oxley, you might reach the same result—going over the head of the CFO—but here, it is probably required. This is because the trigger under this legislation is "becomes aware of evidence,"[32] a standard that has not received a lot of interpretation but clearly is defined as significantly less than "knows."[33] Is the non-disclosure of that letter "evidence of a material violation"—a violation of securities law or fiduciary duty to the organization?[34]

Who does the SEC's Sarbanes-Oxley rules have us report to?

---

30. 17 C.F.R. § 205.2(a).

31. MODEL RULES 1.0(f), 1.13(b); RLGL § 96.

32. 17 C.F.R. § 205.3(b).

33. 17 C.F.R. § 205.2(e)

34. 17 C.F.R. § 205.2(i).

The legislation requires a report to the Chief Legal Officer or the CLO and the CEO of the issuer.[35]

Then are we done?

Hardly. Only if, within a reasonable time, you receive "an appropriate response" are your obligations at an end.[36]

What the hell does that mean? An appropriate response?

One that makes you comfortable that no "material violation" has occurred or is occurring. Certainly something more substantive than what you heard from the CFO.[37]

But the deal closes later today.

Then it's time to move quickly. If you are satisfied with what you hear back, your obligations are at an end.

How will I know? It's a patent issue.

The way you make judgments all the time about matters you as a lawyer don't fully understand.

And if the disquiet continues?

Now you're at a decision tree. If the client has set up a qualified legal compliance committee ("QLCC") of the board, you report to them, and your work is done.[38] If there is no QLCC, ...

I think we never got around to forming one.

Then you must go to either the audit committee, a committee of outside directors, or the entire board.[39]

Is that the end?

No. That's why the QLCC is so valuable to the outside lawyer. If you don't think the board committees or the full board have given you an appropriate response, then you have to explain to all why you remain troubled.[40] The SEC's Sarbanes-Oxley rules even give you permission to notify the SEC.[41]

Even when my state ethics code bars such communication?

---

35. 17 C.F.R. § 205.3(b)(1).

36. 17 C.F.R. § 205.3(b)(3).

37. 17 C.F.R. § 205.2(b).

38. 17 C.F.R. § 205.3(c).

39. 17 C.F.R. § 205.3(b)(3).

40. 17 C.F.R. § 205.3(b)(9).

41. 17 C.F.R. § 205.3(d).

That's the way the regulations read.[42] Whether the federal government could preempt state regulation of lawyers in this way has not been tested. And do keep in mind, some states have adopted Model Rule 1.13, which also permits disclosure outside the organization under certain circumstances.[43]

A lot of responsibility on the lawyer.

You can say that again. One of authors has warned that Section 307 of Sarbanes-Oxley, which required the SEC to adopt regulations in this area, was passed in a frenzy and is not good public policy.[44] Let the clients be responsible for their decision-making, we assert, and leave the lawyers out of it. But it's the law of the land.

So now I've got to get to the bottom of this issue. Quickly.

And don't let your swimming pool cloud your good judgment and professional independence. Better to delay the offering, make additional disclosure, and hope it doesn't squelch investor ardor than to give every investor a '33 Act claim if the shares go south later on.

I guess so.

Figure 11   Obligations of Lawyers under SEC Regulations Adopted Pursuant to Sarbanes-Oxley

1. A Lawyer who provides advice to any client with respect to any matter described or that should have been described in an SEC filing, who becomes aware of credible evidence that a material violation (violation of any federal or state securities law or material breach of fiduciary duty under federal or state law) has likely occurred by the issuer or officers, directors, employees or agents of issuer shall report evidence of the violation to the CLO (Chief Legal Officer) or CLO and CEO of the issuer.
2. CLO or CEO shall investigate whether a violation has occurred.

---

42. 17 C.F.R. § 205.6(c).

43. *See supra* Chapter 4 note 33.

44. Lawrence J. Fox, *William Reece Smith, Jr. Distinguished Lecture In Legal Ethics: Can Client Confidentiality Survive Enron, Arthur Andersen, And The ABA?*, 34 STETSON L. REV. 147 (2004); Lawrence J. Fox, *The Fallout from Enron: Media Frenzy and Misguided Notions of Public Relations Are No Reason to Abandon Our Commitment to Our Clients*, 2003 U. ILL. L. REV. 1243 (2003).

3. Unless the lawyer reasonably believes that CLO or CEO has made an appropriate response that no violation has or is about to occur, that reasonable remedial measures have been undertaken, or with board approval an investigation has been undertaken that will result in either remedial action or a colorable defense to the matter can be asserted, within a reasonable time, lawyer shall report violation to:

An audit committee of the board of directors, or

A committee of outside directors, or

The entire board of directors, or

A qualified legal compliance committee of the board (QLCC).

4. Except where the lawyer has reported to a QLCC, the lawyer has an obligation to assess whether the issuer has appropriately responded. A lawyer who does not reasonably believe that the issuer has made an appropriate response within a reasonable time shall explain his or her reasons therefore to the CLO, CEO and the directors, and may disclose confidential information to the SEC to the extent the lawyer reasonably believes necessary:

To prevent material violations likely to cause substantial injury to the financial interest or property of the issuer or investors;

To prevent the issuer from committing perjury or acts likely to perpetrate a fraud upon the Commission;

To rectify the consequences of a material violation by the issuer that may cause substantial injury to the financial interest or property of the issuer or investors, in furtherance of which the lawyer's services were used.

5. Subordinate lawyers (those who appear or practice before the SEC under the direct supervision or direction of another lawyer) comply by reporting evidence of a material violation to their supervising lawyer, and may take the steps permitted or required above if the subordinate lawyer reasonably believes that the supervisory lawyer to whom he or she has reported has failed to comply with the regulatory requirements.

6. Violation of these regulations can result in discipline by the SEC, including disbarment. The regulations also provide that lawyers who comply cannot be held civilly liable or disciplined under any inconsistent state rule, though this grant of immunity has not been tested to date.

7. Lawyers who are fired for complying with the good regulations may report the firing to the Board of Directors.

8. The SEC has threatened, but to date never decided, to impose mandatory disclosure obligations on lawyers when they do not believe that the entity has made an appropriate response.

✺ Scene II

So I went up the ladder. To the full board. They told me that they had made a business judgment that the need to raise capital now was worth the risk of something coming of that e-mail. I remonstrated about their duty of full disclosure. How all of us might be liable. They responded that I was simply aiding and abetting the enemy. The purpose of the letter was to derail our offering. Now what?

Well, if you think *you* are aiding and abetting a securities fraud, you must withdraw and withdraw any opinions you have offered as well.[45]

I just don't know. Maybe the board is right.

Life is not always as cut and dried as we would like it to be. There is risk everywhere. You must decide, and then stick with your decision.

TABLE 5 **Model Rule 1.13 and Sarbanes-Oxley**

	Model Rule 1.13	*Sarbanes-Oxley*
Client Identification	1.13 (a): organizations acting through duly authorized constituents	*15 U.S.C. § 7245, 17 C.F.R. § 205.3: representation of issuers as organizations before the SEC*
Up-the-Ladder Obligation: Trigger	1.13 (b): L knows	*§ 205.3(b)(1): L becomes aware of credible evidence that it is likely a violation has or will occur*
Up-the-Ladder Obligation: Kind of reportable violations	1.13 (b): violation of legal obligation to organization or violation of law that reasonably might be imputed to organization	*§ 205.2(i)(e): material violations of any applicable U.S. or state securities law & material breaches of fiduciary duty (misfeasance, nonfeasance, abdication of duty, abuse of trust, and approval of unlawful transactions) or similar violations under U.S. or state law*

---

45. MODEL RULES 1.2(d), 4.1(b); RLGL § 94.

TABLE 5 Model Rule 1.13 and Sarbanes-Oxley (Cont'd. . .)

	Model Rule 1.13	Sarbanes-Oxley
Up-the-Ladder Obligation: To whom?	1.13 (b): highest authority that can act on behalf of the organization, determined by applicable law	§ 205.3(b)(1): chief legal officer or chief executive officer or both; 203.3(b)(3): if no appropriate response in reasonable time, to audit committee of issuer's board of directors
Disclosure	1.13 (c): to prevent violations of law that are reasonably certain to result in substantial injury to the organization; 1.6(b)(2)(3); to prevent or mitigate substantial injury to the financial interests or property of another using the lawyer's services	§ 205.3(d): to prevent issuer from committing a material violation likely to cause substantial injury to the financial interest or property of the issuer or investors, or to rectify the consequences of a material violation that caused or may cause substantial injury to the financial interest or property of issuer or investors using the lawyer's services
Lawyer's discharge due to reporting inside or outside organization	1.13 (e): discretion to notify organization's highest authority	§ 203.3(b)(10): May notify board of directors or any committee of board
Penalty	8.4 (a): discipline	§ 205.6: SEC civil penalties and remedies & SEC discipline; no discipline or liability under "inconsistent standards imposed by any state or other United States jurisdiction"

ℳ Up the Ladder and Fiduciary Duty

We have been representing Colossus on acquisitions and divestitures for years. They have a magic touch and no better example than now. We have been working on a sale of their Hong Kong software subsidiary to RKK, the storied private equity fund. All was going smoothly when we found out the CEO of Colossus has a brother who is a 24% limited partner in the RKK fund doing the deal.

That gave you concerns?

For sure. And we weren't happy how we learned it either. Not from the client and, worse than that, this has never been disclosed to the Colossus board.

So you are going to disclose, right?

Not exactly. We talked to General Counsel. She says CEO will go berserk. When she discussed this with him earlier, he said, "a) we have two fairness opinions, and b) my brother is only a limited partner."

So did she persuade you?

Not really. When this finally comes out, it will affect the reputation of Colossus in the market. Might mess up its planned re-capitalization, which is crucial to the company's future. And, for sure, the board is going to be upset when it finds out after the fact.

So have you convinced GC to disclose?

Not yet. Maybe never.

Where does that leave you?

That's why we contacted you. Is this the kind of thing outside counsel has to put directly to the board under Sarbanes if neither the GC or the CEO is willing to? Could be a breach of fiduciary duty by the CEO not to disclose it to the board. But it's a close question.

Precisely the problem with the federal government legislating in an area where the states have been in the drivers' seats. Do you know whether it would be "unreasonable . . . for a prudent and competent attorney not to conclude"[46] that the CEO's failure to disclose his brother's interest in the RKK fund is a "material" breach of fiduciary duty?[47] Is the GC allowed to make the decision? And be wrong? And on close questions the collar gets really tight. If you go forward (that is, around the GC and CEO), will you be clear in your mind that you are doing it because you are required to, or just because you want to "look good" (or not bad) in the eyes of the board. And remember, of course, the old saying: "If you are going to shoot at the king, you better hit him."

---

46. 17 C.F.R. § 205.2 (e).

47. 17 C.F.R. § 205.2 (d).

TWELVE

Unincorporated Associations

※ Introduction: A Group of Individuals

UNINCORPORATED ASSOCIATIONS offer their members the quintessential American opportunity to unite for a common purpose. For lawyers, their relative lack of statutory regulation and varied organizational structures present real client identity issues. In some circumstances, they are viewed as essentially a joint representation of a number of clients; in others as an entity with constituents authorized to make decisions for the group.

We include in this chapter groups united for short- or long-term purposes, such as tenant associations and labor unions. Throughout, we will again note that your ethical obligations to them depend on both their legal structure and your now-growing comprehension of the law governing lawyers. We explore here issues related to identifying your client and your Five C fiduciary obligations in the context of representing unincorporated associations.

We will see throughout the chapter that the number of as well as the relationships among association members shape both their expectations of you and your obligations to them.

※ Who Is My Client?

This is totally scary. The homebuilder's association hired us to draft legislation that would save its members on their taxes. We did what they asked, and you know those homebuilders. Enough clout to get the legislation passed in the pre-holiday rush to adjourn. What a coup. But now one of the members—some builder from Georgia—has sued our firm for malpractice. Says they could have saved even more if we had drafted the bill a different way. I thought you told us the association was our client.

If you follow the entity theory of representation, as our rules do, only the association itself should be able to sue for malpractice.[1]

That's good news, 'cause as far as we know, the association leaders are happy. That's why they rejected the Atlanta guy's demand that they sue.

The problem is that there is case law out there that gives standing to association members to sue the association's lawyers.[2] It may not be the better view, but you have to know about it. So move to dismiss. Under Rule 1.13, your client was the association.[3] But you can expect to see some wrong-headed decisions cited in response.

𝍀 Settlement Authority

I met with the board of the Neighborhood Association to discuss settlement of what turned out to be an uninsured claim brought against the Association by someone injured at the Association's swimming pool. The Association members were adamant and unanimous. They were never going to settle this "fraudulent" claim brought by a former Association member whose injuries my clients said were totally feigned. "We are committed to taking this case to trial," are the Association president's final words. Now I have an offer to settle for $50,000. That will cost each Association member $2500. My instructions are to turn it down, and frankly, I'm afraid even to tell the Association members. They'll take my head off.

If you had the meeting yesterday, you might be justified in not reporting this offer. But, quite honestly, no matter how recently you met with clients, you should run the risk of incurring their ire by at least informing them of the offer.[4] Because, if the case comes out badly and someone learns that they could have settled for $50,000, that offer will appear in a much more favorable light. No matter how adamantly a client's settlement position is expressed, the best view is to pass all offers along because people's views

1. MODEL RULE 1.13(a), cmt. [1]; RLGL § 96, cmt. c; *Ocean Club of Palm Beach Shores Condo. Ass'n v. Estate of Daly*, 504 So. 2d 1377 (Fla. Dist. Ct. App. 1987).

2. *Schwartz v. Broadcast Music, Inc.*, 16 F.R.D. 31 (S.D.N.Y. 1954). *See also Franklin v. Callum*, 804 A.2d 444 (N.H. 2002) (lawyer who represents unincorporated association represents each member as to the association's business, enabling each to see legal bills containing confidential information).

3. *See also* RLGL § 14, cmt. f.

4. MODEL RULE 1.2(a); RLGL § 22.

change over time, and there is something about a concrete offer that could affect a client's thinking. Remember, settlement is one of those areas that is absolutely allocated to the client for decision-making purposes.

𝒲 The Public Union

We represent a police union. Great work and lots of referrals too. But this one has us stumped. One of the union members got in trouble for distributing some controversial pamphlets. The county sheriff's office fired him, and the cop's union asked us to step into the breach. Advise him about a possible settlement. Now our guy has buyer's remorse. Wants to throw the settlement out. And he wants us to testify about our discussions. Threatening to sue us for malpractice, as well. But the union says no way. So we're staying silent until some court tells us otherwise.

Well, you certainly have an obligation to refuse to testify if the union is taking that position. But we have to tell you, even though the union is a client, it looks like the member also was your client for this purpose.[5] The union hired you. The union paid you. But don't be surprised if a court concludes that this was a joint representation, in which case the union can stand on the privilege, but the member can waive it as to matters he communicated to you.[6] The court might even view this as an individual representation in which your ingrate client is free to waive the privilege for whatever reason.[7]

Not unlike an insurance company hiring a lawyer to represent its insured?

Precisely. These association representations give rise to many ambiguous circumstances.

𝒲 A Note to the Members

I've been representing this association for years. Just went to an association board meeting. Real fireworks. I think the group is treating the members unfairly, and I told them so. The board unanimously rejected my advice. So much for my

---

5. RLGL § 14.

6. RLGL § 75.

7. *Bagley v. Searles*, No. 3:06CV00480, 2007 U.S. Dist. LEXIS 4242 (D. Conn. Jan. 19, 2007).

vaunted advocacy. Under the circumstances, I am convinced I should resign. Problem is, I'm worried the association members will not learn how they're getting screwed. Maybe I'll send my resignation letter to all members. "A little note from your lawyer."

We understood the resignation part. You certainly have grounds under Rule 1.16. It does sound like your client is pursuing a course of conduct that you find repugnant.[8]

Yes, and it's not just one member of the board; they're all in agreement.

But your client is the entity. And you owe a duty of confidentiality to the entity, the association.[9] And unless you can assert that the conduct of the association triggers an exception to Rule 1.6, or your jurisdiction has adopted an exception to confidentiality in its version of Rule 1.13,[10] you would breach your duty to your singular client by notifying all the members of your board members' decision and its implications.

But what they're doing is wrong.

If that is so, then the members will have a claim against the board members or the association itself, but that will have to be prompted by knowledge they gain other than from you.

✸ Representing the Trade Association

We were hired by the Securities Industry Association to investigate allocations of IPOs. Back when they were the rage. SIA thought their internal investigation would have more credibility if plaintiffs' lawyers conducted the work. We determined that the industry was pretty clean. Now we've brought suit against Drexel, Lehman & Lambert. By a class of disgruntled customers. And DL&L moved to disqualify us. We never represented them, but, it is true, we did receive information from them in the SIA investigation. If we're conflicted from suing every SIA member, there goes our securities practice.

The good news is that the prohibition is not that broad. There is no blanket ban to taking a position adverse to every member of an association you represent. The entity theory should apply, and therefore the members never

---

8. RLGL § 1.16(b)(4); RLGL § 32(3)(f).

9. MODEL RULES 1.6, 1.13, cmt. [2]; RLGL § 96, cmt. b.

10. *See supra* Chapter 4 note 33.

became clients.[11] But if you received confidential information from association members that could be used in the new representation adverse to the member, then the motion to disqualify is likely to be granted.[12] Another example where non-client information can lead to real ethical problems.

⁊ The Problem with Conflicts

The Homeowner's Association is totally fed up. The president, of all people, is delinquent in paying his assessment. Three years. I have no idea how it got out of control. Now they want to sue the guy. With penalties. Want us to do it. Can we?

Start from the proposition that the Association, not any of its officers, is your client. But that only answers half the question.

You gonna tell me the other half?

Of course. Two things. First, does the president have any reason to think he was your client? I'm sure you referred to him that way, but did you ever do any work—on the side—for him? Or give him any other basis to think you were his lawyer?[13] For example, do you have confidential information about the president that the president would not expect you to share with the Association?

No way. We only dealt with the guy on association business, and he knew that.

Well, assuming that's clear, the next question is whether under Rule 1.7(a)(2) you think you relationship with the president—even if he was never a client—will create a material limitation on your ability to represent the Association?[14] Do you think you might pull your punches going after him, in a way that could affect the representation? In short, would the Association be better off with a different lawyer who doesn't know President Deadbeat?

---

11. ABA Comm. on Ethics and Prof'l Responsibility, Formal Op. 92-365 (1992) (Trade Associations as Clients); *J.G. Ries & Sons, Inc. v. Spectraserv, Inc.*, 894 A.2d 681 (N.J. Super. Ct. App. Div. 2006).

12. RLGL § 121, Illus. 10; *Westinghouse Elec. Co. v. Kerr-McGee Corp.*, 580 F.2d 1311 (7th Cir. 1978) (trade association member who shared confidential information with law firm considered client for purposes of disqualification in subsequent substantially related representation).

13. RLGL § 14, cmt. f, § 131, cmt. e.

14. MODEL RULE 1.7(a)(2); RLGL § 121.

ℳ Business Development

Well, when you represent an association, can you also represent association members? Sounds like a great business development tool.

That it is. Strut your best stuff in front of the group. Maybe some will be impressed and hire you for other things.

So the course is clear?

Not quite.

Your usual answer.

Well, it's another area fraught with the need to proceed cautiously, and the proper analysis is very fact-specific. Say you represent a trade association, and one of the members wants to hire you. Sounds good, but it may be that the association hired you specifically because you represented none of them. They wanted a lawyer who had no particular loyalty to any in the group.

Assuming that's not the case, there are probably a wide range of matters you could take on. Think of representing a condominium association and having one of your colleagues do estate planning for a large number of the members. Totally benign as long as you recognize you could never simultaneously represent the association adverse to these estate planning clients without their consent.[15]

So I'm feeling pretty good about this.

And you should. But remember you also cannot take on any representation where there is a possible conflict between the association and the member. Imagine a homeowner's association member who wants to get a zoning change. The association might oppose it.

Can I represent one member of an association against another?

Your business developments efforts are paying off in strange ways. Again, as with the suit by the association against its deadbeat president, you have to analyze your relationship with the putative defendant. In some associations, the members would not have a reasonable basis to conclude that you were the lawyer for each of them. In others, the reverse might be true. Think a small association. Or what if this association member was one of the key players in forming the association and having you as the association's lawyer? In any event, don't be surprised if your representation is challenged on that basis and be prepared to assert that, other than the members' membership

---

15. MODEL RULE 1.7(a); RLGL § 121.

in the association, there are no other indicia that a lawyer-client relationship was formed.[16]

The effect of this representation on behalf of one member against another also has to be evaluated in relation to your ongoing representation of the association. If the matter is entirely unrelated to association business, you might be free to take it on. But if the representation could be disruptive of the association or implicate confidential information of the association, then Rule 1.7(a)(2) could require you to decline the matter. You certainly do not want to jeopardize your relationship with the association by taking on a matter you never would have been presented if not for the association representation.

Finally, as with any organization, Rule 1.13(g) permits concurrent representation of an association and one of its members subject to the provisions of Rule 1.7. If the organization's consent is required because of a Rule 1.7 conflict of interest, the organization's consent must come from someone other than the individual being represented.

---

16. *E.g., In re Buffalo Coal Co.*, No. 06-366, 2008 Bankr. LEXIS 1259 (Bankr. N.D. W. Va. Apr. 30, 2008).

THIRTEEN

Nonprofits

※ Introduction: The Nonprofit Purpose

NONPROFITS ARE NO DIFFERENT in structure or organization from many corporations, but exist for a purpose apart from profit and often rely on voluntary donations to serve their mission. Many were created by or could not exist without the help of lawyers, who often serve these organizations on a pro bono basis.

We include in this chapter nonprofits that range in size from small shoestring operations to those that operate vast service enterprises. Once again, it should come as no surprise that your ethical obligations to these organizations depend on both their legal structure and your clear-headed application of the law governing lawyers. We explore here issues related to identifying your client, your Five C fiduciary obligations, and some special lawyer code provisions that encourage lawyers to assist nonprofits.

We will see throughout the chapter that both the nonprofit's purpose as well as its management shape its expectations of you as well as your obligations to the organization. Serving these nonprofit purposes can be one of the brightest memories in a lawyer's career, but also can complicate a legal representation. This is especially true if a lawyer views the organization's obligations as less subject to scrutiny because of its nonprofit status.

※ Representing Nonprofits

Well, you sure make representing companies seem so complicated. So many things to worry about. Shareholders, subsidiaries, derivative actions. At least I won't have to worry about all of that for my latest client, the local college; and they'll pay regular hourly rates, too.

Slow down, again. Representing not-for-profit organizations can be just as daunting as representing a public company, just in different ways.[1] And the ethical lawyer has to be just as watchful.

Well, they don't have to make a profit, right?

That's true. But they still must be fiscally sound. They still must be careful to maintain their nonprofit status. And they actually present even more constituents to deal with.

How can that be?

Well, not-for-profits have the usual players: officers, trustees, employees, agents. Then they have some others. Take your little college. It's got faculty who present special issues. It has students who aren't just like the customers at Wal-Mart. It has the student's parents who are likely supporting a large percentage of the annual operating budget through tuition payments. It has alumni, some of whom sit on the board of trustees and some of whom just care about the football team. It has donors; in fact, in some cases they are the organization's lifeline to future success. It has governmental watchdogs, federal and state agencies that fund research and programs. I could go on, but you've got the idea. The legal problems confronting nonprofits require all the sophistication and good judgment of any other representation, maybe more.

Well, we were thinking the great thing would be as counsel, we would get to represent some of the college's top science professors who are always licensing cutting-edge technology.

There you have a perfect example. Can you simultaneously represent the school and a faculty member?[2]

Well, this is one professor's research. The school celebrates that.

It does. But it also might think that, since it partially funded the research, maybe it belongs to the school. Have you read their patent policy?

Hadn't thought of that. Well, anyway, we get to meet the rich donors.

Again, you can't ignore the perfect conflict. When Daddy Warbucks thinks of giving money to Old U, the college is actually directly adverse to Daddy in negotiating the terms of the gift.[3] Does Daddy get to name the new student union? Or get his ne'er-do-well nephew into Old U? So representing him may be problematic.

Hadn't quite thought of it that way.

---

1. MODEL RULE 1.13; RLGL § 96, cmt. c.

2. MODEL RULE 1.7; RLGL § 131.

3. MODEL RULE 1.7(a), cmt. [7]; RLGL § 130.

ℳ The Only Lawyer

I sit on the board of this local food pantry. The work is both eye-opening and rewarding. I really think we are delivering important services to people in need. My concern is that I'm the only lawyer on the board. Not surprisingly, many of the issues that come before the board are legal issues. And when that happens, invariably, the board turns to me for advice. Somehow, these board members think that lawyers know everything.

You raise a great point. Lawyers can bring a lot of special expertise and judgment to a board membership. On the other hand, being a board member creates one set of duties, and being a lawyer to the organization creates another set.[4] But money being tight, there is a huge incentive in securing free advice from a lawyer board member, and warnings that the advice is worth exactly what the client is paying for it are not taken seriously. Your job is to remind people that you are not the lawyer for the organization, to answer those questions where you are confident that you are well within your competence zone, and to demand that the pantry secure outside legal services for all matters that are beyond your expertise.[5] And, of course, to the extent that you do answer what are clearly legal questions, the food pantry becomes a client. So, among other things, you do not want the pantry to become an accidental client of yours with the attendant responsibilities that come with that role. Serving as a pro bono director, a good deed in itself, may not go unpunished if you cross the line.

ℳ The Overbroad Delegation

Another no good deed goes unpunished. The CEO of the local MS Chapter asked me, their volunteer lawyer, to negotiate the best deal I could to get a local for-profit sponsor for the MS Bike-a-thon. What a great job I did. Or so I thought. Got the local Big Bank to pay $250,000. If we agreed to an exclusive five-year deal. So I signed it up. Now the board is furious. Wants to breach the contract. Claims I had no such authority. And Big Bank is upset as well.

---

4. Model Rule 1.7, cmt. [35]; RLGL § 135, cmt. d.

5. Model Rule 1.1, RLGL § 52; Principles of the Law of Nonprofit Organizations § 315 (ALI Tentative Draft 2007).

We're afraid you took on too much. You were delegated to do this. But as the nonprofit's lawyer, you should have recognized that this delegation to the CEO was way too broad.[6] So you either had to seek more explicit instructions or go to the board before you signed off. Now you are caught in a crossfire. The MS Chapter can defend Big Bank's claim on the ground that Big Bank should have recognized that you didn't have final authority. If MS loses on that one, so may you.

Well then, my volunteering to jump into the fray was a good idea.

Only if, separately advised, MS decides it's in their best interests to use you. But you are laboring under a conflict,[7] *and* you could be a key witness.[8]

〽 Biting the Hand

Our agency, Saving Kids, serves abused and neglected foster kids. Wrenching and rewarding work. Always a problem getting enough funding. The program director urges us to come up with a legal strategy to "shake things up." We decide a class action lawsuit is the way to go. Just like the one Children's Rights brought in Philadelphia. So we file, using our most sympathetic three-kid family as plaintiffs suing DHS. Then I am called by the board chairman of Saving Kids. She can't believe we sued the Department of Human Services when they fund 90 percent of our budget. She wants the suit withdrawn.

Well, that's one thing you cannot do.

Why not? She's the highest officer at the agency. Didn't you teach that she becomes the boss?

That would be so if she were your client. But, of course, she is not for two very different reasons.

Two?

Yes. First, your client is an agency. Its highest authority is its board. With this present pickle, the matter certainly should be brought to the attention of the board.[9] Maybe that should have happened much earlier. Accepting the

---

6. PRINCIPLES OF THE LAW OF NONPROFIT ORGANIZATIONS § 325 (ALI Tentative Draft 2007).

7. MODEL RULE 1.7; RLGL § 121.

8. MODEL RULE 3.7.

9. PRINCIPLES OF THE LAW OF NONPROFIT ORGANIZATIONS § 320 (ALI Tentative Draft 2007).

program director's instructions may not have been your most intelligent decision.[10] But, even if the board says withdraw the lawsuit, that decision will hardly be dispositive.

Why not? The board is as high as you can go.

True enough. But you told us you brought the suit on behalf of three children. They are your clients. And we assume you labeled it a class action.

Of course.

So you represent the three. You represent a putative class. Just because you took this step at the urging of the agency does not mean that you don't owe full client rights to your other clients, the children.[11]

But I've been instructed to withdraw the lawsuit by our client, the agency.

That may create a conflict for you. And that may require you to seek withdrawal in favor of other counsel if a substitute can be found *and* if the court will let you out.[12] Otherwise, you may have to continue this representation, even if your original client is unhappy.

What a shame. I let my Good Samaritan view of our work cloud the ethical analysis of what we were doing.

You . . . and so many other well-meaning lawyers.

〽 "Helping" the Charity

Affordable housing is a huge concern in our community. I gladly accepted the position as outside general counsel to the local housing authority. And I thought I was supporting the cause when I learned we had gotten permission from HUD to tear down the old William Penn project and replace it with new turn-key housing, and then our law firm bought the abandoned lot across the street from the dilapidated project, maybe to put in a much-needed supermarket. One of our board members found out (we didn't hide our idea) and reported us to the disciplinary authorities. And they've issued a show cause order.

We feel your pain. But the fact is that you used client confidential information.[13]

---

10. Model Rule 1.13, cmt. [3]; RLGL § 96, cmt. d.

11. Fed. R. Civ. P. 23.

12. Model Rule 1.16; RLGL § 32.

13. Model Rule 1.8(b); RLGL § 60.

But we did it to help the client. A supermarket will make the new housing that much more desirable. Now our residents have to take two buses and walk five blocks to buy toilet paper.

We know your motives were good. But to avoid running afoul of the rules, you either could do nothing or tell the client about the availability of the property, and only if the client were not interested could you explain to the client your hopes and dreams, receive the client's blessing, and then proceed. Even now, you might mitigate matters by following that path, albeit on a tardy basis.[14]

⁂ The Library Board

I was so pleased to be appointed to the library board. When I was a kid, our local library was a magic place. And as the only lawyer, I think I add some special expertise. Besides, they can hardly afford to get paid legal advice. And I get to pump up my pro bono hours.

Go slowly, our friend. Your role as a director makes it perfectly okay to help the board identify legal issues they need to address. For example, can the library pay a local bibliophile who sits on the board for some rare volumes. But once you go beyond that, you are not acting as a well-informed board member, but a lawyer with all the duties that entails.[15] If you know the answer, you can certainly offer it. If not, and you volunteer to find out, you owe the library the same standard of care as any client.[16]

And if the assignment is so big, my partners will insist I charge something?

Then, even though you think you are being nothing but charitable, you will have to proceed as any board member seeking to do business with the library. You cannot participate in the decision to retain counsel. You must remind the board that there are other lawyers who could perform the service, maybe lawyers whose full rates are lower than your charitable ones. You should urge the board to consider advice on retaining you from another

---

14. RLGL § 60, cmt. j; Principles of the Law of Nonprofit Organizations § 330 (ALI Tentative Draft 2007).

15. Model Rule 1.7, cmt. [35]; RLGL § 135, cmt. d.

16. Principles of the Law of Nonprofit Organizations § 315, Illus. 2-4 (ALI Tentative Draft 2007).

lawyer, and the board will have to determine that the transaction is really fair and in the best interests of the library.[17]

Hardly worth all that aggravation.

Maybe so. But these principles have to apply in all contexts, not just for fully paid services to a for-profit corporation.

ℳ The Legal Services Board

I serve on the board of a legal services agency here in town. Really makes me feel good to contribute my time to this effort. But sometimes it gets quite dicey. At the last board meeting, we were asked to authorize a class action lawsuit against Big Bank attacking the bank's pay-day lending practices. I listened to the discussion, even got enthusiastic about the merits of the claims and self-righteous about the need to end these predatory practices, when it suddenly dawned on me that our firm does work for Big Bank, not in the lending area, but defending employment discrimination suits. I felt uncomfortable. Did not actually participate in the final vote, but I sure was vocal in support of this initiative.

Your pride and your dismay are totally justifiable. We want lawyers to serve on boards of agencies that provide legal services on a pro bono basis. Their service can be invaluable. To encourage that, we say that such service is permissible even if some of the agency's matters might be adverse to the lawyer director's clients.[18] But that does come with one big caveat, which is that the lawyer should recuse himself or herself from participating in any board decision that is incompatible with lawyers' duties under Rule 1.7 or an action which could have a material adverse effect on a client of the lawyer.[19] The standard is whether the lawyer does so "knowingly,"[20] which means the lawyer does not have to undertake a conflicts check every time a decision is made; but if the lawyer knows that a client of the lawyer is involved, then the lawyer should stand down.

---

17. Principles of the Law of Nonprofit Organizations § 330 (ALI Tentative Draft 2007).

18. RLGL § 135, cmt. e.

19. Model Rule 6.3.

20. Model Rule 1.0(f).

〰 A Pro Bono Triangle

I am on the board of a women's shelter. We provide housing, food, and food for the soul. Counseling. A little prayer. Whatever helps.

The problem is, so many of our clients need legal services, too. And with the federal cutbacks in Legal Services Corporation funding, Community Legal Services cannot help. So we got this idea. I would round up some volunteer lawyers. Me included. Our agency would train them, give them offices on-site, and they could fill this ethical need.

Will they be employed by the agency?

Only one. The others would be pro bono.

This is perfectly okay so long as your organization is really a nonprofit, the organization charges no fee for the services, and the lawyers (even the paid employee lawyer) recognize they must maintain professional independence from the agency in delivering the legal services to the needy women.[21] This may be hard. Not because the agency will want to interfere. But because the agency may want to tout what it's doing, trumpet its successes, evaluate the program's effectiveness. None of those worthy goals can trump the lawyers' duty of confidentiality or obligation to make decisions as to how to proceed solely on the basis of the best interests of the clients, even if that puts the clients at odds with the agency's goals.[22]

〰 Corporate Lawyers Can Help

The local bar wants to set up a legal hotline. Every Thursday night, volunteers will take questions over the phone. Try to give answers. Or steer folks in the right direction. Could even pick up full-fledged pro bono representations if it works.

Sounds so admirable.

It is. But we're a big firm. So many clients. And those clients—banks, landlords, used car dealers—may be just the folks our callers are having trouble with. I think we'll just have to respectfully decline.

---

21. MODEL RULES 1.8(f), 5.4(c); RLGL § 134.

22. Mo. Formal Op. 121 (2006).

Not quite so fast. There is a new Model Rule. Maybe your state supreme court has embraced it. It says that lawyers who staff hotlines can handle the calls without undertaking a conflicts check.[23]

That would bog things down.

Precisely. So what the rule says is, if you—the person taking the call—do not recognize a conflict off the top of your head, you may proceed to give telephone advice without fear of a disciplinary violation. If the call ripens into a formal representation, then conflict clearance is required. But just to give advice over the phone you may proceed without the formalities.

Sounds enlightened to me.

We hope so.

---

23. MODEL RULE 6.5.

FOURTEEN

Governments

% Introduction: The Public Purpose

GOVERNMENT REPRESENTATION is complicated by governmental structure, which defines the nature and power of the entity. The organic law that created and empowered the government unit also may determine who may represent it (agency lawyers, the attorney general, a prosecutor, or outside private lawyers). As a government lawyer, you are governed by the lawyer codes where you are admitted to practice and other law applicable to lawyers. You also are regulated by constitutional, statutory, and regulatory provisions, which may further specify your obligations.

We explore in this chapter the meaning of some of this complex regulation in the context of identifying your client, your Five C fiduciary duties to that client, and the limits of the law that specifically regulate both your client's and your own activities. Understanding this often very specific law that governs the conduct of government lawyers, as well as the law governing lawyers, will enable you to serve your public client with confidence.

% Representing the Government

We do a lot of state university work for Ohio. Great work—even better if we didn't have to attend so many $500 per plate rubber chicken dinners . . . for both parties. But it's a living, a good living. Anyway, one of our new associates, one of those ACLU types, commenced to take a habeas case. Some thug on death row. But his defense lawyer screwed up big time. Even I felt sorry for the guy. Jail would be fine, but there's no way this lunatic should be on death row. So we agreed to take the case, filed the petition, and we got a call from the State Controller. "What the hell you guys doing, suing your own client?" I don't know what he's talking about. We didn't sue him. Then he explains it's the habeas case. Our suit against the Warden of the penitentiary. "Who do you think he *works for?" our state university benefactor asks with great indignation. "The Governor does not want his really talented law firms representing someone on death row," the Controller screams.*

What you raise is the cognate of the conflicts in the corporate family issue.[1] When you represent a subsidiary, you don't necessarily represent the parent. On the other hand, the parent might get upset. Here, there are no parents and subsidiaries. Just a governmental entity operating through lots of departments and agencies, some with statutory authorization and others set up merely for convenience.

Here, of course, you start off not with an ethical but a business question. Do you really want to incur the wrath of the Governor and the Controller? There is a great principle at stake. Should the state, which enjoys the services of the very best firms in Ohio, be able to limit the pool of those who can represent death row inmates so dramatically that the burden will fall on other firms? But we can understand why any firm might find that principle too costly to defend. If you were to do it, i.e., take on a representation adverse to one part of the state government, risk the state officials' wrath, and assert no conflict, you need to be clear on the relationship between the two government entities.[2]

✺ The Spectacular Contingent Fee

Our firm was hired by the State of Nebraska. They got this crazy idea that they could collect Medicaid expenses for lung cancer patients from the tobacco companies. Everyone told them the idea was ridiculous. Nebraska probably saved money because so many people died so young. Besides, the tobacco companies had never lost a case. In any event, Nebraska put the proposal out for bid, and our firm decided to seek the representation as a pro bono gesture. We would never win, but at least we would be doing a public service on the side of the angels. The Nebraska Attorney General would not even agree to fund our expenses, but she did agree to pay us twenty-five percent of their recovery. We were suing for $3 billion.

---

1. MODEL RULE 1.13, cmt. [9]; RLGL § 97, cmt. c.

2. *People v. Crawford Distrib. Co.*, 382 N.E.2d 1223 (Ill. App. Ct. 1978), *aff'd* 397 N.E.2d 1362 (Ill. 1979) (special Assistant Attorney General for limited type of civil cases owes no duty to Attorney General in criminal matters). Some states expressly provide that the representation of an agency does *not* create a lawyer-client relationship with any other agency, but in New Jersey the agency lacks the power to consent to a conflict with it. *See* note 19 *infra*.

Three years, $25 million in lawyer time and $2 million in expenses, and the tobacco companies agreed to settle. They are going to pay the State $4 billion over the next twenty-five years. And you can imagine the celebration around here when we calculated our fee. But now our ingrate client is claiming the fee is unreasonable. Can you believe that? The day they hired us, they would have been thrilled to hand us $1 billion if we got them 3. In fact the Attorney General said something just like that when questioned about our fee agreement.

We are afraid the way you framed the question probably tells you the answer. There is no doubt that the fee agreement was reasonable when entered into. The case seemed hopeless, and, as you say, your firm really thought of it as a pro bono matter. But you raise two very important public policy issues. The first is whether the client gets a "look back" on the reasonableness of a fee. The American Bar opinion says the client shouldn't.[3] But at least one case and commentator thinks a "look back" is appropriate.[4] Second, you are dealing with a public entity.[5] At least one court has made it clear that under those circumstances, a jury might properly consider the public interest when assessing the fee.[6] In fact, that court asked the jury to consider the image of the profession if such a large fee were awarded. So the lesson is that there is no guarantee that the client won't get a "look back," and, if the client is a public entity, the likelihood of a "look back" is enhanced.

※ We Forgot to Look

We were hired by Cheltenham Township to act as bond counsel on the issuance of some tax-free bonds to help fund a new shopping center the township has

---

3. ABA Comm. on Ethics and Prof'l Responsibility, Formal Op. 94-389 (1994) (Contingent Fees).

4. *E.g., In re Swartz*, 686 P.2d 1236 (Ariz. 1984) (en banc) (lawyer who failed to reduce his one-third contingent fee, reasonable at the outset but which later became excessive because there was no issue about liability and the limits of available insurance, charged a clearly excessive fee despite approval by probate court and State Compensation Fund, suspended for six months and required to return the fee); GEOFFREY C. HAZARD, JR. & W. WILLIAM HODES, THE LAW OF LAWYERING § 8.6 (3d ed., Aspen 2002).

5. *E.g., State v. Am. Tobacco Co.*, 772 So. 2d 417 (Ala. 2000) (contingent fee contract with private counsel hired by governor void for lack of compliance with statutory procedures); *Philip Morris Inc. v. Glendening*, 709 A.2d 1230 (Md. 1998) (twenty-five percent contingent fee authorized by governor, approved by State Board of Public Works, and executed by State Attorney General valid and enforceable).

6. *See* Frank Phillips, *Jury Caps Fees Owed Tobacco Law Firms; Attorney General Cites a Victory,* THE BOSTON GLOBE, Dec. 20, 2003, at A1.

voted to support. Our lawyers prepared the necessary offering statement in which we opined that the bonds complied with all applicable IRS regulations and, therefore, should be tax-exempt. We also put in a warning, however, that all investors in these bonds should consult their own counsel with respect to tax issues.

Now the IRS has asserted that the bonds are, in fact, taxable, and the disgruntled investors have brought a lawsuit against the issuer, Cheltenham Township. Cheltenham Township, in turn, has impleaded our firm. We say we cannot possibly be responsible for this because we warned all of these investors to check with their own counsel.

First, you certainly do not get any special consideration simply because your client is a public entity. Government clients are entitled to the same standard of care as everyone else. If you asserted that these bonds complied with all applicable IRS regulations, that was a representation made with the intent that investors rely upon it.

But we put the disclaimer in.

We are afraid that does not save you. You cannot both make a representation and then claim the person, the third party, shouldn't have relied upon it because of your warning.[7] Moreover, the purchasers are not suing your law firm. It is your client that is doing that, and your client, quite properly, is entitled to a claim against you if, in fact, you were negligent in giving this advice.[8]

Well, we just missed one set of regulations that had been issued two weeks earlier.

Unfortunately, that is not "just."[9] You made a representation that these bonds complied with all applicable regulations, not just the regulations you had in your memory. Having made that representation, you are responsible to your client, the municipality, if it turns out you were negligent.[10] And to the investors as well, at least if you were reckless.[11]

---

7. RLGL § 51, cmt. e.

8. RLGL § 56, cmt. c.

9. *E.g., In re Servance*, 508 A.2d 178 (N.J. 1986) (lawyer subject to discipline for representing investments were sound although he knew "little or nothing about them").

10. RESTATEMENT (SECOND) OF TORTS § 552.

11. RESTATEMENT (SECOND) OF TORTS § 531; *Ultramares Corp. v. Touche*, 174 N.E. 441 (N.Y. 1931).

❧ The Disclosure

Sometimes our government lawyers forget they owe duties of confidentiality. You'd be amazed how many times they'll talk to the press or opposing parties about matters clearly confidential, rationalizing their conduct on some public right to know.

We can tell you that lawyers for the government are subject to the same rules of confidentiality as any other lawyers. Unless they can point to a Rule 1.6 or other exception such as those found in Rules 1.13, 3.3, 3.9, and 4.1, we know of no do-gooder exception.

Well, listen to this. One of my deputies went to a Sierra Club meeting. Wanting to be a hero, he discloses that we are considering some changes to the Commonwealth's regs governing acid rain. What a blunder. When word got out, our agency was in a perfect trap. We lost all flexibility. Ended up stuck with the proposed regs he disclosed.

I want to fire him. Still might. But he insists he was entitled to disclose because by disclosing this same information to an opposing party in a pending case two months earlier, our agency waived privilege. He also asserts that the Sierra Club could have gotten the proposals with a FOIA request. Is he right?

Not even close. The question is not whether he might be forced to testify about the regs, in which case the privilege issues would be relevant. The question is whether he could voluntarily disclose confidential information to this group. And the answer is no. Unless the information is already generally known, the lawyer—even the self-aggrandizing government lawyer—must not disclose the information.[12]

What about his FOIA argument?

Same answer. Rule 1.6 allows disclosure "to comply with other law." But FOIA, the other law, does not require disclosure until a proper request is made.

❧ Government Whistleblowers

I cannot believe this one. I'm the AG's assigned lawyer to the State Insurance Department. Boring. That is, until I was asked to investigate the Madison Group. Turns out they have clearly misstated their reserves. Not writing down their

---

12. *Lawyer Disciplinary Bd. v. McGraw*, 461 S.E.2d 850 (W. Va. 1995).

collateral mortgage obligations to market. So I wrote a report. Recommended prosecution. And I hear nothing. Finally, after months of waiting, I'm told to drop the whole thing. I smell a rat. And one of my friends at the Insurance Department tells me Madison solved this little problem by making a huge charitable contribution to Boys Town. And guess who chairs our Boys Town Chapter? Don't know if I have the guts to go public, but would the rules let me?

What you know is certainly confidential. To the client. Not to the AG.[13] So in the first instance, you should work within the organization to get to the bottom of it. If that will be futile, then you can only go outside if you can find an exception in the rules.

How 'bout our state Whistleblower Statute?

Unlikely that would help. Most of those are permissive. They allow disclosure, but that permission would be trumped by your obligations under Rule 1.6. That is, unless you can find an exception apart from "to comply with other law."

Well, can I?

That would require a careful look at the exceptions to Rule 1.6 in your state. Generally, disclosure under the exception to prevent crime or fraud requires that you know about it, that serious harm is threatened, and that your client used your services to perpetrate the illegal conduct. What you tell us doesn't sound like knowledge, gives us no indication about threatened harm, and you did not assist with the illegal conduct, if any.

That can't be the end of it.

Rule 1.13 might also provide an exception—if your state has adopted the Model Rule, because the amended Rule 1.13 permits disclosure outside an organizational client but only under special circumstances: the lawyer must know; the lawyer must go as far up the organizational ladder as she can; the lawyer then may disclose, but only to prevent substantial injury to the government agency. So you have the necessary check list. Now answer the questions.[14]

Thanks a lot.

---

13. *E.g., Ross v. City of Memphis*, 423 F.3d 596 (6th Cir. 2005) (municipality, not any individual officer, is client for purposes of conversations between municipality's counsel and municipal officials).

14. Kathleen Clark, *Government Lawyers and Confidentiality Norms*, 85 WASH. U. L. REV. 1033 (2007).

ℳ Government Family Conflicts

We love representing county agencies. Good steady work. Pay their bills on time. Gives us a patina of power that recruits other clients. But the conflicts can be difficult to handle.

You are right there. The complexity of government organization can make them even more complicated.

Oh, I know. We have a New Jersey office. Anyway, in the last month we've had two different situations. We have always represented the township school board in employment discrimination cases. We got the work, frankly, because the school board chairman was a high school classmate. Who knew I was doing business development sneaking smokes behind the auditorium? We didn't give these cases a thought when we were asked to help a developer get zoning for a strip mall out by the old quarry. It's the same township for sure, but different officers, different solicitors. And schools have nothing to do with expanding suburban blight.

We hear you. As a fundamental proposition, just as in corporate family conflicts, the client has the right to define who is to be considered a client for this purpose. So, if the school board retained you asserting that you could not take on any representation adverse to any agency of the township, you are stuck with the conflict asserted here.[15]

Actually, I checked, and the only retainer letter is from us to them.

Then you are left with a second question. Did you address the issue in *your* letter? Do you want to incur the wrath of the school board by handling the shopping center matter?

Great question. We thought of that. But my school board buddy tells me he really doesn't care. Can't understand why the township solicitor made him contact me.

Now that we've put the business judgment decision to the side, you are then left with an analysis just like the corporate family one.[16] Is there a basis for treating the township zoning hearing board as a distinct entity for conflicts purposes? Just the fact that the school board hires its own lawyers is instructive. And education and zoning are certainly different areas of endeavor.

---

15. MODEL RULE 1.13, cmt. [9]; RLGL § 97, cmt. c.

16. MODEL RULE 1.7, cmt. [34]; RLGL § 14, cmt. f, § 131, cmt. d.

Your work adverse to the zoning board will have no impact on the educational mission. Also hard to imagine your loyalty to the school board could be compromised.[17]

So we're okay going forward?

You have some great arguments, but nothing definitive. But you said you had two.

This one's a little trickier. Our county counsel asked us to defend a claim by parents that we shouldn't be mandating certain vaccinations. They cause autism, is the claim.

So far so good.

It was, that is, until one of my do-gooder, card-carrying ACLU member partners sued the County Sheriff's Office for police brutality. That's when the County Attorney who hired us in the vaccine case, made the nasty phone call. To me!

And you'd like to handle both?

Of course not. But my partner insists there's no conflict. One's health; the other is policing. Two different agencies. Unrelated topics. Just like you noted as to the first matter.

But there is a difference. Your firm has taken on a quasi-public role—or so it sounds—on the vaccine case. Someone could argue with a straight face that even if these are two different organizations—a fact that is anything but clear—your suit against the police seems inconsistent with the loyalty the county is entitled to on the vaccine case. And it sounds as if the same County Attorney's office is involved—not a helpful fact. Under the circumstances, absent county consent, we think you could be disqualified from the brutality suit, and only you guys can determine whether that representation is worth the fight.[18]

Well, I know how I come out. As for my tree-hugging partner, we'll have to find out.

---

17. *Brown & Williamson v. Pataki*, 152 F. Supp. 2d 276 (S.D.N.Y. 2001) (law firm not disqualified from representing plaintiffs seeking to overturn a statutory prohibition against mail order sale of cigarettes while simultaneously representing the state welfare department in obtaining federal funding; no relationship between the two matters or state employees involved).

18. ABA Comm. on Ethics and Prof'l Responsibility, Formal Op. 97-405 (1997) (Conflicts in Representing Government Entities).

⫻ Getting a Waiver

We are representing a developer in an appeal from a decision by the Zoning Board of the City. We filed the notice of appeal, and almost immediately, a solicitor from the Zoning Board filed a motion to disqualify. We were shocked. But the motion claims that we do work for the City Fire Department, and, therefore, we have a conflict of interest. They are right. We handled employment discrimination suits for the Fire Department, but that is a different entity altogether. This is outrageous! Besides, I'm sure when we took on those discrimination cases, we got a waiver. I even think I remember who I was talking to.

Well, you have a number of issues there. Let's address them in reverse order. The first is whether a municipality can even grant a waiver. In a few states, any waiver of a conflict of interest from a governmental entity is void and totally unenforceable.[19] You choose to represent a governmental entity in those states, and you just have to live with the conflicts and whatever business it requires you to turn down.[20]

No problem in our jurisdiction, and I did get consent from someone in the City.

This raises a question of who is the client in a government setting. The client gets to decide and, if the client takes the position at the time of your initial engagement that in representing any of those agencies, divisions, or operating subsidiaries you shall be deemed to be representing every other division or subsidiary, that view will prevail. If the issue was not addressed by the client, then it will be up to a court to decide the question essentially the same way corporate family issues are decided. Just remember that it is rare that different departments and agencies of a government will in fact be separate legal entities, and, therefore, the entire government may have to be considered your client for conflict-of-interest purposes.

Suppose I got all of these issues right?

There's still one more. You say you remember getting a waiver, or at least you think you did. First, what did the waiver say? Second, this was an advance waiver, which means it is only valid if it reasonably described the

---

19. *See, e.g.,* N.J. Rule Prof. Conduct 1.7(b)(1), 1.8(1), 1.9(d); *State ex rel. Morgan Stanley & Co. v. MacQueen,* 416 S.E.2d 55 (W. Va. 1992) (state not capable of consenting to concurrent representation of government and government employees by outside counsel in the same action, but allowed to amend pleadings to avoid disqualification).

20. *But see* RLGL § 122, cmt. g(ii) (rejecting per se prohibition).

future conflicts as well as the adverse consequences they could have on your client.[21] Third, assuming all this was accomplished, our rules now require that you provide the client with a writing that will fairly reflect the informed consent of the client.[22] So, unless you can find a contemporaneous writing that reflects your discussion—including a discussion of those items essential to securing informed consent—your reliance on the oral advanced waiver will be unavailing.

⁂ Hiring Former Government Lawyers

We are always looking to hire lawyers who work for the state. They bring such great expertise and credibility to our practice. But I must say the conflicts involved certainly drive us crazy. We know the rules let us screen government lawyers, but we don't hire these lawyers to be screened. We hire them to represent parties adverse to their former employer. If they cannot do that, why bother?

Well, you certainly are right about the screening part.[23] Figuring out what they can handle is a more difficult question.

Precisely. We have two situations right now. We hired Julia Davis, who worked at the State Attorney General's office for six years handling employment discrimination cases against state departments. Now we have a new client, Paula Pearson, whose case we would love to assign to Julia. It is a race discrimination claim against the state Department of Taxation. Problem is, Julia handled another race discrimination claim on the defense side against the same department. Should Pearson get the benefit of Julia's experience?

The answer to that question turns on whether she was personally and substantially involved in this matter.[24]

She says she knows nothing about it, but the events giving rise to the claim arose while Julia was still working for the state.

---

21. MODEL RULE 1.7, cmt. [22]; ABA Comm. on Ethics and Prof'l Responsibility, Formal Op. 05-436 (2005) (Informed Consent to Future Conflicts of Interest) (Withdrawal of Formal Op. 94-382).

22. MODEL RULE 1.7(b)(4).

23. MODEL RULE 1.11(b)–(c).

24. MODEL RULE 1.11(a)–(e); RLGL § 133(1), cmt. c; ABA Comm. on Ethics and Prof'l Responsibility, Formal Op. 97-409 (1997) (Conflict of Interest: Successive Government and Private Employment).

Under those circumstances, Julia should be able to represent Ms. Pearson.

But won't they say that Julia knows the Attorney General's "playbook?"

Nothing can guarantee the state can't raise a conflict-of-interest claim and seek to disqualify Julia. Your argument back will be that the "playbook" argument must fit within the "personal and substantial involvement" in this matter. If this requirement is read too broadly, former government lawyers can never take a position adverse to their former clients. No guarantees here, but in our view, you should prevail.[25]

But that only answers one question. We have been asked to represent a local municipality in an antitrust claim against a bus manufacturer, claiming price-fixing. We want to assign Julia to that case because she handled a similar claim on behalf of the state Department of Transportation against the same bus man-ufacturer. When we thought about it, we figured there would be no problem since in this case, Julia would be adverse to the same entity. But one of our colleagues thought this might be a problem.

Your colleague is right. Julia would have to get the permission of her former employer to take on this new representation.[26] That is because, as a public policy matter, we do not want former government lawyers to be able to use, as private sector lawyers, the special access to information they may have gotten as government lawyers unless they first get the former government employer's permission.[27]

𝍖 The Former Government Lawyer as Witness

We've got a double-barreled problem. We have a case with the FDA that's been going on for years. One of their top lawyers is looking to leave the agency. We're drooling to get her. But two years ago, she gave a deposition in our case. If we hire her, does our client have to hire new counsel because of the ethics rules?

Let's focus on hiring someone from the FDA, first. You are certainly free to hire her. The Ethics in Government Act, however, makes it a felony for her to appear or communicate with the FDA about the matter.[28] The Model Rules

---

25. RLGL § 133, cmt. e.

26. *Id.*

27. RLGL § 133, cmt. d.

28. 18 U.S.C. § 207 (2006).

parallel this requirement.[29] If she was not personally and substantially involved in the pending matter, there are no conditions to the hire. If she was so involved, then your firm can continue to handle the matter as long as you notify the government and screen the new lawyer from the matter. Because we want to encourage lawyers to work in public service and not become so many Typhoid Marys when they look for post-government employment (employment which most likely would be with the firms that most often appear before the agency), the rules craft this exception to the treatment of the side-switching private lawyer in the majority of states that still prohibit involuntary screening of the side-switching lawyer to avoid imputation of matters that lawyer worked on at the lawyer's earlier practice setting.

What about the fact that she might be a witness?

The Model Rule, unlike the old Model Code, provides for disqualification of the testifying lawyer, but not the firm, as long as the testimony does not materially and adversely affect the client.[30] You must discuss with your client the possible detriment to the client's case that might arise from calling a witness who is a lawyer at the client's law firm, something you had better do before you hire the FDA lawyer. But assuming the client consents to the arrangement, then there is no reason the representation may not proceed. Cobbling together two exceptions will carry the day here.

✍ Ex Parte Contact with Government Officials

Self-righteous private lawyers. They are always throwing around Rule 4.2 as a sword, threatening to turn us in to the bar for contacting their "clients"—mere employees of their corporate clients—when all we are doing is what the law requires. Pursuing investigative leads to fulfill our law enforcement mandate. But when we announce we represent the government in a litigated matter, these private lawyers have no trouble contacting the head of the department they are suing. It's not fair.

We'll leave fairness to another discussion. The point is, Rule 4.2 does apply to the contacting of government officials, except for one very important exception. The Constitution gives citizens the First Amendment right to petition the government for the redress of grievances. And that right may be

---

29. MODEL RULE 1.11.

30. MODEL RULE 3.7.

exercised through one's lawyer. So when a developer has a fight before the Zoning Board of Appeals, the developer does not lose the right to contact, through her lawyer, the township's zoning officer on a matter of public policy. Even one that affects the case. It's a narrow exception to the reach of 4.2 as to government clients, albeit a very important one.[31]

ℳ Prosecutorial Comment

The DA just held a press conference on the courthouse steps that sounded like a campaign speech and a closing argument all at once. And he had all the networks there, catching "the jury" a week before trial.

There are rules governing trial publicity by lawyers. Defining what is impermissible in the context of the First Amendment and enforcing violations of these trial publicity rules has always been difficult. Nonetheless, what you describe sounds as though it went way beyond the safe harbor of accepted information and in fact was designed to prejudice the proceedings. Don't be surprised when those assertions are met with free speech rhetoric and the need to keep the public informed. But this conduct may give grounds for postponement, a change of venue, and a disciplinary complaint against the DA.[32]

---

31. MODEL RULE 4.2, cmt. 5; RLGL §§ 99(1)(a), 101.

32. MODEL RULE 3.6; RLGL § 109; GEOFFREY C. HAZARD, JR. & W. WILLIAM HODES, THE LAW OF LAWYERING § 32.5 (3d ed., Aspen 2002).

PART THREE

Navigating the Legal Fiction

"Ethically I'm probably at, or perhaps just
a bit below, the national average."

FIFTEEN

Five Steps to Ethically Representing
Your Organizational Client

% Introduction: The Daunting Task

REPRESENTING ORGANIZATIONS CAN BE DAUNTING. We hope we have helped clarify your ethical obligations in this book. In this chapter, we summarize our approach, cross-referencing to prior chapters.

% Step One: Beginning Your Representation
(Section I)

1. Identify Your Client(s) (Chapter One)

Your role as an officer of the legal system creates primary obligations to clients, as well as responsibilities to courts and third parties. All of these obligations require you to identify your clients, an inquiry that can produce unanticipated results.

In most situations, lawyers know who their clients are because they have expressly agreed to represent them. Increasingly, however, the law governing lawyers also has recognized what lawyers may think of as "accidental" clients, those a lawyer did not expect, but those recognized by law as being owed the same fiduciary duties lawyers owe clients they intend to represent.

Entities can create accidental clients because they act only through agents. Model Rule 1.13 adopts the entity theory of representation, making the obvious point that lawyers for entities represent the organization, not any constituent of the latter. Yet, when you represent the entity you must simultaneously stay focused on the organization's interests while interacting with and receiving direction from these constituents. This reality makes it easy to view your client, mistakenly, as the person you deal with, rather than the entity that person represents. Usually, you do not want that person to be your client. You do not want that person to believe you will keep his individual confidences from the organization. You also do not want him to assume you are his lawyer when he needs personal legal advice, especially if his personal interests may conflict with those of the organization.

At the same time, general rules that govern the creation of client-lawyer relationships might make it reasonable for a constituent to believe that you, the entity's lawyer, are the constituent's lawyer as well. Such a joint representation is not presumed, nor is it per se prohibited. But it must be undertaken with the informed consent of both clients, and reconsidered or stopped when their interests conflict. And if the constituent is to become a client under circumstances in which the organization's consent is required, someone in the organization other than the constituent must authorize that consent.

An accidental client can result when that constituent reasonably and personally relies on your legal advice or services apart from the constituent's role as an agent for the organization. They also lurk in prospective client situations. Accidental clients can be created by court appointments, and by imputation. Identifying some clients can be complicated by change, such as by merger, reorganization, or bankruptcy. Some third parties qualify as quasi-clients if your client designates them as third-party beneficiaries.

Once you identify accidental as well as intended clients, you will be in a position to avoid client-lawyer relationships you do not wish to create and embrace those you do. When you know your clients, you will be able to observe your Five C fiduciary duties appropriately.

2. Clarify Your Fee (Chapter Two)

Lawyers are fiduciaries and therefore owe their clients certain pre-contractual duties of fairness in bargaining for fees. Model Rule 1.5 articulates this premise by providing that you may not agree to, charge, or collect an unreasonable fee or expense. Factors determining reasonableness include the time and difficulty of the matter, the fee customarily charged, the amount involved, results obtained, your experience and ability, and the kind of fee. You are free to charge an hourly, flat, contingent, or blended fee, but it must be reasonable. Contingent fees and agreements to split fees must meet specific writing requirements. All fees should be communicated to the client, preferably in writing, along with the scope of representation and the basis or rate at which expenses are charged. Failure to clarify the basis for expenses in such an agreement leaves you with the only option of passing on the actual cost.

In an increasing number of situations, courts determine a reasonable fee. Often this occurs in a statutory fee-shifting case, but it also can occur where a court has jurisdiction to consider the fee as part of its general obligations, for example, in approving the reasonableness of amounts owed by an estate or trustee to a lawyer for the personal representative or trust.

Courts also become involved in common funds cases, especially class actions, by virtue of their obligations under court rules. And, of course, whenever litigation over a fee occurs, courts look to the reasonableness of the fee in deciding the matter. If your fee is subject to judicial scrutiny or approval in any context, imprecise billing practices (including "block billing") will invariably work to your monetary disadvantage.

Once you take on a representation and agree to a fee, fiduciary duties attach, making any attempt to modify a fee after the initial agreement subject to a presumption that you unduly influenced the client. To rebut this presumption, you should recommend that clients have outside advice before agreeing to a fee modification.

Clients also have the right to fire lawyers at any time for any reason, and you must withdraw from a matter if this occurs. You also must withdraw when your other ethical obligations will be violated if you continue a representation. If this happens before you complete a matter, you lose your right to a contract fee, but may recover the lesser of the amount of quantum meruit or the contract fee. Since quantum meruit in most jurisdictions focuses on a reasonable hourly rate times number of hours expended on the matter, you must keep track of your billable hours so that you can document the quantum meruit amount should you not finish the representation.

When you receive an advance "retainer," it is not earned until you provide the legal services. It is therefore the client's money and belongs in your trust account. You may, indeed you should, withdraw sums as you provide services and an appropriate accounting to your client. Calling such an advance retainer "nonrefundable" is a fraud because it's not true (and now you know that). On the other hand, availability retainers—those that assure your attention to a matter in a specific time period—are earned when paid.

𝕄 Step Two: Attending to Fiduciary Duty (Section II)

Lawyers assume five fiduciary duties—what we call the "Five C's"—when an actual or implied client-lawyer relationship is established. These obligations rest on a key principle of agency law now restated in the law governing lawyers, that you assume fiduciary duties of proper deference to client control, communication, competence, confidentiality, and conflict of interest resolution to ensure that the client's best interests are promoted in a representation.

1. Control: Who's in Charge? (Chapter Three)

Like other agents, you have a duty to act on the client-entity's behalf, subject to the client's right to control the objectives of the representation. The law governing lawyers divides client-lawyer authority into three spheres. Clients have sole authority to determine the objective or goals of the representation. Lawyers have sole authority to take actions required by law before tribunals and to refuse to engage in unlawful conduct. Clients and lawyers share authority and are free to negotiate control in the vast middle sphere that governs all other aspects of the representation.

The client's ambit of authority includes the goals of the representation and specific decisions where clients retain sole authority, including whether and when to settle or appeal a matter, and in criminal cases, how to plead, whether to waive a jury trial, and whether to testify. Clients may authorize you to make a particular decision within this area, but the ultimate authority of clients to decide may not be delegated completely. A direct or indirect attempt to limit the client's authority on these issues will likely be found unenforceable and may subject you to discipline.

The lawyer's sphere of sole authority includes refusing to perform, counsel, or assist a client's unlawful act. The lawyer also has sole authority and may bind clients by actions taken before tribunals that are required by law or court order, despite client preferences to the contrary.

The third sphere, where you and your clients share authority, often is labeled the means to accomplish the client's objectives. Tactics are part of this vast middle ground, where you and your client are free to agree to strategy. You may bargain for authority in this middle sphere before a client engages you, and if you do not feel comfortable with your client's later requests, you may withdraw from the representation. This sphere also includes the scope of the representation, which you may reasonably limit with proper client informed consent.

All three spheres of authority require that you initiate communication during a representation. When a client decision arises, you must promptly inform, consult with your client, and clarify your client's decision. When a client insists on illegal conduct, you must inform the client that the conduct is not permitted and explain why. When a client has decided upon an objective, you should consult with the client about the means to accomplish it.

The outcome of these consultations creates your actual authority and empowers you to act on behalf of the client. Clients also can be legally bound by apparent authority, which requires their own holding out to a third party that you are so authorized, even if you in fact are not.

2. Communication: The Foundation of the Five C's (Chapter Four)

Communication is essential to every aspect of the client-lawyer relationship. It defines the initial terms of the representation and is necessary to make each of your fiduciary duties work properly. Clients cannot control the goals of a representation without understanding feasible legal options. You cannot act competently without understanding what your client hopes to accomplish and knowing how to get there. You need facts sufficient to permit you to apply the law to your client's situation, and confidentiality helps you get those facts for the client's benefit. And you must search for and resolve conflicts of interest to avoid favoring your own or some other person's interest over that of your client. A significant percentage of disciplinary complaints are based on a lawyer's failure to fulfill the obligation to communicate in a clear and timely manner.

Communicating with organizational clients means communicating with constituents and therefore requires knowledge about the organization's organic structure to determine who has the authority to speak for the entity. This may mean different people for different purposes. Ordinarily, you should accept the agents' or group of agents' direction, even if you disagree with the decision.

At the same time, you are required to give some measure of scrutiny to these constituent decisions, because the agent you deal with could be acting contrary to the best interests of the organization. When a constituent's decision violates a legal obligation to the organization or otherwise will mean a violation of law attributable to the organization, you must weigh two factors. First, how likely is it that this violation will cause substantial injury to the organization, such as criminal or civil liability or harm to reputation? Second, if substantial injury is threatened, you must consider how to proceed in a manner that promotes the best interests of your client, the organization.

What to do? If the deciding constituent will not reconsider, perhaps after receiving a legal opinion from you or another lawyer, an up-the-ladder trip ordinarily will be necessary. Again, the organization of the entity will determine who has supervisory authority. That supervisory constituent or group should be asked to reconsider the matter.

If a complete up-the-ladder trip to the highest authority within the organization does not change the result, then you face several other ethical dilemmas. Model Rule 1.2(d) requires you to refrain from counseling or assisting unlawful conduct, and may require you to withdraw from the representation. In a case where substantial injury to the organization is reasonably likely, you also may have discretion to disclose beyond the client to prevent the violation.

Throughout the representation, if you stay focused on the best interests of the organization, raise questions when those interests are threatened, go up the ladder when the threat is serious and, when a serious legal violation is likely to cause substantial injury, withdraw, you will do your job admirably. Without your recognition of the governance of the organization, you can misunderstand what your client wishes to accomplish or bind your client to an outcome it does not want.

The key to understanding your communication duty is to recognize that lawyers must initiate the conversation. Seven specific events trigger this obligation. First, when you initially agree to a fee, you should define the scope of a representation and craft an engagement agreement. Second, throughout the representation, you should explain the matter to enable the client to determine the objectives of the representation. Third, you should keep the client reasonably informed about the status of the matter throughout the representation, including changes in your practice, such as a serious illness or a law firm merger. Fourth, you must inform the client when you make a material mistake in a matter. Fifth, you should promptly respond to your client's requests for information. Sixth, you must inform your client whenever the law imposes limits on conduct the client expects you to undertake. Finally, you must specifically obtain your client's informed consent to important decisions, including limiting the scope of a representation, obtaining waivers of fiduciary duties (especially confidentiality and conflicts of interest), and before providing an evaluation for use by third parties that is likely to adversely affect the client's interests.

Like other fiduciary duties, informed consent is viewed from the client's perspective. To obtain informed consent, you must first disclose and explain the risks of the proposed course of conduct and, second, inform the client of alternatives to that option. When considering litigation, disclosure of ADR options is one such alternative.

Overall, communication is essential to becoming a collaborative lawyer, that is, one who avoids the twin dangers of both under- and over-identification with clients. Without communication, you may end up breaching another fiduciary duty or abetting a client's wrongdoing.

3. Competence: Why You Were Hired in the First Place (Chapter Five)

Clients hire you for competent service precisely because they are not able to navigate a complex legal system themselves. . Both tort law and the lawyer codes require "reasonable" competence and diligence. You do not have to be perfect, but you do have to meet or exceed the standard of practice in your jurisdiction. A violation of your Rules of Professional Conduct may be evidence a lapse from the appropriate standard of care.

In both malpractice and disciplinary matters, reasonable care usually is established by expert testimony, although disciplinary agencies typically do not proceed against lawyers for isolated instances of incompetence or lack of diligence. Some errors are deemed so obvious that they are within the common knowledge of a fact finder. These include the failure to file within a mandatory time period, the failure to perform legal or factual research, and the failure to observe core fiduciary duties, such as compliance with client instructions, a failure of communication, or a breach of confidentiality.

Malpractice requires not only that a client prove a lawyer violated the appropriate standard of care, but also that the violation caused the client harm. The same is true of suits for breach of fiduciary duty, which typically allege violation of a well-defined core professional duty such as communication, confidentiality, or conflict of interest.

If you make a material mistake, notify your client, as well as your carrier. You do not need to fall on your sword, but you do need to explain the facts that led to your error, the conflict of interest you now face, and your need to withdraw. Do not attempt to settle the matter yourself, because your client needs to be given an opportunity to seek independent representation before deciding what to do about your mistake. The law of undue influence will invalidate any such agreement, and the potential for serious discipline also should not be overlooked. Above all, avoid any deceit or cover-up of any relevant facts. That constitutes fraud, which brings additional adverse tort and disciplinary consequences.

Lawyers also need to think about competence in a limited but growing class of cases where third-party non-clients seek relief. Third parties who are intended beneficiaries, or who are invited to rely on your representation of a client, may sue for malpractice in many jurisdictions. Third parties also may sue for fraud, which includes intentional as well as reckless misstatements of material fact, as long as the third party reasonably relies on the misstatement and can prove damages. Some courts also grant a cause of action against lawyers for negligent misrepresentation. Less common but also recognized is an action for aiding and abetting a client's breach of fiduciary duty, but only if the lawyer gives substantial assistance to the client's breach, for example by engaging in fraud, a crime, or statutory breach.

Acting with competence is essential to avoiding accountability to your client and, on occasion, to a third party as well. Getting it wrong can mean liability as well as professional discipline.

4. Confidentiality: The Never-Ending Obligation (Chapter Six)

Confidentiality obligations originated in both agency law and the attorney-client privilege, an evidentiary doctrine. The agency fiduciary duty now abides as well in the lawyer disciplinary codes, and protects all information relating to the representation of a client, from the initial prospective client communication, throughout the representation and beyond, even after your client's death or reorganization. The evidentiary privilege is narrower and may be invoked only before a tribunal to block disclosure of confidential communications between client and lawyer for the purpose of seeking or conveying legal advice. The law of evidence also immunizes lawyer work-product from discovery, which includes the lawyer's opinions and mental impressions formed in representing the client in anticipation of litigation.

Organizations as well as individuals are protected by these doctrines. Organizational clients are protected by the client-lawyer privilege whenever the lawyer speaks to a duly authorized constituent concerning a legal matter of interest to the organization.

Both fiduciary duty and the evidence-based privilege recognize parallel exceptions, whose exact dimensions nevertheless may differ substantially, even within the same jurisdiction. When applicable, exceptions to the fiduciary duty usually grant lawyers discretion to disclose, and if you choose to do so, you must only disclose to the extent reasonably necessary to accomplish the narrow purpose of the exception. Once privilege exceptions are established, courts may order lawyers to testify, on pain of contempt if they refuse to do so.

Express or implied client consent allows disclosure or use of client confidences. Remember, however, that your confidentiality obligation belongs to your client organization, not to the constituent employee. The organization therefore determines when to waive the protection, and the folks making that determination may be a different set of constituents from the group that communicated with you in the first place.

Most jurisdictions also recognize a confidentiality exception to prevent future client crime or fraud, on the basis that the client may not use the client-lawyer relationship to accomplish either. Whether criminal or not, the lawyer codes increasingly also recognize future threats of serious bodily harm as an additional sufficiently weighty reason to disclose, even without client consent.

Two exceptions grant you some measure of self-protection. One allows you to employ confidential information to collect fees and to defend yourself against charges of misconduct by clients or others. The other allows you to seek guidance about how to comply with your ethical obligations by sharing otherwise confidential information with another lawyer.

Most jurisdictions also recognize a "to comply with other law or a court order" exception. In the context of the evidentiary privilege or work product protections, the "court order" part of this exception requires you first to claim the privilege (or the client will lose it) and then, if the other side prevails either to comply with the order to testify or produce documents, or to appeal it. The "comply with other law" part of this exception also can allow disclosure when other law, such as a disclosure required by statute, supersedes your ethical obligation.

Confidentiality assures that clients are encouraged to share all relevant information with their lawyers. Without relevant facts, you may fail to understand what your client wishes to accomplish, the law that is relevant to your client's circumstance, and other legal options that might be available to fulfill your client's needs. Breaching confidentiality can result in serious harm to client interests. The law nevertheless recognizes limited non-consensual exceptions when serious countervailing considerations occur.

5. Conflict of Interest Resolution: Your Loyalty Obligation (Chapter Seven)

Your fiduciary duty of loyalty requires you to identify and avoid or resolve conflicts of interest. You derive your power from clients, but your superior knowledge and skill also allow you to overpower your client's interests.

Loyalty imposes the obligation to seek client consent whenever your judgment might reasonably be called into question from the client's point of view. It also prevents client harm by imposing on you the obligation to recognize and respond to any influences that may interfere with your ability to act in the client's best interests as defined by the client.

Both agency law and the lawyer codes recognize that conflicts of interest can arise from several sources, including the lawyer's own personal interests, the interests of other clients, third persons, and former clients. Pursuing the client's best interests requires you to remain vigilant throughout the representation so that we can recognize conflicts when they arise. Once identified, a conflict must be disclosed to your client(s), unless doing so would violate another client's confidentiality. If that occurs, you should resolve the conflict by not proceeding in the matter.

A lawyer's conflicts are imputed to the lawyer's firm. This imputation assumes that lawyers readily interact with each other in firms and that all firm lawyers owe loyalty to all firm clients. Imputation also requires a conflict-of-interest system to check for conflicts whenever a firm takes on a new lawyer, new matter, or new client.

If conflict disclosure will not violate the lawyer's duty of confidentiality, such disclosure is the beginning of the informed consent process, which allows your client to waive the conflict. In some situations, conflicts are so serious that client consent cannot vitiate them. When this occurs, you may not seek a waiver, and must turn down a prospective client or withdraw from representing a current client to avoid the conflict.

Failure to recognize and properly respond to conflicts creates overlapping remedies for clients. If harm is caused, the client may seek tort relief. If harm is threatened, the client may seek disqualification or injunctive relief, ordering you to end the representation of the conflicting interest. If you have proceeded in a representation without disclosing a conflict, your client also can seek fee forfeiture, disgorgement of fees already paid, or a constructive trust of other property that is implicated.

Step Three: Observing the Limits of the Law (Chapter Eight)

Every agency and client-lawyer relationship is subject to one significant limitation: neither your client's power of control nor your obligation of loyalty allows either of you to violate the limits or bounds of the law.

Both of you remain responsible for the consequences of your conduct as autonomous legal persons.

The limits of the law include several familiar bodies of law that are explicitly incorporated into lawyer code provisions. This means that straying over the line can result in professional discipline as well as other legal consequences, such as procedural sanctions, civil and criminal accountability, or equitable relief.

The most obvious legal limits are created by the criminal law, although today's thousands of criminal statutes can create a legal limit unrecognized by an organizational lawyer. Tort law, and in particular the law of fraud, creates similar limitations. The law of evidence, which recognizes the client-lawyer privilege and the work-product doctrine is enforced by contempt orders and sanctions. Courts also impose monetary sanctions for violations of procedural rules, such as Rules 11 and 26. Tribunals further exercise their inherent power when they disqualify, disbar or discipline lawyers, or hold lawyers in contempt.

Lawyer codes impose additional limits on client advocacy. Specific rules govern ex parte contact with opponents, define improper inducements to settle a matter, and regulate lawyers who serve as witnesses in client matters.

All of these bodies of law impose limits or bounds that restrain unfettered client allegiance. If you violate these legal limits or fail to identify them to avoid violation by clients, you also may face professional discipline. Taken together, these limits remind us that client-lawyer relationships do not exempt either client or lawyer from general legal requirements, some of which impose limits on client advocacy. This is not an unfamiliar role, because lawyers have long advised clients about how to avoid illegality. Many of these limits seek to provide a fair and accessible justice system. Others seek to avoid serious wrongdoing. If you become blinded by client over-identification, you can get yourself into more trouble than you could have helped your client avoid.

𝍦 Step Four: Recognizing Remedies (Chapter Nine)

Lawyers owe agency-based fiduciary duties to clients, which trigger equitable as well as legal remedies. These fiduciary duties are the foundation for many of the provisions in lawyer codes, violation of which further triggers professional discipline. Lawyers who fail to understand a legal limit imposed on unrestrained client advocacy also may be accountable to third-party non-clients.

Client legal remedies include claims for breach of contract, malpractice, and breach of fiduciary duty. Equitable remedies for breaches of fiduciary duty also grant clients presumptions of undue influence and allow them to seek a constructive trust, disqualification or injunctive relief, fee forfeiture, or restoration of pre-contractual rights.

Non-clients can seek relief against you if they are identified third-party beneficiaries, invited by you or your client to rely on your legal services, or if you commit crimes or intentional torts against them. In an increasing number of situations, non-clients also seek relief for negligent misrepresentation or aiding and abetting a client's breach of fiduciary duty. Non-clients involved in litigation also can seek procedural sanctions for frivolous actions or discovery abuse.

All of these remedies have been created to support lawyer fiduciary duties or the limits on advocacy imposed by other law. If you understand and observe your Five C fiduciary duties, you should not create grounds for client relief. Identifying and staying within the limits of the law also should keep you out of third-party trouble.

✺ Step Five: Understanding Rules that Govern Specific Legal Fictions (Chapters Ten–Fourteen)

Representing an entity requires you to identify your client by understanding the organic law that governs your client organization and its internal constituents. Some organizations create specific ethical issues because of their structure, governance, or additional legal regulation.

1. Privately Held Businesses (Chapter Ten)

Partners owe fiduciary duties to one another, so that lawyers who represent a partnership need to be aware of these obligations in advising the entity. In some jurisdictions, this means that you represent all the partners; in others, the partnership through its designed agents. Size also matters. In a small partnership, you may have to communicate with all of the partners. In a large partnership, the partners may determine which constituents you should consult. Similarly, communicating with all of the partners should be privileged. But speaking to limited partners may waive the partnership's privilege. When a partner proposes questionable conduct, you need to consider whether it threatens either a breach of fiduciary duty to the entity or might constitute a legal violation of the partnership. If either is the case, your up-the-ladder obligation requires that you consult with others, including all of the partners, if necessary, to resolve the matter.

Privately held companies can range in size from a small family corporation to a large entity. The law that governs them may not require the same degree of public disclosure for many activities, but it does require the fulfillment of fiduciary obligations by those who act on behalf of the entity. On the other hand, the private relationships that make up a family company can complicate your representation. This is especially true where you represent both the entity and individual family members. If they feud, you can find yourself in an impossible situation. If you side with one over the others, the disadvantaged will claim you as lawyer and may allege that you either breached your own or your favored client's fiduciary duty to them.

2. Publicly Held Businesses (Chapter Eleven)

Publicly held businesses are subject to a myriad of laws to assure stockholder rights. Federal and state securities laws impose some of these obligations. The SEC's Sarbanes-Oxley Rules impose up-the-ladder obligations similar but not identical to those imposed by Model Rule 1.13. When a public company fails, lawyers and others are often the subject of litigation, investigation and regulatory review.

3. Unincorporated Associations (Chapter Twelve)

Unincorporated associations present real client identity issues. In some circumstances, they are viewed as essentially a joint representation of a number of clients; in others, as an entity with constituents authorized to make decisions for the group. These rules also play an important role in determining whether the group can sue or be sued as an entity or a group of named individuals.

4. Nonprofits (Chapter Thirteen)

Many nonprofits were created by or could not exist without the help of lawyers, who often serve these organizations on a pro bono basis. In some situations, the lawyer codes encourage this work by creating special rules to govern them. Lawyers who offer short-term, limited scope legal services, or those who serve on the boards of legal services organizations, are assisted by these provisions.

5. Governments (Chapter Fourteen)

Government representation is complicated by governmental structure. You may be asked to represent a government unit, such as a municipality, or a branch of government, such as the executive branch, or a governmental agency or employee. In each situation, the organic law that created the government will determine the nature and power of the entity and may also determine who may represent it (the attorney general alone, or other private lawyers as well). As a government lawyer, you are governed by lawyer codes and the law governing lawyers, but you also may be regulated by constitutional, statutory, and regulatory provisions, which may further specify your obligations.

This complex regulation determines which constituents are authorized to give you direction as a government lawyer. It also determines your up-the-ladder obligations when the constituent you deal with insists on unlawful activity. These provisions may require that you represent several entities within the government, even if their interests conflict. They also may require that you avoid conflicts after leaving government service or face criminal or civil sanctions. While employed by the government, special regulations also may govern your conduct in accepting or reporting gifts or outside compensation.

Prosecutors exercise considerable discretion and power in the criminal justice system and generally are immune from civil liability. If you serve in such a role, you are therefore subject to several constitutional and lawyer code obligations to fairly execute your duties. Further, your access as a government lawyer with investigatory powers makes you privy to confidential information of both your client government and the citizen it is investigating. This access requires you not only to keep government confidences, but also to keep confidential the information your client government is obligated to keep secret.

All of this legal regulation demands careful attention to your government client, your role, and the distinctive remedies created by lawyer codes, statute, or common law. If you understand these aspects of your representations you will serve your clients well. If you do not, you may confuse your client's identity, or worse, misunderstand your own obligations created by lawyer codes or other regulation.

Selected State Rules of Professional Conduct

❧ Indiana Rule 1.13 ("Post-Enron" Rule 1.13)

Organization as Client

(a) A lawyer employed or retained by an organization represents the organization acting through its duly authorized constituents.

(b) If a lawyer for an organization knows that an officer, employee or other person associated with the organization is engaged in action, intends to act or refuses to act in a matter related to the representation that is a violation of a legal obligation to the organization, or a violation of law which reasonably might be imputed to the organization, and that is likely to result in substantial injury to the organization, then the lawyer shall proceed as is reasonably necessary in the best interest of the organization. Unless the lawyer reasonably believes that it is not necessary in the best interest of the organization to do so, the lawyer shall refer the matter to higher authority in the organization, including, if warranted by the circumstances to the highest authority that can act on behalf of the organization as determined by applicable law.

(c) Except as provided in paragraph (d), if

    (1) despite the lawyer's efforts in accordance with paragraph (b) the highest authority that can act on behalf of the organization insists upon or fails to address in a timely and appropriate manner an action, or a refusal to act, that is clearly a violation of law and

    (2) the lawyer reasonably believes that the violation is reasonably certain to result in substantial injury to the organization, then the lawyer may reveal information relating to the representation whether or not Rule 1.6 permits such disclosure, but only if and to the extent the lawyer reasonably believes necessary to prevent substantial injury to the organization.

(d) Paragraph (c) shall not apply with respect to information relating to a lawyer's representation of an organization to investigate an alleged violation of law, or to defend the organization or an officer, employee or other constituent associated with the organization against a claim arising out of an alleged violation of law.

(e) A lawyer who reasonably believes that he or she has been discharged because of the lawyer's actions taken pursuant to paragraphs (b) or (c), or who withdraws under circumstances that require or permit the lawyer to take action under either of those paragraphs, shall proceed as the lawyer reasonably believes necessary to assure that the organization's highest authority is informed of the lawyer's discharge or withdrawal.

(f) In dealing with an organization's directors, officers, employees, members, shareholders or other constituents, a lawyer shall explain the identity of the client when the lawyer knows or reasonably should know that the organization's interests are adverse to those of the constituents with whom the lawyer is dealing.

(g) A lawyer representing an organization may also represent any of its directors, officers, employees, members, shareholders or other constituents, subject to the provisions of Rule 1.7. If the organization's consent to the dual representation is required by Rule 1.7, the consent shall be given by an appropriate official of the organization other than the individual who is to be represented, or by the shareholders.

Comment

The Entity as the Client

[1] An organizational client is a legal entity, but it cannot act except through its officers, directors, employees, shareholders and other constituents. Officers, directors, employees and shareholders are the constituents of the corporate organizational client. The duties defined in this Comment apply equally to unincorporated associations. "Other constituents" as used in this Comment means the positions equivalent to officers, directors, employees and shareholders held by persons acting for organizational clients that are not corporations.

[2] When one of the constituents of an organizational client communicates with the organization's lawyer in that person's organizational capacity, the communication is protected by Rule 1.6. Thus, by way of example, if

an organizational client requests its lawyer to investigate allegations of wrongdoing, interviews made in the course of that investigation between the lawyer and the client's employees or other constituents are covered by Rule 1.6. This does not mean, however, that constituents of an organizational client are the clients of the lawyer. The lawyer may not disclose to such constituents information relating to the representation except for disclosures explicitly or impliedly authorized by the organizational client in order to carry out the representation or as otherwise permitted by Rule 1.6.

[3] When constituents of the organization make decisions for it, the decisions ordinarily must be accepted by the lawyer even if their utility or prudence is doubtful. Decisions concerning policy and operations, including ones entailing serious risk, are not as such in the lawyer's province. Paragraph (b) makes clear, however, that when the lawyer knows that the organization is likely to be substantially injured by action of an officer or other constituent that violates a legal obligation to the organization or is in violation of law that might be imputed to the organization, the lawyer must proceed as is reasonably necessary in the best interest of the organization. As defined in Rule 1.0(f), knowledge can be inferred from circumstances, and a lawyer cannot ignore the obvious.

[4] In determining how to proceed under paragraph (b), the lawyer should give due consideration to the seriousness of the violation and its consequences, the responsibility in the organization and the apparent motivation of the person involved, the policies of the organization concerning such matters, and any other relevant considerations. Ordinarily, referral to a higher authority would be necessary. In some circumstances, however, it may be appropriate for the lawyer to ask the constituent to reconsider the matter; for example, if the circumstances involve a constituent's innocent misunderstanding of law and subsequent acceptance of the lawyer's advice, the lawyer may reasonably conclude that the best interest of the organization does not require that the matter be referred to higher authority. If a constituent persists in conduct contrary to the lawyer's advice, it will be necessary for the lawyer to take steps to have the matter reviewed by a higher authority in the organization. If the matter is of sufficient seriousness and importance or urgency to the organization, referral to higher authority in the organization may be necessary even if the lawyer has not communicated with the constituent. Any measures taken should, to the extent practicable, minimize the risk of revealing information relating to the representation to persons

outside the organization. Even in circumstances where a lawyer is not obligated by Rule 1.13 to proceed, a lawyer may bring to the attention of an organizational client, including its highest authority, matters that the lawyer reasonably believes to be of sufficient importance to warrant doing so in the best interest of the organization.

[5] Paragraph (b) also makes clear that when it is reasonably necessary to enable the organization to address the matter in a timely and appropriate manner, the lawyer must refer the matter to higher authority, including, if warranted by the circumstances, the highest authority that can act on behalf of the organization under applicable law. The organization's highest authority to whom a matter may be referred ordinarily will be the board of directors or similar governing body. However, applicable law may prescribe that under certain conditions the highest authority reposes elsewhere, for example, in the independent directors of a corporation.

Relation to Other Rules

[6] The authority and responsibility provided in this Rule are concurrent with the authority and responsibility provided in other Rules. In particular, this Rule does not limit or expand the lawyer's responsibility under Rules 1.8, 1.16, 3.3 or 4.1. Paragraph (c) of this Rule supplements Rule 1.6(b) by providing an additional basis upon which the lawyer may reveal information relating to the representation, but does not modify, restrict, or limit the provisions of Rule 1.6(b)(1)–(6). Under paragraph (c) the lawyer may reveal such information only when the organization's highest authority insists upon or fails to address threatened or ongoing action that is clearly a violation of law, and then only to the extent the lawyer reasonably believes necessary to prevent reasonably certain substantial injury to the organization. It is not necessary that the lawyer's services be used in furtherance of the violation, but it is required that the matter be related to the lawyer's representation of the organization. If the lawyer's services are being used by an organization to further a crime or fraud by the organization, Rules 1.6(b)(2) and 1.6(b)(3) may permit the lawyer to disclose confidential information. In such circumstances Rule 1.2(d) may also be applicable, in which event, withdrawal from the representation under Rule 1.16(a)(1) may be required.

[7] Paragraph (d) makes clear that the authority of a lawyer to disclose information relating to a representation in circumstances described in paragraph (c) does not apply with respect to information relating to a lawyer's

engagement by an organization to investigate an alleged violation of law or to defend the organization or an officer, employee or other person associated with the organization against a claim arising out of an alleged violation of law. This is necessary in order to enable organizational clients to enjoy the full benefits of legal counsel in conducting an investigation or defending against a claim.

[8] A lawyer who reasonably believes that he or she has been discharged because of the lawyer's actions taken pursuant to paragraph (b) or (c), or who withdraws in circumstances that require or permit the lawyer to take action under either of these paragraphs, must proceed as the lawyer reasonably believes necessary to assure that the organization's highest authority is informed of the lawyer's discharge or withdrawal.

Government Agency

[9] The duty defined in this Rule applies to governmental organizations. Defining precisely the identity of the client and prescribing the resulting obligations of such lawyers may be more difficult in the government context and is a matter beyond the scope of these Rules. See Scope [18]. Although in some circumstances the client may be a specific agency, it may also be a branch of government, such as the executive branch, or the government as a whole. For example, if the action or failure to act involves the head of a bureau, either the department of which the bureau is a part or the relevant branch of government may be the client for purposes of this Rule. Moreover, in a matter involving the conduct of government officials, a government lawyer may have authority under applicable law to question such conduct more extensively than that of a lawyer for a private organization in similar circumstances. Thus, when the client is a governmental organization, a different balance may be appropriate between maintaining confidentiality and assuring that the wrongful act is prevented or rectified, for public business is involved. In addition, duties of lawyers employed by the government or lawyers in military service may be defined by statutes and regulation. This Rule does not limit that authority. See Scope.

Clarifying the Lawyer's Role

[10] There are times when the organization's interest may be or become adverse to those of one or more of its constituents. In such circumstances

the lawyer should advise any constituent, whose interest the lawyer finds adverse to that of the organization of the conflict or potential conflict of interest, that the lawyer cannot represent such constituent, and that such person may wish to obtain independent representation. Care must be taken to assure that the individual understands that, when there is such adversity of interest, the lawyer for the organization cannot provide legal representation for that constituent individual, and that discussions between the lawyer for the organization and the individual may not be privileged.

[11] Whether such a warning should be given by the lawyer for the organization to any constituent individual may turn on the facts of each case.

Dual Representation

[12] Paragraph (g) recognizes that a lawyer for an organization may also represent a principal officer or major shareholder.

Derivative Actions

[13] Under generally prevailing law, the shareholders or members of a corporation may bring suit to compel the directors to perform their legal obligations in the supervision of the organization. Members of unincorporated associations have essentially the same right. Such an action may be brought nominally by the organization, but usually is, in fact, a legal controversy over management of the organization.

[14] The question can arise whether counsel for the organization may defend such an action. The proposition that the organization is the lawyer's client does not alone resolve the issue. Most derivative actions are a normal incident of an organization's affairs, to be defended by the organization's lawyer like any other suit. However, if the claim involves serious charges of wrongdoing by those in control of the organization, a conflict may arise between the lawyer's duty to the organization and the lawyer's relationship with the board. In those circumstances, Rule 1.7 governs who should represent the directors and the organization.

ℳ Delaware Rule 1.13 ("Original" Rule 1.13)

Organization as client

(a) A lawyer employed or retained by an organization represents the organization acting through its duly authorized constituents.

(b) If a lawyer for an organization knows that an officer, employee or other person associated with the organization is engaged in action, intends to act or refuses to act in a matter related to the representation that is a violation of a legal obligation to the organization, or a violation of law which reasonably might be imputed to the organization, and is likely to result in substantial injury to the organization, the lawyer shall proceed as is reasonably necessary in the best interest of the organization. In determining how to proceed, the lawyer shall give due consideration to the seriousness of the violation and its consequences, the scope and nature of the lawyer's representation, the responsibility in the organization and the apparent motivation of the person involved, the policies of the organization concerning such matters and any other relevant considerations. Any measures taken shall be designed to minimize disruption of the organization and the risk of revealing information relating to the representation to persons outside the organization. Such measures may include among others:

(1) asking for reconsideration of the matter;

(2) advising that a separate legal opinion on the matter be sought for presentation to appropriate authority in the organization; and

(3) referring the matter to higher authority in the organization, including, if warranted by the seriousness of the matter, referral to the highest authority that can act on behalf of the organization as determined by applicable law.

(c) If, despite the lawyer's efforts in accordance with paragraph (b), the highest authority that can act on behalf of the organization insists upon action, or a refusal to act, that is clearly a violation of law and is likely to result in substantial injury to the organization, the lawyer may resign in accordance with Rule 1.16.

(d) In dealing with an organization's directors, officers, employees, members, shareholders or other constituents, a lawyer shall explain the identity of the client when the lawyer knows or reasonably should know that the organization's interests are adverse to those of the constituents with whom the lawyer is dealing.

(e) A lawyer representing an organization may also represent any of its directors, officers, employees, members, shareholders or other constituents, subject to the provisions of Rule 1.7. If the organization's consent to the dual representation is required by Rule 1.7, the consent shall be given by an appropriate official of the organization other than the individual who is to be represented, or by the shareholders.

Comment

[1] *The Entity as the Client* An organizational client is a legal entity, but it cannot act except through its officers, directors, employees, shareholders and other constituents. Officers, directors, employees and shareholders are the constituents of the corporate organizational client. The duties defined in this Comment apply equally to unincorporated associations. "Other constituents" as used in this Comment means the positions equivalent to officers, directors, employees and shareholders held by persons acting for organizational clients that are not corporations.

[2] When one of the constituents of an organizational client communicates with the organization's lawyer in that person's organizational capacity, the communication is protected by Rule 1.6. Thus, by way of example, if an organizational client requests its lawyer to investigate allegations of wrongdoing, interviews made in the course of that investigation between the lawyer and the client's employees or other constituents are covered by Rule 1.6. This does not mean, however, that constituents of an organizational client are the clients of the lawyer. The lawyer may not disclose to such constituents information relating to the representation except for disclosures explicitly or impliedly authorized by the organizational client in order to carry out the representation or as otherwise permitted by Rule 1. 6.

[3] When constituents of the organization make decisions for it, the decisions ordinarily must be accepted by the lawyer even if their utility or prudence is doubtful. Decisions concerning policy and operations, including ones entailing serious risk, are not as such in the lawyer's province. However, different considerations arise when the lawyer knows that the organization may be substantially injured by action of a constituent that is in violation of law. In such a circumstance, it may be reasonably necessary for the lawyer to ask the constituent to reconsider the matter. If that fails, or if the matter is of sufficient seriousness and

importance to the organization, it may be reasonably necessary for the lawyer to take steps to have the matter reviewed by a higher authority in the organization. Clear justification should exist for seeking review over the head of the constituent normally responsible for it. The stated policy of the organization may define circumstances and prescribe channels for such review, and a lawyer should encourage the formulation of such a policy. Even in the absence of organization policy, however, the lawyer may have an obligation to refer a matter to higher authority, depending on the seriousness of the matter and whether the constituent in question has apparent motives to act at variance with the organization's interest. Review by the chief executive officer or by the board of directors may be required when the matter is of importance commensurate with their authority. At some point it may be useful or essential to obtain an independent legal opinion.

[4] The organization's highest authority to whom a matter may be referred ordinarily will be the board of directors or similar governing body. However, applicable law may prescribe that under certain conditions the highest authority reposes elsewhere, for example, in the independent directors of a corporation.

[5] *Relation to Other Rules* The authority and responsibility provided in this Rule are concurrent with the authority and responsibility provided in other Rules. In particular, this Rule does not limit or expand the lawyer's responsibility under Rule 1.6, 1.8, 1.16, 3.3 or 4.1. If the lawyer's services are being used by an organization to further a crime or fraud by the organization, Rule 1.2(d) can be applicable.

[6] *Government Agency* The duty defined in this Rule applies to governmental organizations. Defining precisely the identity of the client and prescribing the resulting obligations of such lawyers may be more difficult in the government context and is a matter beyond the scope of these Rules. See Scope [18]. Although in some circumstances the client may be a specific agency, it may also be a branch of government, such as the executive branch, or the government as a whole. For example, if the action or failure to act involves the head of a bureau, either the department of which the bureau is a part or the relevant branch of government may be the client for purposes of this Rule. Moreover, in a matter involving the conduct of government officials, a government lawyer may have authority under applicable law to question such conduct more extensively than that of a lawyer for a private organization in similar circumstances. Thus, when the client is a governmental organization, a different

balance may be appropriate between maintaining confidentiality and assuring that the wrongful act is prevented or rectified, for public business is involved. In addition, duties of lawyers employed by the government or lawyers in military service may be defined by statutes and regulation. This Rule does not limit that authority. See Scope.

[7] *Clarifying the Lawyer's Role* There are times when the organization's interest may be or become adverse to those of one or more of its constituents. In such circumstances the lawyer should advise any constituent, whose interest the lawyer finds adverse to that of the organization of the conflict or potential conflict of interest, that the lawyer cannot represent such constituent, and that such person may wish to obtain independent representation. Care must be taken to assure that the individual understands that, when there is such adversity of interest, the lawyer for the organization cannot provide legal representation for that constituent individual, and that discussions between the lawyer for the organization and the individual may not be privileged.

[8] Whether such a warning should be given by the lawyer for the organization to any constituent individual may turn on the facts of each case.

[9] *Dual Representation* Paragraph (e) recognizes that a lawyer for an organization may also represent a principal officer or major shareholder.

[10] *Derivative Actions* Under generally prevailing law, the shareholders or members of a corporation may bring suit to compel the directors to perform their legal obligations in the supervision of the organization. Members of unincorporated associations have essentially the same right. Such action may be brought nominally by the organization, but usually is, in fact, a legal controversy over management of the organization.

[11] The question can arise whether counsel for the organization may defend such an action. The proposition that the organization is the lawyer's client does not alone resolve the issue. Most derivative actions are a normal incident of an organization's affairs, to be defended by the organization's lawyer like any other suit. However, if the claim involves serious charges of wrongdoing by those in control of the organization, a conflict may arise between the lawyer's duty to the organization and the lawyer's relationship with the board. In those circumstances, Rule 1.7 governs who should represent the directors and the organization.

Government Lawyers

⅋ Maryland Rule 1.11

Special Conflicts of Interest for Former and Current Government Officers and Employees

(a) Except as law may otherwise expressly permit, a lawyer who has formerly served as a public officer or employee of the government:

    (1) is subject to Rule 1.9(c); and

    (2) shall not otherwise represent a client in connection with a matter in which the lawyer participated personally and substantially as a public officer or employee, unless the appropriate government agency gives its informed consent, confirmed in writing, to the representation.

(b) When a lawyer is disqualified from representation under paragraph (a), no lawyer in a firm with which that lawyer is associated may knowingly undertake or continue representation in such a matter unless:

    (1) the disqualified lawyer is timely screened from any participation in the matter and is apportioned no part of the fee therefrom; and

    (2) written notice is promptly given to the appropriate government agency to enable it to ascertain compliance with the provisions of this Rule.

(c) Except as law may otherwise expressly permit, a lawyer having information that the lawyer knows is confidential government information about a person acquired when the lawyer was a public officer or employee, may not represent a private client whose interests are adverse to that person in a matter in which the information could be used to the material disadvantage of that person. As used in this Rule, the term "confidential government information" means information that has been obtained under governmental authority and which, at the time this Rule is applied, the government is prohibited by law from disclosing to the public or has a legal privilege not to disclose and which is not otherwise available to the public. A firm with which that lawyer is associated may undertake or continue representation in the matter only if the disqualified lawyer is timely screened from any participation in the matter and is apportioned no part of the fee therefrom.

(d) Except as law may otherwise expressly permit, a lawyer currently serving as a public officer or employee:

    (1) is subject to Rules 1.7 and 1.9; and

    (2) shall not:

        (i) participate in a matter in which the lawyer participated personally and substantially while in private practice or non-governmental employment, unless the appropriate government agency gives its informed consent, confirmed in writing; or

        (ii) negotiate for private employment with any person who is involved as a party or as lawyer for a party in a matter in which the lawyer is participating personally and substantially, except that a lawyer serving as a law clerk to a judge, other adjudicative officer or arbitrator may negotiate for private employment as permitted by Rule 1.12(b) and subject to the conditions stated in Rule 1.12(b).

(e) As used in this Rule, the term "matter" includes:

    (1) any judicial or other proceeding, application, request for a ruling or other determination, contract, claim, controversy, investigation, charge, accusation, arrest or other particular matter involving a specific party or parties, and

    (2) any other matter covered by the conflict of interest rules of the appropriate government agency.

Comment

[1] A lawyer who has served or is currently serving as a public officer or employee is personally subject to the Maryland Lawyers' Rules of Professional Conduct, including the prohibition against concurrent conflicts of interest stated in Rule 1.7. In addition, such a lawyer may be subject to statutes and government regulations regarding conflict of interest. Such statutes and regulations may circumscribe the extent to which the government agency may give consent under this Rule. See Rule 1.0(f) for the definition of informed consent.

[2] Paragraphs (a)(1), (a)(2) and (d)(1) restate the obligations of an individual lawyer who has served or is currently serving as an officer or employee of the government toward a former government or private client. Rule 1.10 is not applicable to the conflicts of interest addressed by this Rule. Rather, paragraph (b) sets forth a special imputation rule for former government

lawyers that provides for screening and notice. Because of the special problems raised by imputation within a government agency, paragraph (d) does not impute the conflicts of a lawyer currently serving as an officer or employee of the government to other associated government officers or employees, although ordinarily it will be prudent to screen such lawyers.

[3] Paragraphs (a)(2) and (d)(2) apply regardless of whether a lawyer is adverse to a former client and are thus designed not only to protect the former client, but also to prevent a lawyer from exploiting public office for the advantage of another client. For example, a lawyer who has pursued a claim on behalf of the government may not pursue the same claim on behalf of a later private client after the lawyer has left government service, except when authorized to do so by the government agency under paragraph (a). Similarly, a lawyer who has pursued a claim on behalf of a private client may not pursue the claim on behalf of the government, except when authorized to do so by paragraph (d). As with paragraphs (a)(1) and (d)(1), Rule 1.10 is not applicable to the conflicts of interest addressed by these paragraphs.

[4] This Rule represents a balancing of interests. On the one hand, where the successive clients are a government agency and another client, public or private, the risk exists that power or discretion vested in that agency might be used for the special benefit of the other client. A lawyer should not be in a position where benefit to the other client might affect performance of the lawyer's professional functions on behalf of the government. Also, unfair advantage could accrue to the other client by reason of access to confidential government information about the client's adversary obtainable only through the lawyer's government service. On the other hand, the rules governing lawyers presently or formerly employed by a government agency should not be so restrictive as to inhibit transfer of employment to and from the government. The government has a legitimate need to attract qualified lawyers as well as to maintain high ethical standards. Thus a former government lawyer is disqualified only from particular matters in which the lawyer participated personally and substantially. The provisions for screening and waiver in paragraph (b) are necessary to prevent the disqualification rule from imposing too severe a deterrent against entering public service. The limitation of disqualification in paragraphs (a)(2) and (d)(2) to matters involving a specific party or parties, rather than extending disqualification to all substantive issues on which the lawyer worked, serves a similar function.

[5] When a lawyer has been employed by one government agency and then moves to a second government agency, it may be appropriate to treat that second agency as another client for purposes of this Rule, as when a lawyer is employed by a city and subsequently is employed by a federal agency. However, because the conflict of interest is governed by paragraph (d), the latter agency is not required to screen the lawyer as paragraph (b) requires a law firm to do. The question of whether two government agencies should be regarded as the same or different clients for conflict of interest purposes is beyond the scope of these Rules. See Rule 1.13 Comment [8].

[6] Paragraphs (b) and (c) contemplate a screening arrangement. See Rule 1.0(m) (requirements for screening procedures). These paragraphs do not prohibit a lawyer from receiving a salary or partnership share established by prior independent agreement, but that lawyer may not receive compensation directly relating the lawyer's compensation to the fee in the matter in which the lawyer is disqualified.

[7] Notice, including a description of the screened lawyer's prior representation and of the screening procedures employed, generally should be given as soon as practicable after the need for screening becomes apparent.

[8] Paragraph (c) operates only when the lawyer in question has knowledge of the information, which means actual knowledge; it does not operate with respect to information that merely could be imputed to the lawyer.

[9] Paragraphs (a) and (d) do not prohibit a lawyer from jointly representing a private party and a government agency when doing so is permitted by Rule 1.7 and is not otherwise prohibited by law.

[10] For purposes of paragraph (e) of this Rule, a "matter" may continue in another form. In determining whether two particular matters are the same, the lawyer should consider the extent to which the matters involve the same basic facts, the same or related parties, and the time elapsed.

District of Columbia Rule 1.11

Successive Government and Private Employment

(a) A lawyer shall not accept other employment in connection with a matter which is the same as, or substantially related to, a matter in which the lawyer participated personally and substantially as a public officer or employee. Such participation includes acting on the merits of a matter in a judicial or other adjudicative capacity.

(b) If a lawyer is required to decline or to withdraw from employment under paragraph (a) on account of a personal and substantial participation in a matter, no partner or associate of that lawyer, or lawyer with an of counsel relationship to that lawyer, may knowingly accept or continue such employment except as provided in paragraphs (c) and (d) below. The disqualification of such other lawyers does not apply if the sole form of participation was as a judicial law clerk.

(c) The prohibition stated in paragraph (b) shall not apply if the personally disqualified lawyer is timely screened from any form of participation in the matter or representation as the case may be, and from sharing in any fees resulting therefrom, and if the requirements of paragraphs (d) and (e) are satisfied.

(d) Except as provided in paragraph (e), when any of counsel, lawyer, partner, or associate of a lawyer personally disqualified under paragraph (a) accepts employment in connection with a matter giving rise to the personal disqualification, the following notifications shall be required:

  (1) The personally disqualified lawyer shall submit to the public department or agency by which the lawyer was formerly employed and serve on each other party to any pertinent proceeding a signed document attesting that during the period of disqualification the personally disqualified lawyer will not participate in any manner in the matter or the representation, will not discuss the matter or the representation with any partner, associate, or of counsel lawyer, and will not share in any fees for the matter or the representation.

  (2) At least one affiliated lawyer shall submit to the same department or agency and serve on the same parties a signed document attesting that all affiliated lawyers are aware of the requirement that the personally disqualified lawyer be screened from participating in or discussing the matter or the representation and describing the procedures being taken to screen the personally disqualified lawyer.

(e) If a client requests in writing that the fact and subject matter of a representation subject to paragraph (d) not be disclosed by submitting the signed statements referred to in paragraph (d), such statements shall be prepared concurrently with undertaking the representation and filed with Bar Counsel under seal. If at any time thereafter the fact and subject matter of the representation are disclosed to the public or become a part of the public record, the signed statements previously prepared shall be promptly submitted as required by paragraph (d).

(f) Signed documents filed pursuant to paragraph (d) shall be available to the public, except to the extent that a lawyer submitting a signed document demonstrates to the satisfaction of the public department or agency upon which such documents are served that public disclosure is inconsistent with Rule 1.6 or other applicable law.

(g) This rule applies to any matter involving a specific party or parties.

(h) A lawyer who participates in a program of temporary service to the Office of the District of Columbia Attorney General of the kind described in Rule 1.10(e) shall be treated as having served as a public officer or employee for purposes of paragraph (a), and the provisions of paragraphs (b)–(e) shall apply to the lawyer and to lawyers affiliated with the lawyer.

Comment

[1] This rule deals with lawyers who leave public office and enter other employment. It applies to judges and their law clerks as well as to lawyers who act in other capacities. It is a counterpart of Rule 1.9, as applied to an individual former government lawyer, and of Rule 1.10, as applied to a law firm.

[2] A lawyer representing a government agency, whether employed or specially retained by the government, is subject to the Rules of Professional Conduct, including the prohibition against representing adverse interests stated in Rule 1.7 and the protections afforded former clients in Rule 1.9. In addition, such a lawyer is subject to this Rule 1.11 and to statutes and government regulations concerning conflict of interest. In the District of Columbia, where there are many lawyers for the federal and D.C. governments and their agencies, a number of whom are constantly leaving government and accepting other employment, particular heed must be paid to the federal conflict-of-interest statutes. *See, e.g.,* 18 U.S.C. Chapter 11 and regulations and opinions thereunder.

[3] Rule 1.11, in paragraph (a), flatly forbids a lawyer to accept other employment in a matter in which the lawyer participated personally and substantially as a public officer or employee; participation specifically includes acting on a matter in a judicial capacity. Other than as noted in Comment [10] to this rule, there is no provision for waiver of the individual lawyer's disqualification. "Matter" is defined in paragraph (g) so as to encompass only matters that are particular to a specific party or parties. The making of rules of general applicability and the establishment of general policy will ordinarily not be a "matter" within the meaning of Rule 1.11. When a lawyer is forbidden by paragraph (a) to accept private employment in a matter, the partners and associates of that lawyer are likewise forbidden, by paragraph (b), to accept the employment unless the screening and disclosure procedures described in paragraphs (c) through (f) are followed.

[4] The rule forbids lawyers to accept other employment in connection with matters that are the same as or "substantially related" to matters in which they participated personally and substantially while serving as public officers or employees. The leading case defining "substantially related" matters in the context of former government employment is *Brown v. District of Columbia Board of Zoning Adjustment*, 486 A.2d 37 (D.C. 1984) (en banc). There the D.C. Court of Appeals, *en banc*, held that in the "revolving door" context, a showing that a reasonable person could infer that, through participation in one matter as a public officer or employee, the former government lawyer "may have had access to information legally relevant to, or otherwise useful in" a subsequent representation, is *prima facie* evidence that the two matters are substantially related. If this *prima facie* showing is made, the former government lawyer must disprove any ethical impropriety by showing that the lawyer "could not have gained access to information during the first representation that might be useful in the later representation." *Id.* at 49–50. In *Brown*, the Court of Appeals announced the "substantially related" test after concluding that, under former DR 9-101(B), *see* "Revolving Door," 445 A.2d 615 (D.C. 1982) (*en banc*) (*per curiam*), the term "matter" was intended to embrace all matters "substantially related" to one another—a test that originated in "side-switching" litigation between private parties. *See* Rule 1.9, Comments [2] and [3]; *Brown*, 486 A.2d at 39–40 n. 1, 41–42 & n. 4. Accordingly, the words "or substantially related to" in paragraph (a) are an express statement of the judicial gloss in *Brown* interpreting "matter."

[5] Paragraph (a)'s absolute disqualification of a lawyer from matters in which the lawyer participated personally and substantially carries forward a policy of avoiding both actual impropriety and the appearance of impropriety that is expressed in the federal conflict-of-interest statutes and was expressed in the former Code of Professional Responsibility. Paragraph (c) requires the screening of a disqualified lawyer from such a matter as a condition to allowing any lawyers in the disqualified lawyer's firm to participate in it. This procedure is permitted in order to avoid imposing a serious deterrent to lawyers' entering public service. Governments have found that they benefit from having in their service both younger and more experienced lawyers who do not intend to devote their entire careers to public service. Some lawyers might not enter into short-term public service if they thought that, as a result of their active governmental practice, a firm would hesitate to hire them because of a concern that the entire firm would be disqualified from matters as a result.

[6] There is no imputed disqualification and consequently no screening requirement in the case of a judicial law clerk. But such clerks are subject to a personal obligation not to participate in matters falling within paragraph (a), since participation by a law clerk is within the term "judicial or other adjudicative capacity."

[7] Paragraph (d) imposes a further requirement that must be met before lawyers affiliated with a disqualified lawyer may participate in the representation. Except to the extent that the exception in paragraph (e) is satisfied, both the personally disqualified lawyer and at least one affiliated lawyer must submit to the agency signed documents basically stating that the personally disqualified lawyer will be screened from participation in the matter. The personally disqualified lawyer must also state that the lawyer will not share in any fees paid for the representation in question. And the affiliated lawyer must describe the procedures to be followed to ensure that the personally disqualified lawyer is effectively screened.

[8] Paragraph (e) makes it clear that the lawyer's duty, under Rule 1.6, to maintain client confidences and secrets may preclude the submission of any notice required by paragraph (d). If the client requests in writing that the fact and subject matter of the representation not be disclosed, the lawyer must comply with that request. If the client makes such a request, the lawyer must abide by the client's wishes until such time as the fact

and subject matter of the representation become public through some other means, such as a public filing. Filing a pleading or making an appearance in a proceeding before a tribunal constitutes a public filing. Once information concerning the representation is public, the notifications called for must be made promptly, and the lawyers involved may not honor a client request not to make the notifications. If a government agency has adopted rules governing practice before the agency by former government employees, members of the District of Columbia Bar are not exempted by Rule 1.11(e) from any additional or more restrictive notice requirements that the agency may impose. Thus the agency may require filing of notifications whether or not a client consents. While the lawyer cannot file a notification that the client has directed the lawyer not to file, the failure to file in accordance with agency rules may preclude the lawyer's representation of the client before the agency. Such issues are governed by the agency's rules, and Rule 1.11(e) is not intended to displace such agency requirements.

[9] Although paragraph (e) prohibits the lawyer from disclosing the fact and subject matter of the representation when the client has requested in writing that the information be kept confidential, the paragraph requires the lawyer to prepare the documents described in paragraph (d) as soon as the representation commences and to preserve the documents for possible submission to the agency and parties to any pertinent proceeding if and when the client does consent to their submission or the information becomes public.

[10] "Other employment," as used in paragraph (a) of this rule, includes the representation of a governmental body other than an agency of the government by which the lawyer was employed as a public officer or employee, but in the case of a move from one government agency to another the prohibition provided in paragraph (a) may be waived by the government agency with which the lawyer was previously employed. As used in paragraph (a), it would not be other employment for a lawyer who has left the employment of a particular government agency and taken employment with another government agency (e.g., the Department of Justice) or with a private law firm to continue or accept representation of the same government agency with which the lawyer was previously employed.

[11] Paragraph (c) does not prohibit a lawyer from receiving a salary or partnership share established by prior independent agreement. It prohibits

directly relating the attorney's compensation in any way to the fee in the matter in which the lawyer is disqualified. *See* D.C. Bar Legal Ethics Committee Opinion 279.

[12] Rule 1.10(e) provides an exception to the general imputation imposed by Rule 1.10(a) for lawyers assisting the Office of the District of Columbia Attorney General on a temporary basis. Rule 1.10(e) provides that lawyers providing such temporary assistance are not considered to be affiliated with their law firm during such periods of temporary assistance. However, lawyers participating in such temporary assistance programs have a potential for conflicts of interest or the abuse of information obtained while participating in such programs. It is appropriate to subject lawyers participating in temporary assistance programs to the same rules which paragraphs (a)–(g) impose on former government employees. Paragraph (h) effects this result.

[13] In addition to ethical concerns, provisions of conflict of interest statutes or regulations may impose limitations on the conduct of lawyers while they are providing assistance to the Office of the District of Columbia Attorney or after they return from such assignments. *See, e.g.,* 18 U.S.C. §§ 207, 208. Compliance with the Rules of Professional Conduct does not necessarily constitute compliance with all of the obligations imposed by conflict of interest statutes or regulations.

Selected Sections of the Restatement of the Law, Third, The Law Governing Lawyers*

§ 14. Formation of a Client-Lawyer Relationship

A relationship of client and lawyer arises when:
   (1) a person manifests to a lawyer the person's intent that the lawyer provide legal services for the person; and either
      (a) the lawyer manifests to the person consent to do so; or
      (b) the lawyer fails to manifest lack of consent to do so, and the lawyer knows or reasonably should know that the person reasonably relies on the lawyer to provide the services; or
   (2) a tribunal with power to do so appoints the lawyer to provide the services.

Comment:

a. Scope and cross-references. This Section sets forth a standard for determining when a client-lawyer relationship begins. Nonetheless, the various duties of lawyers and clients do not always arise simultaneously. Even if no relationship ensues, a lawyer may owe a prospective client certain duties (see § 15; § 60 & Comment *d* thereto). A lawyer representing a client may perform services also benefiting another person, for example arguing a motion for two litigants, without owing the nonclient litigant all the duties ordinarily owed to a client (see § 19(1)). Even if a relationship ensues, the client may not owe the lawyer a fee (see § 17 & Comment *b* thereto; § 38 & Comment *c* thereto; Restatement Second, Agency § 16). When a fee is due, the person owing it is not necessarily a client (see § 134). Moreover, a client-lawyer relationship may be more readily found in some situations (for example, when a person

---

has a reasonable belief that a lawyer was protecting that person's interests; see Comment *d* hereto) than in others (for example, when a person seeks to compel a lawyer to provide onerous services). In some situations—for example, when a lawyer agrees to represent a defendant without knowing that the lawyer's partner represents the plaintiff—a lawyer is forbidden to perform some duties for the client (continuing the representation) while nevertheless remaining subject to other duties (keeping the client's confidential information secret from others, including from the lawyer's own partner).

When a client-lawyer relationship arises, its scope is subject to the principles set forth in § 19(1), and its termination is governed by §§ 31 and 32. Agency and contract law are also applicable, except when inconsistent with special rules applicable to lawyers. The scope of responsibilities may change during the representation.

b. Rationale. The client-lawyer relationship ordinarily is a consensual one (see Restatement Second, Agency § 15). A client ordinarily should not be forced to put important legal matters into the hands of another or to accept unwanted legal services. The consent requirement, however, is not symmetrical. The client may at any time end the relationship by withdrawing consent (see §§ 31, 32, & 40), while the lawyer may properly withdraw only under specified conditions (see §§ 31 & 32). A lawyer may be held to responsibility of representation when the client reasonably relies on the existence of the relationship (see Comment *e*), and a court may direct the lawyer to represent the client by appointment (see Comment *g*). Lawyers generally are as free as other persons to decide with whom to deal, subject to generally applicable statutes such as those prohibiting certain kinds of discrimination. A lawyer, for example, may decline to undertake a representation that the lawyer finds inconvenient or repugnant. Agreement between client and lawyer likewise defines the scope of the representation, for example, determining whether it encompasses a single matter or is continuing (see § 19(1); § 31(2)(e) & Comment *h*). Even when a representation is continuing, the lawyer is ordinarily free to reject new matters.

c. The client's intent. A client's manifestation of intent that a lawyer provide legal services to the client may be explicit, as when the client requests the lawyer to write a will. The client's intent may be manifest from surrounding facts and circumstances, as when the client discusses the possibility of representation with the lawyer and then sends the lawyer relevant papers or a retainer requested by the lawyer. The client may hire the lawyer to work in its legal department. The client may demonstrate intent by ratifying the lawyer's acts, for example when a friend asks a lawyer to represent an imprisoned person who later manifests acceptance of the lawyer's services. The client's intent may be communicated by someone acting for the client, such as a relative or secretary. (The power of such a representative to act on behalf of the client is determined by the law of agency.) No written contract is required in order to establish the relationship, although a writing may be required by disciplinary or procedural standards (see § 38, Comment *b*). The client need not necessarily pay or agree to pay the lawyer; and paying a lawyer does not by itself create a client-lawyer relationship with the payor if the circumstances indicate that the lawyer was to represent someone else, for example, when an insurance company designates a lawyer to represent an insured (see § 134).

The client-lawyer relationship contemplates legal services from the lawyer, not, for example, real-estate-brokerage services or expert-witness services. A client-lawyer relationship results when legal services are provided even if the client also intends to receive other services. A client-lawyer relationship is not created, however, by the fact of receiving some benefit of the lawyer's service, for example when the lawyer represents a co-party. Finally, a lawyer may answer a general question about the law, for instance in a purely social setting, without a client-lawyer relationship arising.

A client-lawyer relationship can arise even if the client's consent to enter into the relationship is not fully informed. The lawyer should, however, consult with the client about such matters as the benefits and disadvantages of the proposed representation and conflicts of interest. On consultation in general, see § 20. A lawyer who fails to disclose such matters may be subject to fee forfeiture, professional discipline, malpractice liability, and other sanctions (see §§ 15, 20, 37, 48, 121, & 122).

d. Clients with diminished capacity. Individuals who are legally incompetent, for example some minors or persons with diminished mental capacity, often require representation to which they are personally incapable of giving consent (see Restatement Second, Agency § 20). A guardian for such an individual may retain counsel for the incapacitated person, subject in some instances to court approval. A court also may appoint counsel to represent an incompetent party without the party's consent. A person of diminished capacity nevertheless may be able to consent to representation, and to become liable to pay counsel, under the doctrine of "necessaries" (see § 31, Comment *e*; § 39; Restatement Second, Contracts § 12, Comment *f*). Representing a client of diminished capacity is considered in § 24 (see also § 31, Comment *e* (client's incompetence does not automatically end lawyer's authority)).

e. The lawyer's consent or failure to object. Like a client, a lawyer may manifest consent to creating a client-lawyer relationship in many ways. The lawyer may explicitly agree to represent the client or may indicate consent by action, for example by performing services requested by the client. An agent for the lawyer may communicate consent, for example, a secretary or paralegal with express, implied, or apparent authority to act for the lawyer in undertaking a representation.

A lawyer's consent may be conditioned on the successful completion of a conflict-of-interest check or on the negotiation of a fee arrangement. The lawyer's consent may sometimes precede the client's manifestation of intent, for example when an insurer designates a lawyer to represent an insured (see § 34, Comment *f*) who then accepts the representation. Although this Section treats separately the required communications of the client and the lawyer, the acts of each often illuminate those of the other.

Illustrations:

1. Client telephones Lawyer, who has previously represented Client, stating that Client wishes Lawyer to handle a pending antitrust investigation and asking Lawyer to come to Client's headquarters to explore the appropriate strategy for Client to follow. Lawyer comes to the headquarters and spends a day discussing strategy, without stating then or promptly thereafter that Lawyer has not yet decided whether to represent Client. Lawyer has communicated willingness to represent Client by so doing. Had Client simply asked Lawyer to discuss the possibility of representing Client, no client-lawyer relationship would result.

2. As part of a bar-association peer-support program, lawyer A consults lawyer B in confidence about an issue relating to lawyer A's representation of a client. This does not create a client-lawyer relationship between A's client and B. Whether a client-lawyer relationship exists between A and B depends on the foregoing and additional circumstances, including the nature of the program, the subject matter of the consultation, and the nature of prior dealings, if any, between them.

Even when a lawyer has not communicated willingness to represent a person, a client-lawyer relationship arises when the person reasonably relies on the lawyer to provide services, and the lawyer, who reasonably should know of this reliance, does not inform the person that the lawyer will not do so (see § 14(1)(b); see also § 51(2)). In many such instances, the lawyer's conduct constitutes implied assent. In others, the lawyer's duty arises from the principle of promissory estoppel, under which promises inducing reasonable reliance may be enforced to avoid injustice (see Restatement Second, Contracts § 90). In appraising whether the person's reliance was reasonable, courts consider that lawyers ordinarily have superior knowledge of what representation entails and that lawyers often encourage clients and potential clients to rely on them. The rules governing when a lawyer may withdraw from a representation (see § 32) apply to representations arising from implied assent or promissory estoppel.

Illustrations:

3. Claimant writes to Lawyer, describing a medical-malpractice suit that Claimant wishes to bring and asking Lawyer to represent Claimant. Lawyer does not answer the letter. A year later, the statute of limitations applicable to the suit expires. Claimant then sues Lawyer for legal malpractice for not having filed the suit on time. Under this Section no client-lawyer relationship was created (see § 50, Comment *c*). Lawyer did not communicate willingness to represent Claimant, and Claimant could not reasonably have relied on Lawyer to do so. On a lawyer's duty to a prospective client, see § 15.

4. Defendant telephones Lawyer's office and tells Lawyer's Secretary that Defendant would like Lawyer to represent Defendant in an automobile-violation proceeding set for hearing in 10 days, this being a type of proceeding that Defendant knows Lawyer regularly handles. Secretary tells Defendant to send in the papers concerning the proceeding, not telling Defendant that Lawyer would then decide whether to take the case, and Defendant delivers the papers the next day. Lawyer does not communicate with Defendant until the day before the hearing, when Lawyer tells Defendant that Lawyer does not wish to take the case. A trier of fact could find that a client-lawyer relationship came into existence when Lawyer failed to communicate that Lawyer was not representing Defendant. Defendant relied on Lawyer by not seeking other counsel when that was still practicable. Defendant's reliance was reasonable because Lawyer regularly handled Defendant's type of case, because Lawyer's agent had responded to Defendant's request for help by asking Defendant to transfer papers needed for the proceeding, and because the imminence of the hearing made it appropriate for Lawyer to inform Defendant and return the papers promptly if Lawyer decided not to take the case.

The principles of promissory estoppel do not bind prospective clients as readily as lawyers. Clients who are not sophisticated about how client-lawyer relationships arise should not be forced to accept unwanted representation or to pay lawyers for unwanted services. Nevertheless, promissory estoppel may bind a person who has not requested a lawyer's services. That may occur, for example, when a person has regularly retained a lawyer to prepare and file certain reports, knows that the lawyer is preparing and filing the next report, and accepts the benefit of the lawyer's services without warning the lawyer that they are unwanted. Also, a person's knowing acceptance of the benefits of a lawyer's representation, when the person could have chosen not to accept them, may constitute consent by ratification. If an employer, for example, notifies an employee that it has arranged for a lawyer to represent the employee in a prosecution arising out of the employment, and the employee confers with the lawyer and takes no action when the lawyer purports to speak for the employee in court, the employee has ratified the relationship. The client may end the relationship by discharging the lawyer (see §§ 32 & 40).

f. Organizational, fiduciary, and class-action clients. When the client is a corporation or other organization, the organization's structure and organic law determine whether a particular agent has authority to retain and direct the lawyer. Whether the lawyer is to represent the organization, a person or entity associated with it, or more than one such persons and entities is a question of fact to be determined based on reasonable expectations in the circumstances (see Subsection (1)). Where appropriate, due consideration should be given to the unreasonableness of a claimed expectation of entering into a co-client status when a significant and readily apparent conflict of interest exists between the organization or other client and the associated person or entity claimed to be a co-client (see § 131).

Under Subsection (1)(b), a lawyer's failure to clarify whom the lawyer represents in circumstances calling for such a result might lead a lawyer to have entered into client-lawyer representations not intended by the lawyer. Hence, the lawyer must clarify whom the lawyer intends to represent when the lawyer knows or reasonably should know that, contrary to the lawyer's own intention, a person, individually, or agents of an entity, on behalf of the entity, reasonably rely on the lawyer to provide legal services to that person or entity (see Subsection (1)(b); see also § 103, Comment *b* (extent of a lawyer's duty to warn an unrepresented person that the lawyer represents a client with conflicting interests)). Such clarification may be required, for example, with respect to an officer of an entity client such as a corporation, with respect to one or more partners in a client partnership or in the case of affiliated organizations such as a parent, subsidiary, or similar organization related to a client person or client entity. An implication that such a relationship exists is more likely to be found when the lawyer performs personal legal services for an individual as well or where the organization is small and characterized by extensive common ownership and management. But the lawyer does not enter into a client-lawyer relationship with a person associated with an organizational client solely because the person communicates with the lawyer on matters relevant to the organization that are also relevant to the personal situation of the person. In all events, the question is one of fact based on the reasonable and apparent expectations of the person or entity whose status as client is in question.

In trusts and estates practice a lawyer may have to clarify with those involved whether a trust, a trustee, its beneficiaries or groupings of some or all of them are clients and similarly whether the client is an executor, an estate, or its beneficiaries. In the absence of clarification the inference to be drawn may depend on the circumstances and on the law of the jurisdiction. Similar issues may arise when a lawyer represents other fiduciaries with respect to their fiduciary responsibilities, for example a pension-fund trustee or another lawyer.

Class actions may pose difficult questions of client identification. For many purposes, the named class representatives are the clients of the lawyer for the class. On conflict-of-interest issues, see § 125, Comment *f.* Yet class members who are not named representatives also have some characteristics of clients. For example, their confidential communications directly to the class lawyer may be privileged (compare § 70, Comment *c),* and opposing counsel may not be free to communicate with them directly (see § 99, Comment *l).*

Lawyers in class actions must sometimes deal with disagreements within the class and breaches by the named parties of their duty to represent class members. Although class representatives must be approved by the court, they are often initially self-selected, selected by their lawyer, or even (when a plaintiff sues a class of defendants) selected by their adversary. Members of the class often lack the incentive or knowledge to monitor the performance of the class representatives. Although members may sometimes opt out of the class, they may have no practical alternative other than remaining in the class if they wish to enforce their rights. Lawyers in class actions thus have duties to the class as well as to the class representatives.

A class-action lawyer may therefore be privileged or obliged to oppose the views of the class representatives after having consulted with them. The lawyer may also propose that opposing positions within the class be separately represented, that sub-classes be created, or that other measures be taken to ensure broader class participation. Withdrawal may be an option (see § 32), but one that is often undesirable because it may leave the class without effective representation. The lawyer should act for the benefit of the class as its members would reasonably define that benefit.

g. Nonconsensual relationship: appointed counsel. A lawyer may be required to represent a client when appointed by a court or other tribunal with power to do so. A lawyer may discuss the proposed representation with the prospective client and may give the court reasons why appointment is inappropriate or should be terminated.

The appointment may be rejected by the prospective client, except for persons, such as young children, lacking capacity to make that decision. In the case of some parties, for example corporations and other entities, the party may appear in court only through a lawyer. A court may require a criminal defendant to choose between an unwelcome lawyer and self-representation, and in criminal cases standby or advisory counsel may be appointed when the defendant elects self-representation. When a court appoints a lawyer to represent a person, that person's consent may ordinarily be assumed absent the person's rejection of the lawyer's services.

h. Client-lawyer relationships with law firms. Many lawyers practice as partners, members, or associates of law firms (see § 9(1)). When a client retains a lawyer with such an affiliation, the lawyer's firm assumes the authority and responsibility of representing that client, unless the circumstances indicate otherwise. For example, the lawyer ordinarily may share the client's work and confidences with other lawyers in the firm (see § 61, Comment *d*), and the firm is liable to the client for the lawyer's negligence (see § 58). Should the lawyer leave the firm, the client may choose to be represented by the departing lawyer, the lawyer's former firm, neither, or both (see §§ 31 & 32; see also § 9(3)). On the other hand, a client's retention of a lawyer or firm ordinarily does not permit the lawyer or firm, without further authorization from the client, to retain a lawyer outside the firm at the client's expense to represent the client (see Restatement Second, Agency § 18). On imputation of conflicts of interest within a law office, see § 123.

i. Others to whom lawyers owe duties. In some situations, lawyers owe duties to nonclients resembling those owed to clients. Thus, a lawyer owes certain duties to members of a class in a class action in which the lawyer appears as lawyer for the class (see Comment *f*) and to prospective clients who never become clients (see § 15). Duties may be owed to a liability-insurance company that designates a lawyer to represent the insured even if the insurer is not a client of the lawyer, to trust beneficiaries by a lawyer representing the trustee, and to certain nonclients in other situations (see § 134, Comment *f*; see also Comment *f* hereto). What duties are owed can be determined only by close analysis of the circumstances and the relevant law and policies. A lawyer may also become subject to duties to a nonclient by becoming, for example, a trustee, or corporate director. On conflicts between such duties and duties the lawyer owes clients, see § 135; see also § 96. On civil liability to nonclients, see §§ 51 and 56.

§ 73. The Privilege for an Organizational Client

When a client is a corporation, unincorporated association, partnership, trust, estate, sole proprietorship, or other for-profit or not-for-profit organization, the attorney-client privilege extends to a communication that:

(1) otherwise qualifies as privileged under §§ 68–72;

(2) is between an agent of the organization and a privileged person as defined in § 70;

(3) concerns a legal matter of interest to the organization; and

(4) is disclosed only to:

    (a) privileged persons as defined in § 70; and

    (b) other agents of the organization who reasonably need to know of the communication in order to act for the organization.

Comment:

a. Scope and cross-references. This Section states the conditions under which an organization can claim the attorney-client privilege. The requirements of §§ 68–72 must be satisfied, except that this Section recognizes a special class of agents who communicate in behalf of the organizational client (see Comment *d*). The Section also requires that the communication relate to a matter of interest to the organization as such (see Subsection (3) & Comment *f* hereto) and that it be disclosed within the organization only to persons having a reasonable need to know of it (see Subsection (4)(b) & Comment *g* hereto).

Conflicts of interest between an organizational client and its officers and other agents are considered in § 131, Comment *e*. On the application of the privilege to governmental organizations and officers, see § 74.

b. Rationale. The attorney-client privilege encourages organizational clients to have their agents confide in lawyers in order to realize the organization's legal rights and to achieve compliance with law (Comment *d* hereto). Extending the privilege to corporations and other organizations was formerly a matter of doubt but is no longer questioned. However, two pivotal questions must be resolved.

The first is defining the group of persons who can make privileged communications on behalf of an organization. Balance is required. The privilege should cover a sufficiently broad number of organizational communications to realize the organization's policy objectives, but not insulate ordinary intraorganizational communications that may later have importance as evidence. Concern has been expressed, for example, that the privilege would afford organizations "zones of silence" that would be free of evidentiary scrutiny. A subsidiary problem is whether persons who would be nonprivileged occurrence witnesses with respect to communications to a lawyer representing a natural person can be conduits of privileged communications when the client is an organization. That problem has been addressed in terms of the "subject-matter" and "control-group" tests for the privilege (see Comment *d*).

Second is the problem of defining the types of organizations treated as clients for purposes of the privilege. It is now accepted that the privilege applies to corporations, but some decisions have questioned whether the privilege should apply to unincorporated associations, partnerships, or sole proprietorships. Neither logic nor principle supports limiting the organizational privilege to the corporate form (see Comment *c* hereto).

c. Application of the privilege to an organization. As stated in the Section, the privilege applies to all forms of organizations. A corporation with hundreds of employees could as well be a sole proprietorship if its assets were owned by a single person rather than its shares being owned by the same person. It would be anomalous to accord the privilege to a business in corporate form but not if it were organized as a sole proprietorship. In general, an organization under this Section is a group having a recognizable identity as such and some permanency. Thus, an organization under this Section ordinarily would include a law firm, however it may be structured (as a professional corporation, a partnership, a sole proprietorship, or otherwise). The organization need not necessarily be treated as a legal entity for any other legal purpose. The privilege extends as well to charitable, social, fraternal, and other nonprofit organizations such as labor unions and chambers of commerce.

d. An agent of an organizational client. As stated in Subsection (2), the communication must involve an agent of the organization, on one hand,

and, on the other, a privileged person within the meaning of § 70, such as the lawyer for the organization. Persons described in Subsection (4)(b) may disclose the communication under a need-to-know limitation (see Comment *g* hereto). The existence of a relationship of principal and agent between the organizational client and the privileged agent is determined according to agency law (*see generally* Restatement Second, Agency §§ 1–139).

Some decisions apply a "control group" test for determining the scope of the privilege for an organization. That test limits the privilege to communications from persons in the organization who have authority to mold organizational policy or to take action in accordance with the lawyer's advice. The control-group circle excludes many persons within an organization who normally would cooperate with an organization's lawyer. Such a limitation overlooks that the division of functions within an organization often separates decisionmakers from those knowing relevant facts. Such a limitation is unnecessary to prevent abuse of the privilege (see Comment *g*) and significantly frustrates its purpose.

Other decisions apply a "subject matter" test. That test extends the privilege to communications with any lower-echelon employee or agent so long as the communication relates to the subject matter of the representation. In substance, those decisions comport with the need-to-know formulation in this Section (see Comment *g*).

It is not necessary that the agent receive specific direction from the organization to make or receive the communication (see Comment *h*).

Agents of the organization who may make privileged communications under this Section include the organization's officers and employees. For example, a communication by any employee of a corporation to the corporation's lawyer concerning the matter as to which the lawyer was retained to represent the corporation would be privileged, if other conditions of the privilege are satisfied. The concept of agent also includes independent contractors with whom the corporation has a principal-agent relationship and extends to agents of such persons when acting as subagents of the organizational client. For example, a foreign-based corporation may retain a general agency (perhaps a separate corporation) in an American city for the purpose of retaining counsel to represent the interests of the foreign-based corporation. Communications by the general agency would be by an agent for the purpose of this Section.

For purpose of the privilege, when a parent corporation owns controlling interest in a corporate subsidiary, the parent corporation's agents who are responsible for legal matters of the subsidiary are considered agents of the subsidiary. The subsidiary corporation's agents who are responsible for affairs of the parent are also considered agents of the parent for the purpose of the privilege. Directors of a corporation are not its agents for many legal purposes, because they are not subject to the control of the corporation (see Restatement Second, Agency § 14C). However, in communications with the organization's counsel, a director who communicates in the interests and for the benefit of the corporation is its agent for the purposes of this Section. Depending on the circumstances, a director acts in that capacity both when participating in a meeting of directors and when communicating individually with a lawyer for the corporation about the corporation's affairs. Communications to and from nonagent constituents of a corporation, such as shareholders and creditors, are not privileged.

In the case of a partnership, general partners and employees and other agents and subagents of the partnership may serve as agents of the organization for the purpose of making privileged communications (*see generally* Restatement Second, Agency § 14A). Limited partners who have no other relationship (such as employee) with the limited partnership are analogous to shareholders of a corporation and are not such agents.

In the case of an unincorporated association, agents whose communications may be privileged under this Section include officers and employees and other contractual agents and subagents. Members of an unincorporated association, for example members of a labor union, are not, solely by reason of their status as members, agents of the association for the purposes of this Section. In some situations, for example, involving a small unincorporated association with very active members, the members might be considered agents for the purpose of this Section on the ground that the association functionally is a partnership whose members are like partners.

In the case of an enterprise operated as a sole proprietorship, agents who may make communications privileged under this Section with respect to the proprietorship include employees or contractual agents and subagents of the proprietor.

Communications of a nonagent constituent of the organization may be independently privileged under § 75 where the person is a co-client along with the organization. If the agent of the organization has a conflict of interest with the organization, the lawyer for the organization must not purport to represent both the organization and the agent without consent (see § 131, Comment *c*). The lawyer may not mislead the agent about the nature of the lawyer's loyalty to the organization (see § 103). If a lawyer fails to clarify the lawyer's role as representative solely of the organization and the organization's agent reasonably believes that the lawyer represents the agent, the agent may assert the privilege personally with respect to the agent's own communications (compare § 72(2), Comment *f*; see also § 131, Comment *e*).

The lawyer must also observe limitations on the extent to which a lawyer may communicate with a person of conflicting interests who is not represented by counsel (see §103) and limitations on communications with persons who are so represented (see § 99 and following).

e. The temporal relationship of principal-agent. Under Subsection (2), a person making a privileged communication to a lawyer for an organization must then be acting as agent of the principal-organization. The objective of the organizational privilege is to encourage the organization to have its agents communicate with its lawyer (see Comment *d* hereto). Generally, that premise implies that persons be agents of the organization at the time of communicating. The privilege may also extend, however, to communications with a person with whom the organization has terminated, for most other purposes, an agency relationship. A former agent is a privileged person under Subsection (2) if, at the time of communicating, the former agent has a continuing legal obligation to the principal-organization to furnish the information to the organization's lawyer. The scope of such a continuing obligation is determined by the law of agency and the terms of the employment contract (see Restatement Second, Agency § 275, Comment *e*, & § 381, Comment *f*). The privilege covers communications with a lawyer for an organization by a retired officer of the organization concerning a matter within the officer's prior responsibilities that is of legal importance to the organization.

Subsection (2) does not include a person with whom the organization established a principal-agent relationship predominantly for the purpose of providing the protection of the privilege to the person's communications, if the person was not an agent at the time of learning the information. For example, communications between the lawyer for an organization and an eyewitness to an event whose communications would not otherwise be privileged cannot be made privileged simply through the organization hiring the person to consult with the organization's lawyer. (As to experts and similar persons employed by a lawyer, see § 70, Comment *g*).

Ordinarily, an agent communicating with an organization's lawyer within this Section will have acquired the information in the course of the agent's work for the organization. However, it is not necessary that the communicated information be so acquired. Thus, a person may communicate under this Section with respect to information learned prior to the relationship or learned outside the person's functions as an agent, so long as the person bears an agency relationship to the principal-organization at the time of the communication and the communication concerns a matter of interest to the organization (see Comment *f*). For example, a chemist for an organization who communicates to the organization's lawyer information about a process that the chemist learned prior to being employed by the organization makes a privileged communication if the other conditions of this Section are satisfied.

f. Limitation to communications relating to the interests of the organization. Subsection (3) requires that the communication relate to a legal matter of interest to the organization. The lawyer must be representing the organization as opposed to the agent who communicates with the lawyer, such as its individual officer or employee. A lawyer representing such an officer or employee, of course, can have privileged communications with that client. But the privilege will not be that of the organization. When a lawyer represents as co-clients both the organization and one of its officers or employees, the privileged nature of communications is determined under § 75. On the conflicts of interest involved in such representations, see § 131, Comment *e*.

g. The need-to-know limitation on disclosing privileged communications. Communications are privileged only if made for the purpose of obtaining legal services (see § 72), and they remain privileged only if neither the client nor an agent of the client subsequently discloses the communication to a nonprivileged person (see § 79; see also § 71, Comment *d*). Those limitations apply to organizational clients as provided in Subsection (4). Communications become, and remain, so protected by the privilege only if the organization does not permit their dissemination to persons other than to privileged persons. Agents of a client to whom confidential communications may be disclosed are generally defined in § 70, Comment *f*, and agents of a lawyer are defined in § 70, Comment *g*. Included among an organizational client's agents for communication are, for example, a secretary who prepares a letter to the organization's lawyer on behalf of a communicating employee.

The need-to-know limitation of Subsection (4)(b) permits disclosing privileged communications to other agents of the organization who reasonably need to know of the privileged communication in order to act for the organization in the matter. Those agents include persons who are responsible for accepting or rejecting a lawyer's advice on behalf of the organization or for acting on legal assistance, such as general legal advice, provided by the lawyer. Access of such persons to privileged communications is not limited to direct exchange with the lawyer. A lawyer may be required to take steps assuring that attorney-client communications will be disseminated only among privileged persons who have a need to know. Persons defined in Subsection (4)(b) may be apprised of privileged communications after they have been made, as by examining records of privileged communications previously made, in order to conduct the affairs of the organization in light of the legal services provided.

Illustration:

1. Lawyer for Organization makes a confidential report to President of Organization, describing Organization's contractual relationship with Supplier, and advising that Organization's contract with Supplier could be terminated without liability. President sends a confidential memorandum to Manager, Organization's purchasing manager, asking whether termination of the contract would nonetheless be inappropriate for business reasons. Because Manager's response would reasonably depend on several aspects of Lawyer's advice, Manager would have need to know the justifying reason for Lawyer's advice that the contract could be terminated. Lawyer's report to President remains privileged notwithstanding that President shared it with Manager.

The need-to-know concept properly extends to all agents of the organization who would be personally held financially or criminally liable for conduct in the matter in question or who would personally benefit from it, such as general partners of a partnership with respect to a claim for or against the partnership. It extends to persons, such as members of a board of directors and senior officers of an organization, whose general management and supervisory responsibilities include wide areas of organizational activities and to lower-echelon agents of the organization whose area of activity is relevant to the legal advice or service rendered.

Dissemination of a communication to persons outside those described in Subsection (4)(b) implies that the protection of confidentiality was not significant (see § 71, Comment *b*). An organization may not immunize documents and other communications generated or circulated for a business or other nonlegal purpose (see § 72).

h. Directed and volunteered agent communications. It is not necessary that a superior organizational authority specifically direct an agent to communicate with the organization's lawyer. Unless instructed to the contrary, an agent has authority to volunteer information to a lawyer when reasonably related to the interests of the organization. An agent has similar authority to respond to a request for information from a lawyer for the organization. And the lawyer for the organization ordinarily may seek relevant information directly from employees and other agents without prior direction from superior authorities in the organization.

i. Inside legal counsel and outside legal counsel. The privilege under this Section applies without distinction to lawyers who are inside legal counsel or outside legal counsel for an organization (see § 72, Comment *c*). Communications predominantly for a purpose other than obtaining or providing legal services for the organization are not within the privilege (see § 72, Comment *c*). On the credentials of a lawyer for the purposes of the privilege, see § 72(1), Comment *e*.

j. Invoking and waiving the privilege of an organizational client. The privilege for organizational clients can be asserted and waived only by a responsible person acting for the organization for this purpose. On waiver, see §§ 78–80. Communications involving an organization's director, officer, or employee may qualify as privileged, but it is a separate question whether such a person has authority to invoke or waive the privilege on behalf of the organization. If the lawyer was representing both the organization and the individual as co-clients, the question of invoking and waiving the privilege is determined under the rule for co-clients (see § 75, Comment *e*). Whether a lawyer has formed a client-lawyer relationship with a person affiliated with the organization, as well as with the organization, is determined under § 14. Communications of such a person who approaches a lawyer for the organization as a prospective client are privileged as provided in § 72. Unless the person's contrary intent is reasonably manifest to a lawyer for the organization, the lawyer acts properly in assuming that a communication from any such person is on behalf and in the interest of the organization and, as such, is privileged in the interest of the organization and not of the individual making the communication. When the person manifests an intention to make a communication privileged against the organization, the lawyer must resist entering into such a client-lawyer relationship and receiving such a communication if doing so would constitute an impermissible conflict of interest (see § 131, Comment *e*).

An agent or former agent may have need for a communication as to which the organization has authority to waive the privilege, for example, when the agent is sued personally. A tribunal may exercise discretion to order production of such a communication for benefit of the agent if the agent establishes three conditions. First, the agent must show that the agent properly came to know the contents of the communication. Second, the agent must show substantial need of the communication. Third, the agent must show that production would create no material risk of prejudice or embarrassment to the organization beyond such evidentiary use as the agent may make of the communication. Such a risk may be controlled by protective orders, redaction, or other measures.

Illustration:

2. Lawyer, representing only Corporation, interviews Employee by electronic mail in connection with reported unlawful activities in Corporation's purchasing department in circumstances providing Corporation with a privilege with respect to their communications. Corporation later dismisses Employee, who sues Corporation, alleging wrongful discharge. Employee files a discovery request seeking all copies of communications between Employee and Lawyer. The tribunal has discretion to order discovery under the conditions stated in the preceding paragraph. In view of the apparent relationship of Employee's statements to possible illegal activities, it is doubtful that Employee could persuade the tribunal that access by Employee would create no material risk that third persons, such as a government agency, would thereby learn of the communication and thus gain a litigation or other advantage with respect to Corporation.

k. Succession in legal control of an organization. When ownership of a corporation or other organization as an entity passes to successors, the transaction carries with it authority concerning asserting or waiving the privilege. After legal control passes in such a transaction, communications from directors, officers, or employees of the acquired organization to lawyers who represent only the predecessor organization, if it maintains a separate existence from the acquiring organization, may no longer be covered by the privilege. When a corporation or other organization has ceased to have a legal existence such that no person can act in its behalf, ordinarily the attorney-client privilege terminates (*see generally* § 77, Comment *c*).

Illustration:

3. X, an officer of Ajax Corporation, communicates in confidence with Lawyer, who represents Ajax, concerning dealings between Ajax and one of its creditors, Vendor Corporation. Ajax later is declared bankrupt and a bankruptcy court appoints Trustee as the trustee in bankruptcy for Ajax.

Thereafter, Lawyer is called to the witness stand in litigation between Vendor Corporation and Trustee. Trustee has authority to determine whether the attorney-client privilege should be asserted or waived on behalf of the bankrupt Ajax Corporation with respect to testimony by Lawyer about statements by X. X cannot assert a privilege because X was not a client of Lawyer in the representation. Former officers and directors of Ajax cannot assert the privilege because control of the corporation has passed to Trustee.

A lawyer for an organization is ordinarily authorized to waive the privilege in advancing the interests of the client (see § 61 & § 79, Comment *c*). Otherwise, when called to testify, a lawyer is required to invoke the privilege on behalf of the client (see § 86(1)(b)). On waiver, see §§ 78–80.

§ 85. Communications Involving a Fiduciary Within an Organization

In a proceeding involving a dispute between an organizational client and shareholders, members, or other constituents of the organization toward whom the directors, officers, or similar persons managing the organization bear fiduciary responsibilities, the attorney-client privilege of the organization may be withheld from a communication otherwise within § 68 if the tribunal finds that:

(a) those managing the organization are charged with breach of their obligations toward the shareholders, members, or other constituents or toward the organization itself;

(b) the communication occurred prior to the assertion of the charges and relates directly to those charges; and

(c) the need of the requesting party to discover or introduce the communication is sufficiently compelling and the threat to confidentiality sufficiently confined to justify setting the privilege aside.

Comment:

a. Scope and cross-references. The exception recognized in this Section applies primarily in suits by shareholders and similar beneficial owners of private organizations. No jurisdiction has yet recognized this exception in citizen suits against a governmental agency (*cf.* § 74). Because the rule is discretionary with a tribunal, there is no corresponding permission for a lawyer voluntarily to reveal confidential client information.

b. Rationale. Proceeding by analogy from the trustee exception of § 84, the leading decision of Garner v. Wolfinbarger, 430 F.2d 1093 (5th Cir.1970), cert. denied, 401 U.S. 974, 91 S. Ct. 1191, 28 L.Ed.2d 323 (1971), held that a court could, in appropriate circumstances, refuse to enforce a corporation's otherwise valid attorney-client privilege when shareholders attempt to discover a communication between the corporation's officers and its lawyers. The court also relied on the co-client doctrine (compare § 75), the crime-fraud exception (compare § 82), and the statutory and common-law right of shareholders to inspect books and records of their corporation. That exception is stated in this Section.

Two policy considerations support the *Garner* decision. First, directors and managers of an organization acting in that capacity in principle should not keep corporate information secret from their own principal constituents, the members and shareholders of the organization. Their function is to advance the interests of shareholder-investors and members. Second, in litigation against their constituents, the question of waiver may not be decided objectively. Even if the directors and managers personally named in the suit do not make the determination concerning waiver, there usually exists a close personal and business relationship between the directors and managers who are sued and those empowered to determine waiver. This Section in effect provides a disinterested determination by the tribunal based on all relevant considerations, including protecting the organization's legitimate need for privacy and for effective client-lawyer communications (see Comment *c* hereto). Although the *Garner* principle inevitably introduces a measure of uncertainty into the privilege for organization clients, it probably does little to deter communications in good faith between managers who need legal advice and the organization's lawyer.

c. Application of the organizational-fiduciary exception. A court applying this Section weighs the benefits of disclosure against the benefits of continuing confidentiality. The determination should be guided by the following considerations: (1) the extent to which beneficiaries seeking the information have interests that conflict with those of opposing or silent beneficiaries; (2) the substantiality of the beneficiaries' claim and whether the proceeding was brought for ulterior purpose; (3) the relevance of the communication to the beneficiaries' claim and the extent to which information it contains is available from nonprivileged sources; (4) whether the beneficiaries' claim asserts criminal, fraudulent, or similarly illegal acts; (5) whether the communication relates to future conduct of the organization that could be prejudiced;

(6) whether the communication concerns the very litigation brought by the beneficiaries; (7) the specificity of the beneficiaries' request; (8) whether the communication involves trade secrets or other information that has value beyond its character as a client-lawyer communication; (9) the extent to which the court can employ protective orders to guard against abuse if the communication is revealed; and (10) whether the determination not to waive the privilege made in behalf of the organization was by a disinterested group of directors or officers.

The exception in this Section extends to legal assistance in nonlitigation as well as litigation assistance. With respect to the limited applicability of the attorney-client privilege and work-product immunity to litigation reports and underlying communications in derivative actions, see Principles of Corporate Governance: Analysis and Recommendations § 7.13(e).

§ 96. Representing an Organization as Client

(1) **When a lawyer is employed or retained to represent an orga nization:**

   (a) **the lawyer represents the interests of the organization as defined by its responsible agents acting pursuant to the organization's decision-making procedures; and**

   (b) **subject to Subsection (2), the lawyer must follow instructions in the representation, as stated in § 21(2), given by persons authorized so to act on behalf of the organization.**

(2) **If a lawyer representing an organization knows of circumstances indicating that a constituent of the organization has engaged in action or intends to act in a way that violates a legal obligation to the organization that will likely cause substantial injury to it, or that reasonably can be foreseen to be imputable to the organization and likely to result in substantial injury to it, the lawyer must proceed in what the lawyer reasonably believes to be the best interests of the organization.**

(3) **In the circumstances described in Subsection (2), the lawyer may, in circumstances warranting such steps, ask the constituent to reconsider the matter, recommend that a second legal opinion be sought, and seek review by appropriate supervisory authority within the organization, including referring the matter to the highest authority that can act in behalf of the organization.**

Comment:

a. Scope and cross-references. This Section concerns the duties of a lawyer who represents an organization as client and in doing so deals with constituents of the organization. On the definition of organization, see Comment *c*; on the definition of constituent, see Comment *b*. To the extent not inconsistent with § 97, this Section applies to counseling governmental clients.

On forming a client-lawyer relationship with an organizational client, see § 14, Comment *f*. On conflicts of interest involved generally in representing an organization, see § 131; on conflicts involved in representing an organization concurrently with one or more constituents, see § 131, Comments *e* and *f*; on conflicting interests of affiliated organizations, see § 131, Comment *d*. On conflicts of interest that may be involved in providing legal services to an organization while also serving as an officer or director of the organization, see § 135, Comment *d*.

On limitations on advising and assisting a client, see § 94. The attorney-client privilege as applied to corporate and similar clients is considered in § 73.

On disclosing confidential client information with respect to certain unlawful acts of a client, see §§ 66–67. Disclosure under §§ 66–67 differs from action permissible for a lawyer to take under this Section in several respects. First, the purpose of allowing disclosure under §§ 66–67 is to protect third persons or the lawyer, while the purpose of action within the organization under Subsection (2) (see Comments *e* & *f* hereof) is to protect the interests of the organizational client. Second, the crime or fraud warranting disclosure to prevent financial loss under § 67 is that of the client. In situations arising under Subsection (2), a nonclient constituent commits the wrongful act and the client organization is either the victim of the act or is vicariously responsible as a result of the wrongful act of the constituent. Third, permissible disclosure under §§ 66–67 is limited to a future or continuing act of the client (except for disclosure under § 67(2)), and under § 67 is limited to client acts in which the lawyer's legal services were employed by the client. Under Subsection (2), a lawyer may be required to protect the organizational client from past as well as ongoing and future wrongful acts of a constituent (see Comment *e*) and from acts in which the lawyer's services were not employed.

b. Rationale: an organization as client. A lawyer who has been employed or retained to represent an organization as a client owes professional duties of loyalty and competence to the organization. By representing the organization, a lawyer does not thereby also form a client-lawyer relationship with all or any individuals employed by it or who direct its operations or who have an ownership or other beneficial interest in it, such as its shareholders. However additional circumstances may result in a client-lawyer relationship with constituents while the lawyer concurrently represents the organization (see Comment *h* hereto).

A lawyer representing only an organization does not owe duties of care (see § 52), diligence (see § 16), or confidentiality (see § 60) to constituents of the organization. Compare § 132, Comment *g(ii)* (duties of confidentiality to persons about whom lawyer learned confidential information in prior representation of client). Correspondingly, although a lawyer for the organization acts at the direction of its officers, the lawyer for an organization does not possess, solely in that capacity, power to act for officers as their lawyer. Thus, third persons may not reasonably conclude, solely from that capacity, that a lawyer for the organization represents officers individually (compare §§ 26 & 27). Similarly, a lawyer representing only a constituent does not, by virtue of that representation, owe either to the organization employing the constituent or to other constituents obligations that would arise only from a client-lawyer relationship with the organization.

The so-called "entity" theory of organizational representation, stated in Subsection (1), is now universally recognized in American law, for purposes of determining the identity of the direct beneficiary of legal representation of corporations and other forms of organizations. On the definition of organizations within the meaning of this Section, see Comment *c*. Pursuant to the entity theory, the rights and responsibilities of the client-lawyer relationship described in Chapter 2 obtain between the organization and the lawyer.

A lawyer representing an organization deals with individuals such as its officers, directors, and employees, who serve as constituents of the organization. Such individuals acting under the organization's authority retain and direct the lawyer to act on behalf of the organization (see Comment *d* hereto). Nonetheless, personal dealings with such persons do not lessen the lawyer's responsibilities to the organization as client, and the lawyer may not let such dealings hinder the lawyer in the performance of those responsibilities.

A "constituent" of an organization within the meaning of the Section has the same meaning as in Rule 1.13 of the ABA Model Rules of Professional Conduct (1983). A constituent includes an officer, director, or employee of the organization. A shareholder of a stock corporation or a member of a membership corporation is also a constituent within the meaning of this Section, as under Rule 1.13.

A lawyer may represent an organization either as an employee of the organization (inside legal counsel) or as a lawyer in private practice retained by the organization (outside legal counsel). In general, a lawyer's responsibilities to a client organization are the same in both capacities. Special rules for inside legal counsel are stated in § 32, Comment *b*; § 37, Comment *e*; § 58, Comment *c*; and § 123, Comment *d(i)*. However, the nature of the lawyer's work and greater or less access to an organization's channels of information can affect the lawyer's knowledge and thus, for example, the reasonableness of the lawyer's reliance on a constituent of the organization for information and direction.

c. Forms of client organizations. In general, this Section applies to representation of formally constituted organizations. In all events, whether a client-lawyer relationship is formed is to be determined in light of the considerations stated in § 14. Such organizations include for-profit and nonprofit corporations, limited-liability companies, unincorporated associations (such as trade associations and labor unions), general and limited partnerships, professional corporations, business trusts, joint ventures, and similar organizations. An organization client may also be an informal entity such as a social club or an informal group that has established an investment pool. For the purposes of this Section, whether the organization is a formal legal entity is relevant but not determinative. For example, while a sole proprietorship is not treated as an entity for many legal purposes, such an organization may be of sufficient size and complexity to warrant treatment as an organizational client under this Section.

d. The direction of a lawyer's work for a client organization. Persons authorized to act for the organization make decisions about retaining or discharging a lawyer for the organization, determine the scope of the representation, and create an obligation for the organization to compensate the lawyer. As stated in Subsection (1)(b), such persons also direct the activities of the lawyer during the course of the representation (*see generally* §§ 14, 21, & 38). Unless the lawyer withdraws, the lawyer must follow instructions and implement decisions of those persons, as the lawyer would follow instructions and decisions of an individual client. On advising a client respecting nonlegal considerations, see § 94(3) and Comment *h* thereto. A constituent of the organization authorized to do so may discharge the lawyer. On client discharge generally, see § 32; on withdrawal generally, see § 32(2) and (3). As stated in § 23(1), a lawyer is not bound by a constituent's instruction to a lawyer to perform, counsel, or assist future or ongoing acts that the lawyer reasonably believes to be unlawful. Such an instruction also does not remove the lawyer's duty to protect the best interests of the organizational client as stated in Subsection (2) (see Comments e & f hereto).

Who within an organization or among related organizations is authorized to direct the activities of a lawyer representing an organization is a question of organizational law beyond the scope of this Restatement. Such law determines whether, for example, an officer of a parent corporation is authorized to direct the activities of a lawyer representing a subsidiary corporation.

e. A constituent's breach of a legal obligation to the client organization. A lawyer representing an organization is required to act with reasonable competence and diligence in the representation (see § 16(2)) and to use care in representing the organizational client (see § 50). The lawyer thus must not knowingly or negligently assist any constituent to breach a legal duty to the organization. However, a lawyer's duty of care to the organization is not limited to avoidance of assisting acts that threaten injury to a client. A lawyer is also required to act diligently and to exercise care by taking steps to prevent reasonably foreseeable harm to a client. Thus, Subsection (2) requires a lawyer to take action to protect the interests of the client organization with respect to certain breaches of legal duty to the organization by a constituent.

The lawyer is not prevented by rules of confidentiality from acting to protect the interests of the organization by disclosing within the organization communications gained from constituents who are not themselves clients. That follows even if disclosure is against the interests of the communicating person, of another constituent whose breach of duty is in issue, or of other constituents (see § 131, Comment e). Such disclosure within the organization is subject to direction of a constituent who is authorized to act for the organization in the matter and who is not complicit in the breach (see Comment d). The lawyer may withdraw any support that the lawyer may earlier have provided the intended act, such as by withdrawing an opinion letter or draft transaction documents prepared by the lawyer.

Illustration:

1. Lawyer represents Charity, a not-for-profit corporation. Charity promotes medical research through tax-deductible contributions made to it. President as chief executive officer of Charity retained Lawyer to represent Charity as outside general counsel and has extensively communicated in confidence with Lawyer on a variety of matters concerning Charity.

President asks Lawyer to draft documents by which Charity would make a gift of a new luxury automobile to a social friend of President. In that and all other work, Lawyer represents only Charity and not President as a client. Lawyer concludes that such a gift would cause financial harm to Charity in violation of President's legal duties to it. Lawyer may not draft the documents. If unable to dissuade President from effecting the gift, Lawyer must take action to protect the interests of Charity (see Subsection (2) & Comment *f*). Lawyer may, for example, communicate with members of Charity's board of directors in endeavoring to prevent the gift from being effectuated.

f. Proceeding in the best interests of the client organization. Within the meaning of Subsection (2), a wrongful act of a constituent threatening substantial injury to a client organization may be of two types. One is an act or failure to act that violates a legal obligation to the organization and that would directly harm the organization, such as by unlawfully converting its assets. The other is an act or failure to act by the constituent that, although perhaps intended to serve an interest of the organization, will foreseeably cause injury to the client, such as by exposing the organization to criminal or civil liability.

In either circumstance, as stated in Subsection (2), if the threatened injury is substantial the lawyer must proceed in what the lawyer reasonably believes to be the best interests of the organization. Those interests are normally defined by appropriate managers of the organization in the exercise of the business and managerial judgment that would be exercised by a person of ordinary prudence in a similar position. The lawyer's duty of care is that of an ordinarily prudent lawyer in such a position (see ALI Principles of Corporate Governance: Analysis and Recommendations § 4.01, at 148–149 (1994)). In the face of threats of substantial injury to the organization of the kind described in Subsection (2), the lawyer must assess the following: the degree and imminence of threatened financial, reputational, and other harms to the organization; the probable results of litigation that might ensue against the organization or for which it would be financially responsible; the costs of taking measures within the organization to prevent or correct the harm; the likely efficaciousness of measures that might be taken; and similar considerations.

The measures that a lawyer may take are those described in Subsection (3), among others. Whether a lawyer has proceeded in the best interests of the organization is determined objectively, on the basis of the circumstances reasonably apparent to the lawyer at the time. Not all lawyers would attempt to resolve a problem defined in Subsection (2) in the same manner. Not all threats to an organization are of the same degree of imminence or substantiality. In some instances the constituent may be acting solely for reasons of self-interest. In others, the constituent may act on the basis of a business judgment whose utility or prudence may be doubtful but that is within the authority of the constituent. The lawyer's assessment of those factors may depend on the constituent's credibility and intentions, based on prior dealings between them and other information available to the lawyer.

The appropriate measures to take are ordinarily a matter for the reasonable judgment of the lawyer, with due regard for the circumstances in which the lawyer must function. Those circumstances include such matters as time and budgetary limitations and limitations of access to additional information and to persons who may otherwise be able to act. If one measure fails, the lawyer must, if the nature of the threat warrants and circumstances permit, take other reasonably available measures. With respect to the lawyer's possible liability to the organizational client, failure to take a particular remedial step is tested under the general standard of § 50. When the lawyer reasonably concludes that any particular step would not likely advance the best interests of the client, the step need not be taken.

Several options are described in Subsection (3). The lawyer may be able to prevent the wrongful act or its harmful consequences by urging reconsideration by the constituent who intends to commit the act. The lawyer may also suggest that the organization obtain a second legal or other expert opinion concerning the questioned activity. It may be appropriate to refer the matter to someone within the organization having authority to prevent the prospective harm, such as an official in the organization senior in authority to the constituent threatening to act. In appropriate circumstances, the lawyer may request intervention by the highest executive authority in the organization or by its governing body, such as a board of directors or the independent directors on the board, or by an owner of a majority of the stock in the organization. In determining how to proceed, the lawyer may be guided by the organization's internal policies and lines of authority or channels of communication.

In a situation arising under Subsection (2), a lawyer does not fulfill the lawyer's duties to the organizational client by withdrawing from the representation without attempting to prevent the constituent's wrongful act.

However, the lawyer's threat to withdraw unless corrective action is taken may constitute an effective step in such an attempt.

If a lawyer has attempted appropriately but unsuccessfully to protect the best interests of the organizational client, the lawyer may withdraw if permissible under § 32. Particularly when the lawyer has unsuccessfully sought to enlist assistance from the highest authority within the organization, the lawyer will be warranted in withdrawing either because the client persists in a course of action involving the lawyer's services that the lawyer reasonably believes is criminal or fraudulent (see § 32(3)(d)) or because the client insists on taking action that the lawyer considers repugnant or imprudent (see § 32(3)(f)). On proportionality between certain grounds for withdrawal and possible harm to the organizational client that would be caused by withdrawal, see § 32, Comment *h(i)*. On the circumstances in which a lawyer is required to withdraw, see § 32(2). Following withdrawal, if the lawyer had fulfilled applicable duties prior to withdrawal, the lawyer has no further duty to initiate action to protect the interests of the client organization with respect to the matter. The lawyer continues to be subject to the duties owed to any former client, such as the duty not to become involved in subsequent adverse representations (see § 132) or otherwise to use or disclose the former client's confidential information adversely to the former client (see § 60).

Whether the lawyer may disclose a constituent's breach of legal duty to persons outside the organization is determined primarily under §§ 66–67 (see also §§ 61–64). In limited circumstances, it may clearly appear that limited disclosure to prevent or limit harm would be in the interests of the organizational client and that constituents who purport to forbid disclosure are not authorized to act for the organization. Whether disclosure in such circumstances is warranted is a difficult and rarely encountered issue, on which this Restatement does not take a position.

g. A constituent's breach of fiduciary duty to another constituent. One constituent of an organization may owe fiduciary duties to another such constituent, for example in some instances a majority stockholder to a minority holder. A lawyer representing only the organization has no duty to protect one constituent from another, including from a breach by one constituent of such fiduciary duties, unless the interests of the lawyer's client organization are at risk. On communicating with a nonclient constituent, see § 103, Comment *e*. However, if the lawyer represents as a client either the entity or the constituent owing fiduciary duties, the lawyer may not counsel or assist a breach of any fiduciary obligation owed by the constituent to the organization.

Illustrations:

2. Lawyer represents Client, a closely held corporation, and not any constituent of Client. Under law applicable to the corporation, a majority shareholder owes a fiduciary duty of fair dealing to a minority shareholder in a transaction caused by action of a board of directors whose members have been designated by the majority stockholder. The law provides that the duty is breached if the action detrimentally and substantially affects the value of the minority shareholder's stock. Majority Shareholder has asked the board of directors of Client, consisting of Majority Shareholder's designees, to adopt a plan for buying back stock of the majority's shareholders in Client. A minority shareholder has protested the plan as unfair to the minority shareholder. Lawyer may advise the board about the position taken by the minority shareholder, but is not obliged to advise against or otherwise seek to prevent action that is consistent with the board's duty to Client.

3. The same facts as in Illustration 2, except that Lawyer has reason to know that the plan violates applicable corporate law and will likely be successfully challenged by minority shareholders in a suit against Client and that Client will likely incur substantial expense as a result. Lawyer owes a duty to Client to take action to protect Client, such as by advising Client's board about the risks of adopting the plan.

On conflicts of interest in cases of intra-organization disagreement, see § 131, Comment *h*.

The foregoing discussion assumes an entity of substantial size and significant degree of organization. On the other hand, in the case of a closely held organization, some decisions have held that a lawyer may owe duties to a nonclient constituent, such as one who owns a minority interest.

h. Relationships with constituent and affiliated organization. Subject to conflict-of-interest considerations addressed in § 131, a lawyer representing a client organization may also represent one or more constituents of the organization, such as an officer or director of the organization (§ 131, Comment *e*) or an organization affiliated with the client (see § 131, Comment *d*). On whether a lawyer has entered into a client-lawyer relationship with a constituent person or an organization affiliated with a client organization, see § 14, Comment f. On avoiding misleading a corporate constituent about the role of a lawyer for the organization, see § 103, Comment *e*.

§ 99. A Represented Nonclient—The General Anti-Contact Rule

(1) **A lawyer representing a client in a matter may not communicate about the subject of the representation with a nonclient
whom the lawyer knows to be represented in the matter by
another lawyer or with a representative of an organizational
nonclient so represented as defined in § 100, unless:**

    (a) **the communication is with a public officer or agency to
the extent stated in § 101;**

    (b) **the lawyer is a party and represents no other client in the
matter;**

    (c) **the communication is authorized by law;**

    (d) **the communication reasonably responds to an emergency;
or**

    (e) **the other lawyer consents.**

(2) **Subsection (1) does not prohibit the lawyer from assisting the
client in otherwise proper communication by the lawyer's
client with a represented nonclient.**

Comment:

a. Scope and cross-references. This Section states the general rule prohibiting
a lawyer from communicating about a matter involved in a representation
with a nonclient involved in the same matter who is represented by another
lawyer. Several exceptions are then stated. Narrower prohibitions may apply
with respect to communication by a government investigating lawyer
(Comment *h* hereto) and communication with represented governmental
agencies or officials (Subsection (1)(a) & § 101). On remedial orders and
remedies, see Comments *m* and *n*.

Nonclients and representatives of nonclients included within this Section
are defined in § 100 (see also Comment *c* hereto). On limitations on communications with confidential agents of a nonclient, see § 102. On the rule
limiting communications with an unrepresented nonclient, see § 103.

The rule stated in this Section derives from the lawyer codes and a violation is thus subject to professional discipline (see § 5). Unless the lawyer's conduct is otherwise tortious, for example because the communicating lawyer
engages in actionable misrepresentation (*see generally* § 98), a nonclient has
no civil-damage remedy against the offending lawyer (see § 51, Comment *c*).

On other possible remedies, such as disqualification of the offending lawyer or suppression of information or an agreement gained through prohibited contact, see Comment *n* hereto. On court orders relaxing the rule or otherwise regulating contact with represented nonclients, see Comment *h*.

b. Rationale. The rules stated in §§ 99–103, protect against overreaching and deception of nonclients. The rule of this Section also protects the relationship between the represented nonclient and that person's lawyer and assures the confidentiality of the nonclient's communications with the lawyer (see also § 102).

The general exception to the rule stated in Subsection (1)(e) requires consent of the opposing lawyer; consent of the client alone does not suffice (see Comment *j*). The rule accordingly has been criticized for requiring three-stage communications (from client, through lawyer, through another lawyer, or vice versa) that are often more expensive, delayed, and inconvenient than direct communication. In addition, the rule limits client autonomy by requiring that both communication and consent be given by the lawyer (see Comment *j* hereto). Notwithstanding such criticism, the rule is universally followed in American jurisdictions.

A lawyer whose appropriate efforts to communicate with a represented nonclient through that person's lawyer are thus frustrated may in some situations seek the aid of a tribunal to effectuate the communication (see Comment *m*) or complain to an appropriate disciplinary authority. On communications made by a lawyer's client, see Comment *k*.

The anti-contact rule constrains a lawyer who represents another person in the matter. The rule also applies to nonlawyer employees and other agents of a lawyer, such as an investigator. On agents of a client, see Comment *k* hereto.

c. Persons protected by the anti-contact rule. As stated in Subsection (1), the anti-contact prohibition extends to any nonclient that the contacting lawyer knows to be represented by counsel in the matter in which the lawyer is representing a client. It is not limited to situations of opposing parties in litigation or in which persons otherwise have adverse interests. Thus, the rule covers a represented co-party and a nonparty fact witness who is represented by counsel with respect to the matter, as well as a nonclient so represented prior to any suit being filed and regardless of whether such suit is contemplated or eventuates. A lawyer represented by other counsel is a represented person and hence covered by this Section. On inside legal counsel for a corporation or similar organization, see § 100, Comment *c*.

A lawyer who does not represent a person in the matter and who is approached by an already-represented person seeking a second professional opinion or wishing to discuss changing lawyers or retaining additional counsel, may, without consent from or notice to the original lawyer, respond to the request, including giving an opinion concerning the propriety of the first lawyer's representation. If such additional or substituted counsel is retained, an opposing lawyer may, of course, communicate and otherwise deal with new counsel for the nonclient. Thus, a lawyer representing a claimant in an injury case may approach a lawyer personally retained in the matter by an insured defendant even if other counsel have been designated by the defendant's insurer to represent the person in the matter.

d. A communication on an unrelated matter. This Section does not prohibit communications with a represented nonclient in the course of social, business, or other relationships or communications that do not relate to the matter involved in the representation. What matter or matters are involved in a representation depends on the circumstances. For example, a lawyer might know that a witness at a deposition was represented by a lawyer for an opposing party only for purposes of attending the deposition. The lawyer may contact that nonclient following the deposition when representation has ended.

Illustrations:

1. Lawyer A is counsel to Corporation and represents Corporation, among other matters, in connection with a shareholder action filed against it. Officer is separately represented in the matter by Lawyer B. In the course of the other matters on which Lawyer A represents Corporation, Lawyer A and Officer have frequent occasion to speak and correspond. Lawyer A may continue such discussions directly with Officer on matters not related to the matter in which Officer is represented. However, Lawyer A may not discuss with Officer facts or legal issues involved in the shareholder action, unless Lawyer B consents (see Comment *j*).

2. Plaintiff, represented by Lawyer B, has filed a personal-injury action against Defendant. Lawyer A, who is representing Defendant, directs Investigator to make an appointment at Plaintiff's place of business, a beauty parlor. While Plaintiff shampoos, cuts, and sets Investigator's hair, Plaintiff and Investigator engage in small talk unrelated to Plaintiff's lawsuit or physical condition. Investigator reports to Lawyer A, including

several observations indicating that Plaintiff is not physically impaired as alleged. Lawyer A has not violated the rule of this Section because Investigator did not engage Plaintiff in conversation relevant to the matter on which Plaintiff is represented and only engaged Plaintiff in activities that Plaintiff engages in regularly in dealing with the public.

e. A lawyer communicating in a nonrepresentational situation. A lawyer representing his or her own interests pro se may communicate with an opposing represented nonclient on the same basis as other principals (see Subsection (1)(b)). A lawyer representing both a client and the lawyer's own interests in the same matter is subject to the anti-contact rule of the Section.

Illustration:

3. Lawyer A, who rents law-office space from Landlord, receives a letter from Lawyer B, representing Landlord, directing Lawyer A to vacate by a certain date. Lawyer A telephones Landlord without the prior consent of Lawyer B and insists to Landlord that the lease prohibits the eviction. Lawyer A has not violated the rule of this Section.

f. Prohibited forms of communication. Under the anti-contact rule of this Section, a lawyer ordinarily is not authorized to communicate with a represented nonclient even by letter with a copy to the opposite lawyer or even if the opposite lawyer wrongfully fails to convey important information to that lawyer's client (see § 20), such as a settlement offer. The rule prohibits all forms of communication, such as sending a represented nonclient a copy of a letter to the nonclient's lawyer or causing communication through someone acting as the agent of the lawyer (see § 5(2) & Comment *f* thereto) (prohibition against violation of duties through agents). The anti-contact rule applies to any communication relating to the lawyer's representation in the matter, whoever initiates the contact and regardless of the content of the ensuing communication.

Illustration:

4. Wife is represented by Lawyer A in a marriage-dissolution action. Husband is represented by Lawyer B. Meeting without Lawyer A or

Lawyer B, Wife and Husband negotiate the outlines of an agreement providing for property division and child support. Wife then brings Husband to Lawyer A's office to have the agreement reduced to writing. Lawyer A welcomes both Wife and Husband and engages in a discussion of provisions of the agreement with both of them. Lawyer A has violated the rule of this Section.

g. A communication authorized by law. As stated in Subsection (1)(c), direct communication with a represented nonclient is permissible, without consent of the nonclient's lawyer (cf. Comment *j* hereto), when authorized by law. Where such communication is permissible, it may extend no further than reasonably necessary. No complete list of such authorizations is stated here. Several of the important interests are described below. See also § 101 (contact with officers or employees of represented governmental agency). Whether direct communication is authorized depends on the legal justification for the contact in the situation, having regard for the interest in protecting client-lawyer relationships and avoiding overreaching of represented nonclients (see Comment *b*).

An interest sometimes recognized by law is that of transmitting notice directly to a represented nonclient of certain legally significant matters. Among other things, such notice eliminates the possibility of disputes as to the authority of the nonclient's lawyer to receive such notice. For example, law commonly provides for service of process on a defendant, even in instances where the lawyer for the plaintiff knows that the defendant is represented by a lawyer in the matter. However, after initial notice has been transmitted directly to the represented nonclient, the authority of the defendant's lawyer to act on the defendant's behalf can readily be determined (see § 25). Thereafter, communication with the nonclient ordinarily must be conducted through the nonclient's lawyer.

Direct communication may occur pursuant to court order or under the supervision of a court. Thus, a lawyer is authorized by law to interrogate as a witness an opposing represented nonclient during the course of a duly noticed deposition or at a trial or other hearing. It may also be appropriate for a tribunal to order transmittal of documents, such as settlement offers, directly to a represented client.

A tribunal, in the exercise of its authority over advocates appearing before it (see § 1, Comment *c*) and over proceedings generally, may expand the right of a lawyer to make ex parte contact with a nonclient represented by opposing counsel. Such a court order is usually entered after notice and hearing.

For example, although a lawyer for plaintiffs in a certified class action is considered to represent all members of the class (see Comment *l*), the court may permit defense counsel to approach class members directly if in the circumstances the court concludes that such persons will not be subjected to overreaching and that direct contact would otherwise be appropriate. So also, a court may appoint a psychiatrist designated by the prosecutor to conduct a pretrial evaluation of a represented defendant, in contemplation of consultation between the psychiatrist and the prosecutor following the examination.

Contractual notice provisions may explicitly provide for notice to be sent to a designated individual. A lawyer's dispatch of such notice directly to the designated nonclient, even if represented in the matter, is authorized to comply with legal requirements of the contract.

h. A represented nonclient accused or suspected of a crime. Controversy has surrounded the question whether prosecutors are fully subject to the rule of this Section with respect to contact, prior to indictment, with represented nonclients accused or suspected of crime. Certain considerations favor a relaxed anti-contact rule. Law-enforcement officials traditionally have resorted to undercover means of gathering important evidence. If retention of a lawyer alone precluded direct prosecutorial contact, a knowledgeable criminal suspect could obtain immunity from otherwise lawful forms of investigation by retaining a lawyer, while unsophisticated suspects would have no similar protection. Moreover, nonlawyer law-enforcement personnel such as the police are not subject to the rule of this Section. Rigidly extending the anti-contact rule to prosecutors would create unfortunate incentives to eliminate them from involvement in investigations.

On the other hand, certain considerations argue in favor of an anti-contact rule for prosecutors. They are in a position to overreach suspects or interfere in client-lawyer relationships in the same manner as lawyers in private practice and may be tempted to do so to solve a crime. Accordingly, at a minimum, a suspect or accused has constitutional protection of the following kind: against governmental intrusion, including prosecutorial intrusion, into essentials of the client-lawyer relationship, such as attempts to dissuade a nonclient from retaining counsel or from trusting or consulting counsel already retained or assigned; against taking statements from a suspect who is in custody and has not effectively waived the right to counsel; and against such measures as unlawful searches of a lawyer's office or similar threats to client-lawyer confidentiality. Elaboration of such limitations is beyond the scope of this Restatement.

It has been extensively debated whether, beyond such constitutional protections, the anti-contact rule independently imposes all constraints of this Section on prosecutors or, to the contrary, whether the authorized-by-law exception (see Comment *g*) entirely removes such limitations. Both polar positions seem unacceptable. Organizations of prosecutors and lawyers are elaborating rules governing specific situations. The scope of such rules and the law in default of such rules are subjects beyond the scope of this Restatement. Prosecutor contact in compliance with law is within the authorized-by-law exception stated in Subsection (1)(c).

i. A communication reasonably responding to an emergency. Communication with a represented nonclient is authorized to protect life or personal safety and to deal with other emergency situations. As provided in Subsection (1)(d), communication in such situations is permissible to the extent reasonably necessary to deal with the emergency.

Illustration:

5. Lawyer A represents Husband in a divorce action. Wife has retained Lawyer B in connection with the action. Late at night, Wife calls Lawyer A, saying that Husband is threatening to harm her and that she cannot reach Lawyer B. Lawyer A advises Wife to leave the house and that Lawyer A will immediately attempt to calm down Husband. Lawyer A has not violated the rule of this Section.

j. A communication with the consent of the lawyer for the represented nonclient. As stated in Subsection (1)(e), a lawyer otherwise subject to the rule of this Section may communicate with a represented nonclient when that person's lawyer has consented to or acquiesced in the communication. An opposing lawyer may acquiesce, for example, by being present at a meeting and observing the communication. Similarly, consent may be implied rather than express, such as where such direct contact occurs routinely as a matter of custom, unless the opposing lawyer affirmatively protests.

The nonclient's lawyer has a duty to the client to consent when doing so would be in the interest of the client or when the client so instructs the lawyer (see § 21(2)). When determining whether to consent, the lawyer must consider only the client's interest and not the lawyer's personal interest in controlling aspects of the representation.

k. A communication by a client with a represented nonclient. No general rule prevents a lawyer's client, either personally or through a nonlawyer agent, from communicating directly with a represented nonclient. Thus, while neither a lawyer nor a lawyer's investigator or other agent (see Comment *b* hereto) may contact the represented nonclient, the same bar does not extend to the client of the lawyer or the client's investigator or other agent.

As stated in Subsection (2), the anti-contact rule does not prohibit a lawyer from advising the lawyer's own client concerning the client's communication with a represented nonclient, including communications that may occur without the prior consent (compare Comment *j*) or knowledge of the lawyer for the nonclient.

The lawyer for a client intending to make such a communication may advise the client regarding legal aspects of the communication, such as whether an intended communication is libelous or would otherwise create risk for the client. Prohibiting such advice would unduly restrict the client's autonomy, the client's interest in obtaining important legal advice, and the client's ability to communicate fully with the lawyer. The lawyer may suggest that the client make such a communication but must not assist the client inappropriately to seek confidential information, to invite the nonclient to take action without the advice of counsel, or otherwise to overreach the nonclient.

Illustration:

6. Lawyer represents Owner, who has a worsening business relationship with Contractor. From earlier meetings, Lawyer knows that Contractor is represented by a lawyer in the matter. Owner drafts a letter to send to Contractor stating Owner's position in the dispute, showing a copy of the draft to Lawyer. Viewing the draft as inappropriate, Lawyer redrafts the letter, recommending that Client send out the letter as redrafted. Client does so, as Lawyer knew would occur. Lawyer has not violated the rule of this Section.

l. A communication with class members. A lawyer who represents a client opposing a class in a class action is subject to the anti-contact rule of this Section. For the purposes of this Section, according to the majority of decisions, once the proceeding has been certified as a class action, the members of the class are considered clients of the lawyer for the class; prior to certification, only those class members with whom the lawyer maintains a personal client-lawyer relationship are clients. Prior to certification and unless the court orders otherwise, in the case of competing putative class actions a lawyer for one set of representatives may contact class members who are only putatively represented by a competing lawyer, but not class representatives or members known to be directly represented in the matter by the other lawyer.

m. Clarifying, protective, and remedial orders of a tribunal. In situations of doubt involving communication with a represented nonclient, a clarifying ruling may be sought from a tribunal. A party seeking to protect against impermissible contact by an opposing lawyer may seek a protective or reme-dial ruling. A ruling may impose conditions on access and may expand or contract the general rule of this Section as appropriate in light of circum-stances. For example, a ruling permitting access may require the lawyer to inform each contacted nonclient of the identity and interests of the lawyer's client, the right of the nonclient to refuse to be interviewed, and the right of the nonclient to request the presence of a lawyer during an interview. The court may grant access on condition that no statement taken will be admissible in evidence. Contact pursuant to the terms of such a ruling is authorized by law within the meaning of this Section (see Comment *h*).

n. Disqualification, evidence suppression, and related remedies. When con-tact has been made in violation of this Section, a court may disqualify the offending lawyer when necessary to protect against a significant risk of future misuse of confidential information obtained through the contact, when the contact has substantially interfered with the client's relationship with the client's lawyer, or when disqualification is appropriate to deter flagrant or reckless violations. A lawyer violating or threatening to violate the rule may be enjoined from doing so. A lawyer who violates the rule of this Section is also subject to professional discipline. Fines and fee-shifting sanctions may be warranted under applicable procedural law.

A court may also suppress or otherwise exclude from evidence state-ments, documents, or other material obtained in violation of the rule. When a release or other document affecting the interests of a represented nonclient is obtained in violation of the rule, the law against fraud or overreaching may permit the nonclient to obtain a ruling voiding the document. A tribunal may compel production of any statement taken in violation of the rule despite its status otherwise as protected work product (see § 87(3)).

§ 100. Definition of a Represented Nonclient

Within the meaning of § 99, a represented nonclient includes:
   (1) **a natural person represented by a lawyer; and:**
   (2) **a current employee or other agent of an organization represented by a lawyer:**
      (a) **if the employee or other agent supervises, directs, or regularly consults with the lawyer concerning the matter or if the agent has power to compromise or settle the matter;**
      (b) **if the acts or omissions of the employee or other agent may be imputed to the organization for purposes of civil or criminal liability in the matter; or**
      (c) **if a statement of the employee or other agent, under applicable rules of evidence, would have the effect of binding the organization with respect to proof of the matter.**

Comment:

a. Scope and cross-references. This Section defines the scope of the anti-contact rule of § 99 with respect to a client who is a natural person and, in the case of an organizational client, those persons connected with the client whose responsibility within the organization makes application of the anti-contact rule appropriate (see Comment *b*). With respect to a person affiliated with an organization who is independently represented in the matter by a lawyer, see Comment *i*. On the authority of a lawyer to request employees or agents of a client not to speak with lawyers or others representing an opposing party, see § 116(4). The types of "organizations" within Subsection (2) include those listed in § 96, Comment *c*.

With respect to other limitations on contact, see § 102.

b. Rationale. Operation of the anti-contact rule with respect to natural persons ordinarily involves no questions of agency authority. However, with respect to organizational clients, difficult questions of the scope of the rule are presented.

An organization acts only through agents. Thus, certain employees and perhaps other persons are properly regarded as nonclients who may not be contacted under § 99. The definition of Subsection (2) applies whether or not the employee or other representative is personally represented by counsel for the organization. (With respect to the scope of the anti-contact rule when a representative of an organization is personally represented, see Comment *h* hereto.) A very broad definition of such persons, for example one including all present and former employees, would be easily administered but at an unacceptably high cost. Under such a rule, the organization's lawyer (as permitted under § 99 & Comment *j* thereto) could deny permission for the inquiring lawyer to speak to any employee. The opposing party would thus be required to resort to the burdensome process of filing suit (based on less information than would otherwise be available) and obtaining discovery to gain access to relevant information. Moreover, employees may be unwilling to speak as freely or candidly at a deposition in the presence of the lawyers for their employer as in an informal, pretrial interview. There is no justification for permitting one party thus to control entirely the flow of information to opposing parties. Such control is not available to an individual party, whose friends and colleagues may be approached without infringing the rule. The anti-contact rule stated in the Section therefore reflects a balance among the considerations pertinent to the anti-contact rule (see § 99, Comment *b*).

Generally, persons associated with an organization and within this Section will be employees or agents of the organization. However, a nonagent such as an independent contractor or a member of a board of directors may also be within the definitions of Subsections (2)(a)–(2)(c) (see also § 102).

c. A person who regularly consults with an organization's lawyer (Subsection (2)(a)). As stated in Subsection (2)(a), the anti-contact rule of § 99 applies to persons connected with an organization who supervise, direct, or regularly consult with a lawyer for the organization in the matter or who have power to compromise or settle the matter in consultation with the lawyer. Such persons are likely to have confidential information concerning the matter, much of which would be immune from discovery under the attorney-client privilege (§ 68 and following) and the work-product doctrine (§ 87 and following) (see also Subsection (2)(b) & Comment *f* hereto). While such a person may also know discoverable facts, ex parte contact would incur the risk that the person would be unable to distinguish between properly discoverable facts and protected information. In addition, with respect to persons in the organization who supervise or direct the lawyer or who have power to settle or compromise the matter on behalf of the organization, the anti-contact rule also seeks to prevent improvident settlements and impairment of the relationship of trust and confidence with the lawyer (see § 99, Comment *b*).

Agents and others who are in contact with the organization's lawyer may bear different levels of responsibility, for example, a corporate vice president dealing with patent counsel on a patent challenge, a corporate clerk assigned to collect documents for the lawyer, or a production employee providing expert information to the lawyer about a mechanical process that is in issue. On the other hand, agents and others (including managerial employees) who are not within the definition of this Section may be contacted without consent regardless of their position in the organization.

Illustrations:

1. Manager heads the transportation department of Corporation, which is defending against a claim for personal injuries by Plaintiff. Plaintiff, represented by Lawyer A, seeks damages resulting from a traffic accident allegedly caused by Corporation's negligence in hiring Driver who had a bad driving record. Lawyer A knows that Corporation is represented by Lawyer B in defending against the claim. Manager has power to authorize settlement of the matter with Plaintiff on behalf of Corporation. Lawyer A may not contact Manager except with the consent of Lawyer B or as otherwise permitted under § 99.

2. Same facts as stated in Illustration 1, except that authorization to settle claims is reserved to Executive Vice President of Corporation and is not part of Manager's responsibilities. Lawyer A may contact Manager without the consent of Lawyer B, unless contact with Manager is otherwise prohibited by Subsection (2) or by § 102. On the other hand, if the facts were that Manager had responsibility for the allegedly negligent hiring, Manager would be a represented nonclient within Subsection (2)(b).

On avoiding inquiry into confidential matters during the course of otherwise permissible interviews with employees or agents of a represented nonclient, see Comment *i*.

Inside legal counsel for a corporation is not generally within Subsection (2), and contact with such counsel is not generally limited by § 99.

d. A person whose act or omission may be imputed to an organization for purposes of liability (Subsection (2)(b)). As stated in Subsection (2)(b), the anti-contact rule of § 99 also extends to persons connected with an organization, regardless of their rank, whose acts or omissions in the matter may be imputed to the organization for purposes of civil or criminal liability with respect to the matter involved in the representation. Such a person has acted in the matter on behalf of the organization and, save for the separate legal character of the organizational form, would often be directly named as a party in a lawsuit involving the matter. The Subsection applies even if facts are disputed concerning the person's actions, such as whether they are properly imputed to the organization or whether they were the cause of the harm alleged.

Illustrations:

3. Same facts as stated in Illustration 1, except that Lawyer A wishes to interview Driver. Under applicable agency and tort law, Driver has allegedly committed an act for which civil or criminal liability may be imputed to Corporation in the matter involved in Lawyer B's representation of Corporation. Lawyer A may not contact Driver without the consent of Lawyer B or as otherwise permitted under § 99. The result does not change if Corporation has filed an answer asserting that Driver's actions were beyond the scope and course of Driver's duties and thus not imputable to Corporation.

4. Same facts as stated in Illustration 1, except that Lawyer A wishes to interview Brake Mechanic, another employee of Corporation, who repaired the brakes of Driver's vehicle. Lawyer A's objective is to determine whether Brake Mechanic may have negligently made repairs, providing an additional basis for an allegation of Corporation's negligence. In such a case, any negligence of Brake Mechanic would be imputed to Corporation. Lawyer A may not contact Brake Mechanic without the consent of Lawyer B or as otherwise permitted under § 99.

When an individual employee or agent falls within Subsection (2)(b), there may be a conflict of interest between the organizational client and the person. A lawyer for the organization who is requested to represent the individual must comply with conflict-of-interest requirements before undertaking such a representation (see § 131, Comment *e*).

e. An employee or agent whose statement binds an organization under applicable evidence law (Subsection (2)(c)). Under evidence law generally applied a century ago and still in force in some jurisdictions for certain purposes, some employees and agents have the power to make statements that bind the principal, in the sense that the principal may not introduce evidence contradicting the binding statement. When such a binding-admission rule applies, under Subsection (2)(c) an employee or agent with power to make such a statement is a represented nonclient within the anti-contact rule of § 99. Such a person is analogous to a person who possesses power to settle a dispute on behalf of the organization (see Comment *c*).

However, under modern evidence law, employees and agents who lack authority to enter into binding contractual settlements on behalf of the organization have no power to make such binding statements. Modern evidence rules make certain statements of an employee or agent admissible notwithstanding the hearsay rule, but allow the organization to impeach or contradict such statements. Employees or agents are not included within Subsection (2)(c) solely on the basis that their statements are admissible evidence. A contrary rule would essentially mean that most employees and agents with relevant information would be within the anti-contact rule, contrary to the policies described in Comment b.

f. Instructing an employee or agent not to communicate with an opposing lawyer. A principal or the principal's lawyer may inform employees or agents of their right not to speak with opposing counsel and may request them not to do so (see § 116(4) & Comment *e* thereto). In certain circumstances, a direction to do so could constitute an obstruction of justice or a violation of other law. However, even when lawful, such an instruction is a matter of intra-organizational policy and not a limitation against a lawyer for another party who is seeking evidence. Thus, even if an employer, by general policy or specific directive, lawfully instructs all employees not to cooperate with another party's lawyer, that does not enlarge the scope of the anti-contact rule applicable to that lawyer.

g. A former employee or agent. Contact with a former employee or agent ordinarily is permitted, even if the person had formerly been within a category of those with whom contact is prohibited. Denial of access to such a person would impede an adversary's search for relevant facts without facilitating the employer's relationship with its counsel. A former employee or agent of a party may in some circumstances be within the anti-contact rule of § 99 or within the prohibited class of persons described in § 102, Comment *d*. For example a former employee who, as the lawyer knows, continues regularly to consult about the matter with the lawyer for the ex-employer is within Subsection (2)(a); thus no such employee may be contacted except as permitted under § 99. See also § 102, Comment *d*.

h. A nonclient employee or agent independently represented. When a person associated with an organization is independently represented in the matter, contact with that nonclient is governed by § 99. In such a case, consent of the lawyer representing the organization need not also be obtained. See § 99, Comment *d*, Illustration 1; on contact with such nonclients who are unrepresented, see § 103, Comment *e*.

i. Limitations on otherwise permissible contact with an employee or agent. A lawyer may not seek confidential information during the course of an otherwise permissible communication (see § 102). After beginning to communicate with a nonclient, a lawyer may learn that the nonclient is represented in the matter. The lawyer must then cease further communication, unless an exception stated in § 99 applies.

§ 131. Conflicts of Interest in Representing an Organization

Unless all affected clients consent to the representation under the limitations and conditions provided in § 122, a lawyer may not represent both an organization and a director, officer, employee, shareholder, owner, partner, member, or other individual or organization associated with the organization if there is a substantial risk that the lawyer's representation of either would be materially and adversely affected by the lawyer's duties to the other.

Comment:

a. Scope and cross-references. This Section concerns conflict-of-interest issues involving a lawyer for an organization. For the purpose of this Section, an organization includes a corporation (whether for-profit or not-for-profit), limited or general partnership (whether formal or informal), labor union, unincorporated association, joint venture, trust, estate, or similar entity with a recognizable form, internal organization, and relative permanence. Many organizations are recognized as entities for other legal purposes, but such recognition is not invariably required for the purposes of this Section (*see, e.g.,* Comment *f* hereto, Illustration 5).

This Section is a particular application of the general conflicts standard expressed in § 121. The conflict is subject to consent under the limitations and conditions provided in § 122. The conflict is imputed to affiliated lawyers by § 123, an imputation that can be removed as described in § 124. Remedies for violation of the Section include those set forth in § 121,

Comment *f*. A lawyer's violation of this Section that injures the organization renders the lawyer liable to the organization for professional malpractice (see § 48 and following).

Issues of who constitutes a lawyer's client are addressed in § 14 and § 121, Comment *d*. This Section presupposes that the lawyer has a client-lawyer relationship with an organization. On the power of authorized agents of the organization to instruct the lawyer on behalf of the client, see § 96, Comment *d*.

The duty to preserve confidential client information of organizational clients is described in § 60 and the attorney-client privilege for organizations in § 73. A lawyer's role in counseling organizational clients is addressed in § 96; on a lawyer's duties when a person associated with an organizational client threatens to harm the organization, see § 96(2). A lawyer's ownership of an interest in an organizational client is considered in § 126. Representation of two or more individuals who are forming an organization is examined in § 130, Comment *c*. Payment by an organization of the legal expenses of one or more directors, officers, employees, or other individuals, is considered in § 134. Conflicts of interest created by a lawyer's duties as a corporate director or officer is discussed in § 135, Comment *d*.

b. Rationale. An organization with more than a single owner-employee is an aggregation of multiple interests, if only because it is made up of multiple persons or entities. Persons initially forming an organization are linked by a common interest that partly transcends their individual interests. The individuals might have separate lawyers for their other activities and for negotiating the question of their shares or other forms of control in the organization. However, a lawyer might be retained for representation relating to the organization separate from that of any individual associated with the enterprise. An organization's lawyer thus is said to represent the entity and not the elements that make it up. A lawyer for an organization serves whatever lawful interest the organization defines as its interest, acting through its responsible agents and in accordance with its decisionmaking procedures (see § 96(1) and Comment *d* thereto).

c. A challenge to the policy of a client organization. Individuals having responsible roles in an organization can disagree about the definition of its interests. However, that does not by itself indicate that a lawyer representing the organization has a conflict of interest within the meaning of § 121. If conduct of the organization is challenged as unlawful, the lawyer for the organization generally may defend at least until it is ruled upon by the tribunal or changed pursuant to the procedures of the organization. Such a change can occur, for example, because the lawyer is directed to settle the controversy as instructed by the agent (see § 21).

Illustration:

1. The Board of Directors of Corporation, acting pursuant to its articles and by-laws, votes not to declare a preferred stock dividend because of a perceived shortage of working capital. This is done contrary to the recommendation of Lawyer for Corporation, who believes that there is a reasonable argument that the dividend can be omitted but that a tribunal would probably order the dividend declared. Thereafter, Lawyer implements the decision of Board, memorializing its decision in a resolution. Several shareholders file suit to compel Corporation to issue a dividend. Neither Lawyer's earlier advice nor the lawsuit itself creates a conflict of interest that would prevent Lawyer from defending against the suit.

On the lawyer's duty if the responsible agent is acting in violation of a duty to the organization, see § 6(2). On the lawyer's duty if the organization engages in a crime or fraud, see § 67. On the lawyer's right to withdraw from representation because of disagreement with the organizational policy, see § 32. On the lawyer's right to take public positions inconsistent with those of the lawyer's client, see § 125, Comment *e*.

d. Conflicting interests of affiliated organizations. Whether a lawyer represents affiliated organizations as clients is a question of fact determined under § 14 (see Comment *f* thereto). When a lawyer represents two or more organizations with some common ownership or membership, whether a conflict exists is determined primarily on the basis of formal organizational distinctions. If a single business corporation has established two divisions within the corporate structure, for example, conflicting interests or objectives of those divisions do not create a conflict of interest for a lawyer representing the corporation. Differences within the organization are to be resolved through the organization's decisionmaking procedures.

If an enterprise consists of two or more organizations and ownership of the organizations is identical, the lawyer's obligation is ordinarily to respond according to the decisionmaking procedures of the enterprise, subject to any special limitations that might be validly imposed by regulatory regimes such as those governing financial institutions and insurance companies.

On the other hand, when ownership or membership of two or more organizations is not identical, the lawyer must respect the organizational boundaries of each and analyze possible conflicts of interest on the basis that the organizations are separate entities. That is true even when a single individual or organization has sufficient ownership or influence to exercise working control of the organizations (*cf.* § 123, Comment *d(i)*).

Illustration:

2. A Corporation owns 60 percent of the stock of B Corporation. All of the stock of A Corporation is publicly owned, as is the remainder of the stock in B Corporation. Lawyer has been asked by the President of A Corporation to act as attorney for B in causing B to make a proposed transfer of certain real property to A at a price whose fairness cannot readily be determined by reference to the general real-estate market. Lawyer may do so only with effective informed consent of the management of B (as well as that of A). The ownership of A and B is not identical and their interests materially differ in the proposed transaction.

e. Representation of an organization and an individual constituent. Representation of a client organization often is facilitated by a close working relationship between the lawyer and the organization's officers, directors, and employees. However, unless the lawyer and such an individual person enter into a client-lawyer relationship (see § 14, Comment *f*), the individual is not a client of the lawyer (see § 121, Comment *d*). With respect to the attorney-client privilege attaching to communications with a person affiliated with an organization, see § 73, Comment *j*.

When a lawyer proposes to represent both an organization and a person associated with it, such as an officer, director, or employee, whether a conflict exists is determined by an analysis of the interests of the organization as an entity and those of the individuals involved. That is true whether the multiple representation involves civil (see § 128) or criminal (see § 129) litigation or a nonlitigated matter (see § 130). The interests of the organization are those defined by its agents authorized to act in the matter (see § 96, Comment *d*). For example, when an organization is accused of wrongdoing, an individual such as a director, officer, or other agent will sometimes be charged as well, and the lawyer representing the organization might be asked also to represent the individual. Such representation would constitute a conflict of interest when the individual's interests are materially adverse to the interests of the organization (see § 121). When there is no material adversity of interest, such as when the individual owns all of the equity in the organization or played a routine role in the underlying transaction, no conflict exists. In instances of adversity, concurrent representation would be permissible with the consent of all affected clients under the limitations and conditions stated in § 122.

Consent by an organization can be given in any manner consistent with the organization's lawful decisionmaking procedures. Applicable corporate law may provide that an officer who is personally interested in the matter may not provide consent in the matter. In deciding whether to consent to multiple representation by outside counsel, the organization might rely upon the advice of inside legal counsel. Issues concerning informed consent by public organizations to otherwise conflicted representations are discussed in § 122, Comment *c*.

Illustrations:

3. President, the chief executive officer of Corporation, has been charged with discussing prices with the president of a competing firm. If found guilty, both President and Corporation will be subject to civil and criminal penalties. Lawyer, who is representing Corporation, has concluded after a thorough investigation that no such pricing discussions occurred. Both Corporation and President plan to defend on that ground. President has asked Lawyer to represent President as well as Corporation in the proceedings. Although the factual and legal defenses of President and Corporation appear to be consistent at the outset, the likelihood of conflicting positions in such matters as plea bargaining requires Lawyer to obtain the informed consent of both clients before proceeding with the representation (see § 129, Comment *c*).

4. The same facts as in Illustration 3, except that after further factual investigation both President and Corporation now concede that the pricing discussions took place. One of President's defenses will be that the former general counsel of Corporation told President that discussion of general pricing practices with a competitor was not illegal. Corporation denies that such was the advice given and asserts that President acted without authority. The conflict between President and Corporation is so

great that the same lawyer could not provide adequate legal services to both in the matter. Thus, continued representation of both is not subject to consent (see § 122, Comment *g(iii)*, & §§ 128 & 129).

If a person affiliated with an organization makes an unsolicited disclosure of information to a lawyer who represents only the organization, indicating the person's erroneous expectation that the lawyer will keep the information confidential from the organization, the lawyer must inform the person that the lawyer does not represent the person (see § 103, Comment *e*). The lawyer generally is not prohibited from sharing the communication with the organization. However, the requirements stated in § 15, Comment *c*, with respect to safeguarding confidential information of a prospective client may apply. That would occur when the person reasonably appeared to be consulting the lawyer as present or prospective client with respect to the person's individual interests, and the lawyer failed to warn the associated person that the lawyer represents only the organization and could act against the person's interests as a result (see § 103, Comment *e*). With respect to a lawyer's duties when a person associated with the organization expressed an intent to act wrongfully and thereby threatens harm to the organization client, see § 96(2) and Comment *f* thereto.

Issues considered in this Comment may be particularly acute in the case of close corporations, small partnerships, and similar organizations in which, for example, one person with substantial ownership interests also manages. Such a manager may have a corresponding tendency to treat corporate and similar entity distinctions as mere formalities. In such instances, when ownership is so concentrated that no nonmanaging owner exists and in the absence of material impact on the interests of other nonclients (such as creditors in the case of an insolvent corporation), a lawyer acts reasonably in accepting in good faith a controlling manager's position that the interests of all controlling persons and the entity should be treated as if they were the same. Similar considerations apply when a close corporation or similar organization is owned and managed by a small number of owner-managers whose interests are not materially in conflict.

f. A challenge by a client organization to the action of an associated person. Both Subsections of this Section can be applicable when the organization challenges the action of one or more of its associated persons, such as an officer, director, or employee. The policy of the organization in the matter will be that established according to the organization's decisionmaking procedures (see § 96(1)(a)). Because the interests of the organization and the associated person are necessarily adverse, the conflict of interest ordinarily will not be subject to consent (see § 122(2)(c)). On the lawyer's dealing with threatened wrongdoing by a person associated with an organizational client, see § 96(2); see also §§ 66–67.

Illustration:

5. Treasurer, the chief financial officer of Club, a private investment trust, has been accused of converting $25,000 of Club's assets for personal use. Responsible other officers of Club, acting on Club's behalf, retain Lawyer to recover the money from Treasurer. They direct Lawyer not to reveal the loss or file suit until other collection efforts have been exhausted. Lawyer may properly represent Club and in doing so must proceed in the manner directed. Further, although the matter is not yet in litigation, the interests of Club and Treasurer are so adverse that even informed consent of both would not permit their common representation by Lawyer in the matter (see § 122, Comment *g*).

g. Derivative action. When an organization such as a business corporation is sued in a derivative action, the organization is ordinarily aligned as an involuntary plaintiff. Persons associated with the organization who are accused of breaching a duty to the organization, typically officers and directors of the organization, are ordinarily named as defendants. The theory of a derivative action is that relief is sought from the individuals for the benefit of the organization. Even with informed consent of all affected clients, the lawyer for the organization ordinarily may not represent an individual defendant as well (see § 128, Comment *c*). If, however, the disinterested directors conclude that no basis exists for the claim that the defending officers and directors have acted against the interests of the organization, the lawyer may, with the effective consent of all clients, represent both the organization and the officers and directors in defending the suit (see § 122).

In a derivative action, if the advice of the lawyer acting for the organization was an important factor in the action of the officers and directors that gave rise to the suit, it is appropriate for the lawyer to represent, if anyone, the officers and directors and for the organization to obtain new counsel. Because the lawyer would be representing clients with interests adverse to the corporation, consent of the corporation would be required. That would be true even if the lawyer withdrew from representing the corporation in order to represent the individuals (see § 132, Comment *c*). Whom the lawyer should represent in the matter, if anyone, should be determined by responsible agents of the organization. Ordinarily, those will be persons who are not named and are not likely to be named parties in the case.

If an action challenging an act of an organization is not a derivative action, whether a conflict exists is determined under § 128, Comment *d(ii)*.

h. Proxy fights and takeover attempts. Outsiders or insiders might challenge incumbent management for control of organizations. Incumbent management, shareholders, creditors, and employees will all be affected by such a contest in various ways. When the challenge to incumbent management comes from outside the management group, the role of the lawyer representing the organization must be to follow policies adopted by the organization, in accordance with the organization's decisionmaking procedures. Persons authorized to act on behalf of the organization determine the organization's interest in responding to the challenge (see § 96(1)).

When all or part of incumbent management seeks to obtain control of the organization, typically by restructuring ownership of and authority in the organization, a conflict of interest is presented between the individual interests of those members of management and the holders of ownership and authority. Because of their personal interests, those members of management ordinarily would not be appropriate agents to direct the work of a lawyer for the organization with respect to the takeover attempt. Whether a lawyer's personal interests, for example, those based on longtime association with incumbent management, preclude the lawyer from representing the organization or the managers seeking control depends on whether the lawyer's personal interests create a substantial risk of material and adverse effect on the representation (see § 125).

Illustrations:

6. The Board of Directors of Company A expects soon to receive a letter from Company B offering to purchase a controlling interest in Company A at a price 20 percent above current market value of the stock. The Board of Directors decides to resist the takeover attempt and directs Lawyer, the general counsel of Company A, to prepare a by-law amendment making it more difficult for Company B to gain control. In such circumstances, the Board of Directors, not Lawyer, has the legal responsibility to determine whether or not the by-law change is in the best interests

of Company A. Lawyer may advise the Board of Directors concerning the proposed by-law.

7. The same facts as in Illustration 6, except that President and Treasurer of Company A have proposed to transform Company A into a privately held corporation in which they would hold all the shares. Without effective consent, Lawyer's responsibilities to Company A would not permit Lawyer to represent President and Treasurer in the transaction. If Lawyer participates in the matter at all, it should be to represent Company A's interest as defined by the members of Company A's Board of Directors who are empowered to act.

Similar considerations apply when a contest over ownership or control arises within a closely held corporation or similar small organization such as a two-person partnership. If the lawyer also represents a principal in such an enterprise personally, the possibility of conflict is increased if the lawyer undertakes to represent that person in such a contest. When it reasonably appears that the lawyer can serve effectively in the role of conciliator between contending factions, the lawyer may undertake to do so with effective consent of all affected clients (see § 130, Comment *d*). In other cases, however, the lawyer will be required to withdraw from representing all of the individual interests (see § 132).

Table of Cases

Table of Professional Rule Citations

Table of Restatement Sections

Index